The
Golden
Treasury
of
Scottish
Verse

The Golden Treasury of Scottish Verse

Edited by Kathleen Jamie,
Don Paterson and
Peter Mackay

CANONGATE

First published in Great Britain, the USA and Canada in 2021
by Canongate Books Ltd, 14 High Street, Edinburgh EH1 1TE

Distributed in the USA by Publishers Group West
and in Canada by Publishers Group Canada

canongate.co.uk

1

British Library Cataloguing-in-Publication Data
A catalogue record for this book is available on request from the British Library

The publisher acknowledges support from the National Lottery
through Creative Scotland towards the publication of this title.

ISBN 978 1 83885 261 0

Typeset in Apollo MT by 3btype.com

Printed and bound in Great Britain by Clays Ltd, Elcograf S.p.A.

Contents

xii

Introduction

We present *The Golden Treasury of Scottish Verse*.

From our vantage of the early twenty-first century, we have looked back a thousand years and more, and made a personal choice of poems which still speak to us. Some are anonymous, having been passed from mouth to ear through the generations, with the poet's name lost to time. Others are from well-known names; yet others from people less well-known, folk who nonetheless had one fine poem in them. Many are by our own living contemporaries.

This book is not a 'definitive' collection. It makes no attempt to either present or challenge a Scottish poetic canon. Like Frances Palgrave's original *Golden Treasury of English Verse*, it's a work of simple enthusiasm. Think of it as a sightseeing tour, guided by three poet-editors who, between them, have come to know the territory reasonably well – stopping at this breathtaking or heartbreaking view, an old monument, a battleground here or curiosity there. Our task is mainly to entertain, while showing you the range and depth of poetry written since Scotland became a nation. (Well, just a little before. Our earliest piece here is attributed to Columba; we could not imagine Scotland without the silvery, intricate glint of Celtic Christianity.)

One of our earliest poets is John Barbour and his epic 'The Bruce' (though as we include no very long poems, our chosen passage is more of an appetiser). Barbour was, conveniently, reputed to have been born in 1320 – the same year as the Declaration of Arbroath was stamped with its many seals and the nation of Scotland became fully visible. None of our poets was born after 1979. This was the year of the first Scottish devolution referendum, and arguably the year that the question of Scottish political, national and cultural identity became a conscious and genuinely common concern in the modern era.

There were three editors, but no committee decisions: one single claim could win out, if it was expressed vigorously enough. We've tried to make a book with something for everyone, which all readers – young or old, Scots or non-Scots – can open with pleasure and anticipation. Although we include an account of Bannockburn, we hope this book wears its nationality lightly and unselfconsciously, as befits a nation finally relaxing into its identity. We haven't sought out poems which particularly spoke to our political or constitutional situation, nor did we demand that they were 'Scottish' in any sense other than that they were written here. For our *Treasury*, we had in mind something like the Monymusk Reliquary, with its mixed materials, its fusion of Pictish, Gaelic and Anglo-Saxon design. As we read and selected poems from across the centuries to be placed inside it, we simply asked ourselves – does this still speak to us? Does this poem still sing? Does this poem still shock, delight, move, or blindside us? Does this poem still conjure the living present out of which it was written? Does it open windows to unexpected vistas? Does it enlighten us? By the end both the 'yes' and the 'no' pile held many surprises; but we were left with a book we'd want to read ourselves.

The *Treasury* holds work in all our language traditions: Scots, early and modern; English, Gaelic, and a sprinkling of Latin, presented in translation. The English translations appear directly after the original poems. All are present in the room, all are whispering into each other's ears, 'Scotland, small?' Despite the challenges they have faced, Scots and Gaelic are still living languages. Scots, especially, has proven itself receptive to the influences of the new communities Scotland has welcomed over the centuries. Our plurality of languages and dialects is a birthright, one which we should embrace wholly, and protect from class, political and religious affiliation. It is especially in our poetry that this diversity continues to flourish.

Speaking of class: the idea that poetry is largely an upper-class, courtly or 'educated' pursuit has never really taken root in Scotland. Certainly, these pages carry works by the nobility and aristocracy – though even these poems bear the Scottish trait of the 'common concern', and fret about the human business of love, birth and death. But always, always, we have the folk. The folk are aye singing, and weaving their loves and laments and best tales into the form they can best remember. Poetry and song are sister arts, and at times they have become culturally indistinguishable (we are arguably entering such a time again); in Scotland we have, of course, the great ballad tradition that Hamish Henderson declared our cultural gift to the world, and it is well represented here. The ballads were a people's poetry, shaped and streamlined in the wind tunnel of their repeated telling. Of the people, too, was the work of Burns: his rallying cries to equality were a global sensation, his songs are still sung today, and the full extent of his work on the traditional songbook still unknown. Poetry here has never been *de haut en bas* – and our mixed, mongrel, diglossic language traditions saw to that. An earthly and earthy Scots was ever present. The Enlightenment was the product of the Edinburgh tenement, and the conversations it enabled between social classes helped to align Enlightenment ideas with social reality; the street has subtly informed our poetic speech ever since. (Arguably this may limit us too, and our tendency to 'not get above ourselves' has been a self-censoring influence on our poetry. In our natural suspicion of high-flown rhetoric, poetry after the Makars generally kept its heid doon: we had no Metaphysicals, and barely any Romantics.)

As we read through the centuries, we were struck by the sudden shrivelling of Lowland poetry post-Reformation. It practically disappears. After Knox, after the loss of the royal court, not only the theatres fell dark: the ability to turn a decent line of verse seems also to have been lost or forgotten, for all we will have kept singing under our breath. The literature recovered, but the long silence alarms. The Victorian era produced some strange eccentricities – Scotland churned out its fair, wretched share of rill and hills, brooks and nooks (invariably babbling and shady) – as well as an impressive line in Music Hall daftness. Then, of course, there's the Kailyard, that cultural cringe wrapped in a couthy tale presented in a shortie tin. All this was ably expunged by Hugh MacDiarmid, whose political enthusiasms and personal flaws should never detract from the great corrective he was. But the nineteenth century also saw the emergence of a proletarian voice – of miners, mill-girls and weavers. The voices of women strengthen, becoming properly audible and de-anonymised in the twentieth century.

We have deliberately chosen to slightly over-represent more recent poetry – both to make the book engaging to a contemporary reader, but also to offer a sense of the stream of tradition becoming a delta, on whose banks we stand. That said, we've included no one without what we might call a 'proven reputation'. Our 1979 cut-off point means we've also stopped a little short of the most recent concerns that animate the work of younger poets: identity and its complexities, constitutional disputes (as ever), ecological anxiety, the huge cultural changes wrought by the Internet and social media. Future anthologies will also enjoy the advantage of being more diverse, in half a dozen different senses; they will embrace new Scots and new ideas of Scottishness. In terms of gender balance, our numbers are still far from ideal, though we have done our best to correct the eliding and marginalisation of women's voices that marked previous anthologies.

We can talk of the streams of language, of regional tradition, of spans of time – but we have chosen to present these poems in a way that confounds it: the poems are not offered chronologically, but rather alphabetically by their titles; an Index of Authors has been supplied, and their dates can be found there. The result, we believe, allows for surprise and serendipity, strange bedfellows and startling connections. (It also disguises those dead centuries that we conveniently forget when we talk of our great poetic tradition.) We made this book during the Covid pandemic. Social interaction has been impossible for almost a year; the thought of bumping into a friend in the street or an old pal in a crowded pub or cafe for a casual blether, let alone an intimate conversation, seems like the stuff of fantasy. We long to be all mixter-maxter again! Well – our book is a mixter-maxter, and, we think, all the better for it.

We'd like to thank the editors, colleagues and friends who have helped shape this anthology, and offered fine suggestions we otherwise would have overlooked: Joanna Dingley, Francis Bickmore, Megan Reid, Leila Cruickshank and Rebecca Bonallie at Canongate. Prof. Rhiannon Purdie, Prof. Kirstie Blair, the staff of the Scottish Poetry Library. Debs Warner, Eugenie Todd, Helen Bartlett and Senga Fairgrieve. We have tried to make a book all readers can enjoy. Students, cultural nomads, old hands and newcomers, folk interested in their own culture, be it inherited or adopted, folk who don't know quite where to start. Please start here, and open anywhere.

KATHLEEN JAMIE, DON PATERSON and PETER MACKAY, 2021

A Boy's Song

Where the pools are bright and deep,
Where the grey trout lies asleep,
Up the river and over the lea,
That's the way for Billy and me.

Where the blackbird sings the latest,
Where the hawthorn blooms the sweetest,
Where the nestlings chirp and flee,
That's the way for Billy and me.

Where the mowers mow the cleanest,
Where the hay lies thick and greenest,
There to track the homeward bee,
That's the way for Billy and me.

Where the hazel bank is steepest,
Where the shadow falls the deepest,
Where the clustering nuts fall free,
That's the way for Billy and me.

Why the boys should drive away
Little sweet maidens from the play,
Or love to banter and fight so well,
That's the thing I never could tell.

But this I know, I love to play
Through the meadow, among the hay;
Up the water and over the lea,
That's the way for Billy and me.

JAMES HOGG

A Childhood

The last bottle of lemonade is nodding
in the rock pool, keeping cold. A childhood,
put away for later. I'm too busy to notice
the sun is going, that they're packing up,
that it's almost time for home. The low waves

warm round my knees as I dig in,
panning for light, happy to be here, dreaming
of the evening I'll wake on the lilo
singing my head off, somewhere
in the sea-lanes to Stavanger, or Oslo.

ROBIN ROBERTSON

A Continuity Problem

1.
Machines for fixing
machines for fixing machines
for fixing machines.

2.
For a waiting-room,
it's perfect. We don't even
realise we're there.

3.
'I'd rather like a
second opinion on the
entire universe.'

4.
'Please don't worry. His
hands will stop trembling once he
starts to operate.'

5.
Even the ones who
did not make it are also
carried through the sky.

6.
Blood flows down the fine
stairway into the street then
turns to right and left.

FRANK KUPPNER

A Dead Mole

Strong-shouldered mole,
That so much lived below the ground,
Dug, fought and loved, hunted and fed,
For you to raise a mound
Was as for us to make a hole;
What wonder now that being dead
Your body lies here stout and square
Buried within the blue vault of the air?

ANDREW YOUNG

A Description of Tyme

Tak tyme in tym, or tym will not be tane;
Thairfor tak tent how thou this tyme suld tak:
Sho hes no hold, to hold hir by, bot ane;
A toppe befor, bot beld behind hir bak.
Let thou hir slippe, or slipperly grow slak,
Thou gettis no grippe agane fra sho be gane.
If thou wald speid, remember what I spak;
Tak tyme in tyme, or tym will not be tane.

For I haif hard in adagies of auld,
That tyme dois waist and weir all things away;
Then trow the taill that trew men oft hes tauld —
A turne in tyme is ay worth other tway.
Siklyk, I haif hard oft-tymis suith men say,
That negligence yit nevir furtherit nane;
Als, seindle tymis luck folowes long delayis.
Tak tyme in tyme, or tyme will not be tane.

ALEXANDER MONTGOMERIE

A Man's a Man for A' That

Is there for honest poverty
That hings his head, an' a' that;
The coward-slave – we pass him by,
We dare be poor for a' that!
For a' that, an' a' that.
Our toils obscure an' a' that,
The rank is but the guinea's stamp,
The man's the gowd for a' that.

What though on hamely fare we dine,
Wear hoddin grey, an' a' that?
Gie fools their silks, and knaves their wine;
A man's a man for a' that.
For a' that, and a' that,
Their tinsel show, an' a' that,
The honest man, tho' e'er sae poor,
Is king o' men for a' that.

Ye see yon birkie ca'd a lord,
Wha struts, an' stares, an' a' that,
Tho' hundreds worship at his word,
He's but a coof for a' that.
For a' that, an' a' that,
His ribband, star, an' a' that,
The man o' independent mind
He looks an' laughs at a' that.

A prince can mak a belted knight,
A marquise, duke, an' a' that;
But an honest man's aboon his might,
Gude faith, he maunna fa' that!
For a' that, an' a' that,
Their dignities, an' a' that,
The pith o' sense an' pride o' worth,
Are higher rank than a' that.

Then let us pray that come it may,
(As come it will for a' that,)
That Sense and Worth, o'er a' the earth,

Shall bear the gree, an' a' that.
For a' that, an' a' that,
That man to man, the world o'er
Shall brithers be for a' that.

ROBERT BURNS

A mhic Iain 'ic Sheumais

A mhic Iain, 'ic Sheumais
Tha do sgeul air m' aire
   air farail ail ò
   air farail ail ò
Gruaidh ruiteach na fèileachd
Mar èibhil ga garadh.
   Hi ò hì rì ho gì èileadh
   è ho hao rì i bho
   rò ho ì o chall èile
   bhò hi rì ò ho gì ò ho

On latha thug thu an cuan ort
Laigh gruaim air na beannaibh.

Laigh smal air na speuran,
Dh'fhàs na reultan salach.

Latha Blàr a' Chèithe
Bha feum air mo leanabh.

Latha Blàr na Fèitheadh
Bha do lèine na ballan.

Bha an t-saighead na spreòd
Throimh chorp seòlta na glaineadh.

Bha fuil do chuim chùbhraidh
A' drùdhadh throimh 'n anart.

Bha fuil do chuirp uasail
Air uachdar gach fearainn.

Bha mise ga sùghadh
Gus na thùch air m' anail.

Cuime nach do ghabh thu 'm bristeadh
Latha leigeadh na faladh?

Nam biodh agam currach
Gun cuirinn air chuan i,

Feuch am faighinn naidheachd
No brath an duine uasail,

No am faighinn beachd sgeula
Air ogha Sheumais a' chruadail,

A chuir iad ann an crìochaibh
Eadar Niall is Sìol Ailein.

'S nam biodh agam dorsair
Gum fosglainn a-mach thu,

No gille math iuchrach
A thruiseadh na glasaibh.

A MHUIME NIC CÒISEAM

Son of John, son of James

Son of John, son of James
your tale's on my mind.
      air farail ail ò
      air farail ail ò
Your festive red cheeks
like hot-glowing coals.
      hi ò hi ri ho gi èileadh
      è ho hao rì i bhò
      rò ho ì o chall èile
      bhò hi rì ò ho gì ò ho

6

Since you went to sea
the hills have been sullen.

The skies have been dimmed,
and the stars grown dirty.

At the Battle of Cèith
they needed my darling.

At the battle of Fèith
your shirt was blood-splattered.

The arrow was jutting
from your agile white body.

The blood of your sweet chest
had soaked through the linen.

The blood of your proud body
covered the land:

and I sucked it up
till it choked my breath.

How were you not broken
on the day of blood-letting?

If I had a coracle
I'd put her to sea,

to try and get word
or news of the noble,

or to hear the story
of hardy James's grandson

whom they put in the bounds
between Neil and Clanranald.

If I had a door-keeper
I would let you out

or a boy good with keys
who'd collect the locks.

Trans. Peter Mackay and Iain S. MacPherson

A Mother to Her Waking Infant

Now in thy dazzling half-oped eye,
Thy curled nose and lip awry,
Uphoisted arms and noddling head,
And little chin with crystal spread,
Poor helpless thing! what do I see,
That I should sing of thee?

From thy poor tongue no accents come,
Which can but rub thy toothless gum:
Small understanding boasts thy face,
Thy shapeless limbs nor step nor grace:
A few short words thy feats may tell,
And yet I love thee well.

When wakes the sudden bitter shriek,
And redder swells thy little cheek
When rattled keys thy woes beguile,
And through thine eyelids gleams the smile,
Still for thy weakly self is spent
Thy little silly plaint.

But when thy friends are in distress.
Thou'lt laugh and chuckle n'ertheless,
Nor with kind sympathy be smitten,
Though all are sad but thee and kitten;
Yet puny varlet that thou art,
Thou twitchest at the heart.

Thy smooth round cheek so soft and warm;
Thy pinky hand and dimpled arm;

Thy silken locks that scantly peep,
With gold tipped ends, where circle deep,
Around thy neck in harmless grace,
So soft and sleekly hold their place,
Might harder hearts with kindness fill,
And gain our right goodwill.

Each passing clown bestows his blessing,
Thy mouth is worn with old wives' kissing;
E'en lighter looks the gloomy eye
Of surly sense when thou art by;
And yet, I think, whoe'er they be,
They love thee not like me.

Perhaps when time shall add a few
Short years to thee, thou'lt love me too;
And after that, through life's long way,
Become my sure and cheering stay;
Wilt care for me and be my hold,
When I am weak and old.

Thou'lt listen to my lengthened tale,
And pity me when I am frail –
But see, the sweepy spinning fly
Upon the window takes thine eye.
Go to thy little senseless play;
Thou dost not heed my lay.

JOANNA BAILLIE

A Scottish Assembly

Circuitry's electronic tartan, the sea,
Libraries, fields – I want the lot

To fly off and scatter, but most of all
Always to come home to roost

In this unkempt country where a handicapped printer,
Engraver of dog collars, began with his friends

The ultimate encyclopedia.
Don't expect any rhyme or reason

For Scotland remaining an explosion reversed
Or ordinariness a fruited vine

Or why I came back here to choose my union
On the side of the ayes, remaining a part

Of this diverse assembly – Benbecula, Glasgow, Bow of Fife –
Voting with my feet, and this hand.

ROBERT CRAWFORD

Aberdeen

The grey sea turns in its sleep
disturbing seagulls from the green rock.

We watched the long collapse, the black drop
and frothing of the toppled wave; looked out
on the dark that goes to Norway.

We lay all night in an open boat, that rocked
by the harbour wall – listening to the tyres creak
at the stone quay, trying to keep time –
till the night-fishers came in their arc, their lap
of light: the fat slap of waves, the water's
sway, the water mullioned with light.

The sifting rain, italic rain; the smirr
that drifted down for days; the sleet.
Your hair full of hail, as if sewn there.
In the damp sheets we left each other sea-gifts,
watermarks: long lost now in all these years
of the rip-tide's swell and trawl.

All night the feeding storm banked up
the streets and houses. In the morning
the sky was yellow, the frost ringing.

The grey sea turns in its sleep
disturbing seagulls from the green rock.

ROBIN ROBERTSON

Ad Henricum Scotorum Regem

Caltha suos nusquam vultus a sole reflectit,
        illo oriente patens, illo abeunte latens:
nos quoque pendemus de te, sol noster, ad omnes
        expositi rerum te subeunte vices.

To Henry Darnley, King of Scots

The marigold nowhere turns from the sun.
        Opening at dawn, it closes in the dusk.
We too depend on you, our sun. To all
        Your turns of fortune we are left exposed.

Trans. Robert Crawford

GEORGE BUCHANAN

Address to a Haggis

Fair fa' your honest, sonsie face,
Great chieftain o' the pudding-race!
Aboon them a' ye tak your place,
Painch, tripe, or thairm:
Weel are ye wordy o'a grace
As lang's my arm.

The groaning trencher there ye fill,
Your hurdies like a distant hill,
Your pin wad help to mend a mill
In time o'need,
While thro' your pores the dews distil
Like amber bead.

His knife see rustic Labour dight,
An' cut you up wi' ready sleight,
Trenching your gushing entrails bright,
Like ony ditch;
And then, O what a glorious sight,
Warm-reekin', rich!

Then, horn for horn, they stretch an' strive:
Deil tak the hindmost! on they drive,
Till a' their weel-swall'd kytes belyve
Are bent like drums;
Then auld Guidman, maist like to rive,
Bethankit! hums.

Is there that owre his French ragout
Or olio that wad staw a sow,
Or fricassee wad make her spew
Wi' perfect sconner,
Looks down wi' sneering, scornfu' view
On sic a dinner?

Poor devil! see him owre his trash,
As feckless as wither'd rash,
His spindle shank, a guid whip-lash;
His nieve a nit;
Thro' bloody flood or field to dash,
O how unfit!

But mark the Rustic, haggis-fed,
The trembling earth resounds his tread.
Clap in his walie nieve a blade,
He'll mak it whissle;
An' legs an' arms, an' heads will sned,
Like taps o' thrissle.

Ye Pow'rs, wha mak mankind your care,
And dish them out their bill o' fare,
Auld Scotland wants nae skinking ware
That jaups in luggies;
But, if ye wish her gratefu' prayer
Gie her a haggis!

ROBERT BURNS

Address to the Unco Guid, Or the Rigidly Righteous

My Son, these maxims make a rule,
An' lump them aye thegither;
The Rigid Righteous is a fool,
The Rigid Wise anither:
The cleanest corn that ere was dight
May hae some pyles o' caff in;
So ne'er a fellow-creature slight
For random fits o' daffin.
      Solomon (Eccles. ch. vii. verse 16)

O ye wha are sae guid yoursel',
Sae pious and sae holy,
Ye've nought to do but mark and tell
Your neibours' fauts and folly!
Whase life is like a weel-gaun mill,
Supplied wi' store o' water;
The heaped happer's ebbing still,
An' still the clap plays clatter.

Hear me, ye venerable core,
As counsel for poor mortals
That frequent pass douce Wisdom's door
For glaikit Folly's portals:
I, for their thoughtless, careless sakes,
Would here propone defences
Their donsie tricks, their black mistakes,
Their failings and mischances.

Ye see your state wi' theirs compared,
And shudder at the niffer;
But cast a moment's fair regard,
What maks the mighty differ;
Discount what scant occasion gave,
That purity ye pride in;
And (what's aft mair than a' the lave),
Your better art o' hidin.

Think, when your castigated pulse
Gies now and then a wallop!
What ragings must his veins convulse,

That still eternal gallop!
Wi' wind and tide fair i' your tail,
Right on ye scud your sea-way;
But in the teeth o' baith to sail,
It maks a unco lee-way.

See Social Life and Glee sit down,
All joyous and unthinking,
Till, quite transmugrified, they're grown
Debauchery and Drinking:
O would they stay to calculate
Th' eternal consequences;
Or your more dreaded hell to state,
Damnation of expenses!

Ye high, exalted, virtuous dames,
Tied up in godly laces,
Before ye gie poor Frailty names,
Suppose a change o' cases;
A dear-lov'd lad, convenience snug,
A treach'rous inclination –
But let me whisper i' your lug,
Ye're aiblins nae temptation.

Then gently scan your brother man,
Still gentler sister woman;
Tho' they may gang a kennin wrang,
To step aside is human:
One point must still be greatly dark, –
The moving Why they do it;
And just as lamely can ye mark,
How far perhaps they rue it.

Who made the heart, 'tis He alone
Decidedly can try us;
He knows each chord, its various tone,
Each spring, its various bias:
Then at the balance let's be mute,
We never can adjust it;
What's done we partly may compute,
But know not what's resisted.

ROBERT BURNS

Ae Fond Kiss

Ae fond kiss, and then we sever;
Ae fareweel, and then for ever!
Deep in heart-wrung tears I'll pledge thee,
Warring sighs and groans I'll wage thee.
Who shall say that Fortune grieves him,
While the star of hope she leaves him?
Me, nae cheerful twinkle lights me;
Dark despair around benights me.

I'll ne'er blame my partial fancy,
Naething could resist my Nancy:
But to see her was to love her;
Love but her, and love for ever.
Had we never lov'd sae kindly,
Had we never lov'd sae blindly,
Never met – or never parted –
We had ne'er been broken-hearted.

Fare-thee-weel, thou first and fairest!
Fare-thee-weel, thou best and dearest!
Thine be ilka joy and treasure,
Peace, Enjoyment, Love and Pleasure!
Ae fond kiss, and then we sever!
Ae fareweel alas, for ever!
Deep in heart-wrung tears I'll pledge thee,
Warring sighs and groans I'll wage thee.

ROBERT BURNS

after Issa

disnae matter
how ye look at it –
ma heid's cauld

ALAN SPENCE

Ailein Duinn

Ailein Duinn, ò hi shiùbhlainn leat,
Hao ri rì iu ò hì o hù gò rionn ò;
Ailein Duinn, ò hì shiùbhlainn leat.

'S mòr an diù tha tighinn fa-near dhomh:
Fuachd na sìneadh 's meud na gaillinn
A dh'fhuadaich na fir on charraig
'S a chuir iad a bhòid' gan ainneoin –

Cha b' e siud mo rogha cala,
Caolas Shiadair anns na Hearadh
Far am faicte fèidh air bearraidh,
Coileach dubh air bhàrr gach meangain.

Ailein Duinn, a mhiann nan leannan,
Chuala mi gun deach thu fairis
Air a' bhàta chrìon dhubh dharaich;
Mas fìor sin, cha bhi mi fallain –
O, a-chaoidh cha dèan mi banais.

Gura mise tha gu deurach:
Chan e bàs nan uan sa Chèitein
No tainead mo bhuaile sprèidheadh
Ach an fhlichead tha ad lèinidh
'S tu air bàrr nan stuagh ag èirigh
'S mucan-mara ga do reubadh.

'S truagh, a Rìgh, nach mì bha là' riut –
Ge b' e sgeir no bogh' an tàmh thu,
Ge b' e tiùrr am fàg an làn thu –
Cùl do chinn am bac mo làimheadh.

Ailein Duinn, gun tug mi spèis dhut
Nuair a bha thu 'n sgoil na Beurla
Far an robh sinn òg le chèile.

Ailein Duinn, gun d' fhuair thu 'n urram,
Fhuair thu 'n urram air na fearaibh:
An ruith 's an leum 's an streup 's an carachd,
'S ann an cur na cloiche fairis.

16

Ailein Duinn, gun tug mi gràdh dhut
Nach tug mi dh'athair no mhàthair,
'S nach tug mi phiuthar no bhràthair,
'S nach tug mi chinneadh no chàirdean.

Nar dhìoladh Dia siud air d' anam –
Na fhuair mi dhe d' shùgradh falaich,
'S na fhuair mi dhe d' chuid gun cheannach:
Pìosan daora caol' an anairt,
'S nèapaigear dhen t-sìoda bhallach
'S ribinn gus mo ghruag a cheangal.

'S dh'òlainn deoch, ge b' oil le m' chàirdean,
Chan ann de dh'uisge, no de shàile,
'S chan ann de dh'fhìon dearg na Spàinneadh –
A dh'fhuil do chuim, do chlèibh 's do bhràghad,
A dh'fhuil do chuim, 's tu 'n dèis do bhàthadh.

M' iarratas air Rìgh na Cathrach
Gun mo chur an ùir no 'n gaineamh
No an talamh toll no 'n àite falaich
Ach sa bhall a bheil thus', Ailein,
Ged a b' ann san liadhaig fheamainn
No am broinn na muice-mara.

ANNA CHAIMBEUL

Brown-haired Alan

Brown-haired Alan, I'd go with you,
Hao ri rì iu ò hì o hù gò rionn ò;
Brown-haired Alan, I'd go with you.

Huge worries are wracking me.
The storm's cold, the strong gale,
Has cleared men from the rocks
And carried them away helpless.

I'd not have chosen your harbour
In Harris, in the straits of Shader,
Where deer are seen on ridges
And black cockerels sit on the branches.

Brown-haired Alan, desire of lovers,
I heard that you were drowned.
The mean black oak boat went over,
If it's true I'll never come round.
Oh, I'll never be married.

My heart is broken
Not from the death of lambs in May
Or my cattlefold, empty and bare,
But the soaking of your plaid
As you're carried over the waves,
Whales tearing you apart.

God, I wish I was with you
Whichever rock or reef holds you,
Whatever wreck the tides leave you:
Your head crooked in my arm.

Brown-haired Alan, I admired you
When you were in the English school
When we were together in our youth.

Alan, you won each honour,
Honour over all the others:
You ran, jumped, played, wrestled,
And threw the stone better.

I loved you more than any other,
More than a father or mother,
More than a sister or brother,
More than kith and kin.

Let God not damn your soul
For our secret flirtation,
What you gave me without condition:
Scarfs of flecked silk and satin,

And strips of dearest, fine linen
To tie my hair in ribbons.

Despite my people I'd drink
Not water or brine,
Or red Spanish wine –
But the blood of your breast,
Of your sea-drowned chest.

I ask, King of us all,
Don't bury me in sand or soil,
Or in an earthy hole,
But wherever, Alan, you are;
Whether in the tangled sea-oak
Or the belly of the whale.

Trans. Peter Mackay and Iain S. MacPherson

ANNE CAMPBELL

air an fhàinne, fada bho 'shàbaid'

rovaniemi, suomi, am faoilleach, 1998

mac is athair
dol tarsainn na h-aibhne gil
o bhruach gu bruach
san tìr a tuath
a' coiseachd bàrr an uisge
mheanbh-shreamach shèimh
eadr baile nan solas
agus a' choille ghorm
seirm nan clag dòmhnaich
sanas air an cùlaibh
muinntir dhè gan gairm
dhan tional eòlach
mac is athair
paisgte mar phàistean
an clòimh 's an gàire
eadr faiceall is faodail

anail air an àile
braonach ris 'an fhìrinn'
a' laighe sgrath de shiùcar
air màilin agus ciabhag
coigrich anns an t-saoghal seo,
a' leantainn làrach bhonn,
mise 's mo mhac
a' cur earbs' anns an fhuachd
ar n-air' air nì ach
taobh thall a ruigheachd
(eadar cur is cur)
agus tilleadh dìon

AONGHAS MACNEACAIL

on the circle, far from the 'Sabbath'

rovaniemi, finland, january, 1998

son and father
crossing the white river
from bank to bank
in the northern land

walking the water's
quiet rippled surface
between village of lights
and the green forest

chorus of sabbath bells
signalling behind them
god's people being called
to the familiar gathering

son and father
wrapped like children
in wool and laughter
between caution and chance

breath on the air
drizzly as 'the truth'
laying a rind of sugar
on eyebrow and ringlet

strangers in this world,
following in the other's footsteps,
me and my son
putting trust in the cold

our attention on only
reaching the other side
(between blizzard and blizzard),
and returning secure

Translated by author

AONGHAS MACNEACAIL

Alas! Poor Queen

She was skilled in music and the dance
And the old arts of love
At the court of the poisoned rose
And the perfumed glove,
And gave her beautiful hand
To the pale Dauphin
A triple crown to win —
And she loved little dogs
      And parrots
    And red-legged partridges
And the golden fishes of the Duc de Guise
And a pigeon with a blue ruff
She had from Monsieur d'Elboeuf.

Master John Knox was no friend to her;
She spoke him soft and kind,
Her honeyed words were Satan's lure
The unwary soul to bind.
'Good sir, doth a lissome shape

And a comely face
Offend your God His Grace
Whose Wisdom maketh these
Golden fishes of the Duc de Guise?'

She rode through Liddesdale with a song;
'Ye streams sae wondrous strang,
Oh, mak' me a wrack as I come back
But spare me as I gang.'
While a hill-bird cried and cried
Like a spirit lost
By the grey storm-wind tost.

Consider the way she had to go,
Think of the hungry snare,
The net she herself had woven,
Aware or unaware,
Of the dancing feet grown still,
The blinded eyes –
Queens should be cold and wise,
And she loved little things,
            Parrots
        And red-legged partridges
And the golden fishes of the Duc de Guise
And the pigeon with the blue ruff
She had from Monsieur d'Elboeuf.

                                        MARION ANGUS

Bho Alasdair à Gleanna Garadh

[. . .]

Bu tu 'n lasair dhearg gan losgadh,
'S bu tu sgoltadh iad gu 'n sàiltibh,
Bu tu guala chur a' chatha,
Bu tu 'n laoch gun athadh làimhe,
Bu tu 'm bradan anns an fhìor-uisg,
Fìor-eun air an eunlainn as àirde,

22

Bu tu 'n leòmhann thar gach beathach,
Bu tu damh leathann na cràice.

Bu tu 'n loch nach faodte thaomadh,
Bu tu tobar faoilidh na slàinte,
Bu tu Beinn Nibheis thar gach aonach,
Bu tu 'chreag nach faodte theàrnadh;
Bu tu clach-mhullaich a' chaisteil,
Bu tu leac leathann na sràide,
Bu tu leug lòghmhor nam buadhan,
Bu tu clach uasal an fhàinne.

Bu tu 'n t-iubhar thar gach coillidh,
Bu tu 'n darach daingeann làidir,
Bu tu 'n cuileann, 's bu tu 'n draigheann,
Bu tu 'n t-abhall molach blàthmhor;
Cha robh meur annad den chritheann,
Cha robh do dhlighe ri feàrna;
Cha robh do chàirdeas ri leamhan –
Bu tu leannan nam ban àlainn.

Bu tu cèile na mnà prìseil,
'S oil leam fhìn ga dìth an dràsd' thu;
Ged nach ionann dhòmhsa 's dhìse,
'S goirt a fhuair mi fhìn mo chàradh;
H-uile bean a bhios gun chèile,
Guidheadh i Mac Dè na àite,
O 's E 's urra bhi ga còmhnadh
Anns gach bròn a chuireas càs oirr'.

Guidheam t' anam a bhith sàbhailt'
On a chàireadh anns an ùir thu;
Guidheam sonas air na dh'fhàg thu
Ann ad àros 's ann ad dhùthaich:
'S math leam do mhac a bhith 'd àite
Ann an saidhbhreas, am beairteas 's an cùram:
Alasdair à Gleanna Garadh,
Thug thu 'n-diugh gal air mo shùilean.

SÌLEAS NA CEAPAICH

From Alasdair of Glengarry

[...]

You were the red torch who burned,
you would split them to their heels,
you were the shoulder for the battle,
the hero with unflinching hand,
you were the salmon in fresh water,
the eagle in the highest flight,
the lion above all other creatures,
you were the broad-antlered stag.

You were the loch that couldn't be emptied,
the generous well of health,
Ben Nevis above other mountains,
the cliff that couldn't be scaled;
you were the capstone on the castle,
the broad flagstone of the street,
the precious jewel of goodness,
the proud stone of the ring.

You were the yew above each wood,
you were the strong, steadfast oak,
you were the holly, you were the blackthorn,
the rough-barked, flowering apple;
you hadn't a single twig of aspen,
you were not the alder's due,
you had no friendship with the lime-tree,
you were the darling of fine women.

The husband of a dear wife,
I'm sad she now mourns you;
though she and I are different,
my healing too was painful;
every wife without a husband
would pray God's son take his place,
since He could give her comfort
in every sadness she will face.

I pray your soul be saved,
now that you're laid in earth;
I pray joy for those you've left,
in your country and your home:
I'm glad your son is in your place,
with wealth, riches and safekeeping –
Alasdair of Glen Garry,
you brought tears to my eyes today.

Trans. Peter Mackay

JULIA MacDONALD

All Changeth

The angrye winds not ay
Doe cuffe the roring deep,
And though Heauens often weep
Yet doe they smyle for joy when com'd is May,
Frosts doe not euer kill the pleasant flowres
And loue hath sweets when gone are all the sowres.
This said a shepheard closing in his armes
His Deare, who blusht to feele loues new alarmes.

WILLIAM DRUMMOND OF HAWTHORNDEN

A.M.

'Dè man a tha thu?'
Wet, your hair gleams. Heather dew.
Gems. Dharmadhatu.

KEVIN MacNEIL

Bho Am Bruadar

Air bhith dhòmhsa ann am shuain
    A' bruadar dìomhain, mar tha càch,
Bhith glacadh sonais o gach nì
    'S e gam dhìbreadh anns gach àit',

Ar leam gun tàinig neach am chòir
    'S gun tuirt e rium gur gòrach mi
Bhith smuainteach' greim a ghleidheadh den ghaoith
    No gun lìon an saoghal mo chrìdh.

''S dìomhain duit bhith 'g iarraidh sàimh
    'N aon nì no 'n àit' air bith fon ghrèin;
Cha chlos do d' chorp an taobh seo 'n uaigh
    No t' anam 'n taobh seo shuaimhnis Dè.

'An tràth dh'ith Àdhamh 'm meas an tùs,
    Am peacadh dhrùidh e air gach nì,
Lìon e a h-uile nì le saothair
    'S dh'fhàg e 'n saoghal 'na bhristeadh crìdh.

[. . .]

'An nì bu mhò don tug thu miann,
    Nach d'fhàg a mhealtainn riamh e searbh?
Tha tuilleadh sonais ann an dùil
    Na th'ann an crùn le bhith 'na shealbh.

'Ceart mar an ròs ata sa ghàr',
    Seargaidh a bhlàth nuair thèid a bhuain:
Mun gann a ghlacas tu e 'd làimh
    Trèigidh àile e 's a shnuadh.

'Nì bheil neach o thrioblaid saor
    Am measg a' chinne-daonn' air fad:
'S cho lìonmhor osna aig an rìgh
    Is aig an neach as ìsle staid.

'Tha smùdan fhèin às ceann gach fòid
    Is dòrainn ceangailt' ris gach math,
Tha 'n ròs a' fàs air drisibh geur
    'S an taic a chèil' tha mhil 's an gath.

[. . .]

'Nam faigheadh toil na feòl' a rùn
    D'a mianna brùideil dh'iarradh sàth:
Flaitheas a b' àird' chan iarradh i
    Na annta siud bhith sìorraidh 'snàmh.

'Ach ged a b' ionmhainn leis an fheòil
    Air talamh còmhnachadh gach rè,
Bhiodh dùrachd t' àrdain agus t' uaill'
    Cho àrd a-suas ri cathair Dhè.

'Ach nam b' àill leat sonas buan,
    Do shlighe tabhair suas do Dhia,
Le dùrachd, creideamh agus gràdh –
    Is sàsaichidh e t' uile mhiann.

'Tha 'n cuideachd siud gach nì san t-saoghal
    Tha 'n comas dhaoine shealbhach' fìor:
Biadh is aodach agus slàint',
    Is saorsa, càirdeas agus sìth.'

An-sin do mhosgail às mo shuain
    Is dh'fhàg mo bhruadar mi air fad,
Is leig mi dhiom bhith ruith gach sgàil
    Is dh'fhàs mi toilichte le m' staid.

DÙGHALL BOCHANAN

From **The Dream**

Once when I had been asleep
    Dreaming idly, as do others,
Of seizing happiness from everything
    While it forsakes me everywhere,

I thought a being came where I was
      And said to me that I'm a fool
To believe that I can grasp the wind
      Or that the world will fill my heart.

'It's vain for you to be seeking joy
      In any thing or place on earth;
There's no rest for your body this side of the grave
      Or for your soul this side of the peace of God.

'When Adam ate the fruit in the beginning,
      The sin penetrated everything,
It filled everything with toil
      And left the world a disappointment.

[. . .]

'The thing you ever wanted most,
      Didn't enjoying it always leave it bitter?
There's more happiness in looking ahead
      Than in real possession of a crown.

'Just like the rose that's in the garden,
      Its blossom withers when it's plucked:
You've scarcely grasped it in your hand
      When it's abandoned by its scent and hue.

'No one person is free from oppression
      Throughout the whole of the human race:
Just as frequently sighs the king
      As does he of the lowest state.

'Each lump of peat emits its smoke
      And grief to every good is tied,
The rose it grows upon sharp thorns
      With sting and honey side by side.

[. . .]

'If fleshly desire were to get its way
 It would try to fulfil its brutish lusts:
No higher kingdom would it seek
 Than forever to be swimming around in those.

'But though the flesh would be delighted
 To live at all times upon the earth,
Your pride's and vanity's desire
 Would be up as high as the throne of God.

'But if you'd like to have joy eternal,
 Your path surrender now to God,
With sincerity, faith and love –
 And He'll fulfil your every wish.

'That brings all things in the world
 Which men can really possess:
Food and clothing and health,
 And freedom, friendship and peace.'

Then I woke up from my sleep
 And my dream left me completely,
And I ceased to chase each spectre
 And grew content with my condition.

Trans. Ronald Black

DUGALD BUCHANAN

An àiteigin, an oisean dhe mo bhith

An àiteigin, an oisean dhe mo bhith,
tha i fhathast maireann, an aisling sin

gun coinnich sinn ri chèile anns a' bhaile
ghrianach, rèidh, an ceann bliadhna no dhà,

is leus an là ann mar gum biodh a' phlanaid
glacte ann an truinnsear de dh'airgead

chun a lainnir is a neart gu lèir
a chruinneachadh, gun anbharr no gairge,

oir cha bhi boinne fliche anns an adhar,
is giùlainidh na daoin' an teas gun strì.

Rachainn a chadal leis na h-uinneagan
làn-fhosgailte, is nochdadh tu san leabaidh

gun eòlas dhomh, oir b' annsa leat bhith anmoch,
is nuair a thòisicheadh an là a' bristeadh

bhiodh tu 'g èirigh, mar dhuine tha a' triall
gun dùsgadh, gus na còmhlaichean a dhùnadh,

's tiughad a thoirt air ais don dorchadas,
air neo bhitheadh a' chamhanach gad bhuaireadh.

Dh'fhanainn car sealain is mo shùilean fosgailt',
's mo chuimhn' a' dol air grad-theàrnadh na h-oidhche

sa cheàrnaig mhòir is mi, 'nam shuidh', a' coimhead
air siubhal deireannach nan corra-bàn.

CRÌSDEAN MACILLEBHÀIN

Somewhere, in a corner of my being

Somewhere, in a corner of my being,
it still lives on, the dream that we will meet

each other when a year or two have passed,
in the sunny, level city, where

daylight is as if the sun had been
caught in a golden ashet, so that all

its brilliance and its energy can be
concentrated, without surplus or

excess, for in the air there's not a drop
of moisture, and the heat's easy to bear.

When I went to bed, I'd leave the windows
wide open and, without me noticing,

you would arrive, given that you were fond
of sitting up late. Once the day began

to dawn, you'd get up and – you could have been
walking in your sleep – would close the shutters,

returning all its substance to the darkness
so the half-light did not keep you awake.

I'd lie there for a while with open eyes,
remembering how swiftly night had fallen

in the big square, while I would sit and watch
the storks rise in the sky for the last time.

Translated by author

CHRISTOPHER WHYTE

Bho An Claigeann

'S mi 'm shuidh' aig an uaigh,
Ag amharc mu bruaich,
Feuch claigeann gun snuadh air làr;
Do thog mi e suas,
A' tiomach' gu truagh,
Ga thionndadh mun cuairt am làimh.

Gun àille, gun dreach,
Gun aithne, gun bheachd
Air duine thèid seach na dhàil;
Gun fhiacail na dheud,
No teanga na bheul,
No slugan a ghleusas càil.

Gun ruiteag na ghruaidh,
'S e rùisgte gun ghruaig,
Gun èisteachd na chluais dom dhàn;
Gun anail na shròin
No àile den fhòid,
Ach lag far 'm bu chòir bhith àrd.

Gun deàlradh na shùil
No rosg uimpe dùn',
No fradharc ri h-iùl mar b' àbhaist,
Ach durraga crom
A chleachd bhith san tom
Air cladhach dà tholl nan àit'.

Tha 'n t-eanchainn bha 'd chùl
Air tionndadh gu smùr,
Gun tionnsgal no sùrd air d' fheum;
Gun smuainteach' ad dhàil
Mu philleadh gu bràth
A cheartach' na dh'fhàg thu 'd dhèidh.

Chan innis do ghnùis
A-nise cò thu,
Mas rìgh no mas diùc thu fèin —
'S ionann Alasdair Mòr
Is tràille dhìth lòin
A dh'eug air an òtrach bhreun.

Fhir-dhèanamh na h-uaigh',
Nach cogair thu 'm chluais
Cò 'n claigeann seo fhuair mi 'm làimh,
'S gun cuirinn ris ceist
Mu ghnàths mun do theasd,
Ged nach freagair e 'm-feasd mo dhàn.

'M bu mhaighdeann deas thu
Bha sgiamhach ad ghnùis,
'S deagh shuidheach' ad shùil da rèir,
Led mhaise mar lìon
A' ribeadh mu chridh'
Gach òganaich chitheadh thu fèin?

Tha nise gach àgh
Bha cosnadh duit gràidh
Air tionndadh gu gràin gach neach;
Marbhphaisg air an uaigh,
A chreach thu den bhuaidh
Bha ceangailt' ri snuadh do dhreach.

No 'm breitheamh ceart thu
Le tuigs' agus iùl
Bha rèiteach gach cùis don t-sluagh;
Gun aomadh le pàirt
Ach dìteadh gu bàs
Na h-eucoir bha dàicheil, cruaidh?

No 'n d' reic thu a' chòir
Air ghlacaid den òr
On dream gan robh stòras pailt,
Is bochdan an t-sluaigh,
Fo fhòirneart ro-chruaidh,
A' fulang le cruas na h-airc?

[. . .]

DÙGHALL BOCHANAN

From The Skull

As I sit by the grave,
Looking over its edge,
On the ground – an expressionless skull;
I picked it up
And melted with pity,
Turning it round in my hand.

No beauty, no colour,
No knowledge nor thoughts
Of people who pass its way;
No teeth in its jaw,
No tongue in its mouth,
No throat to make a tune.

No blush in its cheek,
Stripped of its hair,
No ear to hear my song;
No breath in its nose,
No smell of the earth,
Just a hole where it should jut out.

No shining of eyes,
No lids to close on them,
No sight that once gave guidance.
Instead crooked worms
That lived in knolls
Have dug two holes in their place.

The brain behind them
Has turned to dust,
No ingenuity, no wit to relieve you.
No thoughts will cross it
Of ever returning
To repair what you left behind.

Your face will not tell
Now who you are,
If you were a king or a duke,
Alexander the Great,
Or a hungry slave
Who died on a fetid midden.

O digger of graves,
Whisper in my ear
Whose skull I have here in my hand,
So I can ask of it
Its habits in life,
Though it will never answer my song.

Were you a sharp young lass
With a handsome face,
Whose eyes were elegantly set,
Your beauty a net
That caught the hearts
Of every young man who saw you?

Now each attribute
That won you their love
Makes you the object of everyone's hate;
A curse on the grave
That ruined the effects
Of your appearance and shape.

Or were you a just judge
With wisdom and sense,
Who settled each case for the people;
Who'd be impartial
But sentence to death
Any crime that was probable and vicious?

Or did you sell justice
For a handful of gold
From those of plentiful means,
While those who were poor
And violently used
Suffered the hardness of poverty?

[. . .]

Trans. Peter Mackay

DUGALD BUCHANAN

An Dàrna Eilean

Nuair a ràinig sinn an t-eilean
bha feasgar ann
's bha sinn aig fois,
a' ghrian a' dol a laighe
fo chuibrig cuain
's am bruadar a' tòiseachadh às ùr.

Ach anns a' mhadainn
shad sinn dhinn a' chuibhrig
's anns an t-solas gheal sin
chunnaic sinn loch anns an eilean

is eilean anns an loch,
is chunnaic sinn
gun do theich am bruadar pìos eile bhuainn.

Tha an staran cugallach
chon an dàrna eilein,
tha a' chlach air uideil
tha a' dìon nan dearcag,
tha chraobh chaorainn a' crìonadh,
fàileadh na h-iadhshlait a' faileachdainn oirnn a-nis.

RUARAIDH MacTHÒMAIS

The Second Island

When we reached the island
it was evening
and we were at peace,
the sun lying down
under the sea's quilt
and the dream beginning anew.

But in the morning
we tossed the cover aside
and in that white light
saw a loch in the island,
and an island in the loch,
and we recognised
that the dream had moved away from us again.

The stepping-stones are chancy
to the second island,
the stone totters
that guards the berries,
the rowan withers,
we have lost now the scent of the honeysuckle.

Translated by author

DERICK THOMSON

Bho An Geamhradh

Do theirig an samhradh,
'S tha 'n geamhradh tighinn dlùth oirnn,
Fìor nàmhaid na chinneas
Tighinn a mhilleadh ar dùthcha,
Ga saltairt fo chasaibh,
'S da maise ga rùsgadh;
Gun iochd ann ri dadam,
Ach a' sladadh 's a' plùnndrainn.

Sgaoil oirnne a sgiathan,
'S chuir e grian air a chùlaibh;
As an nead thug e 'n t-àlach,
Neo-bhàidheil gar sgiùrsadh;
Sneachd iteagach glè-gheal,
O na speuraibh tighinn dlùth oirnn,
Clocha-meallain 's gaoth thuathach,
Mar luaidh is mar fhùdar.

Nuair shèideas e anail,
Chan fhàg anam am flùran;
Tha bhilean mar shiosar
Lomadh lios de gach ùr-ròs;
Cha bhi sgeadach' air coille
No doire nach rùisg e;
No sruthan nach tachd e
Fo leacanna dùbh-ghorm.

Fead reòta a chlèibhe,
Tha sèideadh na doininn,
Chuir beirm anns an fhairge,
'S a dh'at garbh i na tonnaibh;
'S a bhinntich an clàmhain,
Air àirde gach monaidh,
'S ghlan sgùr e na reultan
Dar pèile len solus.

Tha gach beathach is duine
Nach d'ullaich na shèasan
Gan sgiùrsadh le gaillinn,

Gun talla, gun eudach;
'S an dream a bha gnìomhach
Fàs iargalt, mì-dhèirceil;
Nach toir iasad do leisgean,
Anns an t-sneachda, ged eug e.

Tha 'n seillean 's an seangan,
A bha tional an stòrais
Le gliocas gun mhearachd,
Tabhairt aire don dòrainn;
'G ithe bìdh 's ag òl meala,
Gun ghainne air lòn ac',
Fo dhìon anns an talamh
O anail an reòta.

Tha na cuileaga ciatach
Bha dìomhain san t-samhradh,
Sna gathanaibh grèine
Gu h-èibhinn a' dannsa,
Gun deasach, gun chùram
Roimh dhùdlach a' gheamhraidh;
Tha iad nise a' bàsach'
Anns gach àite le teanntachd.

Ach èisd rium, a shean-duin',
'S tuig an samhladh tha 'm stòraidh;
Tha 'm bàs a' tighinn teann ort,
Siud an geamhradh tha 'm òran;
'S ma gheibh e thu 'd leisgean,
Gun deasach fa chòmhdhail,
Cha dèan àithreachas crìche
Do dhìonadh on dòrainn.

[. . .]

DÙGHALL BOCHANAN

From The Winter

Now summer's exhausted
And winter closes on us,
The true enemy of all growth,
It comes wrecking our country;
Trampling it underfoot,
Stripping its beauty;
With no mercy for anything,
As he pillages and plunders.

He spread his wings on us,
Hiding the sun,
Took the brood from the nest,
Lashing us, unkindly;
Pure white feathery snow,
Falling thick from the skies,
Hailstones and a north wind,
Like lead and like powder.

When he blows his breath,
The flowers lose their souls;
His lips are like scissors
Pruning the gardens of roses;
No wood will have finery,
No copse be unstripped;
He'll smother every stream
Under black-blue slopes.

The frozen creel's whistle
Blows in his tempest,
Puts yeast in the ocean,
A rough swell in the waves;
And the sleet curdles
On the tops of each mountain;
And he scrubs clean the stars
That tingle with their cold light.

Every animal and person
Unprepared in the season
Is scourged by tempests

With no hall and no clothes:
And the group who were busy
Grow uncharitable, forbidding,
They won't lend to an idler,
Though he'd die in the snow.

The bee and the ant
Gathered their stores,
With unfailing wisdom,
To fend off hardship;
They eat and drink honey
With no shortage of food,
Safe in the ground,
From the breath of the freeze,

The attractive flies
That lazed through the summer,
In the rays of the sun,
Dancing so gaily;
With no care or preparation
Before the depths of the winter;
They are now dying,
Everywhere in austerity.

But listen to me, old folks,
And get the point of my 'story':
Death's on your doorstep –
The winter of my song;
And if you are an idler
Not prepared for your journey,
No repentance of heart
Will protect you from hardship.

[. . .]

Trans. John Mackenzie

DUGALD BUCHANAN

An Tiona

Nuair a bha mi sa bhun-sgoil
fhuair mi tiona sleamhainn tana
far an cuirinn m' fhaclan
sgrìobhte air sgoltaidhean pàipeir.

Chan eil cuimhne agam air inneach
ach air cho doirbh 's a bha e fhosgladh
gun ainmearean 's gnìomhairean a' leum
a-mach às mar bhradain à lìon –

iorghail bhalbh mo chànain
a' snàmh gu sìorraidh gu dachaigh chaillte.
Nam cheann tha an tiona air meirgeadh,
's cha tèid fhosgladh gun bhristeadh saillte.

PÀDRAIG MaCAOIDH

The Tin

when I was in primary school
I got this thin-walled tin
where I'd stash my words
writ on splinters of paper

I can't remember the design
but how difficult it was to open
without names and deeds leaping out
like salmon from a net

the dumb babble of my languages
swimming forever towards their lost ground
the tin in my head rusted not to be opened
without breaking its crust of salt

Trans. Ciaran Carson

PETER MACKAY

Ane Dreame

I dreamit ane dreame, or that my dreame were trew!
    Me thocht my maistris to my chalmer came,
And with hir harmeles handis the cowrteingis drew,
And sueitlie callit on me be my name:
'Art ye on sleip,' quod sche, 'o fy for schame!
    Haue ye nocht tauld that luifaris takis no rest?'
Me thocht I ansuerit, 'trew it is, my dame,
    I sleip nocht, so your luif dois me molest.'
With that me thocht hir nicht-gowne of sche cuist,
    Liftit the claiths and lichtit in my armis;
Hir Rosie lippis me thocht on me sche thirst,
    And said, 'may this nocht stanche yow of your harmes!'
'Mercy, madame,' me thoucht I menit to say,
Bot quhen I walkennit, alace, sche was away.

ALEXANDER MONTGOMERIE

From Ane Metaphoricall Invention of a Tragedie Called Phoenix

For I complaine not of sic common cace,
Which diversely by divers means dois fall:
But I lament my Phoenix rare, whose race,
Whose kynde, whose kin, whose offspring, they be all
In her alone, whome I the Phoenix call.
That fowle which only one at onis did live,
Not lives, alas! though I her praise revive.

And thow (o reuthles Death) sould throw devore
Her? who not only passed by all mens mynde
All other fowlis in hewe, and shape, but more
In rarenes (sen there was none of her kynde
But she alone) whome with thy stounds thow pynde:
And at the last, heth perced her through the heart,
But reuth or pitie, with thy mortall dart.

Yet worst of all, she lived not half her age.
Why stayde thou Tyme at least, which all dois teare
To worke with her? O what a cruell rage,

To cut her off, before her threid did weare!
Wherein all Planets keeps their course, that yeare
It was not by the half yet worne away,
Which sould with her have ended on a day.

KING JAMES VI

From Ane New Yeir Gift to the Quene Mary, quhen scho come first Hame, 1562

Welcum, illustrat Ladye, and oure Quene!
Welcum, oure lyone with the Floure-delyce!
Welcum, oure thrissill with the Lorane grene!
Welcum, oure rubent roiss vpoun the ryce!
Welcum, oure jem and joyfull genetryce!
Welcum, oure beill of Albion to beir!
Welcum, oure plesand Princes maist of pryce!
God gif the grace aganis this guid new yeir.

This guid new yeir, we hoip, with grace of God,
Salbe of peax, tranquillitie, and rest:
This yeir sall rycht and ressone rewle the rod,
Quhilk sa lang seasoun hes bene soir supprest;
This yeir ferme faith sall frelie be confest,
And all erronius questionis put areir;
To laboure that this lyfe amang ws lest
God gife the grace aganis this guid new yeir.

Heirfore addres the dewlie to decoir
And rewle thy regne with hie magnificence;
Begin at God to gar sett furth his gloir,
And of his gospell gett experience;
Caus his trew Kirk be had in reuerence;
So sall thy name and fame spred far and neir:
Now, this thy dett to do with diligence,
God gif the grace aganis this guid new yeir.

ALEXANDER SCOTT

Annie Laurie

Maxwelton braes are bonnie
Where early fa's the dew,
And it's there that Annie Laurie
Gie'd me her promise true –
Gie'd me her promise true,
Which ne'er forgot will be.
And for bonnie Annie Laurie
I'd lay me doun and dee.

Her brow is like the snaw-drift;
Her throat is like the swan.
Her face is the fairest
That e'er the sun shone on –
That e'er the sun shone on –
And dark blue is her ee;
And for bonnie Annie Laurie
I'd lay me doun and dee.

Like dew on the gowan lying
Is the fa' o' her fairy feet.
And like the winds in summer sighing,
Her voice is low and sweet –
Her voice is low and sweet.
And she's a' the world to me.
And for bonnie Annie Laurie
I'd lay me doun and dee.

WILLIAM DOUGLAS

Bho Ar sliocht Gaodhal ó Ghort Gréag

Ar sliocht Gaodhal ó Ghort Gréag
ní fheil port ar a gcoimhéad,
 dá dteagmhadh nach b' aordha leat
 sliocht Gaodhal do chur tharat.

Is dú éirighe i n-aghaidh Gall,
nocha dóigh éirighe udmhall;
    faobhair claidheamh, reanna ga,
    cóir a gcaitheamh go h-aobhdha.

Ré Gallaibh, adeirim ribh,
sul ghabhadar ar ndúthaigh;
    ná léigimid ar ndúthaigh dhínn,
    déinimid ardchogadh ainmhín,
        ar aithris Gaoidheal mBanbha,
        caithris ar ar n-athardha.

[· · ·]

Ó nach mair acht fuidheall áir
do Ghaoidhlibh ó ghost iomgháidh,
    teagair lé chéile na fir,
    's cuir th'eagal féine ar náimhdibh.

Saigh ar Ghallaibh 'na dtreibh féin:
bi id dhúsgadh, a Mheic Cailéin:
    d'fhear cogaidh, a fholt mar ór,
    ní math an codal ramhór.

GUN URRA

From The Race of Gaels from the Land of Greece

The race of Gaels from the land of Greece
will have no place in their power
    if you should think it no disgrace
    to ignore the Gaelic lineage.
It is right to rise against outsiders,
no bungled strike do we anticipate,
    but swords' edge, spears' tip,
    rightly plied with spirit.

Against outsiders, I tell ye,
in case they take our country;
    let's not throw away our land,
    let us make no gentle warfare;

in imitation of the Gaels of Ireland,
let us watch over our fatherland.

[. . .]

Since only the dregs of the slain
remain of the Gaels from the field of peril,
    bring the men together
    and put fear of yourself in the enemy.

Attack the Goill on their own soul,
rouse yourself, O son of Cailean,
    for a man of war, O hair like gold,
    too long a sleep is no benison.

Trans. Meg Bateman

ANON.

Armies in the Fire

The lamps now glitter down the street;
Faintly sound the falling feet;
And the blue even slowly falls
About the garden trees and walls.

Now in the falling of the gloom
The red fire paints the empty room:
And warmly on the roof it looks,
And flickers on the backs of books.

Armies march by tower and spire
Of cities blazing, in the fire; −
Till as I gaze with staring eyes,
The armies fade, the lustre dies.

Then once again the glow returns;
Again the phantom city burns;
And down the red-hot valley, lo!
The phantom armies marching go!

Blinking embers, tell me true
Where are those armies marching to,
And what the burning city is
That crumbles in your furnaces!

ROBERT LOUIS STEVENSON

Arran

Arann na n-oigheadh n-iomdha,
        tadhall fairrge re a formna;
oiléan i mbearntar buidhne,
        druimne i ndeargthar gaoi gorma.

Ard ós a muir a mullach,
        caomh a luibh, tearc a tonnach;
oiléan gorm groigheach glennach,
        corr bheannach dhoireach dhrongach.

Oighe baotha ar a beannaibh,
        mónainn mhaotha ina mongaibh,
uisge uar ina haibhnibh,
        meas ar a dairghibh donnaibh.

Míolchoin ghéara agus gadhair,
        sméara is airne dubh droighin,
dlúth a froigh ris na feadhaibh,
        doimh ag deabhaidh 'na doiribh.

Díoghlaim chorcra ar a cairrgibh,
        féar gan lochta ar a leargaibh,
ós a creagaibh caon cumhdaigh,
        surdghail laogh bric ag beadhgaigh.

Mín a magh, méith a muca,
        suairc a guirt (sgéal is creite),
cno for bharraibh a fiodhcholl,
        seóladh na siothlong seice.

Aoibhinn dóibh ó thig soineann,
    breac fá bhruachaibh a habhann;
freagraid faolinn 'má fionnall;
    aoibhinn gach ionam Arann!

ANON.

Arran

Arran of the many deer,
    ocean touching its shoulders;
island where troops are ruined,
    ridge where blue spears are blooded.

High above the sea its summit,
    dear its green growth, rare its bogland;
blue island of glens, of horses,
    of peaked mountains, oaks and armies.

Frisky deer on its mountains,
    moist bogberries in its thickets,
cold waters in its rivers,
    acorns on its brown oak-trees.

Hunting dogs and keen greyhounds,
    brambles, sloes of dark blackthorn;
close against the woods its dwellings;
    stags sparring in its oak-groves.

Purple lichen from its rocks,
    faultless grass on its greenswards;
on its crags, a shielding cloak;
    fawns capering, trout leaping.

Smooth its plain, well-fed its swine,
    glad its fields – believe the story! –
nuts upon its hazels' tops,
    the sailing of longships past it.

Fine for them when good weather comes –
    trout beneath its river banks;
gulls reply round its white cliff –
    fine at all times is Arran.

Trans. Thomas Owen Clancy

ANON.

Atá Fleasgach ar mo Thí

Atá fleasgach ar mo thí,
    a Rí na ríogh go rí leis!
a bheith sínte ré no bhroinn
    agus a choim ré mo chneis!

Dá mbeith gach ní mar mo mhian,
    ní bhiadh cian eadrainn go bráth,
gé beag sin dá chur i gcéill,
    's nach tuigeann sé féin mar tá.

Acht ní éadtrom gan a luing,
    sgéal as truaighe linn 'nar ndís:
esan soir is mise siar,
    mar nach dtig ar riar a rís.

ISEABAIL NÍ MHEIC CAILÉIN

There's a Young Man on My Trail

There's a young man on my trail –
    King of Kings, bring him success!
O to have him stretched beside me
    With his chest on my breast.

If this world was as I want it
    We'd be together evermore;
But now there's little chance
    And he doesn't yet know the score.

With no sign of his boat, there can be no joy,
    The tale brings us both pain:
He is east and I am west,
    What we desire won't come again.

Trans. Peter Mackay and Iain S. MacPherson

ISEABAIL NÍ MHEIC CAILÉIN

From Auld Reikie

Auld Reikie, wale o' ilka toun,
That Scotland kens beneath the moon!
Whare couthy chiels at e'ening meet
Their bizzing craigs and mous to weet;
And blythly gar auld care gae by
Wi' blinkit and wi' bleering eye:
O'er lang frae thee the Muse has been
Sae frisky on the simmer's green,
Whan flowers and gowans wont to glent
In bonny blinks upo' the bent;
But now the leaves o' yellow dye,
Peel'd frae the branches, quickly fly;
And now frae nouther bush nor brier
The spreckl'd mavis greets your ear;
Nor bonny blackbird skims and roves
To seek his love in yonder groves.
Then Reikie, welcome! Thou canst charm
Unfleggit by the year's alarm;
Not Boreas, that sae snelly blows,
Dare here pap in his angry nose:
Thanks to our dads, whase biggin stands
A shelter to surrounding lands.
Now morn, wi' bonny purple smiles,
Kisses the air-cock o' St. Giles;
Rakin their ein, the servant lasses
Early begin their lies and clashes;
Ilk tells her friend o' saddest distress,
That still she brooks frae scawling mistress,
And wi' her joe in turnpike stair

She'd rather snuff the stinking air,
As be subjected to her tongue,
When justly censur'd i' the wrong.
On stair wi' tub, or pat in hand,
The barefoot housemaids loe to stand,
That antrin fock may ken how snell
Auld Reikie will at morning smell:
Then, with an inundation big as
The burn that 'neath the Nor Loch brig is,
They kindly shower Edina's roses,
To quicken and regale our noses.
Now some for this, wi' satire's leesh,
Hae gi'en auld Edinbrough a creesh:
But without souring nocht is sweet;
The morning smells that hail our street,
Prepare and gently lead the way
To simmer canty, braw and gay:
Edina's sons mair eithly share
Her spices and her dainties rare,
Than he that's never yet been call'd
Aff frae his plaidie or his fauld.
Now stair-head critics, senseless fools,
Censure their aim, and pride their rules,
In Luckenbooths wi' glouring eye,
Their neighbours sma'est fauts descry:
If ony loun shou'd dander there,
O' aukward gate, and foreign air:
They trace his steps, till they can tell
His pedigree as weel's himsell.
Whan Phaebus blinks wi' warmer ray,
And schools at noon-day get the play,
Then, bus'ness, weighty bus'ness, comes,
The trader glours; he doubts, he hums:
The lawyers eke to cross repair,
Their wings to shaw, and toss an air:
While busy agent closely plies,
And a' his kittle cases tries.
Now night, that's cunzied chief for fun,
Is wi' her usual rites begun;
Thro' ilka gate the torches blaze,
And globes send out their blinkin rays.

The usefu' cadie plies in street,
To bide the profits o' his feet;
For by thir lads Auld Reikie's fock
Ken but a sample o' the stock
O' thieves, that nightly wad oppress,
And mak baith goods and gear the less.
Near him the lazy chairman stands,
And wats na how to turn his hands;
Till some daft birky, ranting fu',
Has matters somewhare else to do;
The chairman willing gi'es his light
To deeds o' darkness and o' night.
It's never saxpence for a lift
That gars thir lads wi' fu'ness rift;
For they wi' better gear are paid,
And whores and culls support their trade.
Near some lamp-post, wi' dowy face,
Wi' heavy ein, and sour grimace,
Stands she that beauty lang had kend,
Whoredom her trade, and vice her end.
But see whare now she wins her bread
By that which Nature ne'er decreed;
And vicious ditties sings to please
Fell Dissipation's votaries.
Whane'er we reputation lose,
Fair chastity's transparent gloss!
Redemption seenil kens the name,
But a's black misery and shame.
Frae joyous tavern, reeling drunk,
Wi' fiery phiz, and ein half sunk,
Behad the bruiser, fae to a'
That in the reek o' gardies fa'
Close by his side, a feckless race
O' macaronies shaw their face,
And think they're free frae skaith or harm,
While pith befriends their leader's arm:
Yet fearfu' aften o' their maught,
They quit the glory o' the faught
To this same warrior wha led
Thae heroes to bright honour's bed;
And aft the hack o' honour shines

In bruiser's face wi' broken lines:
O' them sad tales he tells anon,
Whan ramble and whan fighting's done;
And, like Hectorian, ne'er impairs
The brag and glory o' his sairs.
Whan feet in dirty gutters plash,
And fock to wale their fitstaps fash;
At night the macaroni drunk,
In pools and gutters aftimes sunk:
Hegh! what a fright he now appears,
Whan he his corpse dejected rears!
Look at that head, and think if there
The pomet slaister'd up his hair!
The cheeks observe, where now cou'd shine
The scansing glories o' carmine!
Ah, legs! in vain the silk-worm there
Display'd to view her eident care;
For stink, instead of perfumes, grow,
And clarty odours fragrant flow.

[. . .]

ROBERT FERGUSSON

Aw Jock Tamson's

Moonrise, an maudlin in the mirk,
we coorie in, hoose selt, hame hawked,
oor labour thirled tae yesterday,
the morra pawned fur brick-a-brack.

Thieves tout the mercat, flashin cash
in credit caird tricks yince cried tick.
Gowks gawp. It's easy money. Hauns
dip threidbare pooches skint by lees;

yin cat feeds fat, an hunners sterve.
Dunderheids, we bocht intae grief,
gied up sense fur greed, furgoat brass
barters work, its worth inventit.

A dreich rain faws oan rentit roofs.
We pey tae drain the run-aff, pey
again tae pipe it back. Nae debt
is gain. If lochs fill, mountains droon.

Yit bairns sleep an dream, fit tae bigg
a warld whaur love gies shelter, breid
daily, care redds up, prood tae bide
an fecht whaur fowk cry foul at cheats:

nae man worth mair. It's wha we are.
Tak tent. Waukened, sleeves rowed up,
drookit, set tae work, a new stert.
Day breks, mornin sun ay rises.

JANET PAISLEY

Back-Green Odyssey

I

The sun's oot. I sit, my pipe alunt, and puff.
The claes-line's pegged wi washin. They could be
sails. (Let them) Hou they rax and thraw, and yet
caa naething forrit. Gress grouws on my deck.

Thro the wheepcracks o my sails the blue
wine o the sea is blinkin to the bouwl rim
o the horizon whaur my classic tap
the Berwick Law hides oor nothrin Athens.

Nae watters for an Odyssey ye'll think
whaur jist ilers, coasters, seine-netters ply.
Still, ablow this blue roof and burst o sun

my mind moves amon islands. Ulysses
dominie, I cast aff the tether-tow
and steer my boat sittin on my doup-end.

2

The central belt unbuckles on the sands.
The only reek here is the cloods; the croods
are swaws that brakkin, skyte quicksiller baas.
The blue view is bigger nor Glesga toun.

The air is cowpin pints and nips for free;
the sun's a bargain, cheaper nor Majorca.
Fowk swap a peely-wally white for broun,
like chips, wi troosers or bikinis on.

They tak a dauner oat at nichts or jig
on the Folly; hing aff the pier for fish;
sheet at targets for Hongkong trok. But still

fowk hae a duty to enjoy theirsels.
Aulder nor the thrum o their transistors
the sea is duntin dymbals to the moon.

3

I saw ye Penelope hingin oat claes;
a lang deem, lookin as gin ye didna
ken ye were lookt at; your brou, stern runkles,
and your mou set for a dour horizon

like the times ye tell me I'm hyne awa.
Then, naething steers me to the slams o your een
and the silence is hotterin wi the bile
o auld wars (twice as lang as dung doun Troy)

You are the lang island I cam hame till
in the beddit dark when I see your glims,
the only stams the pit-mirk hasna dowsed.

The herbour crooks its airms. Tethert I ligg
at last. I listen. The soond o the sea!
I smell its tides forgaither in your sough.

4

In my young days I hae navigatit
alang the lane shores o Dalmatia.
On the face o the sea keekit up sma
clinty islands whaur a bird whiles hovert

hawk-studyin its kill; they were happit
wi tangle, sliddery, in the sunlicht
skinklin like emeralds. When the tap-flood
and nicht-mirk smoored them, sails pit oat to leeward

mair to the open sea, to jouk the saw-teeth
o the skellies. My kingdom nou is yon
nae man's land. The herbour kinilles its lichts

for ithers. The unshakkable spirit
and the sad-hertit love for life caas me
still forrit intill the deeps o the sea.

'Ulisse' — fae the Italian o Umberto Saba

5

My main deck is a green. Near the foreheid
the kitchen plot. I am weel stockit wi
vittles. On the starboard gunwales, flooers
and bushes whaur the birds scutter and pleep.

I sit here, the captain and the haill crew
and keep my sun-birsled watches dwaumin.
Whiles I scour the sky-line, whiles I scrieve drauchts
in the log-book o my tethert vaigin;

the sea's a ticht blue swatch; a thin skraichin
o bairns rises fae the beach; a sea gull
peenges like a wean and oars the air back.

I canna read my Homer in this sun.
I feel the reid meat o my body fry.
My Odyssey is jist a doverin.

6

The reid pantile roof-taps crawstep doun to
the skellies cowpit at the back-green wa,
the last cuddle o hooses afore ye socht
the horizon's threshauld aifter threshauld.

Aifter Troy was smush the ports o distance
gantit wide. Ootlin, gangrel, guest, wrack-wid,
the ocean bouffit ye fae ploy to ploy;
Calypso, Nausicaa, Circe . . . Yet

thro aa the sauty variorums o
your life it was a herbour's crookt fore-airm
and her, muckle-tholin Penelope

that drave ye ower the back-bane o the sea,
hert-hankerin for the last tether-tow,
white ainns clippin ye that winna let go.

7

Me Odysseus? I mind a man, auld noo
mair your marraw that sailed his hame-made boat
biggit wi sang fae the timmer o deid words
made in Scotland – the main mast was a thistle –

alang sea routes nane afore heard tell o.
It was a drucken boat for he was fou
on whisky and the moonlicht's barmy wine.
Capax mundi, he took on near aathing

for he had a mind aye to cowp the boat
and daur her bows thro sic ootlandish seas
the mind's wind pechit, He saw sic sichts

aneth the kythin o eternity,
he couldna spik for thinkin and fell mum.
A mind dumfoonert in its Odyssey.

8

The haar-wa at my palin stobs! I think
o that skeely skipper Sir Patrick Spens
nae ten miles aff Norway in a mirk lyft
when he began his last fecht wi the sea.

There was nae priggin wi Poseidon here.
He strave wi wind-boufft watter and the skirls
o coort leddies plyterin to their deaths
'mang silken falderals and feather beds.

A rickle o wrack-wid showdin on the faem
and Frenchy hats nid-noddin withoot heids
and weemin wringin hands on castle waas.

His Homer was a kenless makar chiel
that made his ballad Odyssey. It smells
yet o haar and smirr and Ithaca blin.

9

Happy the man that's made a braw viage
like Ulysses or him that won the fleece,
and syne cams hame wyce wi experience
to bide wi his fowk the lave o his days.

Och me, when will I see aince mair the lums
o my village reekin, when will I see
the gairden o my sma-bit sclatit hoose
that was the world to me and mair forby.

Mair to me this hame my forebears biggit
nor Roman palaces wi prood façades,
mair to me trig sclate nor teuch hard marble.

Mair to me the Loire nor Roman Tiber,
mair to me Liré nor the Palatine,
mair the douce air o Anjou nor the sea,

      fae the French o Joachim du Bellay

10

Ach, flesh is dowie and I've read aa the tomes.
To flee hyne awa . . . amon birds fou on
fremmit faem and lyfts. Naething can tether
this sea-sweeled hert – nae auld gairdens

skinklin in the lochans o the een, nor O the nichts! –
the lamp's lowe whitenin the virgin snawdrift
o my drauchts, or the bairn sookin its mither's briest.
I'm for aff! Steamer showdin your masts, up

anchor for paradisal landfass! Ennui,
doun-moued wi deid hopes still lippens on
the hankie's fare-ye-weels. And the masts

that beckon storms are yon mebbe the skail winds
yark ower ships, tint, tint and nae palm islands . . .
But O listen hert to the sang the sailors sing!

'Brise Marine' – fae the French o Mallarmé

11

The concrete airms o the pier clauchtin air;
and the boats plooin the herbour-mou, plat-calm
in this spell, for the runkled open loof
o the Firth or the seven seas. 'Cast aff'

is the sang the engines thrum. And the nets hairst
the shoals in the cauld causeys o the fish;
gut and box thro the watches o the nicht
as the bows fur hamewards wi the siller crans.

The toun's laich starns; syne the reid aster heid
o the quay-neb licht. The herbour opens
its airms and they sail intill a braid hug

and tie up whaur aince they slippit the tow.
A herbour is a tension atween twa pulls,
the beck o horizons and the rug o hame.

12

My sunflooers face the sea, burnt sienna
in their herts, and wi their petals scouthert
a bleed-tashed bronze, yalla loup o the lowe,
suns, hemmert in the smiddy o the sun.

I smell on the deck whaur the last flooers bleeze,
the blue reek o September's stibble burn.
Month o the pyres! and the ess o the deid
mells wi the hell o tubers and tap-reets.

I feel my erdfast boat brak up in bits
o wizzent leaves and shaws and bruckle stauks.
The yirth's beddit doun, aa the fushion's gane

save for yon late suns that heist up their fires
still, thro aa the deid-thraws o the season
and let their greeshoch dwine forenent the sea.

13

Streekit oot ahint the winbreak I let
Homer drap. The print jobs my een. Instead
I watch a sma green-like beastie craalin
ower the blindrift o sunsheen on the page.

It sang o him blattered by Poseidon
ower the mirk wineskin o the sea. I watcht
this sudden drappin fae the air on till
the hexameters. Whaur was his Ithaca?

I felt like the yird-shakker himsel then
heich abeen this nochtie o a craitur.
I let him streetch his pins a bit. A god

can bide his time and wyle it tae, whit's mair.
Atween ennui and yokey fingers
I skytit him aff the page. Yaawned syne.

14

The rose finger-nebs o the day-sky, this
is aa that Homer sings o the sunlicht
as far as I can mind. Naething ava
o the sun-scaudit prickly aifterneens

when a body keeps thrawin on a spit
till aa his meat, sair-done, is weel-done tae.
Ye fair enjoy whit gars ye fidge fu fain,
gie ower the ploy and turn Lotus-eater

pairt-time, wi nocht to dae but sprauchle on
the gress, sookin ice-cream or suppin tea;
listenin till a gowff-ba's quick intak o

breath, or the speugs yabblin in the bushes.
I steek my een. And syne I canna mind
whitever was it I was thinkin on.

15

I mind on Ungaretti's sma bit poem,
twa lines jist; m 'illumino d 'immenso.
White sheets hing forfochen on the lyft's blue thairm
thrummin wi heat till a ticht horizon.

My boat's dwaumin. Het haar theeks my islands.
I sit. I hear the splyterins o the wash.
I listen till the seven syllables —
oar-blades thrashin thro the lee-lang blue

toomness aneth the licht's ae Cyclops ee . . .
Na, my Scots canna dae't, this orra tongue:
Polyphemus clyterin ower the craigs

duntin doun boolders on the bilin starn
that jouks his dingin rattle-stanes, and him
eeless and bumbazed in a giant birr.

16

And syne the rains came and the sky-line's smoored.
Blae wabs o smirr were steekit to the sea.
I waitit on inside a mochy skull's
grey bane-waas that cam nearer as I gaupt.

Inside nou, I saw the Aegean trintlin
doun the gless. Three weeks I had been leein!
A drap rain and I swappit seas rate quick.
Poetry, but nae haill watter, is a swick.

I couldna play the deck-cheer Ulysses
that day Geoff, but bade inside and frettit
at the sair begunk the lyft had gien me.

I lookt at the weet green. Twa three blackie
were listenin thro their cleuks. Up thro the deck
they ruggit bits o reid twine wi their nebs.

'The bare-nakit epochs' o Baudelaire!
I sit here and plot and yet winna strip.
(The neebors like) I think o the heroes,
swack bodies soopled wi an athlete's virr.

There was nae neurosis in that sea air
when Ulysses met wi Nausicaa
washin claes and him nakit amon leaves.
An orra sailor man wid fleg a quine.

He faced her wi a tunic of torn sprays;
It was the decent thing to dae jist then.
The douce-like cleedin o his mind nae less.

A kinna original sinlessness.
Like liggin wi Calypso. Aa the time
it was the bare thocht o Penelope.

18

I'm nae Ulysses and never will be.
The unkent is the next poem. My sky-lines
are the blue lines o a page whaur my watches
are listenin for silence to say something.

I'm mair like bide-at-hame Penelope
deaved wi suitors, pesterin my mind fasht
wi waitin for that kent face I dinna ken
until I scrieve it doun. Yet for aa that

I need his nous, his tod-like uptak that
smells aa the options and at a blink, loups
wi aa the grace instinctive kennin gies.

Unsiccar work to be baith, ill to come
at. I think o her rippin up her wab
mair than him, Pallas Athene's byspale.

19

I met amon the chitterin o the deid.
a gleg-eed thickset phantom. I stoppit.
"You there sir, a word wi ye" I cryit.
The shape sklentit at me thro the pit-mirk.

"Whit's your will?" And me, "Are you Ulysses?"
"Whiles" he said. Up gaed the wicks o his mou
like an auld tod smirkin. "Whit ploy nou prince,
for hell is oot o the sough o the sea?"

And him, "Say nae mair. My blin frien's yonder.
Aa the deid think on is their lives. Thin scrats.
I am a paradox amon ghaists. See.

Hell is a makkin and nae a mindin.
I tryst my life amon the asphodels.
I meet in sang a chiel I seem to ken."

20

Blue lyft, I've come fae the howe-holes o the deid
to hear the sea's bool-backit swaws splyterin
timed thunders and watch the galleys snoove fae
pit-mirk dawns in the wake o gowden oars.

My hands aa leefu-lane cry back the kings.
My finger-nebs aince kittled their saut beards.
I grat. They sang o their sma-bit tulzies
and the sautjaws o the gulfs whummlin their starns.

I hear the howe mous o the conches stound,
the bugles blawpin to the sweeshin oars,
the rowers' liltin smoors the brass stramash.

And the gods heezit on heroic prows
smilin their auld smile the sea-spire spits on
rax me their chisellt and indulgent airms.

                'Hélène' – fae the French o Valéry

21

My last scrieve. I sit ablow the het drap
o my ae starn's electric licht, dear Geoff.
My boat's a winter wreck lang syne. I keep
my lee-lane watches in a sittin room.

It wisna a drucken boat mine; it kept
its keel in a watter-drap. Gin it was bung-fou
it was wi the sun or sleep or dwaumin.
Its wid-dreams were a dominie's. Jist so.

Tak then frien, thae viages I hae made
sittin on my doup forenent the sea. Nou
like Henryson I beek before the lowe,

and think o the worm-casts howkin my deck,
and deep doun in the mooly netherwarld
my timmers, sleepin in the yird's mirk sleep.

                                    ALASTAIR MACKIE

Ballad of Our Lady

Hale, sterne superne, hale, in eterne
  In Godis sicht to schyne,
Lucerne in derne for to discerne,
  Be glory and grace devyne.
Hodiern, modern, sempitern,
  Angelicall regyne,
Our tern inferne for to dispern,
  Helpe, rialest rosyne.
Aue, Maria, gracia plena.
  Haile, fresche flour femynyne,
Yerne, ws guberne, wirgin matern,
  Of reuth baith rute and ryne.

2

Haile, yhyng benyng fresche flurising,
  Haile, Alphais habitakle.
Thy dyng ofspring maid ws to syng
  Befor his tabernakle.
All thing maling we dovne thring
  Be sicht of his signakle,
Quhilk king ws bring vnto his ryng
  Fro dethis dirk vmbrakle.
Aue, Maria, gracia plena.
  Haile, moder and maide but makle,
Bricht syng, gladyng our languissing
  Be micht of thi mirakle.

3

Haile, bricht be sicht in hevyn on hicht,
  Haile, day sterne orientale,
Our licht most richt in clud of nycht,
  Our dirknes for to scale.
Haile, wicht in ficht, puttar to flicht
  Of fendis in battale,
Haile, plicht but sicht, haile, mekle of mycht,

Haile, glorius virgin, haile.
Aue, Maria, gracia plena.
  Haile, gentill nychttingale,
Way stricht, cler dicht, to wilsome wicht
  That irke bene in travale.

4

Haile, qwene serene, haile, most amene,
  Haile, hevinlie hie emprys,
Haile, schene, vnseyne with carnale eyne,
  Haile, ros of paradys,
Haile, clene bedene, ay till conteyne,
  Haile, fair fresche flour delyce,
Haile, grene daseyne, haile fro the splene,
  Of Ihesu genitrice.
Aue, Maria, gracia plena.
  Thow bair the prince of prys,
Our teyne to meyne and ga betweyne,
  As hvmile oratrice.

5

Haile, more decore than of before
  And swetar be sic sevyne,
Our glore forlore for to restor
  Sen thow art qwene of hevyn.
Memore of sore, stern in aurore,
  Lovit with angellis stevyne,
Implore, adore, thow indeflore,
  To mak our oddis evyne.
Aue, Maria, gracia plena.
  With lovingis lowde ellevyn,
Quhill store and hore my youth devor,
  Thy name I sall ay nevyne.

6

Empryce of prys, imperatrice,
  Bricht polist precious stane,
Victrice of wyce, hie genitrice

Of Ihesu, lord souerayne,
Our wys pavys fro enemys,
    Agane the feyndis trayne,
Oratrice, mediatrice, saluatrice,
    To God gret suffragane.
Aue, Maria, gracia plena.
    Haile, sterne meridiane,
Spyce, flour delice of paradys,
    That bair the gloryus grayne.

7

Imperiall wall, place palestrall
    Of peirles pulcritud,
Tryvmphale hall, hie trone regall
    Of Godis celsitud,
Hospitall riall, the lord of all
    Thy closet did include,
Bricht ball cristall, ros virginall,
    Fulfillit of angell fude.
Aue, Maria, gracia plena.
    Thy birth has with his blude
Fra fall mortall originall
    Ws raunsound on the rude.

WILLIAM DUNBAR

The Banishment of Poverty by His Royal Highness James Duke of Albany

Pox fa that pultron Povertie,
Wae worth the time that I him saw;
Sen first he laid his fang on me,
Myself from him I dought ne'er draw.

His wink to me has been a law.
He haunts me like a penny-dog;
Of him I stand far greater aw
Than pupill does of pedagogue.

The first time that he met with me,
Was at a clachan in the west;
Its name I trow Kilbarchan be,
Where Habbie's drones blew many a blast;

There we shook hands, cauld be his cast;
An ill dead may that custron die;
For there he gripped me full fast,
When first I fell in cautionrie.

Yet I had hopes to be reliev'd,
And fre'ed from that foul laidly lown;
Fernzier, when Whiggs were ill mischiev'd,
And forc'd to fling their weapons down,

When we chased them from Glasgow town,
I with that swinger thought to grapple;
But when Indemnity came down,
The laydron pow'd me by the thrapple.

But yet in hopes of some relief,
A rade I made to Arinfrew,
Where they did bravely buff my beef,
And made my body black and blew.

FRANCIS SEMPILL

Basking Shark

To stub an oar on a rock where none should be,
To have it rise with a slounge out of the sea
Is a thing that happened once (too often) to me.

But not too often – though enough. I count as gain
That once I met, on a sea tin-tacked with rain,
That roomsized monster with a matchbox brain.

He displaced more than water. He shoggled me
Centuries back – this decadent townee
Shook on a wrong branch of his family tree.

Swish up the dirt and, when it settles, a spring
Is all the clearer. I saw me, in one fling,
Emerging from the slime of everything.

So who's the monster? The thought made me grow pale
For twenty seconds while, sail after sail,
The tall fin slid away and then the tail.

NORMAN MacCAIG

Beachcomber

Monday I found a boot –
Rust and salt leather.
I gave it back to the sea, to dance in.

Tuesday a spar of timber worth thirty bob.
Next winter
It will be a chair, a coffin, a bed.

Wednesday a half can of Swedish spirits.
I tilted my head.
The shore was cold with mermaids and angels.

Thursday I got nothing, seaweed,
A whale bone,
Wet feet and a loud cough.

Friday I held a seaman's skull,
Sand spilling from it
The way time is told on kirkyard stones.

Saturday a barrel of sodden oranges.
A Spanish ship
Was wrecked last month at The Kame.

Sunday, for fear of the elders,
I sit on my bum.
What's heaven? A sea chest with a thousand gold coins.

GEORGE MACKAY BROWN

Beinn na Caillich

Sheas mi air mullach
Beinn na Caillich an t-Sratha
'S thug mi sùil
Bhuam a-null
Air Beinn na Caillich, Caol Reatha

'S chunnaic mi feareigin
A bha thall 's a dhìrich am bealach
A' toirt sùil a-nall orm fhìn
A' sealltainn
A-null air fhèin
Air mullach Beinn na Caillich, Caol Reatha
Air mullach Beinn na Caillich an t-Sratha.

RODY GORMAN

beinnnacaillicholdwifiewitchmoormountain

i stopstood on the roofsummit of
beinnnacaillicholdwifiewitchmoormountain
in the dellmeadowstrath of strath and cast
an eye farawaywantingfromme over onto
beinnnacaillicholdwifiewitchmoormountain in kylereanarrow

and i saw someman who had been overthere and
panegyricclimbed the mountainglengapgateway casting an
eye from there on me showlooking over at himself on the
roofsummit of beinnnacaillicholdwifiewitchmoormountain
in kylereanarrow on the roofsummit of
beinnnacaillicholdwifiewitchmoormountain in the
dellmeadowstrath of strath

Translated by author

RODY GORMAN

Benighted in the Foothills of the Cairngorms: January

Cauld, cauld is Alnack . . .
Cauld is the snaw wind and sweet.
The maukin o' Creagan Alnack
Has snaw for meat.

Nae fit gangs ayont Caiplich
Nae herd in the cranreuch bricht.
The troot o' the water o' Caiplich
Dwells deep the nicht.

On a' the screes, by ilk cairn
In the silence nae grouse is heard,
But the eagle abune Geal Charn
Hings like a swerd.

Yon's nae wife's hoose ayont A'an
In the green lift ava
Yon's the cauld lums o' Ben A'an
Wha's smeek is sna.

A' the lang mountains are silent
Alane doth wild Alnack sing.
The hern, the curlew are silent.
Silent a' thing.

OLIVE FRASER

The Bewteis of the Fute-Ball

Brissit brawnis and broken banis,
Strife, discord, and waistis wanis,
Crookit in eild, syne halt withal –
Thir are the bewteis of the fute-ball.

ANON.

The Big Mistake

the shepherd on the train told me

is to clip hill milking ewes too soon

I put my newspaper down;
he'd got my attention.

Nothing puts the milk off them quicker
than just a day like last Wednesday.
And when it goes off at this time of year,
it never comes back.

His warning continues

They never get so rough in the backend,
and have less protection
against the storms and the winter chill.

He glances up,
checks his crook in the luggage rack

And another thing
is that the wool neither weighs so heavy
nor looks so well. It's the new growth
that brings down the scales.

A fleece from a ewe that's near
hasn't the same feel as one from a ewe
that has plenty of rise and a good strong stoan.

In the beginning of July the new wool on a thin ewe
will grow more in one week under the fleece
than it will do in three with the fleece clipped off.

He summarised his argument for me

Experienced flock masters never clip hill stocks
before the second week of July.
In terms of the sheep's sufferings
a strong sun is little less severe than a cold rain.

He stopped there
looked out the window at the passing fields
then fell asleep to Waverley
content that a stranger in a suit
had listened to his wisdom
this wisdom I now share with you.

JIM CARRUTH

Bho Birlinn Clann Raghnaill

An fhairge ga maistreadh 's ga sluistneadh
Troimh a chèile,
Gun robh ròin is mialan-mòra
'M barrachd èiginn;
Anfhadh is confadh na mara
'S falbh na luinge
Sradadh an eanchainnean geala
Feadh gach tuinne,
Iad ri nuallanaich àrd, uaimhinneach,
Searbh-thùrsach,
Ag èigheach gur ìochdarain sinne
Dragh chum bùird sinn.
Gach mion-iasg a bha san fhairge
Tàrr-gheal, tionndaidht',
Le gluasad confadh na gailbhinn
Marbh gun chùnntas;
Clachan is maorach an aigeil
Teachd an uachdar,
Air am buain a-nìos le slacraich
A' chuain uaibhrich;
An fhairg' uile 's i na brochan
Strioplach, ruaimleach
Le fuil 's le gaorr nam biast lorcach
'S droch dhath ruadh oirr',
Na biastan adharcach, iongnach,
Pliutach, lorcach,
Làn cheann 's iad nam beòil gu 'n giallaibh,
'S an craos fosgailt.
An àibheis uile làn bhòcan

Air an cràgradh,
Le spògan 's le earbaill mhòr-bhiast
Air a màgradh.
Bu sgreamhail an ròmhan sgriachaidh
Bhith da èisdeachd,
Thogbhadh iad air caogad mìlidh
Aotrom cèille:
Chaill an sgioba càil an claisneachd
Ri bhith 'g èisdeachd
Ceilearadh sgreadach nan deamhan
'S mothar bhèistean.
Foghar na fairge, 's a slachdraich
Gleac r' a darach,
Fosghaoir a toisich a' bocsaich
Mhuca-mara.

[. . .]

Cha robh tarrang ann gun trochladh
Cha robh calpa ann gun lùbadh,
Cha robh aon bhall bhuineadh dhìse
Nach robh nas miosa na thùbhradh.
Ghairm an fhairge sìoth-shàimh ruinne
Air crois Chaol Ìle;
'S gun d' fhuair a' gharbh-ghaoth shearbh-ghlòireach
Òrdan sìnidh.
Thog i uainne do dh'ionadaibh
Uachdrach an aeir,
'S chinn i dhuinn na clàr rèidh mìn-gheal,
An dèidh a tabhainn.
Thug sin buidheachas don Àrd-rìgh
Chum na dùilean
Deagh Chlann Raghnaill a bhith sàbhailt
O bhàs brùideil.

'S an sin bheum sinn a siùil thana
Bhallach, thùilinn;
'S leag sinn a croinn mhìn-dearg, ghasda
Fad a h-ùrlair.
'S chuir sinn a-mach ràimh chaola bhasgant
Dhaite, mhìne,

74

Den ghiuthas a bhuain MacBharrais
An Eilean Fhìonain.
Rinn sinn an t-iomramh rèidh tulganach,
Gun dearmad:
'S ghabh sinn deagh longphort aig barraibh
Charraig Fhearghais.
Thilg sinn acraichean gu socair
Anns an ròd sin;
Ghabh sinn biadh is deoch gun airceas,
'S rinn sinn còmhnaidh.

ALASDAIR MAC MHAIGHSTIR ALASDAIR

From The Galley of Clan Ranald

The ocean is mashing and sluicing
Through itself,
Seals and leviathans
In great distress;
The raging and roaring of the sea,
And the moving of the ship
Dashing their white brains
Through each wave;
And them howling loudly in terror,
Bitter, sad,
Screaming – we are the underlings,
Drag us on board.
All the tiny fish in the ocean,
Their white bellies upturned
By the raging of the gale –
Countless dead;
Stones and shellfish from the bottom
Come to the surface,
Reaped upwards by the thrashing
Of the proud sea;
The ocean a complete mess,
Dirty and turbid,
With the blood and gore of crawling beasts,
Coloured dank red.
Horned, clawed beasts

Splay-footed, crawling,
Many-headed and to the jaws
Their gob wide open.
The abyss full of ghosts,
All fumbling,
With paws and tails of great beasts
On all fours.
That screeching groan was awful
To hear,
They'd make fifty warriors
Lose their reason.
The crew lost their sense of hearing
Listening to
The horrible warbling of the demons
And the loud cries of beasts.
The harvesting of the sea, her threshing,
Wrestling with the oakbeams,
The huge rumble of her bow
Thumping whales.

[. . .]

All the nails were loosened,
All the shanks were bent,
Every bit of her structure
Was worse than could be wrought.
The sea declared peace
At the cross of the Sound of Islay,
The rough bitter-voiced wind
Was demobbed.
She left us for the higher
Halls of the air,
She became a smooth flat-white plain,
After all her chaos.
We gave thanks to the High King,
To the elements,
That good Clan Ranald was saved
From a brutal death.

Then we lowered her thin spotted
Linen sails;

And laid her fine-red, lovely masts
Down the length of her deck;
And we put out smooth, slender, coloured
Singing oars
Of the pine MacVarish cut
On Islandfinnan.
We rowed with a smooth, flawless,
Rocking:
And made a good harbour at the tip
Of Carrickfergus.
We gently dropped anchor
In that haven;
We took food and drink without stint
And we stayed there.

Trans. Peter Mackay and Iain S. MacPherson

ALEXANDER MacDONALD

The Birth of Antichrist

Lucina shining in silence of the nicht.
The heaven being all full of sternis bricht,
To bed I went, bot there I took no rest,
With heavy thocht I was so sore opprest,
That sair I langit after dayis licht.

Of Fortune I complenit heavely,
That sho to me stood so contrariously;
And at the last, when I had turnit oft,
For weariness on me ane slummer soft
Come with ane dreaming and a fantasy.

Me thocht Deme Fortune with ane fremmit cheer
Stood me beforne and said on this manner,
Thou suffer me to work gif thou do weil,
And preis thee nocht to strive againis my wheel,
Whilk every warldly thing does turn and stear.

Full mony ane man I turn unto the hicht,
And makis als mony full law to doun licht;
Up on my staigis or that thou ascend,
Trat weil thy trouble near is at an end,
Seeing thir taikinis, wherefore thou mark them richt.

Thy trublist gaist sall near more be degest,
Nor thou in to no benefice beis possest,
While that ane abbot him cleith in ernes pens,
And fle up in the air amangis the crenes,
And as ane falcon fare fro east to west.

He sall ascend as ane horrible grephoun,
Him meet sall in the air ane sho dragon;
Thir terrible monsters sall togidder thirst,
And in the cloudis get the Antichrist,
While all the air infleck of their poison.

Under Saturnus fiery region
Simon Magus sall meet him, and Mahoun,
And Merlin at the moon sall him be bydand
And Jonet the widow on ane bussome rydand,
Of witches with ane winder garrison.

And syne they sall descend with reek and fire,
And preach in earth the Antichrists empire,
Be then it sall be near this warldis end.
With that this lady soon fra me did wend;
Sleepand and wankand was frustrate my desire.

When I awoke, my dream it was so nice,
Fra every wicht I hid it as a vice;
While I heard tell be mony soothfast wy,
Fle wald ane abbot up in to the sky,
And all his fethrem made was at device.

Within my hairt confort I took full soon;
'Adieu,' quod I, 'My dreary days are done;
Full weil I wist to me wald never come thrift,
While that twa moons were seen up in the lift,
Or while ane abbot flew above the moon.'

WILLIAM DUNBAR

Birthmark

On my decline, a millipede
Helped me to keep count;
For every time I slipped a foot
Farther down the mountain

She'd leave a tiny, cast-off limb
Of crimson on my cheek
As if to say –
You're hurting us both, Mick . . .

I saw in this gradual sacrifice
No end of merriment:
A broken vein or two; hardly
Memento mori.

This thousandth morning after, though
(Or thousand-and-first)
I miss her, and a bedside mirror
Bellows the worst –

A big, new, bilberry birthmark, stamped
From ear to livid ear,
Her whole body of blood's
Untimely smear.

She must have found, shaking her sock
For warnings, that the hoard was spent,
And had to stain me with her death
To show what she meant:

That it's as bad to fall astray
As to start from the wrong place.
Now I have earned the purple face.
It won't go away.

MICK IMLAH

Bisearta

Chì mi rè geard na h-oidhche
dreòs air chrith 'na fhroidhneas thall air fàire,
a' clapail le a sgiathaibh,
a' sgapadh 's a' ciaradh rionnagan na h-àird' ud.

Shaoileadh tu gun cluinnte,
ge cian, o 'bhuillsgein ochanaich no caoineadh,
ràn corraich no gàir fuatha,
comhart chon cuthaich uaidh no ulfhairt fhaolchon,
gun ruigeadh drannd an fhòirneirt
on fhùirneis òmair iomall fhéin an t-saoghail.
Ach siud a' dol an leud e
ri oir an speur an tostachd olc is aognaidh.

C' ainm nochd a th' orra,
na sràidean bochda anns an sgeith gach uinneag
a lasraichean 's a deatach,
a sradagan is sgreadail a luchd thuinidh,
is taigh air thaigh ga reubadh
am broinn a chéile am brùchdadh toit a tuiteam?
Is có an nochd tha 'g atach
am Bàs a theachd gu grad 'nan cainntibh uile,
no a' spàirn measg chlach is shailthean
air bhàinidh a' gairm air cobhair, is nach cluinnear?
Cò a-nochd a phàigheas
seann chìs àbhaisteach na fala cumant?

Uair dearg mar lod na h-àraich,
uair bàn mar ghile thràighte an eagail éitigh,
a' dìreadh 's uair a' teàrnadh,
a' sìneadh le sitheadh àrd 's a' call a mheudachd,
a' fannachadh car aitil
's ag at mar anail dhiabhail air dhéinead,
an t-Olc 'na chridhe 's 'na chuisle,
chì mi 'na bhuillean a' sìoladh 's a' leum e.
Tha 'n dreòs 'na oillt air fàire,
'na fhàinne ròis is òir am bun nan speuran,

a' breugnachadh 's ag àicheadh
le shoillse sèimhe àrsaidh àrd nan reultan.

DEÒRSA MAC IAIN DEÒRSA

Bizerta

I see during the night guard
a blaze flickering, fringeing the skyline over yonder,
beating with its wings
and scattering and dimming the stars of that airt.

You would think that there would be heard
from its midst, though far away, wailing and lamentation,
the roar of rage and the yell of hate,
the barking of frenzied dogs from it or the howling of wolves,
that the snarl of violence would reach
from yon amber furnace the very edge of the world;
but yonder it spreads
along the rim of the sky in evil, ghastly silence.

What is their name tonight,
the poor streets where every window spews
its flame and smoke,
its sparks and the screaming of its inmates,
while house upon house is rent
and collapses in a gust of smoke?
And who tonight are beseeching
Death to come quickly in all their tongues,
or are struggling among stones and beams,
crying in frenzy for help, and are not heard?
Who tonight is paying
the old accustomed tax of common blood?

Now red like a battlefield puddle,
now pale like the drained whiteness of foul fear,
climbing and sinking,
reaching and darting up and shrinking in size,
growing faint for a moment
and swelling like the breath of a devil in intensity,

I see Evil as a pulse
and a heart declining and leaping in throbs.
The blaze, a horror on the skyline,
a ring of rose and gold at the foot of the sky,
belies and denies
with its light the ancient high tranquillity of the stars.

Translated by author

GEORGE CAMPBELL HAY

The Black Wet

It's raining stair-rods and chairlegs,
it's raining candelabra and microwaves,
it's raining eyesockets.
When the sun shines through the shower
it's raining the hair of Sif,
each strand of which is real gold
(carat unknown).

It's raining jellyfish,
it's raining nuts, bolts and pineal glands,
it's raining a legion of fly noyades,
it's raining marsupials and echnidae,
it's raining anoraks in profusion.
It's siling, it's spittering, it's stotting, it's teeming,
it's pouring, it's snoring, it's plaining, it's Spaining.

People look up, open their mouths momentarily,
and drown.
People look out of windows and say,
'Send it down, David.'
Australians remark, 'Huey's missing the bowl.'
Americans reply, 'Huey, Dewie and Louie
are missing the bowl.'

It is not merely raining,
it's Windering and Thirling, it's Buttering down.
It's raining lakes, it's raining grass-snakes,

it's raining Bala, Baikal, and balalaikas,
it's raining soggy sidewinders and sadder adders.
It's raining flu bugs, Toby jugs and hearth-rugs,
it's raining vanity.

The sky is one vast water-clock
and it's raining seconds, it's raining years:
already you have spent more of your life looking at the rain
than you have sleeping, cooking, shopping and making love.
It's raining fusilli and capeletti,
it's raining mariners and albatrosses,
it's raining iambic pentameters.

Let's take a rain-check:
it's raining houndstooth and pinstripe,
it's raining tweed. This is the tartan of McRain.
This is the best test of the wettest west:
it is not raining locusts – just.
Why rain pests
when you can rain driving tests?

It is raining through the holes in God's string vest.

W. N. HERBERT

The Blue Jacket

When there comes a flower to the stingless nettle,
To the hazel bushes, bees,
I think I can see my little sister
Rocking herself by the hazel trees.

Rocking her arms for very pleasure
That every leaf so sweet can smell,
And that she has on her the warm blue jacket
Of mine, she liked so well.

Oh to win near you, little sister!
To hear your soft lips say –
'I'll never tak' up wi' lads or lovers,
But a baby I maun hae.

'A baby in a cradle rocking,
Like a nut, in a hazel shell,
And a new blue jacket, like this o' Annie's,
It sets me aye sae well.'

MARION ANGUS

The Boat's Blueprint

THE BOAT'S BLUEPRINT

water

IAN HAMILTON FINLAY

Bod Bríoghmhor Atá ag Donncha

Bod bríoghmhor atá ag Donncha,
fada féitheach fíordhorcha,
    reamhar druimleathan díreach,
    sleamhan cuirneach ceirtíneach.

Cluaisleathan ceannramhar crom,
go díoghainn data dubhghorm;
    atá breall ag an fhleascach,
    is e ceannsa (?) go conachtach (?).

Maolshrónach mallghormtha glas,
fuachdha forránach fíorchas;
    go cronánach ceannghorm cruaidh,
    móirbhéimneach i measc banshluaigh.

An fheam tá ag Donncha riabhach,
dar leam, nocha tuilsciamhach –
    síorullamh, a-muigh 's a-mach,
    fíorchruaidh feargach fionnfadhach.

Fomhóir fliuchshúileach faitheach (?),
steallach stuaghach starraighteach;
  bannlamh as a bhalg a-mach –
  an fheamlorg airgtheach fháthach.

Go collach, ciabhach, ciorclach,
dona cursta cuisleannach;
  is fada rámhach 's is rod:
  is annsa linn an rábhod.

          Bod.

Go súghmhor, sáiteach, salach,
lúthmhor láidir lomcharrach (?),
  ceannramhar borrfadhach borb,
  druimneach deigheól an dubhlorg.

Sreamaillseach seól an sonn
bhuadhaigheas cath is comhlann;
  go teascaightheach teilgthe te,
  is treabhraighthe fíoch na fleisce.

SIR DONNCHADH CAIMBEUL GHLINN URCHAIDH

Duncan Has a Powerful Prick

Duncan has a powerful prick:
broad-backed, upright, thick,
  long, sinewy, real dark,
  slick, wattled, bees-waxed.

Broad-eared, big-headed, bent,
it turns indigo when it's vehement:
  the knob of this young stallion
  can be calm – or act the hallion.

Green, slow-blue, sleek-nosed,
impetuous, oppressive, bellicose,
  blue-headed, blunt, bumbling,
  its whacks send women tumbling.

Grizzled Duncan's equipment
is really not just an ornament –
    it's ever-ready, in and out,
    furious, firm, fit for a rout.

Wet-eyed, colossal, gigantic,
its swash swells like the Atlantic's:
    a fathom long out of its sack,
    his humungous silvery pack.

Round, shaggy and sensual,
evil, sinewy, sinful:
    it foams, is long and stiff-oared;
    we're proud of this prick-fort.

      Prick.

Satisfying, juicy, dirty,
fire-rough, potent, mighty,
    barbaric, fatheaded, massive,
    a ridge-backed, brighteyed blackstaff.

A hero, spunky and skilful,
who wins every brawl and battle,
    hurling itself, hasty and hot:
    oh, the harrowing rage of his rod.

Trans. Peter Mackay and Iain S. MacPherson

SIR DUNCAN CAMPBELL OF GLEN ORCHY

The Bonny Boat

Has she got a good high heed, your boat?
Is she laid-in right?
Does she look weel? Or does she coower hor heed, hor stan
Cocked up aheight?

An' has she got a right dip gripe, yon boat?
Does she draa' plenty watter?
Them modern boats, the heeds just blaa's awa'.
The forefoot winna haa'd hor.

So ha' ye got two masts aboard your boat
An' your lang tiller?
An' is your pitch-pine ruther dip withaa'
So ye can sail hor?

An' ha' ye got a right peak on your sail?
Your mast raked back?
Nowth-country boats could dae hor, lad.
One tack

For' Beadlin up t' Amble. O, a bonny boat
Will aye gan weel.
There's varnigh not a bonny boat been built
That winna sail.

KATRINA PORTEOUS

From The Book of the Howlet

[. . .]

Sa come the rook with a rerd and a rane roch,
A bard ont of Ireland with Banachadee.
Said: 'Gluntow guk dynyd dach hala mishy doch;
Raike her a rug of the rost, or sho sall ryive thee.
Mich macmory ach mach mometer moch loch;
Set her doune, give her drink; what Dele ailis she?
O Deremine, O Donnall, O Dochardy droch;
(Thir are his Ireland kingis of the Irishery:)
O Knewlyn, O Conochor, O Gregre Makgrane;
The Shenachy, the Clarshach,
The Ben shene, the Ballach,
The Crekery, the Corach,
Sho kens them ilk ane.'

Mony lesingis he made; wald let for no man
To speak while he spokin had, sparit no things.
The dean rural, the raven, reprovit him than,
Bad him his lesingis leave before they lordings.
The bard worth brain-wood, and bitterly couth ban;
'How corby messenger,' quoth he, 'with sorrory now sings.
Thou ishit out of Noahs ark, and to the erd wan,
Taryit as a traitor, and brocht na tythings.
I sall ryive thee, Raven, baith guts and gall.'
The dean rural worthit reid,
Staw for shame of the steid;
The bard held a great pleid
In the high hall.

In come twa flyrand fools with a fond fair,
The tuchet and the gukkit golk, and yeid hiddy giddy;
Rushit baith to the bard, and ruggit his hair;
Callit him thryss thieves-neck, to thrawe in a widdy.
The fylit him fra the fortop to the foot there.
The bard, smaddit like a smaik smorit in a smiddy,
Ran fast to the door, and gave a great rair;
Socht water to wesh him there out in ane eddy.
The lordis leuch upon loft, and liking they had
That the bard was so bet;
The fools fond in the flet,
And mony mowis at mete
On the floor made.

Syne for ane figonale of fruit they strave in the steid;
The tuchet gird to the golk, and gave him a fall,
Rave his tail fra his rig, with a rath pleid;
The golk gat up again in the great hall,
Tit the Tuchet be the top, oertervit his head,
Flang him flat in the fire, feathers and all.
He cried: 'Alas,' with ane rair, 'revyn is my reid!
I am ungraciously gorrit, baith guts and gall.'
Yet he lap fra the low richt in a line.
When they had remelis raucht,
They forthought that they faucht,

Kissit samyn and saucht;
And sat down syne.

[...]

RICHARD HOLLAND

The Book of the World

Of this fair volume which we World do name
If we the sheets and leaves could turn with care,
Of him who it corrects and did it frame,
We clear might read the art and wisdom rare:
Find out his power which wildest powers doth tame,
His providence existing everywhere,
His justice which proud rebels doth not spare,
In every page, no, period of the same.
But silly we, like foolish children, rest
Well pleased with coloured vellum, leaves of gold,
Fair dangling ribands, leaving what is best,
On the great writer's sense ne'er taking hold;
Or if by chance our minds do muse on ought,
It is some picture on the margin wrought.

WILLIAM DRUMMOND OF HAWTHORNDEN

Bothan Àirigh am Bràigh Raineach

Gur e m' anam is m' eudail
chaidh an-dè do Ghleann Garadh:
fear na gruaig' mar an t-òr
is nam pòg air bhlas meala.

O hi ò o hu ò, o hi ò o hu ò,
Hi rì ri ò hu eile,
O hì ri ri ri ò gheallaibh ò

Is tu as fheàrr dhan tig deise
dhe na sheasadh air talamh;
's tu as fheàrr dhan tig culaidh
dhe na chunna mi dh'fhearaibh.

'S tu as fheàrr dhan tig osan
is bròg shocrach nam barrall:
còta Lunnainneach dubh-ghorm,
's bidh na crùintean ga cheannach.

'S math thig triubhais on iarann
air sliasaid a' ghallain,
's math thig bonaid le fàbhar
air fear àrd a' chùil chlannaich.

An uair a ruigeadh tu 'n fhèill
is e mo ghèar-sa thig dhachaigh;
mo chriosan is mo chìre
is mo stìomag chaol cheangail,

is mo làmhainnean bòidheach
is deis òir air am barraibh;
thig mo chrios à Dùn Èideann
is mo bhrèid à Dùn Chailleann.

Cuim a bhitheamaid gun eudail
agus sprèidh aig na Gallaibh?
Gheibh sinn crodh as a' Mhaorainn
agus caoraich à Gallaibh.

'S ann a bhios sinn gan àrach
air àirigh 'm Bràigh Raineach.
ann am bothan an t-sùgraidh
's gur e bu dùnadh dha barrach.

Bidh a' chuthag 's an smùdan
a' gabhail ciùil dhuinn air chrannaibh;
bidh an damh donn 's a bhùireadh
gar dùsgadh sa mhadainn.

GUN URRA

A Sheiling Bothy on Brae Rannoch

My soul and my treasure
went to Glengarry yesterday:
the man with golden hair
and honey-tasting kisses.

O hi ò o hu ò, o hi ò o hu ò,
Hi rì ri ò hu eile,
O hì ri ri ri ò gheallaibh ò

Your clothes suit you better
than any man on earth;
your garments suit you better
than any man I've ever seen.

Your stockings fit you best,
and elegant laced shoes,
and a navy London coat
bought with crowns.

Ironed trousers well become
this young man's thigh;
a cockaded bonnet well suits
this richly curled tall man.

When you get to the fair
my gear will come home;
my belt and my comb,
and my dainty headband.

And my gorgeous gloves
with gold trim at the cuff:
my belt will come from Edinburgh,
my head-shawl from Dunkeld.

Why should we lack cattle
while Lowlanders have livestock?
We'll get cows from the Mearns
and sheep from Caithness.

We shall rear them
at a sheiling on Brae Rannoch
in a little love-bothy
closed in by brushwood.

The cuckoo and the rock-dove
will serenade us from trees;
and the brown stag in rut
will wake us in the morning.

Trans. Peter Mackay and Iain S. MacPherson

ANON.

Braes of Balquhidder

Will you go lassie go
    To the braes of Balquhidder
Where the high mountains run
    And the bonnie blooming heather
Where the ram and the deer
    They go bounding together
Spend a long summer day
    By the braes of Balquhidder

Oh no sir, she said,
    I am too young to be your lover
For my age is scarce sixteen
    And I dare not for my mother
And beside being so young
    I am afraid you're some deceiver
That have come to charm me here
    By the braes of Balquhidder

Your beauty soon will alter
    I will deprive you of this chance
And live happy with some other
    I will roam this world all over
Until I find some maid of honour

That will go along with me
To the braes of Balquhidder

Oh come back, oh come back
    For I think you're no deceiver
Oh come back, oh come back
    I will never love none other
I will leave all my friends
    Father, Mother, Sister, Brother
And I will go along with you
    To the braes of Balquhidder

Oh now they have gone
    To that bonnie highland mountain
For to view the green fields
    Likewise its silvery fountain
It's there they are united
    And joined in love together
Spend a long summer day
    By the braes of Balquhidder

ROBERT TANNAHILL

Braid Claith

Ye wha are fain to hae your name
Wrote in the bonny book of fame,
Let merit nae pretension claim
    To laurel'd wreath,
But hap ye weel, baith back and wame,
    In gude Braid Claith.

He that some ells o this may fa,
An' slae-black hat on pow like snaw,
Bids bauld to bear the gree awa,
    Wi a' this graith,
Whan bienly clad wi' shell fu braw
    O' gude Braid Claith.

Waesuck for him wha has na fek o't!
For he's a gowk they're sure to geck at,
A chiel that ne'er will be respekit
While he draws breath,
Till his four quarters are bedeckit
Wi gude Braid Claith.

On Sabbath-days the barber spark,
When he has done wi scrapin wark,
Wi siller broachie in his sark,
Gangs trigly, faith!
Or to the Meadow, or the Park,
In gude Braid Claith.

Weel might ye trou, to see them there,
That they to shave your haffits bare,
Or curl an' sleek a pickle hair,
Would be right laith,
Whan pacing wi' a gawsy air
In gude Braid Claith.

If ony mettl'd stirrah grien
For favour frae a lady's een,
He maunna care for being seen
Before he sheath
His body in a scabbard clean
O' gude Braid Claith.

For, gin he come wi coat thread-bare,
A feg for him she winna care,
But crook her bonny mou fu sair,
And scald him baith.
Wooers shoud ay their travel spare
Without Braid Claith.

Braid Claith lends fock an unco heese,
Makes mony kail-worms butter-flees,
Gies mony a doctor his degrees
For little skaith:
In short, you may be what you please
Wi gude Braid Claith.

For thof ye had as wise a snout on
As Shakespeare or Sir Isaac Newton,
Your judgment fouk would hae a doubt on,
I'll tak my aith,
Till they coud see ye wi a suit on
O' gude Braid Claith.

ROBERT FERGUSSON

Brendon Gallacher

He was seven and I was six, my Brendon Gallacher.
He was Irish and I was Scottish, my Brendon Gallacher.
His father was in prison; he was a cat burglar.
My father was a Communist Party full-time worker.
He had six brothers and I had one, my Brendon Gallacher.

He would hold my hand and take me by the river
where we'd talk about his family being poor.
He'd get his mum out of Glasgow when he got older.
A wee holiday some place nice. Some place far.
I'd tell my mum about my Brendon Gallacher.

How his mum drank and his daddy was a cat burglar.
And she'd say, 'Why not have him round to dinner?'
No, no, I'd say he's got big holes in his trousers.
I like meeting him by the burn in the open air.
Then one day after we'd been friends for two years,

one day when it was pouring and I was indoors,
my mum says to me, 'I was talking to Mrs Moir
who lives next door to your Brendon Gallacher.
Didn't you say his address was 24 Novar?
She says there are no Gallachers at 24 Novar.

There have never been any Gallachers next door.'
And he died then, my Brendon Gallacher,
flat out on my bedroom floor, his spiky hair,
his impish grin, his funning flapping ear.
Oh Brendon. Oh my Brendon Gallacher.

JACKIE KAY

Brither Worm

I saw a lang worm snoove throu the space atween twa stanes,
pokan its heid, if it had ane, up throu a hole in the New Toun,
up throu a crack ye wad hardly hae seen in an area of stane,
unkenn'd upliftit tons of mason-wark piled on the soil
wi causey-streets, biggit of granite setts, like blank waas flat on the grund,
plainstane pavements of Thurso slabs laid owre the staneaircht cellars,
the area fifteen feet doun, wi weill-fittan flagstanes, Regency wark.
Nou, in my deedit stane-and-lime property awntert a nesh and perfect worm,
and I was abasit wi thochts of what was gaun-on ablow my feet,
that the feu'd and rentit grand was the soil of the Drumscheuch Forest,
and that life gaed on inunder the grund-waa-stane and had sent out a spy,
jalousan some Frien of the Worms had brocht a maist welcome shoure,
whan I on my side of the crust had teemit a pail of water,
meaning to gie the place a guid scrub-doun wi a stable-besom.
Sae a lang, saft, sappy and delicate pink and naukit cratur
neatly wan out frae atween thae weil-fittan chiselled, unnaitural stanes.
I watched and thocht lang of the wonders of Nature, and didna muve,
and thocht of the deeps of the soil, deeper nor the see, and I made nae sound.
A rat raxt frae a crack atween twa stanes.
My hale body sheuk wi the grue.
It keekit at me, and was gane.

ROBERT GARIOCH

Brostughadh-Catha Chlann Domhnaill, Là Chatha Gharbhaich

A Chlanna Cuinn, cuimhnichibh
Cruas an am na h-iorghaile:
Gu h-àirneach, gu h-arranta,
Gu h-athlamh, gu h-allanta,
Gu beòdha, gu barramhail,
Gu brìoghmhor, gu buan-fheargach,
Gu calma, gu curanta,
Gu cròdha, gu cath-bhuadhach,
Gu dùr is gu dàsannach,
Gu dian is gu deagh-fhulang,
Gu h-èasgaidh, gu h-eaghnamhach,
Gu h-èitidh', gu h-eireachdail,

Gu fortail, gu furachail,
Gu frithir, gu forniata,
Gu gruamach, gu gràineamhail,
Gu gleusta, gu gaisgeamhail,
Gu h-ullamh, gu h-iorghaileach,
Gu h-olla-bhorb, gu h-àibheasach,
Gu h-innil, gu h-inntineach,
Gu h-iomdha, gu h-iomghonach,
Gu laomsgar, gu làn-ath lamh,
Gu làidir, gu luath-bhuilleach,
Gu mearghanta, gu mór-chneadhach,
Gu meanmnach, gu mileanta,
Gu neimhneach, gu naimhdeamhail,
Gu niatach, gu neimh-eaglach,
Gu h-obann, gu h-olla-ghnìomhach,
Gu h-oirdheirc, gu h-oirbheartach,
Gu prap is gu prìomh-ullamh,
Gu prosta, gu prionnsamhail,
Gu ruaimneach, gu ro-dhàna,
Gu ro-bhorb, gu rìoghamhail,
Gu sanntach, gu sèanamhail,
Gu socair, gu sàr-bhuailteach,
Gu teannta, gu togarrach,
Gu talcmhor, gu traigh-èasgaidh,
Gu h-urlamh, gu h-ùr-mhaiseach,
Do chosnadh na cath-làthrach
Re bronnaibh bhar bhiodhbhadha.
A Chlanna Cuinn Cèad-chathaich,
A nois uair bhar n-aitheanta,
A chuileanan confadhach,
A bheithrichean bunanta,
A leòmhannan làn-ghasta,
A onchonaibh iorghaileach,
Chaoiribh chròdha, churanta
De Chlanna Cuinn Cèad-chathaich –
A Chlanna Cuinn, cuimhnichibh
Cruas an am na h-iorghaile.

LACHLANN MÒR MacMHUIRICH

The Harlaw Brosnachadh

Children of Conn, recall now
courage in time of combat:
be attentive, audacious,
agile, ambitious,
be bold, beautiful,
brawny, belligerent,
contumacious, courageous,
clever, combative,
deliberate, destructive,
deadly, enduring,
be eager, expert,
well-equipped, elegant,
be forceful, fitful,
fervent, feisty,
be grim, gruesome,
gymnastic, glorious,
alert, awesome,
intractable, impetuous,
well-accoutred, ardent,
innumerable, incisive,
be lethal, lusty,
swiftly lopping, giving it laldy,
mirthful, mortally-wounding,
mettlesome, military,
be noxious, nasty,
never-daunted, never-fearing,
overwhelming, omnipotent,
outshining, outreaching,
precipitate, prepared,
powerful, princely,
be robust, reckless,
ruinous, regal,
be sharp, sainèd,
steady, sure-hitting,
tight, triumphant,
tenacious, tripping,
youthful and yearning
to beat in battle
the foe's forces.

O Children of Conn of a hundred conflicts,
now is the hour for honour,
O warring whelps,
O bulky bears,
O leading lions,
O obstinate otters,
live, courageous coals
of the Children of Conn of a hundred conflicts –
O Children of Conn, recall now
courage in time of combat.

Trans. Meg Bateman

LACHLANN MÒR MacMHUIRICH

From The Bruce, Book I

A! fredome is a noble thing!
Fredome mays man to haiff liking;
Fredome all solace to man giffis:
He levys at es that frely levys.
A noble hart may haiff nane es,
Na ellys nocht that may him ples,
Gyff fredome failyhe: for fre liking
Is yharnyt our all othir thing.
Na he, that ay has levyt fre,
May nocht knaw weill the propyrte,
The angyr, na the wrechyt dome,
That is cowplyt to foule thyrldome.
Bot gyff he had assayit it,
Than all perquer he suld it wyt;
And suld think fredome mar to prys,
Than all the gold in warld that is.
Thus contrar thingis evir-mar,
Discoveryngis off the tothir ar.
And he that thryll is has nocht his;
All that he has enbandownyt is
Till hys lord, quhat-evir he be.
Yheyt has he nocht sa mekill fre
As fre liking to leyve, or do

99

That at hys hart hym drawis to.
Than mays clerkis questioun,
Quhen thai fall in disputacioun,
That gyff man bad his thryll owcht do,
And in the samyn tym come him to
His wyff, and askyt hym hyr det,
Quhethir he his lordis neid suld let,
And pay fryst that he awcht, and syne
Do furth his lordis commandyne;
Or leve onpayit his wyff, and do
It that commaundyt is him to?
I leve all the solucioun
Till thaim that ar off mar renoun.
Bot sen thai mek sic comperyng
Betwix the dettis off wedding,
And lordis bidding till his threll,
Yhe may weile se, thoucht nane yhow tell,
How hard a thing that threldome is.
For men may weile se, that ar wys,
That wedding is the hardest band,
That ony man may tak on hand:
And thryldome is weill wer than deid;
For quhill a thryll his lyff may leid,
It merrys him, body and banys;
And dede anoyis him bot anys.
Schortly to say, is nane can tell
The halle condicioun off a threll.

JOHN BARBOUR

From The Bruce, Book XIII

In this tyme that I tell of her,
That the battall on this maner
Wes strikin, quhar on athir party
Thai war fechtand richt manfully,
Yhemen, swanys, and poueraill,
That in the Parc to yheyme vittale
War left; quhen thai wist but lesing
That thair lordis, with fell fichtyng,

On thair fais assemblit war,
Ane of them-selvyne that wes thar
Capitane of thame all thai maid;
And schetis, that war sum-deill braid,
Thai festnyt in steid of baneris
Apon lang treis and on speris,
And said that thai wald se the ficht,
And help thar lordis at thar mycht.
Quhen her-till all assentit war,
And in a rowt assemblit ar,
Fiften thousand thai war and ma.
And than in gret hy thai can ga
With thair baneris all in a rout,
As thai had men beyn stith and stout.
Thai com, with all that assemble,
Richt quhill thai mycht the battale se;
Than all at anys thai gaf ane cry,
'Sla! sla! Apon thaim hastily!'
And thar-with all cumand ar thai:
Bot thai war yheit weill far away,
And Inglis men, that ruschit war
Throu fors of ficht, as I said air,
Quhen thai saw cum with sic a cry
Toward thame sic ane cumpany,
That thai thoucht weill als mony war
As at war fechtand with thame thar,
And thai befor had thame nocht seyne,
Than, wit yhe weill, withouten weyne,
Thai war abasit so gretumly,
That the best and the mast hardy
That war in-till the oost that day,
Wald with thair mensk have beyn away.

The King Robert be thair relyng,
Saw thai war neir discomfyting,
And his ensenyhe can hely cry.
Than, with thame of his cumpany,
His fais presit so fast that thai
Wer than in-till sa gret effray,
That thai left place ay mar and mar.
For all the Scottis men that war thar,

Quhen thai saw thame eschew the ficht,
Dang on thame swa with all thar mycht,
That thai scalit in tropellis ser,
And till discumfitur war ner;
And sum of thame fled all planly.
Bot thai that wicht war and hardy,
That schame letit till ta the flicht,
At gret myschef mantemyt the ficht,
And stithly in the stour can stand.
And quhen the King of Ingland
Saw his men fle in syndry place,
And saw his fais rout, that was
Worthyn so wicht and so hardy,
That all his folk war halely
Swa stonayit, that thai had no mycht
To stynt thair fais in the ficht,
He was abaysit so gretumly
That he and all his cumpany,
Fif hundreth armyt weill at rycht,
In-till a frusche all tuk the flycht,
And till the castell held ther way.

JOHN BARBOUR

Ca' the Yowes to the Knowes

Ca' the yowes to the knowes,
Ca' them where the heather grows,
Ca' them where the burnie rowes,
My bonie dearie

As I gaed down the water-side,
There I met my shepherd lad:
He row'd me sweetly in his plaid,
And he ca'd me his dearie.

Will ye gang down the water-side,
And see the waves sae sweetly glide
Beneath the hazels spreading wide,
The moon it shines fu' clearly.

Ye sall get gowns and ribbons meet,
Cauf-leather shoon upon your feet,
And in my arms ye'se lie and sleep,
An' ye sall be my dearie.

If ye'll but stand to what ye've said,
I'se gang wi' thee, my shepherd lad,
And ye may row me in your plaid,
And I sall be your dearie.

While waters wimple to the sea,
While day blinks in the lift sae hie,
Till clay-cauld death sall blin' my e'e,
Ye sall be my dearie.

ROBERT BURNS

Cacmhor an Comann na Goill

Cacmhor an comann na Goill,
    daoine don chloinn dána a-riamh;
ní bhíd faoi phrabadh ré rádh
    gan chacadh fá sháth nó biadh.

Cacaid ag aonach 's ag ól,
    go h-ionntódh na slógh má seach;
tar cheann a gcacaid fó chéad
    cacaid séad ar mhith 's ar mhath.

Ránán ar gach guth dhá nglór,
    fir is mná 's a dtón gan smacht;
má roinnid foireann na dtoll
    ní roinnid bonn as an bhac.

Truagh nach dáilid a gcuid séad
    mar dháilid séad a gcuid cac;
ó nach cuireann séad i mbrígh
    aon rann seach rainn i mbí a gcac,
lén leas leanais cac go barr:
    bidh a n-adhmad nan Gall cac!

DONNCHADH MAC DHUBHGHOILL MHAOIL

The Lowlanders Are a Shitty Crowd

The Lowlanders are a shitty crowd
men of the impudent tribe as ever;
they're never known to hesitate
from shitting at meal-time or at food.

They shit at an assembly and when drinking,
till every company in turn is repelled,
for all they shit, a hundred times,
they shit upon peasantry and nobility.

Every word of their speech is a roar,
men and women with arses out of control;
if the (arse)hole squad are dealing,
they don't deal a *sou* from the stack.

Sad that they don't distribute their wealth
in the way they distribute their shit;
since they don't think it of importance
whatever airt their shit is in,
shit adheres to their haunches to the top:
shit is always in the make-up of the Lowlanders!

Trans. William Gillies

DUNCAN MacGREGOR

Caller Herrin'

Wha'll buy my caller herrin'?
They're bonnie fish and halesome farin';
Wha'll buy my caller herrin',
New drawn frae the Forth?

When ye were sleepin' on your pillows,
Dreamed ye aught o' our puir fellows.
Darkling as they faced the billows,
A' to fill the woven willows?
Buy my caller herrin',
New drawn frae the Forth.

Wha'll buy my caller herrin'?
They're no brought here without brave darin';
Buy my caller herrin',
Hauled through wind and rain.

Wha'll buy my caller herrin'?
Oh, ye may ca' them vulgar farin':
Wives and mithers maist despairin'
Ca' them lives o' men.

When the creel o' herrin' passes,
Ladies, clad in silks and laces,
Gather in their braw pelisses,
Cast their heads and screw their faces.
Wha'll buy my caller herrin'? etc.

Caller herrin's no got lightlie:
Ye can trip the spring fu' tightlie;
Spite o' tauntin', flauntin', flingin',
Gow has set you a' a-singin'.
Wha'll buy my caller herrin'? etc.

Neebor wives, now tent my tellin':
When the bonny fish ye're sellin',
At ae word be in ye're dealin', –
Truth will stand when a' thing's failin'.

CAROLINA OLIPHANT (LADY NAIRNE)

Caller Oysters

O' A' the waters that can hobble
A fishing yole or sa'mon coble,
An' can reward the fisher's trouble,
Or south or north,
There's nane sae spacious an' sae noble
As Frith o' Forth.

In her the skate an' codlin sail,
The eel fu' souple wags her tail,
Wi' herrin, fleuk, and mackarel,
An' whitins dainty:
Their spindle-shanks the labsters trail,
Wi' partans plenty.

Auld Reikie's sons blyth faces wear;
September's merry month is near,
That brings in Neptune's caller cheer,
New oysters fresh;
The halesomest and nicest gear
O' fish or flesh.

O! then we needna gie a plack
For dand'ring mountebank or quack,
Wha o' their drugs sae baldly crack,
An' spread sic notions,
As gar their feckless patients tak
Their stinkin' potions.

Come prie, frail man! for gin thou art sick,
The oyster is a rare cathartic,
As ever doctor patient gart lick
To cure his ails;
Whether you hae the head or heart ake,
It ay prevails.

Ye tiplers open a' your poses,
Ye wha are fash'd wi' pluky hoses,
Fling owr your craig sufficient doses,
You'll thole a hunder,
To fleg awa' your simmer roses,
An' naething under.

Whan big as burns the gutters rin,
Gin ye hae catcht a droukit skin,
To Lucky Middlemist's loup in,
An' sit fu' snug
Owr oysters and a dram o' gin,
Or haddock lug.

Whan auld Saunt Giles, at aught o'clock
Gars merchant lowns their shopies lock,
There we adjourn wi' hearty fock
To birle our bodles,
An' get wharewi' to crack our joke,
An' clear our noddles.
Whan Phœbus did his winnocks steek,
How aften at that ingle cheek
Did I my frosty fingers beek,
An' prie gude fare!
I trow there was na hame to seek
Whan steghin there.

While glakit fools, owr rife o' cash,
Pamper their wames wi' fousom trash,
I think a chiel may gayly pass;
He's nae ill boden
That gusts his gab wi' oyster sauce,
An' hen well sodden,

At Musselbrough, an' eke Newhaven,
The fisher wives will get top livin,
When lads gang out on Sunday's even
To treat their joes,
An' tak o' fat pandores a priven,
Or mussel brose.
Then sometimes, ere they flit their doup,
They'll ablins a' their siller coup
For liquor clear frae cutty stoup,
To weet their wizzen,
An' swallow owr a dainty soup,
For fear they gizzen.

A' ye wha canna staun sae sicker,
Whan twice you've toom'd the big-ars'd bicker,
Mix caller oysters wi' your liquor,
An' I'm your debtor,
If greedy priest or drouthy vicar
Will thole it better.

ROBERT FERGUSSON

Canadian Boat-Song

Listen to me, as when ye heard our fathers
Sing long ago, the song of other shores –
Listen to me, and then in chorus gather
All your deep voices, as ye pull your oars:

Fair these broad meads – these hoary woods are grand;
But we are exiles from our fathers' land.

From the lone shieling of the misty island
Mountains divide us, and the waste of seas –
Yet still the blood is strong, the heart is Highland,
And we in dreams behold the Hebrides:

We ne'er shall tread the fancy-haunted valley,
Where 'tween the dark hills creeps the small clear stream,
In arms around the patriarch banner rally,
Nor see the moon on royal tombstones gleam:

When the bold kindred, in the time long-vanished,
Conquer'd the soil and fortified the keep –
No seer foretold the children would be banish'd,
That a degenerate Lord might boast his sheep:

Come foreign rage – let Discord burst in slaughter!
O then for clansman true, and stern claymore –
The hearts that would have given their blood like water,
Beat heavily beyond the Atlantic roar.

ANON.

Canedolia

oa! hoy! awe! ba! mey!

who saw?
rhu saw rum. garve saw smoo. nigg saw tain. lairg saw lagg.
rigg saw eigg. largs saw haggs. tongue saw luss. mull saw yell.
stoer saw strone. drem saw muck. gask saw noss. unst saw cults.
echt saw banff. weem saw wick. trool saw twatt.

how far?
from largo to lunga from joppa to skibo from ratho to shona from
ulva to minto from tinto to tolsta from soutra to marsco from
braco to barra from alva to stobo from fogo to fada from gigha to
gogo from kelso to stroma from hirta to spango.

what is it like there?
och it's freuchie, it's faifley, it's wamphray, it's frandy, it's
sliddery.

what do you do?
we foindle and fungle, we bonkle and meigle and maxpoffle. we
scotstarvit, armit, wormit, and even whifflet. we play at crosstobs
leuchars, gorbals, and finfan. we scavaig, and there's aye a bit of
tilquhilly. if it's wet, treshnish and mishnish.

what is the best of the country?
blinkbonny! airgold! thundergay!

and the worst?
scrishven, shiskine, scrabster, and snizort.

listen! what's that?
catacol and wauchope, never heed them.

tell us about last night?
well, we had a wee ferintosh and we lay on the quiraing. it was
pure strontian!

but who was there?
petermoidart and craigenkenneth and cambusputtock and
ecclemuchty and corriehulish and balladolly and altnacanny and
clauchanvrechan and stronachlochan and auchenlacher and
tighnacrankie and tilliebruaich and killiehara and invervannach
and achnatudlem and machrishellach and inchtamurchan and
auchterfechan and kinlochculter and ardnawhallie and
invershuggle.

and what was the toast?
schiehallion! schiehallion! schiehallion!

EDWIN MORGAN

Cead Deireannach nam Beann

Bha mi 'n dè 'm Beinn Dòbhrain
's na còir cha robh mi aineolach;
chunna mi na gleanntan
's na beanntaichean a b' aithne dhomh:
b' e sin an sealladh èibhinn,
bhith 'g imeachd air na slèibhtean
nuair bhiodh a' ghrian ag èirigh
's a bhiodh na fèidh a' langanaich.

'S aobhach a' ghreigh uallach
nuair ghluaiseadh iad gu faramach,
's na h-èildean air an fhuaran,
bu chuannar na laoigh bhallach ann;
na maoislichean 's na ruadh-bhuic,
na coilich dhubha 's ruadha –
's e 'n cèol bu bhinne chualas
nuair chluinnt' am fuaim sa chamhanaich.

'S togarrach a dh'fhalbhainn
gu sealgaireachd nam bealaichean,
dol mach a dhìreadh garbhlaich
's gum b' anmoch tighinn gu baile mi;
an t-uisge glan 's am fàile
th' air mullach nam beann àrda,
chuidich e gu fàs mi,
's e rinn domh slàint' is fallaineachd.

Fhuair mi greis dem àrach
air àirighean a b' aithne dhomh,
ri cluiche 's mire 's mànran
's bhith 'n coibhneas blàth nan caileagan;
bu chùis an aghaidh nàdair
gum maireadh sin an-dràst' ann –
's e b' èiginn bhith gam fàgail
nuair thàinig tràth dhuinn dealachadh.

Nis on bhuail an aois mi,
fhuair mi gaoid a mhaireas domh,
rinn milleadh air mo dheudach

's mo lèirsinn air a dalladh orm;
chan urrainn mi bhith treubhach
ged a chuirinn feum air,
's ged bhiodh an ruaig am dhèidh-sa,
cha dèan mi ceum ro chabhagach.

Ged tha mo cheann air liathadh
's mo chiabhagan air tanachadh,
's tric a leig mi mial-chù
ri fear fiadhaich ceannardach;
ged bu toigh leam riamh iad,
's ged fhaicinn air an t-sliabh iad,
cha tèid mi nis gan iarraidh,
on chaill mi trian na h-analach.

Ri àm dol anns a' bhùireadh
bu dùrachdach a leanainn iad,
's bhiodh uair aig sluagh na dùthcha,
toirt òran ùra 's rannachd dhaibh;
greis eile mar ri càirdean
nuair bha sinn anns na campan –
bu chridheil anns an àm sinn,
's cha bhiodh an dram oirnn annasach.

Nuair bha mi 'n toiseach m' òige,
's i ghòraich' a chùm falamh mi;
's e Fortan tha cur oirnne
gach aon nì còir a ghealladh dhuinn;
ged tha mi gann a stòras,
tha m' inntinn làn de shòlas,
on tha mi ann an dòchas
gun d' rinn nighean Deòrs' an t-aran domh.

Bha mi 'n dè san aonach
's bha smaointean mòr air m' aire-sa,
nach robh 'n luchd-gaoil a b' àbhaist
bhith siubhal fàsaich mar rium ann;
's a' bheinn as beag a shaoil mi
gun dèanadh ise caochladh,
on tha i nis fo chaoraibh,
's ann thug an saoghal car asam.

Nuair sheall mi air gach taobh dhìom,
chan fhaodainn gun bhith smalanach,
on theirig coill is fraoch ann,
's na daoine bh' ann, cha mhaireann iad;
chan eil fiadh ra shealg ann,
chan eil eun no earb ann –
am beagan nach eil marbh dhiubh,
's e rinn iad falbh gu baileach às.

Mo shoraidh leis na frìthean,
o 's mìorbhailteach na beannan iad,
le biolair uaine 's fìor uisg',
deoch uasal rìomhach cheanalta;
na blàran a tha prìseil
's na fàsaichean tha lìonmhor,
o 's àit a leig mi dhìom iad,
gu bràth mo mhìle beannachd leo.

DONNCHADH BÀN MAC AN T-SAOIR

Last Farewell to the Mountains

Yesterday I was on Ben Doran,
no stranger to its slopes;
I saw the glens
and the mountains I knew so well;
that was a splendid sight,
to be walking over the hillside
when the sun was rising
and the deer were bellowing.

Happy was the gallant herd
when they moved off noisily;
and the hinds by the spring,
the speckled calves looked bonny there;
the does and the roe-bucks,
the black-cocks and the grouse –
the sweetest music ever heard
was their sound at dawn.

Happily I would go
stalking on the mountain passes,
going out to climb the rough heights,
and getting home late;
the fresh rain and the air
on the high mountain-tops
helped me to grow up,
with good health and wellbeing.

I spent part of my upbringing
on the sheilings that I knew so well,
having fun and games and flirting
and enjoying the warm friendship of the girls;
it would be going against nature
to expect it to be unchanged –
we knew we'd have to leave all that
when the time came for us to go.

And now that old age has struck me
I find it's a complaint I can't shake off,
which has wrought havoc upon my teeth
and clouded my vision;
I can no longer be adventurous
even if I needed to be,
and even if the hunt was after me
I can't move very fast.

Although my head has greyed
and my sideburns have thinned,
I often loosed a greyhound
after an imperious, wild one;
although I've always liked them,
and though I see them on the slopes,
I won't now go after them
since I've lost a third of my breath.

When the time came to bellowing,
the pursuit of them is fervent;
and an hour comes when the countryfolk
will give them songs and rhymes;
another while, as with friends,

when we were in the camps –
jolly were those times
and drams were not unknown.

When I was at the start of my youth,
foolishness kept me empty;
it is Fortune that puts on us
each kind thing that we are promised;
although I'm short of treasures,
my mind is full of solace,
since I have every hope
George's daughter's made me bread.

Yesterday I was on the moor
and heavy thoughts lay on my mind,
that my beloved friends who used
to roam the wastelands with me were no longer there;
and the mountain that I little thought
would ever change,
now that she is covered in sheep,
I think the world has played a trick on me.

When I look around me,
I cannot but be sorrowful,
since the wood and heather's gone,
so too the people who were there;
there are no deer to hunt there,
no bird nor hind –
the few that weren't killed
have all completely fled.

Farewell to the deer-forests,
oh! what wonderful mountains they are,
with green water-cress and spring water,
a noble, royal, pleasant drink;
the moors which are so precious,
and the pastures which are so plentiful,
oh, joyfully I take my leave of them –
my thousand blessings on them forever.

Trans. Anne Lorne Gillies and Peter Mackay

DUNCAN MacINTYRE

Ceumannan

Sheòl thu
a-steach na mo rian mar reul
ùr
chun an speuradair –
gealach
a dh'fhoillsich grian air falach:
aoibhneas fiosrachaidh;
's shìn mi mo làmhan chun a' gharaidh.

Cha do shìn mi mo làmhan gus do ghlacdh;
bha ùghdarras eile gan riaghladh,
bha iad air an lapadh
ann an seirbheis chuairteil m' iunaibhears –
gun de dh'earbsa na saorsa
na sgaoileadh an car às a' char ud.

Is chaidh an tràth seachad.

Thachair thu an-dè rium
air sràid
lasair shùilean is clò gorm
's ruith mi air mo theanga a' lorg
facail a chanainn –

ach bha iad gu lèir air chall;
's tro eighealaich bhalbh
mo thost
dh'èist mi air an t-sràid
brag ceum an dèidh ceum do chois
a' seòladh gorm-bhlàth-dhali
leat seachad; is air falbh.

Bha an latha geal ann
an-diugh
mus do chaidil mi;
chaith mi an oidhche gu h-anshocair
a' sgrùdadh reultan is ghealaichean
(is bheachdaich mi air faire nam bàrd!)
O! nam b' urrainn dhomh a ràdha

gur tusa chùm na mo chaithris mi
– air dòigh dhe na dhà . . .

ach's ann a chaidh an cadal
ceàrr orm
(a leannain)
– mas e an fhìrinn as fheàrr . . .

DOMHNALL MacAMHLAIGH

Steps

You sailed
into my vision like a star
new
to the astronomer;
a moon
revealing a sun hidden:
joy of discovery;
and I stretched out my hands to the warmth.

I did not stretch out my hands to seize you;
another authority ruled them,
they had become numbed
in the ritual service of my universe –
not trusting in freedom enough
to unravel that ancient twist.

And the opportunity passed.

I met you yesterday
on a street
a flame of eyes and blue tweed
and I searched my tongue
for words to speak –

but they were all lost;
and through my numb and wordless
silence
I listened on the street

to thundering step after step of your feet
as they sailed with you blue-flower-blind
past me and away.

It was bright daylight
today
before I slept;
I spent the night very uncomfortably,
scrutinising stars and moons
(and I meditated on the poets' vigil!)
Oh! if I could only say
it was you who kept me awake
– one way or the other . . .

but I quite simply
could not get to sleep
(my love)
– if the truth is to be preferred . . .

Translated by author

DONALD MacAULAY

Chan e Dìreadh na Bruthaich

Chan e dìreadh na bruthaich a dh'fhàg mo shiubhal gun treòir,
No teas ri là grèine nuair a dh'èireadh i oirnn.
Laigh an sneachd seo air m' fheusaig is cha lèir dhomh mo bhròg.

'S gann is lèir dhomh nì 's fhaisge ceann a' bhata nam dhòrn.
'S e mo thaigh mòr na creagan, 's e mo dhaingeann gach fròg:
'S e mo thubhailte m' osan, 's e mo chopan mo bhròg.

Ged a cheannaichinn am buideal chan fhaigh mi cuideachd nì òl.
'S ged a cheannaichinn seipean chan fhaigh mi creideas a' stòip.
'S ged a dh'fhàdainn an teine chì fear foille dheth ceò.

'S i do nighean-sa, Dhonnchaidh, chuir an iomagain seo oirnn –
Tè gam beil an cùl dualach o guaillean gu bròg,
Tè gam beil an cùl bachlach 's a dhreach mar an t-òr.

117

Dheòin a Dhia cha bhi gillean riut a' mire 's mi beò:
Ged nach dèanainn dhut fighe, bhiodh iasg is sitheann mud bhòrd.
'S truagh nach robh mi 's tu, ghaolaich, anns an aonach 'm bi 'n ceò.

Ann am bothaig bhig bharraich 's gun bhith mar rium ach d' fheòil,
Agus pàistean beag leanaibh a cheileadh ar glòir:
'S mì a shnàmhadh an caolas airson faoilteachd do bheòil.

Nuair a thigeadh am Foghar b' e mo roghainn bhith falbh
Leis a' ghunna nach diùltadh 's leis an fhùdar dhubh-ghorm,
Nuair a gheibhinn cead frìth' bhon àn rìgh 's on Iarl' Òg.

Gum biodh fuil an damh chabraich ruith le altaibh mo dhòrn,
Agus fuil a' bhuic bhioraich sìor sileadh feadh feòir;
Ach 's i do nighean-sa, Dhonnchaidh, chuir an iomagain seo oirnn.

FEARCHAR MACRATH

It's Not Climbing the Brae

It's not climbing the brae that has weakened my step
or a sunny day's heat when the sun's at its height:
this snow has lain on my beard and I can't see my shoe.

I can barely see nearby things – the staff-head in my fist;
my great house is the rocks, my stronghold each cranny,
my towel is my stocking, my cup is my shoe.

If I should buy a bottle, I'd find no one to share it,
and if I bought a chopin, I'd not get credit for a stoup.
If I should light a fire, I'd be betrayed by its smoke.

It's your daughter, Duncan, who's caused me this trouble –
the girl with curly hair from her shoulder to her shoe,
the girl with wavy hair the colour of gold.

God willing, no lads would dally with you while I live:
Though I wouldn't weave for you, there'd be fish and game on your table.
It's a shame, my love, we weren't on the misty hill together.

In a wee brushwood bothy, with only you, in the flesh,
and a little child who'd keep our conversation secret:
how I would swim the kyle for your welcoming mouth.

When the Autumn came, I would choose to be away
with the gun that never misfires, and the black-blue powder,
with permission to hunt from the King and the young Earl.

The antlered stag's blood would flow through my hands,
and the pointed buck's blood pour across the grass;
but it's your daughter, Duncan, who caused me this trouble.

Trans. Peter Mackay

FARQUHAR MACRAE

Christmas Oranges

Clementines—
this pile of votive planets
on the fridge-top,
caught in their nylon net.

Some
baggily-skinned, so
hooking a thumb
easily under, then
the whole skin off in a one-er; some
tighter, more
reluctant to be separate
from their hearts of sun.
(Danger of making a juice-sticky mess of those.)

Then breaking them open—
fragrance of orange on the tips of the fingers—
peeling away
like a plaster from skin
                              segment by segment
held up to this morning light
that's coloured the juice of an orange, each

segment veined like the petal of a rose—
to check for the shades of pips
in the cool translucence—
the thrawn wee buggers, the embryos

lavish with thought of perpetual groves.

GERRY CAMBRIDGE

Chrysalis

We found it on a bunch of grapes and put it
In cotton-wool, in a matchbox partly open,
In a room in London in winter-time, and in
A safe place, and then forgot it.

Early in the cold spring we said, 'See this!
Where on earth has the butterfly come from?'
It looked so unnatural whisking about the curtain:
Then we remembered the chrysalis.

There was the broken shell with what was once
The head askew; and what was once the worm
Was away out of the window, out of the warm,
Out of the scene of the small violence.

Not strange, that the pretty creature formalised
The virtue of its dark unconscious wait
For pincers of light to come and pick it out.
But it was a bad business, our being surprised.

MURIEL SPARK

Chunnaic mi an t-Òg Uasal

Hao ri ri ri hó,
Hó ho ro hó, hao hó.

Chunnaic mi an t-òg uasal
    Seachad suas 'n-seo an-dé.

'S le ghunn' air a ghualainn
    Gura uallach a cheum.

'S ghabh e suas orm seachad
    Air each glas nan ceum réidh.

Cha do dh'fhiosraich, cha d' dh'fharraid,
    Cha do ghabh e bhuam sgeul.

'S mun taca seo 'n-uiridh
    Bu leam t' fhuran ro cheud.

'S cha mhutha mi am-bliadhna
    Seach ianlaith nan speur.

'S gu bheil sac air mo chridhe
    Nach tog fidheall nan teud.

Trom mhulad, trom mhulad,
    Trom mhulad 'nad dhéidh.

S truagh, a Rìgh, nach mi 'n gunna
    Ris an cuireadh tu 'n gleus.

S truagh, a Rìgh, nach mi 'n garbhlach
    Air am marbhadh tu na féidh,

S truagh, a Rìgh, nach mi 'm bàta
    Ris an càireadh tu 'm bréid.

S truagh, a Rìgh, nach mi 'm breacan
    Thug thu dhachaigh on fhéill.

'S nuair a thilleadh on fhasrach
    Bhithinn paisgte fo d' sgéith.

'S nuair a rachadh i fhàsgadh
    Bhithinn a-rithist 'nam dhéidh

Gun i thoirt a gaol falaich
    Do dhuine tha fon ghréin.

Bidh iad briathrach a' tighinn
    'S rùn an cridh' aca fhéin.

GUN URRA

I Saw the Well-Born Youth

Hao ri ri ri hó,
Hó ho ro hó, hao hó.

I saw the well-born youth
    Going up past here yesterday.

And with his gun on his shoulder
    Distinguished was his step.

And he climbed up past me
    On the smooth-stepping grey horse.

He didn't ask, he didn't seek,
    He didn't get from me my news.

And about this time last year
    You greeted me before a hundred.

Yet no more am I this year
    Than the bird-flocks of the skies.

And on my heart there's a burden
    That no stringed fiddle will lift.

Deep sadness, deep sadness,
    Deep sadness comes after you.

I wish, my King, I were the gun
    That you'd prepare to fire.

I wish, my King, I were the rough ground
    On which you'd kill the deer.

I wish, my King, I were the boat
    On which you'd hoist the sails.

I wish, my King, I were the plaid
    You brought home from the fair.

For when you got out of the rain
    I'd be wrapped under your arm.

And when she'd been wrung
    I'd be spread out in the sun.

And my advice to a girl
    Who'd follow my footsteps

Is not to give love in secret
    To any man under the sun.

They come loaded with words
    But keep their hearts to themselves.

Trans. Ronald Black

ANON.

From The City of Dreadful Night

II

Because he seemed to walk with an intent
    I followed him; who, shadowlike and frail,
Unswervingly though slowly onward went,
    Regardless, wrapt in thought as in a veil:
Thus step for step with lonely sounding feet
We travelled many a long dim silent street.

At length he paused: a black mass in the gloom,
      A tower that merged into the heavy sky;
Around, the huddled stones of grave and tomb:
      Some old God's-acre now corruption's sty:
He murmured to himself with dull despair,
Here Faith died, poisoned by this charnel air.

Then turning to the right went on once more
      And travelled weary roads without suspense;
And reached at last a low wall's open door,
      Whose villa gleamed beyond the foliage dense:
He gazed, and muttered with a hard despair,
Here Love died, stabbed by its own worshipped pair.

Then turning to the right resumed his march,
      And travelled street and lanes with wondrous strength,
Until on stooping through a narrow arch
      We stood before a squalid house at length:
He gazed, and whispered with a cold despair,
Here Hope died, starved out in its utmost lair.

When he had spoken thus, before he stirred,
      I spoke, perplexed by something in the signs
Of desolation I had seen and heard
      In this drear pilgrimage to ruined shrines:
Where Faith and Love and Hope are dead indeed,
Can Life still live? By what doth it proceed?

As whom his one intense thought overpowers,
      He answered coldly, Take a watch, erase
The signs and figures of the circling hours,
      Detach the hands, remove the dial-face;
The works proceed until run down; although
Bereft of purpose, void of use, still go.

Then turning to the right paced on again,
      And traversed squares and travelled streets whose glooms
Seemed more and more familiar to my ken;
      And reached that sullen temple of the tombs;
And paused to murmur with the old despair,
Hear Faith died, poisoned by this charnel air.

I ceased to follow, for the knot of doubt
    Was severed sharply with a cruel knife:
He circled thus forever tracing out
    The series of the fraction left of Life;
Perpetual recurrence in the scope
Of but three terms, dead Faith, dead Love, dead Hope.

JAMES THOMSON

The Clearances

The thistles climb the thatch. Forever
this sharp scale in our poems,
as also the waste music of the sea.

The stars shine over Sutherland
in a cold ceilidh of their own,
as, in the morning, the silver cane

cropped among corn. We will remember this.
Though hate is evil we cannot
but hope your courtier's heels in hell

are burning: that to hear
the thatch sizzling in tanged smoke
your hot ears slowly learn.

IAIN CRICHTON SMITH

Clerk Sanders

1   Clark Sanders and May Margret
    Walkt ower yon graveld green,
    And sad and heavy was the love,
    I wat, it fell this twa between.

2   'A bed, a bed,' Clark Sanders said,
    'A bed, a bed for you and I;'
    'Fye no, fye no,' the lady said,
    'Until the day we married be.

3 'For in it will come my seven brothers,
  And a' their torches burning bright;
  They'll say, We hae but ae sister,
  And here her lying wi a knight.'

4 'Ye'l take the sourde fray my scabbord,
  And lowly, lowly lift the gin,
  And you may say, your oth to save,
  You never let Clark Sanders in.

5 'Yele take a napken in your hand,
  And ye'l ty up baith your een,
  An ye may say, your oth to save,
  That ye saw na Sandy sen late yestreen.

6 'Yele take me in your armes twa,
  Yele carrey me ben into your bed,
  And ye may say, your oth to save,
  In your bower-floor I never tread.'

7 She has taen the sourde fray his scabbord,
  And lowly, lowly lifted the gin;
  She was to swear, her oth to save,
  She never let Clerk Sanders in.

8 She has tain a napkin in her hand,
  And she ty'd up baith her eeen;
  She was to swear, her oth to save,
  She saw na him sene late yestreen.

9 She has taen him in her armes twa,
  And carried him ben into her bed;
  She was to swear, her oth to save,
  He never in her bower-floor tread.

10 In and came her seven brothers,
  And all their torches burning bright;
  Says thay, We hae but ae sister,
  And see there her lying wi a knight.

11 Out and speaks the first of them,
     'A wat they hay been lovers dear;'
     Out and speaks the next of them,
     'They hay been in love this many a year.'

12 Out an speaks the third of them,
     'It wear great sin this twa to twain;'
     Out an speaks the fourth of them,
     'It wear a sin to kill a sleeping man.'

13 Out an speaks the fifth of them,
     'A wat they'll near be twaind by me;'
     Out an speaks the sixt of them,
     'We'l tak our leave an gae our way.'

14 Out an speaks the seventh of them,
     'Altho there wear no a man but me,
     . . . .
     I bear the brand, I'le gar him die.'

15 Out he has taen a bright long brand,
     And he has striped it throw the straw,
     And throw and throw Clarke Sanders' body
     A wat he has gard cold iron gae.

16 Sanders he started, an Margret she lapt,
     Intill his arms whare she lay,
     And well and wellsom was the night,
     A wat it was between these twa.

17 And they lay still, and sleeped sound,
     Untill the day began to daw;
     And kindly till him she did say
     'It's time, trew-love, ye wear awa.'

18 They lay still, and sleeped sound,
     Untill the sun began to shine;
     She lookt between her and the wa,
     And dull and heavy was his eeen.

19 She thought it had been a loathsome sweat,
    A wat it had fallen this twa between;
    But it was the blood of his fair body,
    A wat his life days wair na lang.

20 'O Sanders, I'le do for your sake
    What other ladys would na thoule;
    When seven years is come and gone,
    There's near a shoe go on my sole.

21 'O Sanders, I'le do for your sake
    What other ladies would think mare;
    When seven years is come and gone,
    Ther's nere a comb go in my hair.

22 'O Sanders, I'le do for your sake
    What other ladies would think lack;
    When seven years is come an gone,
    I'le wear nought but dowy black.'

23 The bells gaed clinking throw the towne,
    To carry the dead corps to the clay,
    An sighing says her May Margret,
    'A wat I bide a doulfou day.'

24 In an come her father dear,
    Stout steping on the floor;
    . . . .
    . . . .

25 'Hold your toung, my doughter dear,
    Let all your mourning a bee;
    I'le carry the dead corps to the clay,
    An I'le come back an comfort thee.'

26 'Comfort well your seven sons,
    For comforted will I never bee;
    For it was neither lord nor loune
    That was in bower last night wi mee.'

ANON.

Clio's

Am I to be blamed for the state of it now? – Surely not –
Her poor wee fractured soul that I loved for its lightness and left?
Now she rings up pathetically, not to make claims of me,
Only to be in her wild way solicitous:
'Do you know of a restaurant called *Clio's* – or something like that –
At number *forty-three* in its road or street, – and the owner
Is beautiful, rich and Italian – you see, I dreamt of it,
And I can't relax without telling you never to go there,
Divining, somehow, that for you the place is *danger* –'

(But I dine at Clio's every night, poor lamb.)

MICK IMLAH

The Cloud's Anchor

THE CLOUD'S ANCHOR

s w a l l o w

IAN HAMILTON FINLAY

The Coin

We brushed the dirt off, held it to the light.
The obverse showed us *Scotland*, and the head
of a red deer; the antler-glint had fled
but the fine cut could still be felt. All right:
we turned it over, read easily *One Pound*,
but then the shock of Latin, like a gloss,
Respublica Scotorum, sent across
such ages as we guessed but never found
at the worn edge where once the date had been
and where as many fingers had gripped hard
as hopes their silent race had lost or gained.
The marshy scurf crept up to our machine,
sucked at our boots. Yet nothing seemed ill-starred.
And least of all the realm the coin contained.

EDWIN MORGAN

The Collier's Ragged Wean

He's up at early morning, howe'er the win' may blaw,
Lang before the sun comes roun' to chase the stars awa';
And 'mang a thoosand dangers, unkent in sweet daylight,
He'll toil until the stars again keek through the chilly night.
See the puir wee callan', 'neath the cauld clear moon!
His knees oot through his troosers and his taes oot through his shoon;
Wading through the freezing snaw, thinking owre again
How happy every wean maun be that's no a collier's wean.

His cheeks are blae wi' cauld, and the chittering winna cease,
To gie the hungry callan' time to eat his mornin' piece;
His lamp is burning on his head wi' feeble flickerin' ray,
And in his heart the lamp o' Hope is burning feebly tae.
Nae wonner that the callan's sweert to face his daily toil,
Nae wonner he sae seldom greets the morning wi' a smile;
For weel he kens he's growing up to face the cauld disdain
That lang the world has measured oot to every collier's wean.

The puir wee hirpling laddie! how mournfully he's gaun,
Ayd dichting aff the ither tear wi's wee hard hackit haun'!
Sair, sair he's tempit 'mang the snaw to toom his flask o' oil,
But ah! – ae flash o' faither's ire were waur than weeks o' toil.
In vain the stars look down on the youth wi' merry twinkling een,
Through clouds o' care sae dense as his their glory is nae seen;
He thinks 'twad been a better plan if coal had boon-most lain,
And wonners why his faither made a collier o' his wean.

Oh! ye that row in Fortune's lap, his waefu' story hear;
Aft sorrows no sae deep as his hae won a pitying tear;
And lichter wrangs than he endures your sympathy hae won –
Although he is a collier's, mind, he's still a Briton's son.
And ye wha mak' and mend oor laws, tak' pity on the bairn;
Oh! bring him sooner frae the pit, and gie him time to learn:
Sae shall ye lift him frae the mire 'mang which he lang has lain,
And win a blessing frae the heart o' every collier's wean.

DAVID WINGATE

Comhairle air na Nigheanan Òga

An toiseach m' aimsir is mo dhòigh ri bargan
Gun robh mi 'g earbsa nach cealgte orm;
Cha chòmhradh cearbach air ro-bheag leanmhainn
Bho aois mo leanbaidh chaidh fheuchainn dhòmhs';
Ach nis bho chì mi cor nan daoine,
An comann gaolach gur faoin a ghlòr,
Cha dèan mi m' aontadh ri neach fon t-saoghal;
Chan eil gach aon dhiubh air aon chainnt beòil.

Nach fhaic sibh òigear nam meall-shùil bòidheach,
Le theangaidh leòmaich 's e labhairt rium?
Le spuir 's le bhòtan, le ad 's le chleòca,
Le chorra-cheann spòrsail an òr-fhuilt duinn;
Saoilidh gòrag le bhriathraibh mòrach
Ga cur an dòchas le glòr a chinn:
'A ghaoil, gabh truas rium 's na leig gu h-uaigh mi;
Do ghaol a bhuair mi bho ghluais mi fhìn.'

'Le d' theangaidh leacaich nam briathran tearca,
'S e saobhadh d' fhacail dh'fhàg sac gam leòn;
Gu bheil mi 'g altram am thaobh an tacaid
A rinn mo ghlacadh 's mo ghreas fon fhòid.'
Mar shamhladh dhà siud gaoth a' Mhàirt ud
Thig bho na h-àirdibh 's nach taobh i seòl:
Nuair gheobh e mhiann dith gun toir e bhriathra
Nach fhac' e riamh i, 's car fiar na shròin.

Na geallan breugach air bheag reusan,
Fallsail, eucorach, neo-ghlan rùn,
Air eagal bhreugan no masladh fhaotainn
'S ann leam nach b' èibhinn taobhsann riuth';
A chlann, na èistibh rin glòr gun èifeachd,
'S na toiribh spèis do fhear caogaidh shùil;
Gur h-adhbhar reusain dhuibhs' an trèigeadh –
'S ann annta fhèin a bhios gnè nan lùb.

Bha mi uair nuair a bha mi 'm ghruagaich
Gum faighinn uaigneas gun fhios do chàch;
Mar shamhladh bruadair an-diugh ga luaidh rium,

131

Gun dad de bhuannachd ach buaidh mar ghnàth,
Na geallan glè-mhòr a gheobhainn fhèin bhuap'
Air chor 's nach trèigeadh iad mi gu bràth;
A-nis is lèir dhomh na rinn mi dh'eucoir
'S a' mheud 's a dh'èist mi d' am breugan bàth.

Ach, a fhearaibh òga, ge mòr nur bòlaich,
'S math 's aithne dhòmhsa cuid mhòr d' ur gnàths:
Gu barrail, bòidheach sibh tighinn am chòmhdhail,
Ler teangaidh leòmaich 's ler còmhradh tlàth;
Ghabhte ceòl leibh an aodann gòraig,
'S mur bi i eòlach gun gabh i à:
Nuair bhios e stòlda 's nuair gheobh e leòr dhith,
Gum bi Ochòin aic' an lorg bhith bàth.

A ghruagach chèillidh, na creid fhèin iad,
An car-fon-sgèith sin bhios ann an gràdh;
Chan eil san t-saoghal nach creid an saoradh,
Ach 's mise dh'fhaodadh a chaochladh ràdh;
Taobh an inntinn mar as cinnteach,
Is theirig aotram air ghaol thoirt dàibh:
Dh'aindeoin fhacail 's a bhriathra brosgail,
Na dèan do lochd leis an t-sochar-dhàil.

A ghruagach dheud-gheal an fhuilt theud-bhuidhe,
Cum do cheutaidh fo d' cheud-bharr ùr;
Na creid am breugan 's na tog droch-sgeula,
Ged robh fear leumnach nan dèidh mar chùl;
Dh'aindeoin uaigneis is raspars uasal,
Na leig e 'n uachdar air chruas a ghlùin,
Ach cum e 'n ìochdar ge b' oil le fhiacail,
Mur toir e bhriathar gur fhiach leis thu.

Am fear a thriallas a dhol a dh'iarraidh
Na mnà as miannaiche bhios da rèir,
Gur cailinn shuairc i nach fhuiling mì-stuamachd,
Na dhol an uaignes le neach fon ghrèin;
Mar shamhladh bhà siud, a bhrìgh a nàire,
Dhol nas dàine na mànran bèil;
Bheir fear gun riaghailt an sin a bhriathar
Gu bheil i fiadhta 's nach fhiach a gnè.

Ma bhios i glèidhteach air nì 's air feudail,
Their fear gun reusan gum bi i crìon,
'S ma bhios i pàirteach air nithe àraidh,
Gun abair càch rith' gum b' fheàirrd' i ciall;
An tè tha stròdhail, cha bhuin i dhòmhsa
Mar chèile-pòsta bhon tha i fial;
Gur cailinn shàmhach nach fhuiling tàmailt,
A mòid no mànran an-àirde miann.

SÌLEAS NA CEAPAICH

Advice to Young Girls

When I was young and weighing a bargain
I had faith I'd not be deceived:
In my childhood I'd never heard
Twisted words you couldn't believe.
Now I see what people are like,
How love's fellowship's based on vain words
That for no two men mean the same thing –
I'd hook up with no man in the world.

Take this loving, leering-eyed laddie
Chatting me up with his arrogant tongue,
His spurs and boots, his hat and his cloak,
He's dirty-blonde, giddy and young.
His conceit would make silly girls think
They can trust in his elegant lies:
'My love for you's ruined my life;
Love, pity me, don't let me die.'

'I'm hurt by your double-talk,
Flagstone tongue and curt asides;
You're hurrying me under the turf
With the dart I nurse in my side.'
But like those winds in March
That buffet skies but fill no sails,
He'll turn up his nose when he gets what he wants;
'I don't know her,' he will maintain.

False promises based on no reason,
Unsavoury motives and unjust lies;
For fear of the shame and the scandal,
I'd get no pleasure in taking their side.
Young girls, ignore winking men,
Pay no attention to their false bravado;
It's their nature to be lewd and perverse –
Good reason to give them the heave-ho.

Back when I was still a young woman
I'd seek solitude, away from them all;
Those days now seem like a dream
As substanceless, as ephemeral.
From men I'd get huge, splendid promises
Vowing that they'd never leave me;
Now it's clear that I did myself wrong
By listening to so much dishonesty.

Young men, though your bragging's great,
I'm accustomed to your wicked ways:
You act genteel and fawning when with me,
With glib tongues and mellow parlay;
You'll play music for pretty young girls,
And if they're naïve, you will take them in:
But when you're finished and had your fill
They'll cry *Alas!* for being foolishly vain.

Sensible girls, don't believe them,
Deceit hides in their affections;
The whole world'd have them acquitted
With just me for the prosecution.
Trust your intelligence, the surest thing
When in love, and always tread lightly:
Don't be misled by flattering friendships:
Their talk's false and their words are flighty.

Girl of white-teeth, harp-string-gold hair,
Keep your affections tightly locked up,
Don't fall for their lies or tall stories,
No matter how leapingly they're backed up.
Don't give him control (despite his hard knees),

Ignore your loneliness and his pretensions;
Keep him down (in spite of his teeth),
Till he proves he rates your attention.

The man who goes far to get what he wants
Will want a polite girl, and so will shun
Those who are immodest, and who wander off
With anyone under the sun;
He'll want a girl who's shy, who says no
If asked, when flirting, to be bolder:
And men with no morals will claim
She's sullen and not worth the bother.

If she's frugal with stock and with kine
The unjust man will say she's tight-fisted;
But if she's generous with her fine goods
Others will say she's slow-witted;
I wouldn't marry a big-spending girl
Because of her loose generosity:
But a quiet girl who'd run from disgrace,
Whose speech rings clear with nobility.

Trans. Peter Mackay and Iain S. MacPherson

JULIA MacDONALD

The Coming of the Wee Malkies

Haw missis, whit'll ye dae when the wee Malkies come,
If they dreep doon affy the wash-hoose dyke,
An pit the hems oan the sterrheid light,
An play wee heidies oan the clean close wa,
Missis, whit'll ye dae?

Whit'll ye dae when the wee Malkies come,
If they chap yir door an choke yir drains,
An caw the feet fae yir sapsy weans,
An tummle thur wulkies through yir sheets,
An tip thur ashes oot in the street,
Missis, whit'll ye dae?

Whit'll ye dae when the wee Malkies come,
If they chuck thur screwtaps doon the pan,
An stick the heid oan the sanitry man,
When ye hear thum shauchlin doon yir loaby,
Chanting, 'Wee Malkies! The gemme's a bogey!'
Haw, missis, whit'll ye dae?

STEPHEN MULRINE

Complaint of the Common Weill of Scotland

And thus as we were talking to and fro
We saw a busteous berne come owre the bent,
But horse, on fute, as fast as he micht go,
Whose rayment was all raggit, riven and rent,
With visage lean, as he had fastit Lent:
And fodwart fast his wayis he did advance,
With ane richt malancolious countenance.

With scrip on hip, and pykestaff in his hand,
As he had purposit to pass fra hame.
Quod I: 'Gude man, I wald fain understand,
Gif that ye plesit, to wit what were your name?'
Quod he: 'My son, of that I think great shame;
Bot sen thou wald of my name have ane feill,
Forsooth, they call me John the Common weill.'

'Schir Common weill, who has you so disguisit?'
Quod I: 'or quhat makis you so miserabill?
I have marvel to see you so supprysit,
The whilk that I have sene so honorabill.
To all the warld ye have bene profitable,
And weill honorit in everilk natioun:
How happenis, now, your tribulatioun?'

'Allace!' quod he, 'thou sees how it dois stand
With me, and how I am disherisit
Of all my grace, and mon pass of Scotland,
And go, afore whare I was cherisit.
Remain I here, I am bot perisit;

For there is few to me that takis tent,
That garris me go so raggit, riven and rent.

'My tender friendis are all put to the flycht;
For Policy is fled again in France.
My sister, Justice, almost hath tint her sicht,
That she can nocht hold evenly the balance.
Plain wrang is plain capitane of Ordinance,
The whilk debarris Lawtie and Reason,
And small remeid is found for oppin treason.

'Into the South, allace, I was near slain:
Ower all the land I culd find no relief;
Almost betwixt the Merse and Lochmabane
I culd nocht knaw ane leill man be ane thief.
To schaw their reif, thift, murder, and mischief,
And vicious werkis, it wald infect the air:
And als, langsum to me for to declare.
'Into the Highland I culd find no remeid,
Bot suddenly I was put to exile.
Tha sweir swyngeoris they took of me none heed,
Nor amangs them let me remain ane while.
Als, in the out Ilis and in Argyle,
Unthrift, sweirness, falset, poverty and strife
Pat Policy in danger of her life.

'In the Lawland I come to seek refuge,
And purposit there to mak my residence;
Bot singular profit gart me soon disluge,
And did me great injuries and offence,
And said to me: "Swith, harlot, hie thee hence:
And in this countre see thou tak no curis,
Sa lang as my auctoritie enduris."

'And now I may mak no langer debait;
Nor I wate nocht quhome to I suld me mene;
For I have socht throw all the Spirituall stait,
Quhilkis tuke na compt for to heir me complene.
Thare officiaries, thay held me at disdane;
For Symonie, he rewlis up all that rowte;
And Covatyce, that Carle, gart bar me oute.

'Pryde haith chaist far frome thame humilitie;
Devotioun is fled unto the freris;
Sensuale plesour hes baneist Chaistitie;
Lordis of Religioun, thay go lyke Seculeris,
Taking more compt in tellyng thare deneris
Nor thay do of thare constitutioun,
Thus ar thay blyndit be ambitioun.

'Oure gentyll men ar all degenerate;
Liberalitie and Lawte, boith, ar loste;
And Cowardyce with Lordis is laureate;
And knychtlie curage turnit in brag and boste;
The Civele weir misgydis everilk oist.
Thare is nocht ellis bot ilk man for hym self,
That garris me go, thus baneist lyke ane elf.

'Therefore, adieu, I may no langer tarry." '
'Fair weill', quod I, and with Sanct John to borrow.
Bot wit ye weill my heart was wonder sarye,
When Common weill so sopit was in sorrow.
Yit after the nicht comis the glad morrow;
'Wharefore, I pray you, shaw me in certain,
When that ye purpose for to comw again.'

'That questioun, it sall be soon decidit',
Quod he: 'thare sall na Scot have comforting
Of me, till that I see the country guidit
Be wisdom of ane gude, auld prudent king,
Whilk sall delight him maist abune all thing,
To put justice till executioun,
And on strang traitouris mak punitioun.

'Als yet to thee I say ane other thing:
I see richt weill that proverb is full true.
Woe to the realm that has owre young a king.'
With that he turnit his back and said 'adieu'.
Over firth and fell richt fast fra me he flew,
Whose departing to me was displesand.
With that, Remembrance took me by the hand.

And soon, me thocht, she brocht me to the roche,
And to the cove whare I began to sleep.
With that ane ship did speedily approach,
Full plesandlie sailing upon the deep;
And syne did slack her sailis, and gan to creep
Towart the land, anent where that I lay:
Bot, wit you weill, I gat ane felloun fray.

All her cannounis she let crack off at onis:
Down shook the streameris from the top-castell;
Thay sparit nocht the poulder, nor the stonis;
Thay shot their boltis and doun their anchoris fell;
The marineris they did so youte and yell,
That hastily I stert out of my dream,
Half in ane fray, and speedily past hame.

And lichtly dinit, with lyste and appetite,
Syne efter, past intil ane oritore,
And took my pen, and than began to write
All the visioun that I have shawin before.
Sir, of my dream as now thou gettis no more,
Bot I beseik God for to send thee grace
To rule thy realm in unity and peace.

SIR DAVID LYNDSAY

Coulter's Candy

Ally bally, ally bally bee,
Sittin' on yer mammy's knee,
Greetin' for a wee bawbee,
Tae buy some Coulter's Candy.

Poor wee Jeanie's gettin' awfy thin,
A rickle o' banes covered ower wi' skin,
Noo she's gettin' a wee double chin,
Wi' sookin' Coulter's Candy.

Mammy gie's ma thrifty doon,
Here's auld Coulter comin' roon',
Wi' a basket on his croon,
Selling Coulter's Candy.

When you grow old, a man to be,
you'll work hard and you'll sail the seas,
an' bring hame pennies for your faither and me,
Tae buy mair Coulter's Candy.

Coulter he's a affa funny man,
He maks his candy in a pan,
Awa an greet to yer ma,
Tae buy some Coulter's Candy.

Little Annie's greetin' tae,
Sae whit can puir wee Mammy dae,
But gie them a penny atween them twae,
Tae buy mair Coulter's Candy.

ROBERT COLTART

Craigo Woods

Craigo Woods, wi' the splash o' the cauld rain beatin'
I' the back end o' the year,
When the clouds hang laigh wi' the weicht o' their load o' greetin'
And the autumn wind's asteer;
Ye may stand like gaists, ye may fa' i' the blast that's cleft ye
To rot i' the chilly dew,
But when will I mind on aucht since the day I left ye
Like I mind on you – on you?

Craigo Woods, i' the licht o' September sleepin'
And the saft mist o' the morn,
When the hairst climbs to yer feet, an' the sound o' reapin'
Comes up frae the stookit corn,
And the braw reid puddock-stules are like jewels blinkin'
And the bramble happs ye baith,
O what do I see, i' the lang nicht, lyin' an' thinkin'
As I see yer wraith – yer wraith?

There's a road to a far-aff land, an' the land is yonder
Whaur a' men's hopes are set;
We dinna ken foo lang we maun hae to wander,
But we'll a' win to it yet;
An' gin there's woods o' fir an' the licht atween them,
I winna speir its name,
But I'll lay me doon by the puddock-stules when I've seen them,
An' I'll cry 'I'm hame – I'm hame!'

VIOLET JACOB

Cumha Ghriogair MhicGriogair Ghlinn Sreith

Moch madainn air latha Lùnast'
    Bha mi sùgradh mar ri m'ghràdh,
Ach mun tàinig meadhan-latha
    Bha mo chridhe air a chràdh.

Ochain, ochain, ochain uiridh,
    Is goirt mo chridhe, a laoigh,
Ochain, ochain, ochain uiridh,
    Cha chluinn d'athair ar caoidh.

Mallachd aig maithibh 's aig càirdean
    Rinn mo chràdh air an-dòigh,
Thàinig gun fhios air mo ghràdh-sa
    Is a thug fo smachd e le foill.

Nam biodh dà fhear dheug d'a chinneadh
    Is mo Ghriogair air an ceann,
Cha bhiodh mo shùil a' sileadh dheur,
    No mo leanabh fhèin gun dàimh.

Chuir iad a cheann air ploc daraich,
    Is dhòirt iad fhuil mu làr:
Nam biodh agamsa an sin cupan,
    Dh'òlainn dith mo shàth.

[. . .]

Ged tha mnathan chàich aig baile
       Nan laighe is nan cadal sàmh,
Is ann bhios mise aig bruaich do lice
       A' bualadh mo dhà làimh.

Is mòr a b'annsa bhith aig Griogair
       Air feadh coille is fraoich
Na bhith aig baran crìon na Dalach
       An taigh cloiche is aoil.

Is mòr a b'annsa bhith aig Griogair
       Cur a' chruidh don ghleann
Na bhith aig baran crìon na Dalach
       Ag òl air fìon is air leann.

Is mòr a b'annsa bhith aig Griogair
       Fo bhrata ruibeach ròin
Na bhith aig baran crìon na Dalach
       A' giùlan sìoda is sròil.

Ged a bhiodh ann cur is cathadh
       Is latha nan seachd sìon,
Gheibheadh Griogair dhomhsa cragan
       San caidlimid fo dhìon.

Ba hu, ba hu, àsrain bhig,
       Chan eil tha fhathast ach tlàth:
Is eagal leam nach tig an là
       Gun dìol thu d'athair gu bràth.

MÒR CHAIMBEUL

Lament for MacGriogair of Glenstrae

Early on Lammas morning
       I was sporting with my love,
but before noon came upon us
       my heart had been crushed.

Alas, alas, alas and alack,
    sore is my heart, my child,
alas, alas, alas and alack,
    your father won't hear our cries.

A curse on nobles and relations
    who brought me to this grief,
who came on my love unawares
    and took him by deceit.

Had there been twelve of his kindred
    and my Griogair at their head,
my eye would not be weeping
    nor my child without a friend.

They put his head on an oaken block
    and spilled his blood on the ground,
if I had had a cup there
    I'd have drunk my fill down.

[. . .]

Though others' wives are safe at home
    lying sound asleep,
I am at the edge of your grave
    beating my hands in grief.

I'd far rather be with Griogair
    roaming moor and copse
than be with the niggardly Baron of Dull
    in a house of lime and stone.

I'd far rather be with Griogair
    driving the cattle to the glen
than be with the niggardly Baron of Dull
    drinking beer and wine.

I'd far rather be with Griogair
    under a rough hairy skin
than be with the niggardly Baron of Dull
    dressed in satin and silk.

Even on a day of driving snow
    when the seven elements reel
Griogair would find me a little hollow
    where we would snugly sleep.

Ba hu, ba hu, little waif,
    you are still only young,
but the day when you revenge your father
    I fear will never come.

Trans. Meg Bateman

MARION CAMPBELL

Da Boat Biggir's Nefjoo

Quhan da bærns chap da windoo
he hadds up da sjip ati'da bottil,
sjaaks his hed – awa!

An da aald fokk sae –
'Tink næthin o'it.'
'Tym'll tell.' 'Du'll fin dy nitch.'

He tinks – Foo dæs'it kum t'gjing insyd?
No a trikk, bit maachikk.
Dønna shaa me, I waant it ta happin.

An da aald fokk sae –
'Quhar dir's a will, dir's a wy.
Aniddir skurtfoo fæ da skroo.'

He tinks – Nyntents o an ysberg's hoidit.
Ungkil Alan wis a quhælir.
Dær's da mukkil atlas a'da windoo.

An da aald fokk sæ –
'Du'll miss'it if du blinks.'
'Hadd tyght noo.' 'Dønna aks me, I dønna ken.'

144

Da njoo kaaf's brølin ati'da byr.
Da aald koo's rekkin trow da widdin slats –
A pæl a'jalloo mylk fir da jungstir.

An da aald fokk sæ –
'Heir da burn rush noo!' 'Ir da hens in?'
'We'll fieniesh it da moarn, Gød willin.'

An Mammie sæs – 'A'll læv de lyght a staart.
Pit by da book noo. Læjie up da Kuttie Sark.
Sall I tell de foo hit's don?'

When the children tap the window, he holds up the ship in the bottle,
    shakes his head – Away!
And the old folk say – 'Think nothing of it.' 'Time will tell.' 'You'll
    find your niche.'
He thinks – How does it come to go inside? Not a trick, but magic.
    Don't show me, I want it to happen.
And the old folk say – 'Where there's a will there's a way. Another
    armful from the haystack.'
He thinks – Nine-tenths of an iceberg's hidden. Uncle Alan was a
    whaler. There's the big atlas in the window.
And the old folks say – 'You'll miss it if you blink.' 'Hold tight now.'
    'Don't ask me, I don't know.'
The new calf's crying in the byre. The old cow's tongue is reaching
    through the slats. A pail of yellow milk for the youngster.
And the old folks say – 'Hear the stream rush now!' 'Are the hens in?'
    'We'll finish it tomorrow, God willing.'
And Mammie says – 'I'll leave your light on a bit. Put the book aside.
    Set up the Cutty Sark. Shall I tell you how it's done?'

ROBERT ALAN JAMIESON

Da cockle shall

Bousta, Sannis

Gyo o Bousta, roond as a cockle: we'd watch
fur sels here, skyip steyns, kyemp fur da finest shalls.

145

We'd barely lift wir een ta see hits shape:
dat sam shall pattren at spread hitsel
owre midders' makkin: thirteen loops taen in
dan löt oot slowly on a oppenwark o gengs:
waves at shadit ta inky-blueness wi da wind.

Daday, ooers swittle trowe dy fingers
as du seeks, as eence I sowt, da perfect steyn
ta skyip. Tree skyips 'll dö, een mair as last year.
Da rings du maks spread fast. Last simmer here
eicht selkies bobbit laek bowes: eyed wis, dived,
eyed wis again. Dey left nae spreadin rings:
art hoidin artistry. I watch dy steyn dance,

defy da wyes o watter, da skyip o years.
Wi dee A'm richt back: we skile fur sels,
seek cockle shalls, weigh da import o steyns;
skyip an höve dem, fur da sea ta bring back,
ta lay up and mak again in time's lap.

CHRISTINE DE LUCA

Dàn do Eimhir IV

A nighean a' chùil bhuidhe, throm-bhuidh, òr-bhuidh,
fonn do bheòil-sa 's gaoir na h-Eòrpa,
a nighean gheal chasarlach aighearach bhòidheach,
cha bhiodh masladh ar latha-ne searbh nad phòig-sa.

An tugadh t' fhonn no t' àilleachd ghlòrmhor
bhuamsa gràinealachd mharbh nan dòigh seo,
a' bhrùid 's am meàirleach air ceann na h-Eòrpa
's do bheul-sa uaill-dhearg san t-seann òran?

An tugadh corp geal is clàr grèine
bhuamsa cealgaireachd dhubh na brèine,
nimh bhùirdeasach is puinnsean crèide
is dìblidheachd ar n-Albann èitigh?

An cuireadh bòidhchead is ceòl suaimhneach
bhuamsa breòiteachd an adhbhair bhuain seo,
am mèinnear Spàinnteach a' leum ri cruadal
is 'anam mòrail dol sìos gun bhruaillean?

Dè bhiodh pòg do bheòil uaibhrich
mar ris gach braon den fhuil luachmhoir
a thuit air raointean reòthta fuara
nam beann Spàinnteach bho fhòirne cruadhach?

Dè gach cuach ded chual òr-bhuidh
ris gach bochdainn, àmhghar 's dòrainn
a thig 's a thàinig air sluagh na h-Eòrpa
bho Long nan Daoine gu daors' a' mhòr-shluaigh?

SOMHAIRLE MacGILL-EAIN

The Cry of Europe

Girl of the yellow, heavy-yellow, gold-yellow hair,
the song of your mouth and Europe's shivering cry,
fair, heavy-haired, spirited, beautiful girl,
the disgrace of our day would not be bitter in your kiss.

Would your song and splendid beauty take
from me the dead loathsomeness of these ways,
the brute and the brigand at the head of Europe
and your mouth red and proud with the old song?

Would white body and forehead's sun take
from me the foul black treachery,
spite of the bourgeois and poison of their creed
and the feebleness of our dismal Scotland?

Would beauty and serene music put
from me the sore frailty of this lasting cause,
the Spanish miner leaping in the face of horror
and his great spirit going down untroubled?

What would the kiss of your proud mouth be
compared with each drop of the precious blood
that fell on the cold frozen uplands
of Spanish mountains from a column of steel?

What every lock of your gold-yellow head
to all the poverty, anguish and grief
that will come and have come on Europe's people
from the Slave Ship to the slavery of the whole people?

Translated by author

SORLEY MacLEAN

Dàn do Eimhir XXII

Choisich mi cuide ri mo thuigse
a-muigh ri taobh a' chuain;
bha sinn còmhla ach bha ise
a' fuireach tiotan bhuam.

An sin thionndaidh i ag ràdha:
A bheil e fìor gun cual
thu gu bheil do ghaol geal àlainn
a' pòsadh tràth Diluain?

Bhac mi 'n cridhe bha 'g èirigh
'nam bhroilleach reubte luath
is thubhairt mi: Tha mi cinnteach;
carson bu bhreug e bhuam?

Ciamar a smaoinichinn gun glacainn
an rionnag leugach òir,
gum beirinn oirre 's gun cuirinn i
gu ciallach 'na mo phòc?

Cha d' ghabh mise bàs croinn-ceusaidh
an èiginn chruaidh na Spàinn
is ciamar sin bhiodh dùil agam
ri aon duais ùir nan dàn?

Cha do lean mi ach an t-slighe chrìon
bheag ìosal thioram thlàth,
is ciamar sin a choinnichinn
ri beithir-theine ghràidh?

Ach nan robh 'n roghainn rithist dhomh
's mi 'm sheasamh air an àird,
leumainn à nèamh no iutharna
le spiorad 's cridhe slàn.

SOMHAIRLE MacGILL-EAIN

The Choice

I walked with my reason
out beside the sea.
We were together but it was
keeping a little distance from me.

Then it turned saying:
is it true you heard
that your beautiful white love
is getting married early on Monday?

I checked the heart that was rising
in my torn swift breast
and I said: most likely;
why should I lie about it?

How should I think that I would grab
the radiant golden star,
that I would catch it and put it
prudently in my pocket?

I did not take a cross's death
in the hard extremity of Spain
and how then should I expect
the one new prize of fate?

I followed only a way
that was small, mean, low, dry, lukewarm,
and how then should I meet
the thunderbolt of love?

But if I had the choice again
and stood on that headland,
I would leap from heaven or hell
with a whole spirit and heart.

Translated by author

SORLEY MacLEAN

Dà Thaibhse

Anns an dìg dhomhainn aig ceann na buaile,
bhiodh na cailleachan ag ràdh chaidh murt a dhèanamh,
bu tric a chunnacas taibhse a' gluasad
air oir an rathaid, ri fèath 's ri siantan.

Is iomadh feasgar a ghabh mi seachad
air oir na h-iomagain is mi 'nam bhalach,
eadar coiseachd 's ruith, air eagal sealladh
fhaotainn a-chaoidh den taibhs' gun anail.

'S ged ruiginn ceann na buaile an-dràsta
tha fhios gu bheil tannasg truagh a' tàmh ann,
ach dhèanainn an-diugh am barrachd dàlach
ri taibhse a' bhalaich a chaidh a bhàthadh.

RUARAIDH MacTHÒMAIS

Two Ghosts

In the deep ditch at the field-end
the old women said there had been a murder;
often a ghost was seen moving
at the edge of the road, in calm or storm.

Many an evening I passed the place,
on edge and anxious when I was a boy,
half running, for fear of catching
a glimpse of the ghost with no breath in its body.

Though I were to reach the field-end now
I'm sure there's a ghost staying there,
but today I'd wait a little longer
for the ghost of the boy who has been drowned.

Translated by author

DERICK THOMSON

Daed-traa

I go to the rockpool at the slack of the tide
to mind me what my poetry's for.

It has its ventricles, just like us —
pumping brine, like bull's blood, a syrupy flow.

It has its theatre —
hushed and plush.

It has its Little Shop of Horrors.
It has its crossed and dotted monsters.

It has its cross-eyed beetling Lear.
It has its billowing Monroe.

I go to the rockpool at the slack of the tide
to mind me what my poetry's for.

For monks, it has barnacles
to sweep the broth as it flows, with fans,
grooming every cubic millimetre.

It has its ebb, the easy heft of wrack from rock,
like plastered, feverish locks of hair.

It has its *flodd*.
It has its welling god
with puddle, podgy cheeks and jaw.

It has its holy hiccup.

Its minute's silence.

daed-traa.

I go to the rockpool at the slack of the tide
to mind me what my poetry's for.

JEN HADFIELD

The Daft-Days

Now mirk December's dowie face
Glowrs owr the rigs wi sour grimace,
While, thro' his minimum of space,
The bleer-ey'd sun,
Wi blinkin light and stealing pace,
His race doth run.

From naked groves nae birdie sings,
To shepherd's pipe nae hillock rings,
The breeze nae od'rous flavour brings
From Borean cave,
And dwyning nature droops her wings,
Wi visage grave.

Mankind but scanty pleasure glean
Frae snawy hill or barren plain,
Whan winter, 'midst his nipping train,
Wi frozen spear,
Sends drift owr a' his bleak domain,
And guides the weir.

Auld Reikie! thou'rt the canty hole,
A bield for many caldrife soul,
Wha snugly at thine ingle loll,
Baith warm and couth,
While round they gar the bicker roll
To weet their mouth.

When merry Yule-day comes, I trou,
You'll scantlins find a hungry mou;
Sma are our cares, our stamacks fou
O' gusty gear,
And kickshaws, strangers to our view,
Sin fairn-year.

Ye browster wives, now busk ye braw,
And fling your sorrows far awa;
Then come and gie's the tither blaw
Of reaming ale,
Mair precious than the well of Spa,
Our hearts to heal.

Then, tho' at odds wi a' the warl',
Amang oursels we'll never quarrel;
Tho' Discord gie a canker'd snarl
To spoil our glee,
As lang's there's pith into the barrel
We'll drink and 'gree.

Fidlers, your pins in temper fix,
And roset weel your fiddle-sticks;
But banish vile Italian tricks
Frae out your *quorum*,
Not *fortes* wi *pianos* mix –
Gie's *Tulloch Gorum*.

For nought can cheer the heart sae weel
As can a canty Highland reel;
It even vivifies the heel
To skip and dance:
Lifeless is he wha canna feel
Its influence.

Let mirth abound, let social cheer
Invest the dawning of the year;
Let blithesome innocence appear
To crown our joy;
Nor envy wi sarcastic sneer
Our bliss destroy.

And thou, great god of *Aqua Vitae*!
Wha sways the empire of this city,
When fou we're sometimes capernoity,
Be thou prepar'd
To hedge us frae that black banditti,
The City Guard.

ROBERT FERGUSSON

Dèan Cadalan Sàmhach

Dèan cadalan sàmhach, a chuilein mo rùin,
Dèan fuireach mar tha thu 's tu 'n-dràst' an àit' ùr;
Bidh òigearan againn làn beairteis is cliù,
'S ma bhios tu nad airidh 's leat feareigin dhiùbh.

Gur ann an Ameireagaidh tha sinn an-dràst'
Fo dhubhar na coille nach teirig gu bràth;
Nuair dh'fhalbhas an dùbhlachd 's a thionndaidh's am blàths,
Bidh cnothan, bidh ùbhlan 's bidh siùcar a' fàs.

'S ro bheag orm fhèin cuid den t-sluagh a tha ann
Len còtaichean drògaid 's ad mhòr air an ceann,
Lem briogaisean goirid 's iad sgoilte gum bainn,
Chan fhaicear an t-osan, 's e bhochdainn sin leam.

Tha sinne nar n-Innseanaich cinnteach gu leòr,
Fo dhubhar nan craobh cha bhi h-aon againn beò;
Coin-allaidh is bèistean ag èigheach 's gach fròg,
Gu bheil sinn nar n-èiginn bhon thrèig sinn Rìgh Deòrs'.

Mo shoraidh le fàilte 'Chinn Tàile nam bò
Far an d' fhuair mi greis m' àrach 's mi 'm phàiste beag òg,
Bhiodh fleasgaichean donn' air am bonnaibh ri ceòl,
Is nìonagan dualach 's an gruaidh mar an ròs.

An toiseach an fhoghair bu chridheil ar sunnd,
Gheibht' fiadh às an fhireach, is bradan à grunnd,
Bhiodh luingeas an sgadain a' tighinn fo shiùil,
Le h-iasgairean tapaidh nach faicte fo mhùig.

IAIN MacRATH

Sleep Peacefully

Sleep peacefully, my darling wee one,
Stay as you are now in this new place;
We'll have young men who are rich and famous;
If you are worthy, you'll get one of them.

This is America we are in now,
In the shade of the unending forest;
When winter goes and turns to warmth,
Nuts and apples and sugar will grow.

I don't much care for the people here,
With their drugget coats and large hats,
With their short trousers split up to the belt –
No one, more's the pity, wears stockings.

We are, sure enough, Indians,
None of us will survive in the gloomy trees;
Wolves and wild beasts growl in each nook;
We're in dire straits since deserting King George.

My greeting and welcome to Kintail of the cattle,
Where I was raised a while when a child;
Dark-haired young men would dance to music,
Wavy-haired girls whose cheeks were like roses.

At the beginning of autumn our mood would be merry,
We'd get deer from the forest, salmon from the river;
The herring boats would come in under sail,
Strapping fishermen you'd never see scowl.

Trans. Peter Mackay

JOHN MacRAE

The Destruction of Sennacherib

I
The Assyrian came down like the wolf on the fold,
And his cohorts were gleaming in purple and gold;
And the sheen of their spears was like stars on the sea,
When the blue wave rolls nightly on deep Galilee.

II
Like the leaves of the forest when Summer is green,
That host with their banners at sunset were seen;
Like the leaves of the forest when Autumn hath blown
That host on the morrow lay withered and strown.

III
For the Angel of Death spread his wings on the blast,
And breathed in the face of the foe as he passed;
And the eyes of the sleepers waxed deadly and chill,
And their hearts but once heaved – and for ever grew still!

IV
And there lay the steed with his nostril all wide,
But through it there rolled not the breath of his pride;
And the foam of his gasping lay white on the turf,
And cold as the spray of the rock-beating surf.

V
And there lay the rider distorted and pale,
With the dew on his brow, and the rust on his mail:
And the tents were all silent – the banners alone –
The lances unlifted – the trumpet unblown.

VI

And the widows of Ashur are loud in their wail,
And the idols are broke in the temple of Baal;
And the might of the Gentile, unsmote by the sword,
Hath melted like snow in the glance of the Lord!

LORD BYRON

Bho Do Dh'Iain Garbh Mac Gille Chaluim Ratharsaigh

Mo bheud 's mo chràdh
Mar dh'èirich dhà
'N fhear ghleusta ghràidh
Bha treun gu spàirn
'S nach fhaicear gu bràth an Ratharsaigh.

'S tu am fear curanta mòr
'S math cuma agus treòir
Od uileann gud dhòrn,
Od mhullach gud bhròig:
Mhic Mhuire mo leòn
Thu bhith 'n innis nan ròn 's nach faighear thu.

Bu tu sealgair a' gheòidh,
Làmh gun dearmad gun leòn,
Air 'm bu shuarach an t-òr
Thoirt a bhuantach' a' cheòil,
'S gun d' fhuair thu nas leòr 's na chaitheadh tu.

Bu tu sealgair an fhèidh
Leis an deargtadh na bèin;
Bhiodh coin earbsach air èill
Aig an Albannach threun;
Càit am faca mi fèin
Ri shireadh fo ghrèin
Aon nì air nach gleusta ghabhadh tu?

Spailp nach dìobradh
Am baiteal strìthe,
Casan dìreach

Fada finealt:
Mo chreach dhìobhail,
Chaidh thu dhìth oirnn
Le neart sìne,
Làmh nach dìobradh caitheamh oirr.

Och, m' eudail uam
Gun sgeul sa chuan
Bu ghlè mhath snuadh
Ri grèin 's ri fuachd –
'S e chlaoidh do shluagh
Nach d'fheud thu an uair a ghabhail orr.

'S math thig gunna nach diùlt
Air curaidh mo rùin
Am mullach a' chùirn,
Air uileann nan stùc:
Gum bi fuil ann an tùs an spreadhaidh sin.

'S e dh'fhàg silteach mo shùil
Faicinn d' fhearann gun sùrd
'S do bhaile gun smùid
Fo charraig nan sùgh,
Dheagh Mhic Caluim an tùir à Ratharsaigh.

MÀIRI NIGHEAN ALASDAIR RUAIDH

From For Iain Garbh, Macleod of Raasay

My pity and my pain's
What's happened to
The well-loved clever man
Who was strong in a struggle,
Who won't be seen again in Raasay.

You were a great brave man,
Well-made and vigorous
From your elbow to your fist.
From your head to your shoe.

Son of Mary, I'm wounded,
Since you won't be found; you're resting with seals.

You were a hunter of geese,
Your hand attentive and flawless,
Who didn't stint with gold
When supporting music,
For you got more than you spent.

You were a hunter of deer,
Who reddened the hides;
Trusty dogs held on leashes
By the strong Scotsman;
Where would I find,
Searching under the sun,
Something you couldn't do skilfully?

A proud man who'd not shrink
In battle or conflict,
Legs that were straight,
Long and elegant:
My destruction and ruin
That you have been lost
In the strength of a gale –
One who wouldn't fear pushing on.

Och, my treasure has gone,
Lost in the sea,
Who looked good
In sun or in cold –
It's tormented your people
You couldn't reach them in that hour.

A gun that never fails
Befits the hero I love
At the top of the cairn
And the corners of the crags:
Blood will come from that firing.

I have tears in my eyes,
Seeing your land without cheer
Your village without smoke
Under the wave-beaten rock,
Good MacCalum of the tower from Raasay.

Trans. Peter Mackay

MARY MACLEOD

Do Mhac Leòid

'S mòr mo mhulad 's mo phràmhan
'S mi gun mhacnas gun mhànran
Anns an talla am bu ghnàth le Mac Leòid.

Taigh mòr macnasach meadhrach
Nam macaomh 's nam maighdean
Far 'm bu tartarach gleadhraich nan còrn.

Tha do thalla mòr priseil
Gun fhasgadh gun dìon ann,
Far am faca mi fìon bhith ga òl.

Aig oighre Shìol Tormaid:
Fear th' eugais chan eòl domh –
Chan i an fhoill a chuir às dhuit no an stròdh.

Cuid dha d' àbhaist 's dha d' bheusan
A bhith gu fuilteach tric bèin-dearg
Air chuideacha chèir-gheal nan cròc.

Leat bu mhiann na coin lùthmhor
Dhol a shiubhal nan stùc-bheann,
Is an gunna nach diùltadh re òrd.

'S i do làmh nach robh tuisleach
Dhol a chaitheamh a' chuspair
Le d' bhogha cruaidh ruiteach deagh-neòil.

Bhiodh glac throm air do shliasaid
'S i gun ghaiseadh gun fhiaradh,
Bàrr dosrach de sgiathaibh an eòin.

Bhiodh cèir air do chrannaibh
Bu neo-èisleineach tarraing
Nuair a leumnadh an tafaid bho ur meòir.

Nuair a leigteadh o d' làimh i
Cha bhiodh aon mhìr gun bhàthadh
Eadar corran a gàinne is a smeòirn.

'S ann sa' chlachan so shios uam
Tha mo chàirdean 's mo dhìslean:
Ciamar thèid mi nam fianais aig bròn?

'S ann na luighe as-teampall
Tha m' aighear is m' annsachd:
Chaoidh cha tèid mi fhèin ann 's gun thu beò.

MÀIRI NIGHEAN ALASDAIR RUAIDH

To MacLeod

Great my dule and dolour
without dalliance or sporting
in the hall that was MacLeod's wonted haunt.

Great joyful blithe castle
of youths and of maidens
where drinking-horns' clatter was loud.

Your brilliant big building
without walls or roof timbers,
where I used to see wine being drunk,

By the heir of Tormod's descendants:
I know no man who bears resemblance –
neither dissoluteness nor deceit left you dead.

A part of your pastime and custom,
often your hide blood-spluttered,
was with the antlered white-buttocked throng.

You loved the lithe deerhounds
roaming the peaked hills
with the gun that always yielded to its lock.

Your hand would not falter
taking aim at the target
with your bow, ruddy and hard of good hue.

On your thigh a heavy quiver,
arrows without twist or defect,
plumed tips of the wings of the fowl.

Your shafts sealed with beeswax
were not sluggish in bending
when the bowstring would leap from your hold.

When it was released from your fingers
no length would be unburied
between its pointed tip and its notch.

Below me in this graveyard
are my friends and relations:
what way can I draw near them in such woe?

Lying in the temple
is my joy and my treasure:
no more will I enter as you have gone.

Trans. Peter Mackay

MARY MACLEOD

Dòbhran Marbh

Tha a' chlosach air ragachadh
mar gun robh e a' snàmh,
spliadh is ceann air an togail,
sùil lainnireach,
bian mar umha.

Tionndaidhidh mi air falbh,
air mo nàrachadh ro mheatair de
dhòbhran fom sgrùdadh,
is am bàs air biast cho falbhach
a ghlacadh.

Air ulbhaig, làrach fhuilteach
a chuinnlean; os a cionn,
sgeilp a' stobadh a-mach
de riasg 's de fhraoch
far an do thuit e

an comhair a chinn dha na creagan fodha,
far an laigh e san dubhar mar chloich eile,
a shròn air a pronnadh, gaoisid na fhiaclan,
's air a chùlaibh, a shaobhaidh ùrail gorm,
dàil-chuach is seòbhrach a' priobadh sa bhruach.

Sìnidh mo làmh gu grad thuige
's mi a' tuigsinn gun deach a nàdar
ceàrr air an drip an earraich,
gun rachadh an dòbhran mòrail
cuideachd air iomrall.

MEG BATEMAN

Dead Otter

Rigor mortis curves the beast
as if swimming,
flat head and webbed foot
raised, eyes gleaming,
pelt of bronze.

I turn away, embarrassed
by a metre of otter
laid out for my scrutiny,
by death's exposure
of so fleet a creature.

On a boulder, the bloody
stamp of its nostrils;
above, a jutting ledge
of tangled, fibrous root
where it must have fallen

headlong to the rocks where it lies in shade
with staved in snout and stillness of stone,
white fur gripped between its teeth,
with its lair behind, lush with liverwort,
and a flicker of violets and primrose in the bank.

I reach out to it, shocked
that in the urgency of spring
instinct could fail it,
shocked that it too
could lose its footing.

MEG BATEMAN

Downe Be Yone River I Ran

Downe be yone river I ran,
Downe be yone river I ran,
Thinkand on Christ sa fre,
That brocht me to libertie,
And I ane sinful man.

Quha suld be my lufe bot he,
That hes onlie savit me,
And be his deith me wan:
On the Croce sa cruellie,
He sched his blude aboundantlie,
And all for the lufe of man.

How suld we thank that Lord,
That was sa misericord,
Be quhome all grace began!
With cruell paine and smart,
He was peirsit throw the hart,
And all for the lufe of man.

That gaif him in the Jewis handis,
To brek bailfull Baliallis bandis,
First quhen he began:
Thair gaif him self to die,
To mak us catives fre,
Remember, sinfull man.

Thay spittit in his face,
All for our lufe, allace!
That Lord he sufferit than,
The cruel panis of deid,
Quhilk was our haill remeid,
Remember, sinfull man.

Love we that Lord allone,
Quhilk deit on the throne,
Our sinnis to refraine:
Pryse him with all our mycht,
Sing till him day and nycht,
The gloir of God and man.

Do all that thow art abill,
Yit thow art unproffitabill
Do all that thow can:
Except thow weschin be,
With Christis blude allanerlie,
Thow art condampnit Man.

And sa I mak ane end,
Christ grant us all to kend,
And steadfast to remaine:
Into Christis Passioun,
Our onlie Salvatioun,
And in nane uther man.

ANON.

Dreaming Frankenstein

for Lys Hansen, Jacki Parry and June Refern

She said she
woke up with him in
her head, in her bed.
Her mother-tongue clung to her mouth's roof
in terror, dumbing her, and he came with a name
that was none of her making.

No maidservant ever
in her narrow attic, combing
out her hair in the midnight mirror
on Hallowe'en (having eaten
that egg with its yolk hollowed out
then filled with salt)
as a spell to summon up her lover
– oh never one had such success as this
she had not courted.
The amazed flesh of her
neck and shoulders nettled
at his apparition.

Later, stark staring awake to everything
(the room, the dark parquet, the white high Alps beyond)
all normal in the moonlight
and him gone, save a ton-weight sensation,
the marks fading visibly where
his buttons had bit into her and
the rough serge of his suiting had chafed her sex,
she knew – oh that was not how –
but he'd entered her utterly.

This was the penetration
of seven swallowed apple pips.
Or else he'd slipped like a silver dagger
between her ribs and healed her up secretly
again. Anyway
he was inside her
and getting him out again

would be agony fit to quarter her,
unstitching everything.

Eyes on those high peaks
in the reasonable sun of the morning,
she dressed in damped muslin
and sat down to quill and ink
and icy paper.

LIZ LOCHHEAD

Edward

I

'Why does your brand sae drop wi' blude,
Edward, Edward?
Why does your brand sae drop wi' blude,
And why sae sad gang ye, O?' –
'O I hae kill'd my hawk sae gude,
Mither, mither;
O I hae killed my hawk sae gude,
And I had nae mair but he, O.'

II

'Your hawk's blude was never sae red,
Edward, Edward;
Your hawk's blude was never sae red,
My dear son, I tell theem, O.' –
'O I hae kill'd my red-roan steed,
Mither, mither;
O I hae kill'd my red-roan steed,
That erst was sae fair and free, O.'

III

'And whatten penance wul ye dree for that,
Edward, Edward?
Whatten penance will ye dree for that?

My deir son, now tell me, O.' –
'I'll set my feet in yonder boat,
Mither, mither;
I'll set my feet in yonder boat,
And I'll fare over the sea, O.'

IV

'And what will ye do wi' your tow'rs and your ha',
Edward, Edward?
And what will ye do wi' your tow'rs and your ha',
That were sae fair to see, O?
'I'll let them stand till they doun fa',
Mither, mither;
I'll let them stand till they doun fa',
For here never mair maun I be, O.'

V

'And what will ye leave to your bairns and your wife,
Edward, Edward?
And what will ye leave to your bairns and your wife,
Whan ye gang owre the sea, O?' –
'The warld's room: let them beg through life,
Mither, mither;
The warld's room, let them beg through life,
For thame never mair will I see, O.'

VI

'And what will ye leave to your ain mither dear,
Edward, Edward?
And what will ye leave to your ain mither dear,
My dear son, now tell me, O?' –
'The curse of hell frae me sall ye bear,
Mither, mither;
The curse of hell frae me sall ye bear:
Sic counsels ye gave to me, O.'

ANON.

The Eemis Stane

I' the how-dumb-deid o' the cauld hairst nicht
The warl' like an eemis stane
Wags i' the lift;
An' my eerie memories fa'
Like a yowdendrift.

Like a yowdendrift so's I couldna read
The words cut oot i' the stane
Had the fug o' fame
An' history's hazelraw
No' yirdit thaim.

HUGH MacDIARMID

Bho Eilean a' Cheò

Ged tha mo cheann air liathadh
Le deuchainnean is bròn,
Is grian mo lethcheud bliadhna
A' dol sìos fo na neòil,
Tha m' aigne air a lìonadh
Le iarratas ro-mhòr
Gum faicinn Eilean Sgiathach
Nan siantannan 's a' Cheò.

Tha còrr 's dà fhichead bliadhna
Bhon thriall mi as dham dheòin,
'S a chuir mi sìos mo lìon
Am meadhan baile mòir;
Is ged a fhuair mi iasgair
A lìon mo thaigh le stòr,
Cha do dhìochuimhnih mi riamh
Eilean Sgiathanach a' Cheò.

[. . .]

An tìr san robh na fiùrain,
'S gach cùis a sheas an còir,

Bha smior as neart nan dùirn,
'S cha b' e 'n sugradh tighinn nan còir;
'S on rinneadh dhuinn an cunntas,
Gu onair, cliù, is glòir,
Na dh'èirich fon a' Chrùn diubh
A Eilean cùbhr' a' Cheò:

Ma thèid mi dhiubh ga innse,
Cha mhearachd brìgh mo sgeòil,
Oir tha e air a sgrìobhadh
Dhan linn sa bheil sinn beò;
Bha còrr agus deich mìle
Fon Rìgh a ghabh an t-òr,
Gu onair 's dìon ar rìoghachd,
A Eilean grinn a' Cheò.

[. . .]

Ach cò aig a bheil cluasan
No cridh' tha gluasad beò
Nach seinneadh leam an duan seo
Mun truaigh' a thàinig oirnn?
Na miltean a chaidh fhuadach,
A' toirt uath' an cuid 's an còir,
A' smaointinn thar nan cuantan,
Gu Eilean uain' a' Cheò.

Ach cuimhnichibh gur sluagh sibh,
Is cumaibh suas ur còir;
Tha beairteas fo na cruachan
Fon d' fhuair sibh àrach òg;
Tha iarann agus gual ann,
Is luaidhe ghlas is òr,
'S tha mèinnean gu ur buannachd
An Eilean uain' a' Cheò.

[. . .]

Beannachd leibh, a chàirdean,
Anns gach ceàrn tha fo na neòil,
Gach mac is nighean màthar

An Eilean àrd a' Cheò;
Is cuimhnichidh sibh Màiri
Nuair bhios i cnàmh fon fhòid –
'S e na dh'fhuiling mi de thàmailt
A thug mo bhàrdachd beò.

MÀIRI MHÒR NAN ÒRAN

From The Island of the Mist

Although my head has greyed
with hardships and with woe,
and the sun of all my fifty years
is setting under clouds,
my spirit is now filled
with a very great desire
to see the Winged Island
of storms and misty sky.

More than forty years have passed
since I left it of my will,
and I let down my net
within a large town's midst,
and though I found a fisher
who filled my house with store,
never once did I forget
Skye's isle, which mist enfolds.

[...]

That land was home to heroes
who stood up for their rights;
their fists were strong and pithy –
to approach them was no joke;
and as we were given a tally
of those who did enlist,
for honour, praise and glory
from the fragrant Isle of Mist:

If I proceed to tell you,
there is no error in my tale,
because it is in writing
for those of our own day;
there were more than ten thousand
who took the King's gold coin
to defend our kingdom's honour,
from the lovely Misty Isle.

[. . .]

But who has ears to listen
or a heart that throbs with life
who would not sing this song with me
about our most hideous plight?
The thousands who have been banished,
having lost their lot and right,
whose thoughts now cross the oceans
to the green Island of the Mist.

Remember that you are a people
and stand up for your rights;
wealth lies beneath those mountains
where you spent your early life;
iron and coal are stored there,
and grey lead, and gold,
and mines to bring you profit
in the green Island of the Mist.

[. . .]

Farewell to you now, my friends,
in each land beneath the clouds,
to every son and daughter
from the lofty Isle of Mist;
you will remember Mary
when she is decaying under the turf;
the humiliation that I endured
was what gave my poetry life.

Trans. Donald Meek

MARY MacPHERSON

Elegy

They are lang deid, folk that I used to ken
their firm set lips aa mowdert and agley,
sherp-tempert een rusty amang the cley:
they are baith deid, thae wycelike, bienlie men,

heidmaisters, that had been in pouer for ten
or twenty year afore fate's taiglie wey
brocht me, a young, weill-harnit, blate and fey
new-cleckit dominie, intill their den.

Ane tellt me it was time I learnt to write —
round-haund, he meant — and saw about my hair:
I mind of him, beld-heidit, wi a kyte.

Ane sneerit quarterly — I cuidna square
my savings bank — and sniftert in his spite.
Weill, gin they arena deid, it's time they were.

ROBERT GARIOCH

Empty Vessel

I met ayont the cairney
A lass wi tousie hair
Singin till a bairnie
That was nae langer there.

Wunds wi warlds to swing
Dinna sing sae sweet,
The licht that bends owre aa thing
Is less ta'en up wi'it.

HUGH MacDIARMID

From Epistle to J. Lapraik

[· · ·]

I am nae poet, in a sense;
But just a rhymer like by chance,
An' hae to learning nae pretence;
    Yet what the matter?
Whene'er my Muse does on me glance,
    I jingle at her.

Your critic-folk may cock their nose,
And say, 'How can you e'er propose,
You wha ken hardly verse frae prose,
    To mak a sang?'
But, by your leave, my learned foes,
    Ye're maybe wrang.

What's a' your jargon o' your schools,
Your Latin names for horns an' stools?
If honest nature made you fools,
    What sairs your grammars?
Ye'd better taen up spades and shools,
    Or knappin-hammers.

A set o' dull, conceited hashes
Confuse their brains in college classes!
They gang in stirks and come out asses,
    Plain truth to speak;
An' syne they think to climb Parnassus
    By dint o' Greek!

Gie me ae spark o' Nature's fire,
That's a' the learnin' I desire;
Then, tho' I drudge thro' dub an' mire
    At pleugh or cart,
My Muse, though hamely in attire,
    May touch the heart.

[· · ·]

ROBERT BURNS

Epitaph on D——C——

Here lies in earth a root of Hell,
Set by the Deil's ain dibble;
This worthless body damned himself,
To save the Lord the trouble.

ROBERT BURNS

Etching of a Line of Trees

I carved out the careful absence of a hill and a hill grew.
I cut away the fabric of the trees
and the trees stood shivering in the darkness.

When I had burned off the last syllables of wind,
a fresh wind rose and lingered.
But because I could not bring myself

to remove you from that hill,
you are no longer there. How wonderful it is
that neither of us managed to survive

when it was love that surely pulled the burr
and love that gnawed its own shape from the burnished air
and love that shaped that absent wind against a tree?

Some shadow's hands moved with my hands
and everything I touched was turned to darkness
and everything I could not touch was light.

JOHN GLENDAY

The Ewe-Buchtin's Bonnie

O, the ewe-buchtin's bonnie, baith e'ening and morn,
When our blithe shepherds play on the bog-reed and horn;
While we're milking, they're lilting, baith pleasant and clear –
But my heart's like to break when I think on my dear.

O the shepherds take pleasure to blow on the horn,
To raise up their flocks o' sheep soon i' the morn;
On the bonnie green banks they feed pleasant and free,
But, alas, my dear heart, all my sighing's for thee!

LADY GRIZEL BAILLIE

The Exiles

The many ships that left our country
with white wings for Canada.
They are like handkerchiefs in our memories
and the brine like tears
and in their masts sailors singing
like birds on branches.
That sea of May running in such blue,
a moon at night, a sun at daytime,
and the moon like a yellow fruit,
like a plate on a wall
to which they raise their hands
like a silver magnet
with piercing rays
streaming into the heart.

IAIN CRICHTON SMITH

faclan, eich-mhara

nam bhruadar bha mi nam ghrunnd na mara
agus thu fhèin nad chuan trom
a' leigeil do chudruim orm
agus d' fhaclan gaoil socair nam chluasan
an dràsda 's a-rithist
òrach grinn ainneamh
man eich-mhara, man notaichean-maise
sacsafonaichean beaga fleòdradh

CAOIMHIN MacNÈILL

words, seahorses

i dreamt i was the seafloor and you were the weight of ocean pressing
down on me, your quiet words of love in my ears now and again, golden,
elegant and strange, like seahorses, like grace-notes, tiny floating
saxophones

Translated by author

KEVIN MacNEIL

Bho Fàilte don Eilean Sgitheanach

O! Fàilt' air do stùcan,
Do choireachan ùdlaidh,
Do bheanntannan sùghmhor,
Far an siùbhlach am meann!
Tha 'n geamhradh le dhùbhlachd
Mu na meallaibh a' dùnadh,
'S gach doire le bhùirean
Air a rùsgadh gu bonn.

Chì mi an Cuiltheann
Mar leòmhann gun tioma,
Le fheusaig den t-sneachd'
Air a phasgadh ma cheann;
'S a ghruaidhean a' sruladh
Le easannan smùideach,
Tha tuiteam nan lùban
Gu ùrlar nan gleann.

Do chreagan gu h-uaibhreach,
Mar challaid mun cuairt dut,
'S na neòil air an iomairt,
A' filleadh mum bàrr;
'S am bonn air a sguabadh
Le srùlaichean gruamach,
Bho bhàrcadh a' chuain
A' toirt nuallain air tràigh.

O càit eil na gaisgich
A dh'àraich do ghlacan,
Bu shuilbhire macnas
Mu stacan a' cheò?
Le fùdar ga sgailceadh
Bhon cuilbheirean glana,
'S na mial-choin nan deannaibh,
Nach fannaich san tòir.

[. . .]

Guma buan a bhios d' eachdraidh,
Agus cliù aig do mhacaibh,
Gus an crìonar an talamh,
'S am paisgear na neòil!
Fhad 's bhios siaban na mara
A' bualadh air carraig,
Bidh mo dhùrachd gun deireas
Do dh'Eilean a' Cheò.

NIALL MacLEÒID

From Hail to the Isle of Skye

O! Hail to your summits,
your gloomy corries,
your substantial mountains
where the young goats wander!
The winter with its gloom
is closing round the peaks,
and each copse by its roaring
is stripped to its roots.

I see the Cuillin
like a dauntless lion,
with a beard of snow
wrapped round its head;
and its cheeks streaming
with misty waterfalls,
tumbling and eddying
to the floor of the glens.

Your cliffs are proud
like a stockade around you
while the clouds, on campaign,
enfold their tops;
their bases are swept
by bleak sucking waves,
the crashing of the ocean,
howling ashore.

O where are the heroes
who were reared in your valleys
who were cheerful and merry
in your misty stacks?
With powder being pelted
from their fine muskets,
and their rushing hounds
who won't flag in the hunt.

[. . .]

May your history live long,
and the fame of your sons,
until the Earth has withered,
the clouds folded away!
As long as the spray of the sea
hits against rocks
I'll give myself, wholehearted,
to the Isle of Mist.

Trans. Peter Mackay

NEIL MacLEOD

Fàire

Anns a' Phràdo, nuair a chunnaic
mi na naoimh aog aig El Greco agus,
bliadhnachan mòr eile, ann am Berlin,
nuair a chunna mi am balla briste,

chuimhnich mi far am biodh tu cumail
dealbh na h-Òighe Moire dìreach
os cionn uisge-coisrigte Lourdes
's cuideachd mar a thuit balla na fainge

sìos, a' fosgladh frith-rathad dhuinn
a-steach gu pàirc a' bhuill-coise faisg
air an sgoil far am faiceamaid, eadar
gach tadhal, a-mach gu fàire na sìorr-

aidheachd, na bàtaichean a' seòladh agus,
gun fhuaim sam bith, jets àrd na h-iarmailt.

AONGHAS PÀDRAIG CAIMBEUL

Horizon

In the Prado, when I first saw
El Greco's gaunt saints and,
much later on, in Berlin,
when I saw the broken wall,

I minded where you kept the
plaster Adoration of the Virgin
just above the Lourdes water-font
and also the way the old sheep-wall

crumbled, allowing us a short-cut
through to the football pitch
by the school, where, resting between
goals, we could see everywhere

the ships sailing and the soundless
plumes of jets high in the blue sky.

Translated by author

ANGUS PETER CAMPBELL

The Fause Knicht

1 'O whare are ye gaun?'
    Quo the fause knicht upon the road:
    'I'm gaun to the scule,'
    Quo the wee boy, and still he stude.

2 'What is that upon your back?'
    'Atweel it is my bukes.'

3 'What's that ye've got in your arm?'
    'Atweel it is my peit.'

4 'Wha's aucht they sheep?'
    'They are mine and my mither's.'

5 'How monie o them are min?'
    'A' they that hae blue tails.'

6 'I wiss ye were on yon tree:'
    'And a gude ladder under me.'

7 'And the ladder for to break:'
    'And you for to fa down.'

8 'I wiss ye were in yon sie:'
    And a gude bottom under me.'

9 'And the bottom for to break:'
    'And ye to be drowned.'

ANON.

Feasgar Luain

Feasgar Luain is mi air chuairt
Gun cualas fuaim nach b' fhuathach leam,
Cèol nan teud gu h-òrdail rèidh
'S còisir d' a rèir os a choinn;
Thuit mi 'n caochladh leis an iongnadh

A dh'aisig mo smaointean a-null,
'S chuir mi 'n cèill gun imthichinn cèin
Le m' aigne fèin, 's e co-streup rium.

Chaidh mi steach an ceann na còisridh
An robh òl, is ceòl, is danns,
Rìbhinnean is fleasgaich òga
'S iad an òrdugh grin gun mheang.
Dhearcas fa-leth air na h-òighean
Le rosg fòil a-null 's a-nall,
'S ghlacadh mo chridhe 's mo shùil cò-luath
'S rinn an gaol mo leòn air ball.

Dhiùchd, mar aingeal, ma mo choinneamh
'N ainnir òg bu ghrinne snuadh:
Seang shlios fallain air bhlàth canaich
No mar eala air a' chuan;
Sùil ghorm, mheallach fo chaoil mhala,
'S caoin a sheallas 'g amharc uath';
Beul tlàth, tairis gun ghnè smalain,
Dh'an gnàth carthannachd gun uaill.

Mar ghath grèin' am madainn Chèitein,
Gun mheath i mo lèirsinn shùl,
'S i ceumadh ùrlair gu rèidh, iùmpaidh
Do rèir pungannan a' chiùil;
Rìbhinn mhòdhail 's fìor-ghlain' fòghlam,
D' fhìon-fhuil mhòrdhalach mo ruin,
Reul nan òighean, grian gach còisridh,
'S i 'n chiall chòmhraidh cheòl-bhinn, chiùin.

'S tearc an sgeula sunnailt t' eugaisg
Bhith ri fheutainn san Roinn-Eòrp,
Tha mais' is fèile, tlachd is ceutaidh,
Nach facas leam fèin fa chòir.
Gach cliù a' fàs riut am mùirn 's an àilleachd,
An sùgradh, 's am mànran beòil,
'S gach buaidh a b' àillidh bh' air Diàna
Gu lèir, mar fhàgail, tha aig Mòir.

'S bachlach, dualach, cas-bhuidh, cuachach
Càradh suaineis gruaig do chinn,
Gu h-àlainn, bòidheach, fàinneach, òrbhuidh,
An caraibh seòighn 's an òrdugh grinn;
Gun chron a' fàs riut dh'fheudte àireamh
O do bhàrr gu sail do bhuinn;
Dhiùchd na buaidhean, òigh, mun cuairt dut,
Gu meudachdainn t' uaill 's gach puinnc.

Bu leigheas eucail, slàn o' n eug,
Do dh'fhear a dh'fheudhadh bhith ma d' chòir;
B' fheàrr na cadal bhith nad fhagaisg
'G èisdeachd agallaidh do bheòil.
Cha robh Bhènus a-measg leugaibh,
Dh'aindeoin feucanntachd, cho bòidheach
Ri Mòir nigh'n mhìn, a leòn mo chrìdh
Le buaidhean, 's mi ga dìth ri m' bheò.

'S glan an fhìon-fhuil as na fhriamhaich
Thu gun fhiaradh mhiar no mheang:
Cinneadh mòrdhalach, bu chròdha
Tional cò-luath chòmhstri lann;
Bhuineadh cùise bhàrr nan Dùbh-Ghall,
Sgiùrsadh iad gu 'n dùthchas thall,
Leanadh ruaig air Cataich fhuara,
'S a' toirt buaidh orr' anns gach ball.

Tha Cabar-fèidh an dlùths do rèir dhut,
Nach biodh euslaineach san t-strì,
Fir nach obadh leis gan togail
Dol a chogadh 'n aghaidh Rìgh;
Bu cholgail, faiceant an stoirm feachdaidh,
Armach, breacanach, air tì
Dol san iomairt gun bhonn gioraig:
'S iad nach tilleadh chaoidh fo chìs.

'S trom leam m' osnadh, 's cruaidh leam m' fhortan,
Gun ghleus socair 's mi gun sùnnt,
'S mi ri smaointean air an aon rùn
A bhuin mo ghaol gun ghaol da chionn.
Throm na Dùilean peanaist dhùbailt

Gus mis' ùmhlachadh air ball,
Thàlaidh Cùpid mi san dùsal
As na dhùisg mi brùite, fann.

Thoir soraidh uam don rìbhinn shuairc,
Den chinneadh mhòr as uaisle gnàths,
'S thoir mo dhùrachd-sa g' a h-iùnnsaigh,
'S mi 'n deagh rùn d' a cùl-bhuidh bàn;
'S nach bruadar cadail a ghluais m' aigne –
'S truagh nach aidich e dhomh tàmh –
'S ge b' ann air chuairt, no thall an cuan,
Gum bi mi smuainteach ort gu bràth.

UILLEAM ROS

Monday Evening

On Monday evening, as I walked,
I heard a sound that pleased me well,
sound of strings played soft with care
and chorus in harmony above;
I was overcome by wonder
which ferried my thoughts across,
and I decided to move away
with my own thoughts that were in turmoil.

I went in and joined the crowd
where there was music, drink and dance,
maidens there and young gallants,
ranged in order, flawless, neat.
I looked at each of the maidens
with gentle eye looking here and there,
and my heart and my eye were transfixed
and love pierced me on the spot.

There appeared, like an angel, before me
the young maid of finest mien:
lithe, healthy form, with skin as white
as cotton-grass or swan on sea;
blue eyes enticing, pencil brows,

yet kindly as they looked at me;
warm, gentle lips, no sign of gloom,
nor pride, their nature always kind.

Like ray of sun on May morning
she softened the look in my eyes,
as she paced the floor, in stately turns,
according to the music's notes;
a modest maid, cleanly nurtured,
one of my proud, beloved clan,
virginal star, sun above all,
whose talk was musical and mild.

Rarely does one hear of your like
in all of Europe to be found,
I for one have never seen
such kindly beauty, virtuous grace.
A reputation for love and beauty,
enjoyment and sweet-lipped talk,
the loveliest virtues that were Diana's
are all inherited now by Mòr.

In pleats and ringlets, yellow, curled
in careful order is your hair,
all lovely, beautiful, curled golden,
in shapes so rare, yet ordered well;
with no fault that can be found
from top of head to sole and heel;
you were surrounded quite by grace,
a cause of pride at every point.

Disease's healing, death's respite
it were to one to be with you;
better than sleep to be near you,
listening to the words you speak.
Venus, surrounded by jewels,
with peacock's preen, was not so fair
as gentle Mòr, whose virtues left
my heart wounded, quite lost to me.

Clean the wine-blood that produced
you, free of twist in branch or twig;
a proud clan that showed valour,
gathering quickly for swords' clash;
winning the Lowlander's tussle,
driving them back to their home,
routing the cold northern clans
and beating them every time.

Close to you too the Mackenzies,
never infirm in the fight,
who would not fail when enlisted
to go and fight against the King;
martial, alert in storm of battle,
armed and plaieded, and keen
to enter battle without panic:
they would never return enslaved.

Heavy my sigh, and hard my fortune,
no ease of mind, no joyful mood,
as I reflect on the dear one
who took my love without return.
The Gods ordained a double penance
to humble me there and then,
Cupid enticed me to slumber
and I wakened bruised and weak.

Take my farewell to the fair maid
who comes of the great and noble clan,
and bring to her my kind regards –
I wish the golden-haired one well;
it is no dream that stirred my thoughts –
alas, it grants to me no rest –
whether away, or over sea,
I'll think of you for evermore.

Trans. Derick Thomson

WILLIAM ROSS

Fhir a Dhìreas am Bealach

Thig trì nithean gun iarraidh, an t-eagal, an t-iadach 's an gaol;
'S gur beag a' chùis mhaslaidh ged ghlacadh leo mis' air a h-aon,
'S a liuthad bean uasal a fhuaradh sa chiont an robh mi,
A thug a gaol fuadain air ro bheagan duaise ga chionn.

Air fàillirinn ìllirinn ùilirinn ò-ho-ro laoi
'S cruaidh fhortan gun fhios a chuir mise fo chuing do ghaoil.

Fhir a dhìreas am bealach, beir soraidh don ghleannan fa thuath;
Is innis dom leannan gur maireann mo ghaol 's gur buan;
Fear eile cha ghabh mi, 's chan fhuiling mi idir a luaidh;
Gus an dèan thu, ghaoil, m' àicheadh, cha chreid mi bho chàch gur fuath.

Fhir nan gorm shùilean meallach on ghleannan am bitheadh an smùid,
Gam bheil a' chaoin mhala mar chanach an t-slèibh fo dhriùchd;
Nuair re'adh tu air t' uilinn bhiodh fuil air fear dhìreadh nan stùc,
'S nam biodh tu, ghaoil, mar rium cha b' anait an cèile leam thu.

Nam faicinn thu tighinn is fios dhomh gur tusa bhiodh ann,
Gun èireadh mo chridhe mar aiteal na grèin' thar nam beann;
'S gun tugainn mo bhriathar gach gaoisdean tha liath 'na mo cheann
Gum fàsadh iad buidhe, mar dhìthein am bruthaich nan allt.

Cha b' ann airson beairteis no idir ro phailteas na sprèidh;
Cha b' fhear do shìol bhodach bha m' osnaich cho trom às a dhèidh.
Ach sàr mhac an duin' uasail fhuair buaidh air an dùthaich gu lèir;
Ged a bhitheamaid falamh 's iomadh caraid a chitheadh oirnn feum.

Mur tig thu fèin tuilleadh gur aithne dhomh 'mhalairt a th' ann
Nach eil mi cho beairteach ri cailin an achaidh ud thall.
Cha tugainn mo mhisneachd, mo ghliocas, is grinneas mo làimh
Air buaile chrodh ballach is cailin gun iùil 'nan ceann.

Ma chaidh thu orm seachad gur taitneach, neo-thuisleach mo chliù:
Cha d' rinn mi riut comann 's cha d' laigh mi leat riamh ann an cùil.
Chan àirichinn arrachd do dhuine chuir ad air a chrùn;
On tha mi cho beachdail 's gun smachdaich mi gaol nach fiù.

Bu lughaid mo thàmailt nam b' airidh ni b' fheàrr a bhiodh ann;
Ach dubh-chail' a' bhuachair nuair ghlacadh i buarach 'na làimh.
Nuair thig an droch earrach 's a chaillear an nì ann sa ghleann;
Bitheas is' air an t-shiulaid gun tuille dhe bunailteas ann.

Esan ga freagairt:
'S truagh nach robh mi 's mo leannan sa chrannaig air stiùireadh le gaoith,
No 'm bùthaig bhig bharraich aig iomall a' ghleannain leinn fhìn,
No 'n lòisdean den daraich ri taobh na mara fo thuinn,
Gun chuimhn' air a' chailin a dh'fhàg mi an caraibh chruidh-laoigh.

NIGHEAN FEAR NA RÈILIG

You Who Are Climbing the Pass

Three things come without asking — fear, envy, and love —
and it's no shame for me to be one of those caught in their weave:
many great ladies have faced the same guilt that I have,
getting little reward for the fleeting love that they gave.

Air fàillirinn illirinn ùilirinn ò-ho-ro laoi
cruel fate put me, unwitting, in the yoke of your love.

You who are climbing the pass, bring my greeting to that northern glen:
tell my lover my love will endure — that it will not fade or abate.
Tell him I'll have no one else, and will not even hear talk of it:
until, my love, you reject me, I won't be convinced of your hate.

You of the teasing blue eyes, you from the glens of the mist,
whose eyebrows are gentle and mild like hill-cotton laden with dew,
when you rest on your elbow, and aim, you blood stags climbing the peaks,
if I had you here as my partner then I would not be ridiculed.

If I saw you approaching and knew that it really was you,
how my heart would leap up — like sunbeams crossing the hills;
and I would give you my promise that every grey hair on my head
would turn yellow like flowers on the banks of a stream.

It was not for riches, nor for an abundance of cows,
nor for a man of ill breeding that I sighed so deeply for you,
but for the great son of a noble, honoured all over the land:
we would never have wanted, so many would have lent a hand.

If you never come back, I'll know the exchange you have made,
I know I'm not as well off as the girl of the fields over there.
But I'd not give my spirit, my wisdom, the skilful work of my hand,
for a fold of bright cattle and a clueless girl at their head.

Even if you've rebuffed me, my honour remains unsullied,
because I never went with you, never lay with you out of sight.
I'd never have raised a runt for one who'd put a hat on his crown:
I'm smart enough to control love not worth its price.

I would have been less offended if she'd been more worthy than me,
but she is dirty-faced, mucky, from handling the fetters of cows:
in the storms of spring when her cattle are astray in the glen,
she'll get her marching orders, her little security gone.

He answers:
O to be with my darling in a boat being steered by the wind,
or in a small leafy bothy on the edge of the glen by ourselves,
or in an oak-wood lodging beside the sea and the waves,
with no thought of the young girl I left looking after the cows.

Trans. Peter Mackay

THE DAUGHTER OF THE LAIRD OF RÈILIG

Fil Súil nGlais

Fil súil nglais
fégbas Érinn dar a hais;
    noco n-aceba íarmo-thá
    firu Érenn nách a mná.

Trans. Anon.

GUN URRA (AM BEUL CHOLUIM CHILLE)

A Blue Eye Turns

A blue eye turns,
watching Ireland fade behind,
  never to see thenceforth
  Ireland's women nor her men.

Trans. Meg Bateman

ANON. (ATTRIBUTED TO COLUMBA)

From Finn, Part V

Finn spies the deer, and sens the dug Bran outbye

In the dreich licht o dawin we're brocht frae wir beds
tae kennle richt quick the fey fire o day
an mak for the mairches, the maist hameless o haunts.
Heich owre hazel-shaw, owre hedder we hechle,
sweit staunan sterk on body an brou,
droukit bi drizzle frae alien airts
we shauchle tae shelter tae pick at wir piece.
Syne cauldrife claitterin, the scree frae the summit
byles up the bluid wi the chance o a chase.
Sae saftlie an slylie we rise frae wir reistin,
creepin richt quietlike owre weit stanes tae see
the great baist o the bellin staun sterk on the sky.
Nou get guid bi thon gully Bran, whaur ye see the whin,
an come up afore me wi the wind in ma ee
that quicklie we'll kep him, syne quaff at the kimmerin
thon weirdest o wines at gied birth tac us baith.

HARVEY HOLTON

Bho Fios Chun a' Bhàird

[. . .]

Ged a roinneas gathan grèine
Tlus nan speur ri blàth nan lòn,
'S ged a chìthear sprèidh air àirigh,
Is buailtean làn de dh'àlach bhò,
Tha Ìle 'n-diugh gun daoine,
Chuir a' chaor' a bailtean fàs;
Mar a fhuair 's a chunnaic mise,
Thoir am fios seo chun a' Bhàird.

Ged thig ànrach aineoil
Gus a' chaladh 's e sa cheò,
Chan fhaic e soills' on chagailt
Air a' chladach seo nas mò;
Chuir gamhlas Ghall air fuadach
Na tha bhuainn 's nach till gu bràth;
Mar a fhuair 's a chunnaic mise,
Thoir am fios seo chun a' Bhàird.

Ged a thogar feachd na h-Alb',
As cliùiteach ainm air faich' an àir,
Bithidh bratach fhraoich nan Ìleach
Gun dol sìos ga dìon le càch;
Sgap mìorun iad thar fairge,
'S gun ach ainmhidhean balbh nan àit';
Mar a fhuair 's a chunnaic mise,
Thoir am fios seo chun a' Bhàird.

Tha taighean seilbh na dh'fhàg sinn
Feadh an fhuinn nan càrnan fuar;
Dh'fhalbh 's cha till na Gàidheil;
Stad an t-àiteach, cur is buain;
Tha stèidh nan làrach tiamhaidh
A' toirt fianais air 's ag ràdh,
'Mar a fhuair 's a chunnaic mise,
Thoir am fios seo chun a' Bhàird'.

Cha chluinnear luinneag òighean,
Sèist nan òran air a' chlèith,
'S chan fhaicear seòid mar b' àbhaist
A' cur bàir air faiche rèidh;
Thug ainneart fògraidh uainn iad;
'S leis na coimhich buaidh mar 's àill;
Mar a fhuair 's a chunnaic mise,
Biodh am fios seo aig a' Bhàird.

Chan fhaigh an dèirceach fasgadh
No 'm fear-astair fois o sgìos,
No soisgeulach luchd-èisdeachd;
Bhuadhaich eucoir, Goill is cìs;
Tha an nathair bhreac 'na lùban
Air na h-ùrlair far an d'fhàs
Na fir mhòr' a chunnaic mise;
Thoir am fios seo chun a' Bhàird.

Lomadh ceàrn na h-Oa,
An Lanndaidh bhòidheach 's Roinn MhicAoidh;
Tha 'n Learga ghlacach ghrianach
'S fuidheall cianail air a taobh;
Tha an Gleann na fhiadhair uaine
Aig luchd-fuath gun tuath, gun bhàrr;
Mar a fhuair 's a chunnaic mise,
Thoir am fios seo chun a' Bhàird.

UILLEAM MAC DHÙNLÈIBHE

From A Message for the Poet

[. . .]

Although beams of sunlight bring
The mildness of the sky to the meadow flowers,
Although cattle can be seen at the sheiling
And enclosures are full of calves,
Islay today has no people –
Sheep have laid waste the villages;
This is as I found and saw it –
Take this message to the poet.

Even if a poor lost soul should come
To the harbour in a mist,
He'll see no light from a hearth
On this shore ever again;
The malice of Lowlanders has cleared
Those who've left never to return;
This is as I found and saw it —
Take this message to the poet.

Even if Scotland's army is raised —
Far famed on the battlefield —
The heather flag of the Islaymen
Won't charge with the rest in its defence;
Ill-will has scattered them overseas,
And only dumb beasts in their place;
This is as I found and saw it —
Take this message to the poet.

The houses of those who've left
Are cold cairns all over the land;
The Gaels have gone, never to return —
No more planting, sowing, reaping;
The foundations of those dismal ruins
Bear witness to this and say,
'This is how I found and saw it —
Take this message to the poet.'

Girls' tunes are no longer heard,
The chorus of their waulking songs,
And there are no more heroes
Scoring goals on level pitches;
The violence of eviction took them —
Strangers have won, as they wished;
With all that I've found and seen
May this message reach the poet.

The beggar will not find shelter
Or the tired traveller get rest,
Or the evangelist find listeners —
Injustice, rent, Foreigners have won;
The speckled adder lies in coils

On the floors where they grew up
Those great men that I saw there;
Take this message to the poet.

Oa has been stripped bare,
Lovely Lanndaidh, the Rhinns of Mackay,
Sunny Learga of the hollows
Has melancholy remnants on its side.
The Glen is a green wilderness
Owned by hate-filled men with no tenants or crops;
This is as I found and saw it –
Take this message to the poet.

Trans. Peter Mackay

WILLIAM LIVINGSTON

The Flowers of the Forest

I've heard them lilting at our ewe-milking,
Lasses a-lilting before the dawn of day;
But now they are moaning on ilka green loaning –
The Flowers of the Forest are a' wede away.

At bughts, in the morning, nae blythe lads are scorning,
The lasses are lonely, and dowie, and wae;
Nae daffin', nae gabbin', but sighing and sabbing,
Ilk ane lifts her leglin and hies her away.

In har'st, at the shearing, nae youths now are jeering,
Bandsters are lyart, and runkled, and gray;
At fair or at preaching, nae wooing nae fleeching –
The Flowers of the Forest are a' wede away.

At e'en, in the gloaming, nae younkers are roaming
'Bout stacks wi' the lasses at bogle to play;
But ilk ane sits drearie, lamenting her dearie –
The Flowers of the Forest are weded away.

Dool and wae for the order sent our lads to the Border!
The English, for ance, by guile wan the day;
The Flowers of the Forest, that fought aye the foremost,
The prime of our land, are cauld in the clay.

We'll hear nae mair lilting at our ewe-milking;
Women and bairns are heartless and wae;
Sighing and moaning on ilka green loaning –
The Flowers of the Forest are a' wede away.

JEAN ELLIOT

From The Flyting of Dunbar and Kennedie

Off Edinburch the boyis as beis owt thrawis
    And cryis owt ay, Heir cumis our awin queir clerk!
Than fleis thow lyk ane howlat chest with crawis,
    Quhill all the bichis at thy botingis dois bark.
    Than carlingis cryis, Keip curches in the merk –
Our gallowis gaipis – lo! quhair ane greceles gais!
    Ane uthir sayis, I se him want ane sark –
    I reid yow, cummer, tak in your lynning clais.

Than rynis thow doun the gait with gild of boyis
    And all the toun tykis hingand in thy heilis;
Of laidis and lownis thair rysis sic ane noyis
    Quhill runsyis rynis away with cairt and quheilis,
    And caiger aviris castis bayth coillis and creilis
For rerd of the and rattling of thy butis;
    Fische wyvis cryis, Fy! and castis doun skillis and skeilis,
    Sum claschis the, sum cloddis the on the cutis.

Loun lyk Mahoun, be boun me till obey,
    Theif, or in greif mischeif sall the betyd;
Cry grace, tykis face, or I the chece and fley;
    Oule, rare and yowle – I sall defowll thy pryd;
    Peilit gled, baith fed and bred of bichis syd
And lyk ane tyk, purspyk – quhat man settis by the!
    Forflittin, countbittin, beschittin, barkit hyd,
Clym ledder, fyle tedder, foule edder: I defy the!

Mauch muttoun, byt buttoun, peilit gluttoun, air to Hilhous,
    Rank beggar, ostir dregar, foule fleggar in the flet,
Chittirlilling, ruch rilling, lik schilling in the milhous,
    Baird rehator, theif of nator, fals tratour, feyindis gett,
    Filling of tauch, rak sauch – cry crauch, thow art oursett;
Muttoun dryver, girnall ryver, yadswyvar – fowll fell the;
    Herretyk, lunatyk, purspyk, carlingis pet,
Rottin crok, dirtin dok – cry cok, or I sall quell the.

[. . .]

In to the Katryne thou maid a foule cahute,
    For thou bedrate hir doune fra starn to stere;
Apon hir sydis was sene that thou coud schute –
    Thy dirt clevis till hir towis this twenty yere:
    The firmament na firth was nevir cler
Quhill thou, Deulbere, devillis birth, was on the see;
The saulis had sonkyn throu the syn of the
    War not the peple maid sa grete prayere.

Quhen that the schip was saynit and undir saile
    Foul brow in holl thou preposit for to pas;
Thou schot, and was not sekir of thy tayle,
    Beschate the stere, the compas and the glas;
    The skippar bad ger land the at the Bas:
Thou spewit and kest out mony a lathly lomp
Fastar than all the marynaris coud pomp,
    And now thy wame is wers than evir it was.

Had thai bene prouvait sa of schote of gune
    By men of were but perile thay had past;
As thou was louse and redy of thy bune
    Thay mycht have tane the collum at the last;
    For thou wald cuk a cartfull at a cast.
Thare is na schip that wil the now ressave;
Thou fylde faster than fyftenesum mycht lave,
    And myrit thaym wyth thy muk to the myd mast.

WALTER KENNEDY

For a Wife in Jizzen

Lassie, can ye say
    whaur ye ha been,
whaur ye ha come frae,
    whatna ferlies seen?

Efter the bluid and swyte,
    the warsslin o yestreen,
ye ligg forfochten, whyte,
    prouder nor onie queen.

Albeid ye hardly see me
    I read it i your een,
sae saft blue and dreamy,
    mindan whaur ye've been.

Anerly wives ken
    the ruits o joy and tene,
      the march o daith and birth,
        the tryst o luve and strife
i the howedumbdeidsunsheen,
    fire, air, water, yirth
        mellan to mak new life,
    lauchan and greetan, feiman and serene.

Dern frae aa men
    the ferlies ye ha seen.

DOUGLAS YOUNG

The Freedom Come-All-Ye

Roch the wind in the clear day's dawin
Blaws the cloods heelster-gowdie ow'r the bay,
But there's mair nor a roch wind blawin
Through the great glen o' the warld the day.
It's a thocht that will gar oor rottans
 – A' they rogues that gang gallus, fresh and gay –
Tak the road, and seek ither loanins
For their ill ploys, tae sport and play

Nae mair will the bonnie callants
Mairch tae war when oor braggarts crousely craw,
Nor wee weans frae pit-heid and clachan
Mourn the ships sailin' doon the Broomielaw.
Broken faimlies in lands we've herriet,
Will curse Scotland the Brave nae mair, nae mair;
Black and white, ane til ither mairriet,
Mak the vile barracks o' their maisters bare.

So come all ye at hame wi' Freedom,
Never heed whit the hoodies croak for doom.
In your hoose a' the bairns o' Adam
Can find breid, barley-bree and painted room.
When MacLean meets wi's freens in Springburn
A' the roses and geans will turn tae bloom,
And a black boy frae yont Nyanga
Dings the fell gallows o' the burghers doon.

HAMISH HENDERSON

Frog Spring

Surprised by my tasting the spring, a golden frog
leaps to the bank. He flies to froggy places,
his ankle-joints stretch the moment.

A puddock from his pop-eyes to his paddle-toes,
he darts out of the vital pool. Immortal frog,
to see him so healthy is a sure sign

the spring will do the same for me.
He hops past my shoulder into the paddy-pipes,
the reed-bed pockets frog. He vanishes through,
each spear of rush keeps its own drop of dew.

VALERIE GILLIES

The Gaberlunzie Man

The pawkie auld carle came o'er the lea,
Wi' mony gude e'ens and days to me,
Saying, Gudewife, for your courtesie,
Will you lodge a silly poor man?
The nicht was cauld, the carle was wat,
And down ayont the ingle he sat;
My dowghter's shouthers he 'gan to clap,
And cadgily ranted and sang.

O wow! quo' he, were I as free,
As first when I saw this countrie,
How blythe and merry wad I be!
And I wad never think lang.
He grew canty, and she grew fain;
But little did her auld minny ken
What thir slie twa together were say'ng,
When wooing they were sae thraug.

And O! quo' he, an' ye were as black
As e'er the crown of my daddy's hat,
'Tis I wad lay thee by my back,
And awa' wi' me thou should gang.
And! quo' she, an' I were as white,
As e'er the snaw lay on the dike,
I'd cleed me braw and lady like,
And awa' wi' thee I would gang.

Between the twa was made a plot;
They raise a wee before the cock,
And wilily they shot the lock,
And fast to the bent are they gane.
Up in the morn the auld wife raise,
And at her leisure pat on her claise;
Syne to the servant's bed she gaes,
To speer for the silly poor man.

She gaed to the bed where the beggar lay,
The strae was cauld, he was away,
She clapt her hands, cry'd, Waladay!

For some of our gear will be gane.
Some ran to coffer, and some to kist,
But nought was stown that cou'd be mist,
She danc'd her lane, cry'd Praise be blest!
I have lodg'd a leal poor man.

Since naething's awa', as we can learn,
The kirn's to kirn, and milk to earn,
Gae butt the house, lass, and waken my bairn,
And bid her come quickly ben.
The servant gade where the doughter lay,
The sheets were cauld, she was away,
And fast to the gudewife 'gan say,
She's aff wi' the gaberlunzie man.

O fy gar ride, and fy gar rin,
And haste ye find these traytors again;
For she's be burnt, and he's be slain,
The wearifu' gaberlunzie man.
Some rade upo' horse, some ran a fit,
The wife was wud, and out o' her wit;
She cou'd na gang, nor yet cou'd she sit,
But aye she curs'd and she bann'd.

Mean time far hind out o'er the lee,
Fu' snug in a glen, where nane could see,
The twa wi' kindly sport and glee,
Cut frae a new cheese a whang:
The priving was good, it pleas'd them baith,
To lo'e her for aye, he ga'e her his aith,
Quo' she To leave thee I will be laith,
My winsome gaberlunzie man.

O kend my minny I were wi' you,
Ill-far'dly wad she crook her mou',
Sic a poor man she'd never trow,
After the gaberlunzie man.
My dear, quo' he, ye're yet o'er young,
And ha'e nae learn'd the beggar's tongue,
To follow me frae town to town,
And carry the gaberlunzie on.

Wi' cauk and keel I'll win your bread,
And spindles and whorles for them wha need,
Whilk is a gentle trade indeed,
To carry the gaberlunzie on.
I'll bow my leg, and crook my knee,
And draw a black clout o'er my e'e,
A cripple or blind they will ca' me,
While we shall be merry and sing.

ANON.

The Gangan Fuit

Whit ist that greets outby the nicht,
that fakes tae fin the sneck?
It's juist the wind, my bonnie lass,
gaen speiran i the dark.

Whit ist that greets outby the nicht
that keens abuin the ruif?
It's juist the glaid, my bonnie lass,
gaen seekin i the lift.

The glaid gangs free, my bonnie lad
kens nocht o daith nor birth,
the wind but cairts aa human pain
tae ilka howe o yirth.

Whit seeks tae come inby the nicht,
nae bield has ever haen,
but haiks its gangrel body whaur
eternities cry doun.

ELLIE MCDONALD

Bho Gaoir nam Ban Muileach

Se chuir m' astar am maillead
'S mo shùilean an doillead

Bhith a' faicinn do chloinne
'S an luchd-foghlaim is oilein
Bhith 'nan ceathairne choille
'S iad gam fògairt gun choire
Gun solas, gun choinneil,
    'S iad gun fhios có an doire 'san tàmh iad,
    'S iad gun fhios có an doire 'san tàmh iad.

Gura goirt leam ri chluinntinn,
'S gura h-oil leam ri iomradh
Nach deach adhbhar ar n-ionndrainn,
Olc air mhath le luchd-diomba,
A thoirt dachaigh d'a dhùthaich –
Gum bu shòlas le d' mhuinntir
Do chorp geal a bhith dlùth dhaibh
    Ann an Ì nam fear cliùiteach le d' chàirdean,
    Ann an Ì nam fear cliùiteach le d' chàirdean.

Och, is mis' th' air mo sgaradh
Nach tug iad thu thairis
Dhol air tìr air an Ealaidh
Dhol fo dhìon anns a' charraig
Ann an réilig nam manach
Mar ri t' athair 's do sheanair
'S ioma treunlaoch a bharrachd
    Far am faodamaid teannadh mu d' chàrnan,
    Far am faodamaid teannadh mu d' chàrnan.

'N deagh bhean mhaiseach sa chì mi,
Si nighean a' bharain, Catrìona,
'S ged nach eil i 'd fhuil dhìreach
'S trom an sac th' air a h-inntinn,
A deòir a' sruthadh gu lìonmhor
'S leann dubh air a cridhe,
Tha do chumh' air a lìonadh –
    S goirt 's gur cruaidh leath' 'n sgrìob th' air do chàirdean,
    S goirt 's gur cruaidh leath' 'n sgrìob th' air do chàirdean.

S mairg a gheibheadh gach buille
A fhuair sinne o 'n-uiridh:
Thàinig tonn air muin tuinne

A dh'fhàg lom sinn 's an cunnart;
Chaidh ar creuchdadh gu guineach,
Dh'fhalbh ar n-éibhneas gu buileach –
Bhrist ar claidheamh 'na dhuille
    Nuair a shaoil sinn gun cumamaid slàn e,
    Nuair a shaoil sinn gun cumamaid slàn e.

MAIREARAD NIGHEAN LACHLAINN

From The Cry of the Mull Women

[...]

What has slackened my pace
And blinded my eyes
Is seeing your children
With their tutors and mentors
As outlaws and wood-kern
Being banished though guiltless
Without light, without candle,
    Without knowing what grove of trees they will rest in,
    Without knowing what grove of trees they will rest in.

I find it bitter to hear
And I hate to relate it
That the cause of our longing,
No matter what foes think,
Has not been brought to his homeland –
Your relatives would be pleased
To have your white body near them
    With your kin in Iona of the celebrated men,
    With your kin in Iona of the celebrated men.

Och, I am distraught
That they brought you not over
To land on the Ealadh
To be sheltered in rock
In the graveyard of the monks

With your father and grandfather
And many other brave heroes
    Where we could gather around your cairn,
    Where we could gather around your cairn.

The good lovely wife whom I see here,
She's the baron's daughter, Catrìona,
And though she's not of your kinfolk,
Her mind's heavily burdened,
Her tears abundantly streaming
And her heart in depression,
Your lament has possessed her –
    She finds the blow to your kind hard and sore,
    She finds the blow to your kind hard and sore.

Pity anyone who got all the blows
That we have suffered since last year:
Wave has come upon wave
And left us bare and in danger;
We've been grievously wounded,
All our happiness has gone –
Our sword has broken in its sheath
    When we thought we could keep it entire,
    When we thought we could keep it entire.

Trans. Ronald Black

MARGARET MacLEAN

Gi'e me a lass

Gi'e me a lass with a lump o' land,
And we for life shall gang thegither;
Tho' daft or wise, I'll ne'er demand,
Or black or fair, it maksna whether.
I'm aff with wit, and beauty will fade,
And blood alane's nae worth a shilling;
But she that's rich, her market's made,
For ilka charm about her's killing.

Gi'e me a lass with a lump o' land,
And in my bosom I'll hug my treasure;
Gin I had ance her gear in my hand,
Should love turn dowf, it will find pleasure.
Laugh on wha likes: but there's my hand,
I hate with poortith, though bonnie, to meddle;
Unless they bring cash, or a lump o' land,
They'se ne'er get me to dance to their fiddle.

There's meikle gude love in bands and bags;
And siller and gowd's a sweet complexion;
But beauty and wit and virtue, in rags,
Have tint the art of gaining affection:
Love tips his arrows with woods and parks,
And castles, and riggs, and muirs, and meadows;
And naething can catch our modern sparks,
But weel-tocher'd lasses, or jointured widows.

ALLAN RAMSAY

Gin I Was God

Gin I was God, sittin' up there abeen,
Weariet nae doot noo a' my darg was deen,
Deaved wi' the harps an' hymns oonendin' ringin',
Tired o' the flockin' angels hairse wi' singin',
To some clood-edge I'd daunder furth an', feth,
Look ower an' watch hoo things were gyaun aneth.
Syne, gin I saw hoo men I'd made mysel'
Had startit in to pooshan, sheet an' fell,
To reive an' rape, an' fairly mak' a hell
O' my braw birlin' Earth, – a hale week's wark –
I'd cast my coat again, rowe up my sark,
An', or they'd time to lench a second ark,
Tak' back my word an' sen' anither spate,
Droon oot the hale hypothec, dicht the sklate,
Own my mistak', an', aince I'd cleared the brod,
Start a'thing ower again, gin I was God.

CHARLES MURRAY

Glasgow

Sing, Poet, 'tis a merry world;
That cottage smoke is rolled and curled
In sport, that every moss
Is happy, every inch of soil; —
Before *me* runs a road of toil
With my grave cut across.
Sing, trailing showers and breezy downs —
I know the tragic hearts of towns.

City! I am true son of thine;
Ne'er dwelt I where great mornings shine
Around the bleating pens;
Ne'er by the rivulets I strayed,
And ne'er upon my childhood weighed
The silence of the glens.
Instead of shores where ocean beats,
I hear the ebb and flow of streets . . .

Afar, one summer, I was borne;
Through golden vapours of the morn,
I heard the hills of sheep:
I trod with a wild ecstasy
The bright fringe of the living sea:
And on a ruined keep
I sat, and watched an endless plain
Blacken beneath the gloom of rain.

O fair the lightly sprinkled waste,
O'er which a laughing shower has raced!
O fair the April shoots!
O fair the woods on summer days,
While a blue hyacinthine haze
Is dreaming round the roots!
In thee, O city! I discern
Another beauty, sad and stern.

Draw thy fierce streams of blinding ore,
Smite on a thousand anvils, roar
Down to the harbour-bars;

Smoulder in smoky sunsets, flare
On rainy nights, while street and square
Lie empty to the stars.
From terrace proud to alley base,
I know thee as my mother's face.

When sunset bathes thee in his gold,
In wreaths of bronze thy sides are rolled,
Thy smoke is dusty fire;
And from the glory round thee poured,
A sunbeam like an angel's sword
Shivers upon a spire.
Thus have I watched thee, Terror! Dream!
While the blue Night crept up the stream . . .

But all these sights and sounds are strange;
Then wherefore from thee should I range?
Thou hast my kith and kin;
My childhood, youth, and manhood brave;
Thou hast that unforgotten grave
Within thy central din.
A sacredness of love and death
Dwells in thy noise and smoky breath.

ALEXANDER SMITH

Glory

I canna' see ye, lad, I canna' see ye,
For a' yon glory that's aboot yer heid,
Yon licht that haps ye, an' the hosts that's wi' ye,
Aye, but ye live, an' it's mysel' that's deid!

They gae'd frae mill and mart; frae wind-blawn places,
And grey toon-closes; i' the empty street
Nae mair the bairns ken their steps, their faces,
Nor stand to listen to the trampin' feet.

Beside the brae, and soughin' through the rashes,
Yer voice comes back to me at ilka turn,
Amang the whins, an' whaur the water washes
The arn-tree wi' its feet amang the burn.

Whiles ye come back to me when day is fleein',
And a' the road oot-by is dim wi' nicht,
But weary een like mine is no for seein',
An', gin they saw, they wad be blind wi' licht.

Deith canna' kill. The mools o' France lie o'er ye,
An yet ye live, O sodger o' the Lord!
For Him that focht wi' deith an' dule afore ye,
He gie'd the life – 'twas Him that gie'd the sword.

But gin ye see my face or gin ye hear me,
I daurna' ask, I maunna' seek to ken,
Though I should dee, wi' sic a glory near me,
By nicht or day, come ben, my bairn, come ben!

VIOLET JACOB

God Send Every Priest ane Wife

God send every priest ane wife,
And every nun ane man,
That they micht live that holy life,
As first the Kirk began.

Sanct Peter, whom nane can reprove,
His life in marriage led.
All guid priestis, whom God did luve
Their maryit wifis had.

Great causis then, I grant, had they
Fra wifis to refrain;
Bot greater causis have they may,
Now wifis to wed again.

For then suld nocht sa mony whore
Be up and down this land.
Nor yet sa mony beggaris poor,
In kirk and merkat stand.

And nocht sa meckle bastard seed,
Through out this country sawin,
Nor good men uncouth fry suld feed,
And all the sooth war knawin.

Sen Cristis law, and commoun law,
And doctoris will admit,
That preistis in that yoke suld draw,
Wha dare say contrair it?

GUDE AND GODLIE BALLADS

The Golden Targe

I

Ryght as the stern of day begouth to schyne,
Quhen gone to bed war Vesper and Lucyne,
I raise and by a rosere did me rest.
Wp sprang the goldyn candill matutyne,
With clere depurit bemes cristallyne,
Glading the mery foulis in thair nest.
Or Phebus was in purpur cape reuest
Wp raise the lark, the hevyns menstrale fyne,
In May in till a morow myrthfullest.

2

Full angellike thir birdis sang thair houris
Within thair courtyns grene in to thair bouris,
Apparalit quhite and rede wyth blomes suete;
Anamalit was the felde wyth all colouris.
The perly droppis schuke in silvir schouris,
Quhill all in balme did branch and leuis flete.
Depart fra Phebus did Aurora grete –

Hir cristall teris I saw hyng on the flouris,
Quhilk he for lufe all drank vp wyth his hete.

3

For mirth of May wyth skippis and wyth hoppis
The birdis sang vpon the tender croppis
With curiouse note, as Venus chapell clerkis.
The rosis yong, new spreding of thair knopis,
War powderit brycht with hevinly beriall droppis,
Throu bemes rede birnyng as ruby sperkis.
The skyes rang for schoutyng of the larkis,
The purpur hevyn, ourscailit in silvir sloppis,
Ourgilt the treis branchis, lef and barkis.

4

Doun throu the ryce a ryuir ran wyth stremys,
So lustily agayn thai lykand lemys
That all the lake as lamp did leme of licht,
Quhilk schadovit all about wyth twynkling glemis.
The bewis bathit war in secund bemys
Throu the reflex of Phebus visage brycht.
On every syde the hegies raise on hicht,
The bank was grene, the bruke vas full of bremys,
The stanneris clere as stern in frosty nycht.

5

The cristall air, the sapher firmament,
The ruby skyes of the orient,
Kest beriall bemes on emerant bewis grene.
The rosy garth, depaynt and redolent,
With purpur, azure, gold and goulis gent
Arayed was by dame Flora, the quene,
So nobily that ioy was for to sene
The roch agayn the riwir resplendent,
As low enlumynit all the leues schene.

6

Quhat throu the mery foulys armony
And throu the ryueris soun, rycht ran me by,
On Florais mantill I slepit as I lay;
Quhare sone in to my dremes fantasy
I saw approch agayn the orient sky
A saill als quhite as blossum vpon spray,
Wyth merse of gold brycht as the stern of day,
Quhilk tendit to the land full lustily,
As falcoun swift desyrouse of hir pray.

7

And hard on burd vnto the blomyt medis
Amang the grene rispis and the redis
Arrivit sche; quharfro anon thare landis
Ane hundreth ladyes, lusty in to wedis,
Als fresch as flouris that in May vp spredis,
In kirtillis grene, withoutyn kell or bandis.
Thair brycht hairis hang gleting on the strandis,
In tressis clere wyppit wyth goldyn thredis,
With pappis quhite and mydlis small as wandis.

8

Discriue I wald, bot quho coud wele endyte
How all the feldis wyth thai lilies quhite
Depaynt war brycht, quhilk to the hevyn did glete?
Noucht thou, Omer, als fair as thou coud wryte,
For all thine ornate stilis so perfyte.
Nor yit thou, Tullius, quhois lippis suete
Off rethorike did in to termes flete.
Your aureate tongis both bene all to lyte
For to compile that paradise complete.

9

Thare saw I Nature and Venus, quene and quene,
The fresch Aurora and lady Flora schene,
Iuno, Appollo and Proserpyna,

Dyane, the goddesse chaste of woddis grene,
My lady Cleo, that help of makaris bene,
Thetes, Pallas and prudent Minerua,
Fair feynit Fortune and lemand Lucina.
Thir mychti quenis in crounis mycht be sene,
Wyth bemys blith, bricht as Lucifera.

10

Thare saw I May, of myrthfull monethis quene,
Betuix Aprile and Iune hir sistir schene,
Within the gardyng walking vp and doun,
Quham of the foulis gladdith all bedene.
Scho was full tender in hir yeris grene.
Thare saw I Nature present hir a goun,
Rich to behald and nobil of renoun,
Off ewiry hew vnder the hevin that bene,
Depaynt and broud be gude proporcion.

11

Full lustily thir ladyes all in fere
Enterit within this park of most plesere,
Quhare that I lay, ourhelit wyth leuis ronk.
The mery foulis blisfullest of chere
Salust Nature, me thoucht, on thair manere;
And ewiry blome on branch and eke on bonk
Opnyt and spred thair balmy leuis donk,
Full low enclynyng to thair quene so clere,
Quham of thair noble norising thay thonk.

12

Syne to dame Flora on the samyn wyse
Thay saluse and thay thank a thousand syse,
And to dame Wenus, lufis mychti quene,
Thay sang ballettis in lufe, as was the gyse,
With amourouse notis lusty to devise,
As thay that had lufe in thair hertis grene.
Thair hony throtis opnyt fro the splene
With werblis suete did perse the hevinly skyes,
Quhill loud resownyt the firmament serene.

13

Ane othir court thare saw I consequent
Cupide, the king, wyth bow in hand ybent
And dredefull arowis grundyn scharp and square.
Thare saw I Mars, the god armypotent,
Aufull and sterne, strong and corpolent.
Thare saw I crabbit Saturn, ald and haire –
His luke was lyke for to perturb the aire.
Thare was Mercurius, wise and eloquent,
Of rethorike that fand the flouris faire.

14

Thare was the god of gardingis, Priapus,
Thare was the god of wildernes, Phanus,
And Ianus, god of entree delytable.
Thare was the god of fludis, Neptunus,
Thare was the god of wyndis, Eolus,
With variand luke rycht lyke a lord vnstable.
Thare was Bacus, the gladder of the table,
There was Pluto, the elrich incubus,
In cloke of grene – his court vsit no sable.

15

And ewiry one of thir in grene arayit
On harp or lute full merily thai playit,
And sang ballettis with michty notis clere.
Ladyes to dance full sobirly assayit,
Endlang the lusty rywir so thai mayit,
Thair obseruance rycht hevynly was to here.
Than crap I throu the leuis and drew nere,
Quhare that I was rycht sudaynly affrayt,
All throu a luke, quhilk I haue boucht full dere.

16

And schortly for to speke, be lufis quene
I was aspyit. Scho bad hir archearis kene
Go me arrest, and thay no tyme delayit.

Than ladyes fair lete fall thair mantillis gren,
With bowis big in tressit hairis schene
All sudaynly thay had a felde arayit.
And yit rycht gretly was I noucht affrayit,
The party was so plesand for to sene.
A wonder lusty bikkir me assayit.

17

And first of all with bow in hand ybent
Come dame Beautee, rycht as scho wald me schent.
Syne folowit all hir dameselis yfere,
With mony diuerse aufull instrument.
Wnto the pres Fair Having wyth hir went,
Fyne Portrature, Plesance and Lusty Chere.
Than come Reson with schelde of gold so clere,
In plate and maille as Mars armypotent.
Defendit me that nobil cheuallere.

18

Syne tender Youth come wyth hir virgyns ying,
Grene Innocence and schamefull Abaising,
And quaking Drede wyth humble Obedience.
The goldyn targe harmyt thay no thing.
Curage in thame was noucht begonne to spring,
Full sore thay dred to done a violence.
Suete Womanhede I saw cum in presence –
Of artilye a warld sche did in bring,
Seruit wyth ladyes full of reuerence.

19

Sche led wyth hir Nurture and Lawlynes,
Contenence, Pacience, Gude Fame and Stedfastnes,
Discrecion, Gentrise and Considerance,
Leuefull Company and Honest Besynes,
Benigne Luke, Mylde Chere and Sobirnes.
All thir bure ganyeis to do me greuance,
Bot Reson bure the targe wyth sik constance,
Thair scharp assayes mycht do no dures
To me, for all thair aufull ordynance.

20

Unto the pres persewit Hie Degree:
Hir folowit ay Estate and Dignitee,
Comparison, Honour and Noble Array,
Will, Wantonnes, Renon and Libertee,
Richesse, Fredom and eke Nobilitee.
Wit ye, thay did thair baner hye display.
A cloud of arowis, as hayle schour, lousit thay
And schot quhill wastit was thair artilye,
Syne went abak reboytit of thair pray.

21

Quhen Venus had persauit this rebute,
Dissymilance scho bad go mak persute
At all powere to perse the goldyn targe;
And scho that was of doubilnes the rute
Askit hir choise of archeris in refute.
Venus the best bad hir go wale at large.
Scho tuke Presence, plicht anker of the barge,
And Fair Callyng, that wele a flayn coud schute,
And Cherising for to complete hir charge.

22

Dame Hamelynes scho tuke in company,
That hardy was and hende in archery,
And broucht dame Beautee to the felde agayn
With all the choise of Venus cheualry.
Thay come and bikkerit vnabaisitly,
The schour of arowis rappit on as rayn.
Perilouse Presence, that mony syre has slayn,
The bataill broucht on bordour hard vs by.
The salt was all the sarar, suth to sayn.

23

Thik was the schote of grundyn dartis kene,
Bot Reson with the scheld of gold so schene
Warly defendit, quho so ewir assayit.

The aufull stoure he manly did sustene,
Quhill Presence kest a pulder in his ene,
And than as drunkyn man he all forvayit.
Quhen he was blynd the fule wyth him thay playit,
And banyst hym amang the bewis grene.
That sory sicht me sudaynly affrayit.

24

Than was I woundit to the deth wele nere
And yoldyn as a wofull prisonnere
To lady Beautee in a moment space.
Me thoucht scho semyt lustiar of chere
(Efter that Reson tynt had his eyne clere)
Than of before, and lufliare of face.
Quhy was thou blyndit, Reson, quhi, allace?
And gert ane hell my paradise appere,
And mercy seme quhare that I fand no grace.

25

Dissymulance was besy me to sile,
And Fair Calling did oft apon me smyle,
And Cherising me fed wyth wordis fair.
New Acquyntance enbracit me a quhile
And fauouryt me, quhill men mycht go a myle,
Syne tuke hir leve. I saw hir nevir mare.
Than saw I Dangere toward me repair.
I coud eschew hir presence be no wyle,
On syde scho lukit wyth ane fremyt fare.

26

And at the last Departing coud hir dresse,
And me delyuerit vnto Hevynnesse
For to remayne, and scho in cure me tuke.
Be this the lord of wyndis with wodenes
(God Eolus) his bugill blew, I gesse,
That with the blast the leuis all toschuke.
And sudaynly in the space of a luke
All was hyne went, thare was bot wildernes,
Thare was no more bot birdis, bank and bruke.

27

In twynklyng of ane eye to schip thai went,
And swyth vp saile vnto the top thai stent,
And with swift course atour the flude thai frak.
Thai fyrit gunnis with powder violent,
Till that the reke raise to the firmament.
The rochis all resownyt wyth the rak,
For rede it semyt that the raynbow brak.
Wyth spirit affrayde apon my fete I sprent,
Amang the clewis so carefull was the crak.

28

And as I did awake of my sueving,
The ioyfull birdis merily did syng
For myrth of Phebus tender bemes schene.
Suete war the vapouris, soft the morowing,
Halesum the vale depaynt wyth flouris ying,
The air attemperit, sobir and amene.
In quhite and rede was all the felde besene,
Throu Naturis nobil fresch anamalyng
In mirthfull May of ewiry moneth quene.

29

O reuerend Chaucere, rose of rethoris all
(As in oure tong ane flour imperiall)
That raise in Britane ewir, quho redis rycht,
Thou beris of makaris the tryumph riall,
Thy fresch anamalit termes celicall
This mater coud illumynit haue full brycht.
Was thou noucht of oure Inglisch all the lycht,
Surmounting ewiry tong terrestriall,
Alls fer as Mayes morow dois mydnycht?

30

O morall Gower and Ludgate laureate,
Your sugurit lippis and tongis aureate
Bene to oure eris cause of grete delyte.

Your angel mouthis most mellifluate
Oure rude langage has clere illumynate
And fair oergilt oure spech, that imperfyte
Stude or your goldyn pennis schupe to write.
This ile before was bare and desolate
Off rethorike or lusty fresch endyte.

31

Thou lytill quair, be ewir obedient,
Humble, subiect and symple of entent
Before the face of ewiry connyng wicht.
I knaw quhat thou of rethorike hes spent.
Off all hir lusty rosis redolent
Is non in to thy gerland sett on hicht.
Eschame tharof and draw the out of sicht.
Rude is thy wede, disteynit, bare and rent,
Wele aucht thou be aferit of the licht.

WILLIAM DUNBAR

The Good Neighbour

Somewhere along this street, unknown to me,
behind a maze of apple trees and stars,
he rises in the small hours, finds a book
and settles at a window or a desk
to see the morning in, alone for once,
unnamed, unburdened, happy in himself.

I don't know who he is; I've never met him
walking to the fish-house, or the bank,
and yet I think of him, on nights like these,
waking alone in my own house, my other neighbours
quiet in their beds, like drowsing flies.

He watches what I watch, tastes what I taste:
on winter nights, the snow; in summer, sky.
He listens for the bird lines in the clouds
and, like that ghost companion in the old

explorers' tales, that phantom in the sleet,
fifth in a party of four, he's not quite there,
but not quite inexistent, nonetheless;

and when he lays his book down, checks the hour
and fills a kettle, something hooded stops
as cell by cell, a heartbeat at a time,
my one good neighbour sets himself aside,
and alters into someone I have known:
a passing stranger on the road to grief,
husband and father; rich man; poor man; thief.

JOHN BURNSIDE

The Good Thief

heh jimmy
yawright ih
stull wayiz urryi
ih

heh jimmy
ma right insane yirra pape
ma right insane yirwanny us jimmy
see it nyir eyes
wanny uz

heh

heh jimmy
lookslik wirgonny miss thi gemm
gonny miss thi GEMM jimmy
nearly three a cloke thinoo

dork init
good jobe theyve gote thi lights

TOM LEONARD

The Great Silkie of Sule Skerrie

1   An eartly nourris sits and sings,
    And aye she sings, Ba, lily wean!
    Little ken I my bairnis father,
    Far less the land that he staps in.

2   Then ane arose at her bed-fit,
    An a grumly guest I'm sure was he:
    'Here am I, thy bairnis father,
    Although that I be not comelie.

3   'I am a man, upo the lan,
    An I am a silkie in the sea;
    And when I'm far and far frae lan,
    My dwelling is in Sule Skerrie.'

4   'It was na weel,' quo the maiden fair,
    'It was na weel, indeed,' quo she,
    'That the Great Silkie of Sule Skerrie
    Suld hae come and aught a bairn to me.'

5   Now he has taen a purse of goud,
    And he has pat it upo her knee,
    Sayin, Gie to me my little young son,
    An tak thee up thy nourris-fee.

6   An it sall come to pass on a simmer's day,
    When the sin shines het on evera stane,
    That I will tak my little young son,
    An teach him for to swim the faem.

7   An thu sall marry a proud gunner,
    An a proud gunner I'm sure he'll be,
    An the very first schot that ere he schoots,
    He'll schoot baith my young son and me.

ANON.

Green Waters

Green Waters
Blue Spray
Grayfish

Anna T
Karen B
Netta Croan

Constant Star
Daystar
Starwood

Starlit Waters
Moonlit Waters
Drift

IAN HAMILTON FINLAY

The Grim Sisters

And for special things
(weddings, school –
concerts) the grown up girls next door
would do my hair.

Luxembourg announced Amami night.
I sat at peace passing bobbipins
from a marshmallow pink cosmetic purse
embossed with jazzmen,
girls with pony tails and a November
topaz lucky birthstone.
They doused my cow's-lick, rollered
and skewered tightly.
I expected that to be lovely
would be worth the hurt.

They read my Stars,
tied chiffon scarves to doorhandles, tried

to teach me tight dancesteps
you'd no guarantee
any partner you might find would ever be able to
keep up with as far as I could see.

There were always things to burn
before the men came in.

For each disaster
you were meant to know the handy hint.
Soap at a pinch
but better nailvarnish (clear) for ladders.
For kisscurls, spit.

Those days womanhood was quite a sticky thing
and that was what these grim sisters came to mean.

'You'll know all about it soon enough.'
But when the clock struck they
stood still, stopped dead.
And they were left there
out in the cold with the wrong skirtlength
and bouffant hair,
dressed to kill,

who'd been
all the rage in fifty eight,
a swish of Persianelle
a slosh of perfume.
In those big black mantrap handbags
they snapped shut at any hint of *that*
were hedgehog hairbrushes
cottonwool mice and barbed combs to tease.
Their heels spiked bubblegum, dead leaves.

Wasp waist and cone breast, I see them yet.
I hope, I hope
there's been a change of more than silhouette.

LIZ LOCHHEAD

Gur ann thall ann an Sòdhaigh

'S gur ann san t-samhradh a shiubhail
Rinn na h-uighean mo lèir-chreach,
Nuair a thugadh bhuam Ìomhar –
Fàth mo mhisneachd gu lèir e.

'S gur ann thall ann an Sòdhaigh
Dh'fhàg mi 'n t-òg nach robh leumach –
Is tu nach fhalbhadh le m' fhacal
'S nach innseadh na breugan.

Thu bhith muigh sa Gheodh' Chumhainn,
Gur cianail dubhach ad dhèidh mi;
'S thu bhith muigh feadh nan stuaghan
'S am muir gad fhuasgladh o chèile.

Ach seachd beannachd do mhàthar
Gad chumail sàmhach ri chèile –
Gun robh d' fhuil air a' chloich ud
Is do lotan air leum oirr'.

'S gur diombach den eug mi,
Cha chaomhail leam fhèin e,
Nach leig thu gu d' mhàthair
Gu i càradh do lèine.

Bidh mo chuid de na h-eunaibh
Anns na neulaibh ag èigheach,
Is mo chuid de na h-uighean
Aig a' bhuidhinn as trèine.

Bliadhn' an t-samhraidh sa 'n-uiridh
Rinn na h-uighean mo lèireadh;
Gur ann thall ann an Sòdhaigh
Dh'fhàg mi 'n t-òg nach robh leumach.

Nuair a thàinig do phiuthar
Cha robh sinn subhach le chèile;
Cha tig thu gu d' mhàthair
Gus càradh do lèine.

GUN URRA

It Was Over in Sòdhaigh

Last summer the egg gathering
devastated me –
Ivor was taken from me,
the source of my courage.

It was over in Sòdhaigh
I left the flawless youth:
you wouldn't repeat my words,
you wouldn't tell any lies.

That you're out in Geodh' Chumhainn
has left me in mourning,
out among the breakers,
the sea tearing you apart.

May your mother's seven blessings
keep you still and intact;
your blood was on that stone,
you bled profusely upon it.

I'm indignant with death,
I don't like it at all:
it won't return you to your mother
so she can fix your shroud.

My share of the birds
will be calling in the skies,
and the bravest of the gatherers
will have my share of the eggs.

A year last summer,
the eggs devastated me;
it was over in Sòdhaigh
I left the flawless youth.

When your sister arrived
we weren't cheerful together;
you won't come to your mother
so I can arrange your shroud.

Trans. Peter Mackay and Jo MacDonald

ANON.

haiku

in silence, out of
the falling snow,
a swan, flying

ALAN SPENCE

haiku

that daft dog
chasing the train
then letting it go

ALAN SPENCE

Hallaig

'Tha tìm, am fiadh, an coille Hallaig'

Tha bùird is tàirnean air an uinneig
trom faca mi an Àird an Iar
's tha mo ghaol aig Allt Hallaig
'na craoibh bheithe, 's bha i riamh

eadar an t-Inbhir 's Poll a' Bhainne,
thall 's a-bhos mu Bhaile Chùirn:
tha i 'na beithe, 'na calltainn,
'na caorann dhìrich sheang ùir.

Ann an Sgreapadal mo chinnidh,
far robh Tarmad 's Eachann Mòr,
tha 'n nigheanan 's am mic 'nan coille
a' gabhail suas ri taobh an lòin.

Uaibhreach a-nochd na coilich ghiuthais
a' gairm air mullach Cnoc an Rà,
dìreach an druim ris a' ghealaich –
chan iadsan coille mo ghràidh.

Fuirichidh mi ris a' bheithe
gus an tig i mach an Càrn,
gus am bi am bearradh uile
o Bheinn na Lice fa sgàil.

Mura tig 's ann theàrnas mi a Hallaig
a dh'ionnsaigh Sàbaid nam marbh,
far a bheil an sluagh a' tathaich,
gach aon ghinealach a dh'fhalbh.

Tha iad fhathast ann a Hallaig,
Clann Ghill-Eain 's Clann MhicLeòid,
na bh' ann ri linn Mhic Ghille Chaluim:
chunnacas na mairbh beò.

Na fir 'nan laighe air an lèanaig
aig ceann gach taighe a bh' ann,
's na h-igheanan 'nan coille bheithe,
dìreach an druim, crom an ceann.

Eadar an Leac is na Feàrnaibh
tha 'n rathad mòr fo chòinnich chiùin,
's na h-igheanan 'nam badan sàmhach
a' dol a Chlachan mar o thùs.

Agus a' tilleadh às a' Chlachan,
à Suidhisnis 's à tìr nam beò;
a chuile tè òg uallach
gun bhristeadh cridhe an sgeòil.

O Allt na Feàrnaibh gus an fhaoilinn
tha soilleir an dìomhaireachd nam beann
chan eil ach coitheanal nan nighean
a' cumail na coiseachd gun cheann.

A' tilleadh a Hallaig anns an fheasgar,
anns a' chamhanaich bhalbh bheò,
a' lìonadh nan leathadan casa,
an gàireachdaich 'nam chluais 'na ceò,

's am bòidhche 'na sgleò air mo chridhe
mun tig an ciaradh air na caoil,
's nuair theàrnas grian air cùl Dhùn Cana
thig peilear dian à gunna Ghaoil;

's buailear am fiadh a tha 'na thuaineal
a' snòtach nan làraichean feòir;
thig reothadh air a shùil sa choille:
chan fhaighear lorg air fhuil rim bheò.

SOMHAIRLE MacGILL-EAIN

Hallaig

'Time, the deer, is in the Wood of Hallaig'

The window is nailed and boarded
through which I saw the West
and my love is at the Burn of Hallaig,
a birch tree, and she has always been

between Inver and Milk Hollow,
here and there about Baile-chuirn:
she is a birch, a hazel,
a straight, slender young rowan.

In Screapadal of my people,
where Norman and Big Hector were,
their daughters and their sons are a wood
going up beside the stream.

Proud tonight the pine cocks
crowing on the top of Cnoc an Ra,
straight their backs in the moonlight —
they are not the wood I love.

I will wait for the birch wood
until it comes up by the cairn,
until the whole ridge from Beinn na Lice
will be under its shade.

If it does not, I will go down to Hallaig,
to the Sabbath of the dead,
where the people are frequenting,
every single generation gone.

They are still in Hallaig,
MacLeans and MacLeods,
all who were there in the time of Mac Gille Chaluim:
the dead have been seen alive.

The men lying on the green
at the end of every house that was,
the girls a wood of birches,
straight their backs, bent their heads.

Between the Leac and Fearns
the road is under mild moss
and the girls in silent bands
go to Clachan as in the beginning,

and return from Clachan,
from Suisnish and the land of the living;
Each one young and light-stepping,
without the heartbreak of the tale.

From the Burn of Fearns to the raised beach
that is clear in the mystery of the hills,
there is only the congregation of the girls
keeping up the endless walk,

coming back to Hallaig in the evening,
in the dumb living twilight,
filling the steep slopes,
their laughter in my ears a mist,

and their beauty a film on my heart
before the dimness comes on the kyles,
and when the sun goes down behind Dun Cana
a vehement bullet will come from the gun of Love;

and will strike the deer that goes dizzily,
sniffing at the grass-grown ruined homes;
his eye will freeze in the wood;
his blood will not be traced while I live.

Translated by author

SORLEY MacLEAN

The Halted Moment

Wha hasna turn'd inby a sunny street
And fund alang its length nae folk were there;
And heard his step fa' steadily and clear
Nor wauken ocht but schedows at his feet.
Shuther to shuther in the reemlin heat
The houses seem'd to hearken and to stare;
But a' were doverin whaur they stude and were
Like wa's ayont the echo o' time's beat.
Wha hasna thocht whan atween stanes sae still,
That had been biggit up for busyness,
He has come wanderin into a place
Lost, and forgotten, and unchangeable;
And thocht the far-off traffic sounds to be
The weary waters o' mortality.

WILLIAM SOUTAR

Hamnavoe

My father passed with his penny letters
Through closes opening and shutting like legends
    When barbarous with gulls
    Hamnavoe's morning broke

On the salt and tar steps. Herring boats,
Puffing red sails, the tillers
    Of cold horizons, leaned
    Down the gull-gaunt tide

And threw dark nets on sudden silver harvests.
A stallion at the sweet fountain
    Dredged water, and touched
    Fire from steel-kissed cobbles.

Hard on noon four bearded merchants
Past the pipe-spitting pier-head strolled,
    Holy with greed, chanting
    Their slow grave jargon.

A tinker keened like a tartan gull
At cuithe-hung doors. A crofter lass
    Trudged through the lavish dung
    In a dream of cornstalks and milk.

Blessings and soup plates circled. Euclidian light
Ruled the town in segments blue and gray.
    The school bell yawned and lisped.
    Down ignorant closes.

In 'The Arctic Whaler' three blue elbows fell,
Regular as waves, from beards spumy with porter,
    Till the amber day ebbed out
    To its black dregs.

The boats drove furrows homeward, like ploughmen
In blizzards of gulls. Gaelic fisher girls
    Flashed knife and dirge
    Over drifts of herring,

And boys with penny wands lured gleams
From the tangled veins of the flood. Houses went blind
    Up one steep close, for a
    Grief by the shrouded nets.

The kirk, in a gale of psalms, went heaving through
A tumult of roofs, freighted for heaven. And lovers
    Unblessed by steeples, lay under
    The buttered bannock of the moon.

He quenched his lantern, leaving the last door.
Because of his gay poverty that kept
    My seapink innocence
    From the worm and black wind;

And because, under equality's sun,
All things wear now to a common soiling,
    In the fire of images
    Gladly I put my hand
    To save that day for him.

GEORGE MACKAY BROWN

He'll Have to Go

I'm waiting in an empty restaurant
dressed up to the nines, but I might
be invisible or wearing another's face.
It feels later than it really is, and darker.

A cold, dark place. Our meeting-place
where you are always absent without apology.
That night I bought myself an hour's grace.
I've been paying for it ever since.

The food is cold. The plates are cracked.
Somewhere, a record I didn't ask for
begins to play. I am somewhere else.
You are at home, still sitting in that chair,

lost in your music while I search everywhere.
Four Walls. He'll Have to Go.
Father, I've sent all the boys away, and still
you won't come back to me.

TRACEY HERD

Hermless

Wi' my hand on my hert
And my hert in my mooth
Wi' erms that could reach ower the sea
My feet micht be big, but the insects are safe
They'll never get stood on by me

Hermless, hermless there's never nae bather fae me
I ging tae the lehbry, I tak oot a book
And then I go hame for my tea

I save a' the coupons that come wi' the soup
And when I have saved fufty three
I send awa fufty, pit three in the drar
And something gets posted to me

Hermless, hermless there's never nae bather fae me
I dae what I'm telt and I tidy my room
And then I come doon for my tea

There's ane or twa lads wha' I could cry my chums
They're canny and meek as can be
There's Tam wi' his pigeons
And Wull wi' his mice
And Robert McLennan and me

Hermless, hermless there's never nae bather fae me
Naebody'd notice that I wasnae there
If I didnae come hame for my tea

MICHAEL MARRA

The High Path

     let's take the high path
that clings to the cliff edge
     through the ripe barley
past the corn marigolds
taking up this and that
     dropping this or that

like a rag or a flag
     space flaps in the wind
fluttering and settling
     between scabious
     and knapweed the sea
flutters lightly away

     trust the tangled path
the sea at your elbow
     it will lead you through
complex information
meadow-grass and bent-grass
     to a fine sea view

in among the grasses
     are the manifold
spaces little places
     where intention is
     no longer gathered
but ramified dispersed

     pale comfrey flowers
linger in green spaces
     in the tall bracken
as if such places were
formed by bracken for
     pale comfrey flowers

melancholy thistle
     rest harrow, milk vetch
climb through the long grasses
     to add at random

a touch of colour
to the drift of colours

the waves are dancing
and the light bounces back
into a larger
atmosphere or climate
that you move in gladly
in receipt of light

over the tall grasses
the blue sky stretches
an unimpeded blue
you can lie back in
crushed grasses and let
your head fill up with blue

swallows swooping low
over the ripe barley
respond as keenly
to the intelligence
as barley to the least
rumour of a breeze

barley combed by the wind
ripples with warm light
as if the light were not
given but contained
given out when combed
by the light-seeking wind

the waves of barley
the ripples of the sea
flow in or out from
your feet as you pass through
the ripples of barley
the waves of the sea

as a hawthorn will show
the prevailing wind
in a motionless gust

of whipped-back branches
    you take the shape of
what you know let it go

THOMAS A. CLARK

The Highland Laird's Song

I have a very large estate,
    All for me, all for me;
My cares are small, my wealth is great,
    All for me, all for me.
Once other people shared my land,
And rented holdings far from grand;
But I have made them understand
    It's all for me, all for me.

The common people I do not
    Like to see, like to see;
A vulgar village is a blot
    On propertie, propertie.
Although they say their homes are dear,
I'll have no vulgar peasants here;
I'll keep my land for sheep and deer,
    All for me, all for me.

The dirty creatures now complain,
    Blaming me, blaming me;
They say, 'We're anxious to remain,
    Let us be, let us be.'
I'll harass them by night and day
Until I drive them all away,
Upon my land not one shall stay,
    It's all for me, all for me.

MARION BERNSTEIN

The Hint o' Hairst

It's dowie in the hint o' hairst,
At the wa-gang o' the swallow,
When the wind grows cauld, and the burns grow bauld,
And the wuds are hingin' yellow;
But oh, it's dowier far to see
The wa-gang o' her the hert gangs wi',
The deid-set o' a shinin' e'e –
That darkens the weary world on thee.

There was mickle love atween us twa –
Oh, twa could ne'er been fonder;
And the thing on yird was never made,
That could ha'e gart us sunder.
But the way of Heaven's abune a' ken,
And we maun bear what it likes to sen' –
It's comfort, though, to weary men,
That the warst o' this warld's waes maun en'.

There's mony things that come and gae,
Just kent, and syne forgotten;
And the flowers that busk a bonnie brae,
Gin anither year lie rotten.
But the last look o' that lovely e'e,
And the dying grip she ga'e to me,
They're settled like eternitie –
Oh, Mary! that I were wi' thee.

HEW AINSLIE

History

St Andrews: West Sands; September 2001

Today
        As we flew the kites
– the sand spinning off in ribbons along the beach
and that gasoline smell from Leuchars gusting across
the golf links;

236

               the tide far out
and quail-grey in the distance;
                              people
jogging, or stopping to watch
as the war planes cambered and turned
in the morning light –

today
        – with the news in my mind, and the muffled dread
of what may come –
                        I knelt down in the sand
with Lucas
            gathering shells
and pebbles
                finding evidence of life in all this
driftwork:
            snail shells; shreds of razorfish;
smudges of weed and flesh on tideworn stone.

At times I think what makes us who we are
is neither kinship nor our given states
but something lost between the world we own
and what we dream about behind the names
on days like this
                        our lines raised in the wind
our bodies fixed and anchored to the shore

and though we are confined by property
what tethers us to gravity and light
has most to do with distance and the shapes
we find in water
                    reading from the book
of silt and tides:
                    the rose or petrol blue
of jellyfish and sea anemone
combining with a child's
first nakedness.

Sometimes I am dizzy with the fear
of losing everything – the sea, the sky,
all living creatures, forests, estuaries:

we trade so much to know the virtual
we scarcely register the drift and tug
of other bodies
                    scarcely apprehend
the moment as it happens: shifts of light
and weather
                    and the quiet, local forms
of history: the fish lodged in the tide
beyond the sands;
                    the long insomnia
of ornamental carp in public parks
captive and bright
                    and hung in their own
slow-burning
                    transitive gold;
                                jamjars of spawn
and sticklebacks
                        or goldfish carried home
from fairgrounds
                    to the hum of radio;
but this is the problem: how to be alive
in all this gazed-upon and cherished world
and do no harm

                        a toddler on a beach
sifting wood and dried weed from the sand
and puzzled by the pattern on a shell

his parents on the dune slacks with a kite
plugged into the sky
                        all nerve and line:
patient; afraid; but still, through everything
attentive to the irredeemable.

JOHN BURNSIDE

Holy Willie's Prayer

O Thou, who in the heavens does dwell,
Who, as it pleases best Thysel',

Sends ane to heaven an' ten to hell,
A' for Thy glory,
And no for ony gude or ill
They've done afore Thee!

I bless and praise Thy matchless might,
When thousands Thou hast left in night,
That I am here afore Thy sight,
For gifts an' grace
A burning and a shining light
To a' this place.

What was I, or my generation,
That I should get sic exaltation,
I wha deserve most just damnation
For broken laws,
Five thousand years ere my creation,
Thro' Adam's cause?

When frae my mither's womb I fell,
Thou might hae plunged me in hell,
To gnash my gums, to weep and wail,
In burnin lakes,
Where damned devils roar and yell,
Chain'd to their stakes.

Yet I am here a chosen sample,
To show thy grace is great and ample;
I'm here a pillar o' Thy temple,
Strong as a rock,
A guide, a buckler, and example,
To a' Thy flock.

O Lord, Thou kens what zeal I bear,
When drinkers drink, an' swearers swear,
An' singin there, an' dancin here,
Wi' great and sma';
For I am keepit by Thy fear
Free frae them a'.

But yet, O Lord! confess I must,
At times I'm fash'd wi' fleshly lust:
An' sometimes, too, in wardly trust,
Vile self gets in:
But Thou remembers we are dust,
Defil'd wi' sin.

O Lord! yestreen, Thou kens, wi' Meg –
Thy pardon I sincerely beg,
O! may't ne'er be a livin plague
To my dishonour,
An' I'll ne'er lift a lawless leg
Again upon her.

Besides, I farther maun avow,
Wi' Leezie's lass, three times I trow –
But Lord, that Friday I was fou,
When I cam near her;
Or else, Thou kens, Thy servant true
Wad never steer her.

Maybe Thou lets this fleshly thorn
Buffet Thy servant e'en and morn,
Lest he owre proud and high shou'd turn,
That he's sae gifted:
If sae, Thy han' maun e'en be borne,
Until Thou lift it.

Lord, bless Thy chosen in this place,
For here Thou hast a chosen race:
But God confound their stubborn face,
An' blast their name,
Wha bring Thy elders to disgrace
An' public shame.

Lord, mind Gaw'n Hamilton's deserts;
He drinks, an' swears, an' plays at cartes,
Yet has sae mony takin arts,
Wi' great and sma',
Frae God's ain priest the people's hearts
He steals awa.

An' when we chasten'd him therefor,
Thou kens how he bred sic a splore,
An' set the warld in a roar
O' laughing at us; —
Curse Thou his basket and his store,
Kail an' potatoes.

Lord, hear my earnest cry and pray'r,
Against that Presbyt'ry o' Ayr;
Thy strong right hand, Lord, make it bare
Upo' their heads;
Lord visit them, an' dinna spare,
For their misdeeds.

O Lord, my God! that glib-tongu'd Aiken,
My vera heart and flesh are quakin,
To think how we stood sweatin', shakin,
An' piss'd wi' dread,
While he, wi' hingin lip an' snakin,
Held up his head.

Lord, in Thy day o' vengeance try him,
Lord, visit them wha did employ him,
And pass not in Thy mercy by 'em,
Nor hear their pray'r,
But for Thy people's sake, destroy 'em,
An' dinna spare.

But, Lord, remember me an' mine
Wi' mercies temp'ral an' divine,
That I for grace an' gear may shine,
Excell'd by nane,
And a' the glory shall be thine,
Amen, Amen!

ROBERT BURNS

Horses

Those lumbering horses in the steady plough,
On the bare field – I wonder, why, just now,
They seemed terrible, so wild and strange,
Like magic power on the stony grange.

Perhaps some childish hour has come again,
When I watched fearful, through the blackening rain,
Their hooves like pistons in an ancient mill
Move up and down, yet seem as standing still.

Their conquering hooves which trod the stubble down
Were ritual that turned the field to brown,
And their great hulks were seraphims of,
Or mute ecstatic monsters on the mould.

And oh the rapture, when, one furrow done,
They marched broad-breasted to the sinking sun!
The light flowed off their bossy sides in flakes;
The furrows rolled behind like struggling snakes.

But when at dusk with steaming nostrils home
They came, they seemed gigantic in the gloam,
And warm and glowing with mysterious fire
That lit their smouldering bodies in the mire.

Their eyes as brilliant and as wide as night
Gleamed with a cruel apocalyptic light,
Their manes the leaping ire of the wind
Lifted with rage invisible and blind.

Ah, now it fades! It fades! And I must pine
Again for the dread country crystalline,
Where the blank field and the still-standing tree
Were bright and fearful presences to me.

EDWIN MUIR

The House of the Hare

At the time I was four years old
I went to glean with the women,
Working the way they told;
My eyes were blue like blue-bells,
Lighter than oats my hair;
I came from the house of the Haldanes
Of work and thinking and prayer
To the God who is crowned with thorn,
The friend of the Boar and the Bear,
But oh when I went from there,
In the corn, in the corn, in the corn,
I was married young to a hare!

We went to kirk on the Sunday
And the Haldanes did not see
That a Haldane had been born
To run from the Boar and the Bear,
And the thing had happened to me
The day that I went with the gleaners,
The day that I built the corn-house,
That is not built with prayer
For oh I was clean set free
In the corn, in the corn, in the corn,
I had lived three days with the hare!

NAOMI MITCHISON

Hydrodamalis Gigas

after G. W. Steller

These beasts are four fathoms long, but perfectly gentle.
They roam the shallower waters like sea-cattle

and graze on the waving flags of kelp.
At the slightest wound their innards will flop

out with a great hissing sound,
but they haven't yet grown to fear mankind:

no matter how many of their number might be killed,
they never try to swim away – they are so mild.

When one is speared, its neighbours will rush in
and struggle to draw out the harpoon

with the blades of their little hooves.
They almost seem to have a grasp of what it is to love.

I once watched a bull return to its butchered
mate two days in a row, butting its flensed hide

and calling out quietly across the shingle till the darkness fell.
The flesh on the small calves tastes as sweet as veal

and their fat is pleasantly coloured,
like the best Dutch butter.

The females are furnished with long, black teats.
Try brushing them with your fingertips

then note what happens next – even on the dead
they will grow firm and the sweet milk bleed.

JOHN GLENDAY

I Leave This at Your Ear

For Nessie Dunsmuir

I leave this at your ear for when you wake,
A creature in its abstract cage asleep.
Your dreams blindfold you by the light they make.

The owl called from the naked-woman tree
As I came down by the Kyle farm to hear
Your house silent by the speaking sea.

I have come late but I have come before
Later with slaked steps from stone to stone
To hope to find you listening for the door.

I stand in the ticking room. My dear, I take
A moth kiss from your breath. The shore gulls cry.
I leave this at your ear for when you wake.

W. S. GRAHAM

Imph-m

When I was a laddie langsyne at the schule,
The maister aye ca'd me a dunce and a fule;
For somehow his words I could ne'er understan'
Unless when he bawl'd, 'Jamie, haud oot yer han'!'
Then I gloom'd and said 'Imph-m' –
I glaunch'd and said 'Imph-m',
I wasna owre proud, but owre dour to say – Aye!

Ae day a queer word, as lang nebbit's himsel',
He vow'd he would thrash me if I widna spell.
Quo' I, 'Maister Quill,' wi' a kin o' a swither,
'I'll spell ye the word if ye'll spell me anither:
Let's hear ye spell "Imph-m",
That common word "Imph-m",
That auld Scotch word "Imph-m", ye ken it means – Aye!'

Had ye seen hoo he glower'd, hoo he scratched his big pate,
An' shouted, 'Ye villain, get oot o' my gate!
Get aff to yer seat, ye're the plague o' the schule!
The deil o' me kens if ye're maist rogue or fule!'
But I only said 'Imph-m',
That pawkie word Imph-m,
He couldna spell 'Imph-m', that stan's for an – Aye!

An' when a brisk wooer, I courted my Jean –
O Avon's braw lasses the pride an' the Queen –
When 'neath my grey plaidie wi' heart beatin' fain,
I speired in a whisper if she'd be my ain,
She blushed and said 'Imph-m',
That charming word 'Imph-m',
A thousan' times better and sweeter than – Aye!

Jist ae thing I wanted my bliss to complete,
A kiss frae her rosy mou', couthie an' sweet;
But a shake o' the heid was her only reply –
Of course that said no, but I kent she meant Aye,
For her sly een said 'Imph-m',
Her red lips said 'Imph-m',
Her hale face said 'Imph-m', and 'Imph-m' means – Aye!

And noo I'm a dad wi' a hoose o' my ain –
A dainty bit wifie, an mair than ae wean;
But the warst o't is this – whan a question I speir,
They put on a look sae auld-farran' an' queer,
But only say 'Imph-m',
That daft-like word 'Imph-m',
That vulgar word 'Imph-m' – they winna say – Aye!

Ye've heard hoo the deil, as he wauchel'd through Beith,
Wi' a wife in ilk oxter and ane in his teeth,
When someone cried oot, 'Will ye tak' mine the morn?'
He wagged his auld tail while he cockit his horn,
But only said 'Imph-m'!
That useful word 'Imph-m',
Wi' sic' a big mouthfu' he couldna say – Aye!

Sae I've gi'en owre the 'Imph-m' – it's no a nice word;
When printed on paper it's perfect absurd;
Sae if ye're owre lazy to open yer jaw,
Just haud ye yer tongue, and say naething ava;
But never say 'Imph-m',
That daft-like word 'Imph-m' –
It's ten times mair vulgar than even braid – Aye!

JAMES NICHOLSON

In Glenskenno Woods

Under an arch o' bramble
Saftly she goes,
Dark broon een like velvet,
Cheeks like the rose.

Ae lang branch o' the bramble
Dips ere she pass,
Tethers wi' thorns the hair
O' the little lass.

Ripe black fruit, an' blossom
White on the spray,
Leaves o' russet an' crimson,
What wad ye say?

What wad ye say to the bairn
That ye catch her snood,
Haudin' her there i' the hush
O' Glenskenno Wood?

What wad ye say? The autumn
O' life draws near.
Still she waits, an' listens,
But canna hear.

HELEN CRUICKSHANK

In My Country

walking by the waters,
down where an honest river
shakes hands with the sea,
a woman passed round me
in a slow, watchful circle,
as if I were a superstition;

or the worst dregs of her imagination,
so when she finally spoke
her words spliced into bars
of an old wheel. A segment of air.
Where do you come from?
'Here,' I said. 'Here. These parts.'

JACKIE KAY

In Orknay

Upon the utmost corners of the warld,
And on the borders of this massive round,
Where fate and fortune hither has me harled
I do deplore my griefs upon this ground;
And seeing roaring seas from rocks rebound
By ebbs and streams of contrar routing tydes,
And Phoebus' chariot in their waves lie drown'd
Wha equally now night and day divides,
I call to mind the storms my thoghts abydes,
Which ever wax and never dois decrease,
For nights of dole day's joys ay ever hides,
And in their vayle doith all my weill suppress:
So this I see, wherever I remove,
I change bot seas, bot cannot change my love.

WILLIAM FOWLER

Is Mairg dá nGalar an Grádh

Is mairg dá ngalar an grádh,
gé bé fáth fá n-abrainn é;
deacair sgarachtainn ré pháirt;
truagh an cás i bhfeilim féin.

An grádh-soin tugas gan fhios,
ó's é mo leas gan a luadh,
mara bhfhaigh mé furtacht tráth,
biaidh ma bhláth go tana truagh.

An fear-soin dá dtugas grádh,
's nach féadtar a rádh ós n-aird,
dá gcuireadh sé mise i bpéin,
gomadh dó féin bhus céad mairg.

Mairg.

ISEABAIL NÍ MHEIC CAILEÍN

248

Pity One for whom Love Is a Sickness

Pity one for whom love is a sickness –
no matter what reasons I give
it's hard to escape from its hold:
I'm in a sorry state.

That love I gave without telling,
since it was better not to declare;
unless I find comfort soon
my bloom will wither and fade.

That man to whom I gave love
(and this shouldn't be said aloud),
if he ever causes me pain,
may he suffer it hundredfold.

Pity.

Trans. Peter Mackay

ISEABAIL NÍ MHEIC CAILÉIN

Is Trom Leam an Àirigh

Is trom leam an àirigh 's a' ghàir seo a th' innt'
Gun a' phàirtinn a dh'fhàg mi bhith 'n-dràst' air mo chinn –
Anna chaol-mhalach chìoch-chorrach shlìob-cheannach chruinn
Is Iseabail a' bheòil mhilis, mhànranaich bhinn.
Heich! Mar a bhà air mo chinn,
A dh'fhàg mi cho cràidhteach 's nach stàth dhomh bhith 'g inns'.

Shiubhail mis' a' bhuaile 's a-suas feadh nan craobh,
'S gach àit' anns am b' àbhaist bhith pàgadh mo ghaoil;
Nuair chunnaic mi 'm fear bàn ud 's e mànran r' a mhnaoi
B' fheàrr leam nach tiginn idir làimh riu', no 'n gaoith –
'S e mar a bhà, air mo chinn,
A dh'fhàg mi cho cràidhteach 's nach stàth dhomh bhith 'g inns'.

On chualas gun gluaiseadh tu uam leis an t-saor
Tha mo shuain air a buaireadh le bruadraichean gaoil,
Den chàirdeas a bhà siud chan fhàir mi bhith saor –
Gun bhàrnaigeadh làimh riut tha 'n gràdh dhomh na mhaor,
Air gach tràth 's mi ann an strì
A' feuchainn r' a àicheadh 's e fàs rium mar chraoibh.

Ach, Anna Bhuidhe nighean Dòmhnaill, nam b' eòl duit mo nì,
'S e do ghràdh gun bhith pàight' leag a-bhàn uam mo chlì;
Tha e dhomh à d' fhianais cho gnìomhach 's nuair chì,
A' diogalladh 's a' smùsach gur ciùrrtach mo chrìdh –
Nis ma thà mi ga do dhìth
Gum b' fheàirrde mi pàg uait mus fàgainn an tìr.

Ach labhair i gu fàiteagach àilgheasach rium:
'Chan fhàir thu bhith làimh rium do chàradh mo chinn –
Tha sianar gam iarraidh o bhliadhna de thìm
'S cha b' àraidh le càch thu thoirt bàrr os an cinn.
Ha ha hà! An d' fhàs thu gu tinn?
'N e 'n gaol-s' a bheir bàs ort? Gum pàigh thu d' a chinn!'

Ach cionnas bheir mi fuath dhuit ged dh'fhuaraich thu rium?
Nuair as feargaich' mo sheanchas mu d' ainm air do chùl,
Thig d' ìomhaigh le h-annsachd na samhladh nam ùidh:
Saoilidh mi 'n sin gun dèan an gaol sin an tùrn
'S thèid air a ràdh gu h-às ùr –
Is fàsaidh e 'n tràth sin cho àrda ri tùr.

ROB DONN MACAOIDH

I'm Depressed by the Sheiling

I'm depressed by the sheiling and the laughing inside,
The party I've left still troubles my mind:
Anna with the sleek hair, pert breasts, round behind,
Isobel, sweet-talking, whispering, refined.
Aich! The state of my mind –
I'm not cured by talking, I'm aching inside.

I wandered the paddock and up through the trees
To all of the places we'd go on a spree,
Overheard a blonde bloke and his wife's pleasantries;
No wish to be seen, I passed them down-breeze.
That was the state of my mind –
I'm not cured by talking, I was aching inside.

Since I heard the joiner would steal you from me
My sleep's been broken by love-baffled dreams.
Yon affair now means I'll never be free:
Without your summons, love's a bailiff to me.
All day long I'm besieged:
I try to deny it, but it grows like a tree.

You don't know what I'm worth, Donald's daughter, blonde Anne,
The way you snub my love leaves me at your command:
With you absent or present, my heart's flames are fanned,
They tickle and suckle and smart like firebrands.
Without you I'm unmanned,
Yet still dream of a kiss before I leave this land.

But full of disdain, condescending, you said:
'You've no chance of caressing my head.
Six men are fighting to be in your stead
And they're all sure *you* won't get close to my bed.
Ha ha! Are you sick in the head?
You think this love'll kill you? Then you'll end up dead.'

You're cold to me, but still I don't hate you,
And though behind your back I slag and slate you
In my mind there's an affectionate you
And I still think my love could elate you.
It's still true:
My love grows tall as a tower for you.

Trans. Peter Mackay and Iain S. MacPherson

ROB DONN MACKAY

John Anderson My Jo

John Anderson, my jo, John,
When we were first acquent;
Your locks were like the raven,
Your bonie brow was brent;
But now your brow is beld, John,
Your locks are like the snaw;
But blessings on your frosty pow,
John Anderson, my jo.

John Anderson, my jo, John,
We clamb the hill the gither;
And mony a canty day, John,
We've had wi' ane anither:
Now we maun totter down, John,
And hand in hand we'll go,
And sleep the gither at the foot,
John Anderson, my jo.

ROBERT BURNS

Johnie Armstrang

1. Sum speikis of Lords, sum speikis of Lairds,
And sick lyke men of hie degrie;
Of a gentleman I sing a sang,
Sum time called Laird of Gilnockie.

2. The King he wrytes a luving letter,
With his ain hand sae tenderly,
And he hath sent it to Johnie Armstrang,
To cum and speik with him speidily.

3. The Eliots and Armstrangs did convene,
They were a gallant cumpanie –
'We'll ride and meit our lawful King,
And bring him safe to Gilnockie.'

4. 'Make kinnen and capon ready then,
And venison in great plentie,
We'll wellcome here our Royal King,
I hope he'll dine at Gilnockie!'

5. They ran their horse on the Langhome howm,
And brak their speirs wi' mickle main;
The Ladies lukit frae their loft windows —
'God bring our men weel back agen!'

6. When Johnie came before the King,
Wi' a' his men sae brave to see,
The King he movit his bonnet to him,
He ween'd he was a King as well as he.

7. 'May I find grace, my Sovereign Leige,
Grace for my loyal men and me?
For my name it is Johnie Armstrang,
And subject of yours, my Liege,' said he.

8. 'Away, away, thou traitor strang!
Out of my sight soon may'st thou be!
I grantit never a traitor's life,
And now I'll not begin wi' thee.' —

9. 'Grant me my life, my Liege, my King!
And a bonny gift I'll gie to thee —
Full four and twenty milk-white steids,
Were a' foaled in a year to me.

10. 'I'll gie thee a' these milk-white steids,
That prance and nicker at a speir;
And as mickle gude Inglish gilt,
As four of their braid backs dow bear.' —

11. 'Away, away, thou traitor strang!
Out of my sight soon may'st thou be!
I grantit nevir a traitor's life,
And now I'll not begin wi' thee!' —

12. 'Grant me my life, my Liege, my King!
And a bonny gift I'll gie to thee –
Gude four and twenty ganging mills,
That gang thro' a' the year to me.

13. 'These four and twenty mills complete,
Shall gang for thee thro' a' the yeir;
And as meikle of gude reid wheit,
As a' thair happers dow to bear.' –

14. 'Away, away, thou traitor strang!
Out of my sight sune may'st thou be!
I grantit nevir a traitor's life,
And now I'll not begin wi' thee.' –

15. 'Grant me my life, my Liege, my King!
And a great gift I'll gie to thee –
Bauld four and twenty sister's sons,
Shall for thee ficht, tho' all should flee!'

16. 'Away, away, thou traitor strang!
Out of my sight sune may'st thou be!
I grantit nevir a traitor's life,
And now I'll not begin wi' thee.' –

17. 'Grant me my life, my Liege, my King!
And a brave gift I'll gie to thee –
All between heir and Newcastle town,
Shall pay their yeirly rent to thee.' –

18. 'Away, away, thou traitor strang!
Out of my sight sune may'st thou be!
I grantit nevir a traitor's life,
And now I'll not begin wi' thee.' –

19. 'Ye leid, ye leid, now King,' he says,
Altho' a King and Prince ye be!
For I've luved naething in my life,
I weel dare say it, but honesty –

20. 'Save a fat horse, and a fair woman,
Twa bonny dogs to kill a deir;
But England suld have found me meil and mault,
Gif I had lived this hundred yeir!

21. 'Sche suld have found me meil and mault,
And beif and mutton in all plentie;
But never a Scots wyfe could have said,
That e'er I skaithed her a pure flee.

22. 'To seik het water beneith cauld ice,
Surely it is a greit folie —
I have asked grace at a graceless face,
But there is nane for my men and me!

23. 'But, had I kenn'd ere I cam frae hame,
How thou unkind wadst been to me!
I wad have keepit the Border side,
In spite of all thy force and thee.

24. 'Wist England's King that I was ta'en,
O gin a blythe man he wad be!
For anes I slew his sister's son,
And on his breist bane brake a trie.' —

25. John wore a girdle about his middle,
Imbroidered ower wi' burning gold;
Bespangled wi' the same metal,
Maist beautiful was to behold.

26. There hang nine targats at Johnie's hat,
And ilk ane worth three hundred pound —
'What wants that knave that a King suld have,
But the sword of honour, and the crown?

27. 'O whair gat thou these targats, Johnie,
That blink sae brawly abune thy brie?'
'I gat them in the field fechting,
Where, cruel King, thou durst not be.

28. 'Had I my horse, and harness gude,
And riding as I wont to be,
It suld have been tald this hundred yeir,
The meeting of my King and me!

29. 'God be with thee, Kirsty, my brother,
Lang live thou Laird of Mangertoun;
Lang mayst thou live on the Border syde,
Ere thou see thy brother ride up and down!

30. 'And God be with thee, Kirsty, my son!
Where thou sits on thy nurse's knee;
But and thou live this hundred yeir,
Thy father's better thoul't never be.

31. 'Farewell! my bonny Gilnock-hall,
Where on Eske side thou standest stout!
Gif I had lived but seven years mair,
I wad hae gilt thee round about.'

32. John murdered was at Carlinrigg,
And all his gallant cumpanie;
But Scotland's heart was near sae wae,
To see sae mony brave men die –

33. Because they saved their country deir,
Frae Englishmen! Nane were sae bauld,
Whyle Johnie lived on the Border syde,
Nane of them durst cum near his hauld.

ANON.

Johnny Cope

Cope sent a challenge frae Dunbar,
Sayin 'Charlie meet me an' ye daur;
An' I'll learn ye the art o' war,
If ye'll meet me in the morning.'

Hey! Johnny Cope, are ye a-waukin' yet?
Or are your drums a-beating yet?
If ye were waukin' I wad wait,
Tae gang tae the coals in the morning.

When Charlie looked the letter upon,
He drew his sword the scabbard from
'Come, follow me my merry men,
And we'll meet Johnny Cope in the morning.'

Now Johnny be as good as your word,
Come, let us try baith fire and sword,
And dinna flee like a frichted bird,
That's chased frae its nest i' the morning.

When Johnny Cope he heard o' this,
He thocht it wouldna be amiss,
Tae hae a horse in readiness,
Tae flee awa in the morning.

Fye now, Johnny, get up an' rin,
The Highland bagpipes mak' a din,
It's better tae sleep in a hale skin,
For it will be a bluidie morning.

When Johnny Cope tae Dunbar cam,
They speired at him, 'Where's a' your men?'
'The de'il confound me gin I ken,
For I left them a' in the morning.'

Now Johnny, troth ye werena blate,
Tae come wi' news o' your ain defeat,
And leave your men in sic a strait,
Sae early in the morning.

In faith, quo Johnny, I got sic flegs
Wi' their claymores an' philabegs,
Gin I face them again, de'il brak my legs,
So I wish you a' good morning.

ADAM SKIRVING

King Worm

What care I for kirk or state?
What care I for war's alarm?
A' are beggars at my yett:
I am King Worm.

Aye a getherin girst I get;
A lippen hairst at time o' hairm:
Want and wastrey mak me fat:
I am King Worm.

The hale world is my heapit plate,
And death the flunkey at my airm:
Wha sae merry owre his meat?
I am King Worm.

WILLIAM SOUTAR

The Laird o' Cockpen

The laird o' Cockpen, he's proud an' he's great,
His mind is ta'en up wi' the things o' the State;
He wanted a wife, his braw house to keep,
But favour wi' wooin' was fashious to seek.

Down by the dyke-side a lady did dwell,
At his table head he thocht she'd look well,
M'Leish's ae dochter o' Clavers-ha' Lea,
A penniless lass wi' a lang pedigree.

His wig was weel pouther'd and as gude as new,
His waistcoat was white, his coat it was blue;
He put on a ring, a sword, and cock'd hat,
And wha could refuse the laird wi' a' that?

He took the grey mare, and rade cannily,
And rapp'd at the yett o' Clavers-ha' Lea;
'Gae tell Mistress Jean to come speedily ben, –
She's wanted to speak to the laird o' Cockpen.'

Mistress Jean she was makin' the elderflower wine;
'An' what brings the laird at sic a like time?'
She put aff her apron, and on her silk goun,
Her mutch wi' red ribbons, and gaed awa' doun.

An' when she cam' ben, he bowed fu' low,
An' what was his errand he soon let her know;
Amazed was the laird when the lady said 'Na',
And wi' a laigh curtsie she turned awa'.

Dumfounder'd was he, nae sigh did he gie,
He mounted his mare – he rade cannily;
An' aften he thought, as he gaed through the glen,
She's daft to refuse the laird o' Cockpen.

CAROLINA OLIPHANT (LADY NAIRNE)

Lament for the Graham

Quhen thai him fand, and gud Wallace him saw,
He lychtyt doun, and hynt him fra thaim aw
In armys up; behaldand his paill face,
He kyssyt him, and cryt full oft; 'Allace!
My best brothir in warld that evir I had!
My a fald freynd quhen I was hardest stad!
My hop, my heill, thou was in maist honour!
My faith, my help, strenthiast in stour!
In thee was wit, fredom, and hardines;
In thee was treuth, manheid, and nobilnes;
In thee was rewll, in thee was governans;
In thee was vertu with outyn varians;
In thee lawte, in thee was gret largnas;
In thee gentrice, in thee was stedfastnas.
Thou was gret caus off wynnyng off Scotland;
Thocht I began, and tuk the wer on hand.
I vow to God, that has the warld in wauld,
Thy dede sall be to Sotheroun full der sauld.
Martyr thou art for Scotlandis rycht and me;
I sall thee venge, or ellis tharfor to die.'

BLIND HARRY

Lament for the Makaris

'Quhen He Wes Sek'

I that in heill west and gladnes,
Am trublit now with gret seiknes,
And feblit wit infermite;
    Timor mortis conturbat me.

Our plesance heir is all vane glory,
This fals warld is bot transitory,
The flesche is brukle, the Fend is sle;
    Timor mortis conturbat me.

The stait of man dois change and vary,
Now sound, now seik, now blith, now sary
Now dansand mery, now like to dee;
    Timor mortis conturbat me.

No stait in erd heir standis sickir;
As with the wynd wavis the wickir,
Wavis this warldis vanite;
    Timor mortis conturbat me.

On to the ded gois Estatis,
Princis, Prelotis, and Potestatis,
Baith riche and pur of al degre;
    Timor mortis conturbat me.

He takis the knychtis in to feild,
Anarmit under helme and scheild;
Victour he is at all mellie;
    Timor mortis conturbat me.

That strang unmercifull tyrand
Takis, on the moderis breist sowkand,
The bab full of benignite;
    Timor mortis conturbat me.

He takis the campion in the stour,
The capitane closit in the tour,
The lady in bour full of bewte;
    Timor mortis conturbat me.

He sparis no lord for his piscence,
Na clerk for his intelligence;
His awfull strak may no man fle;
    Timor mortis conturbat me.

Art, magicianis, and astrologgis,
Rethoris, logicianis, and theologgis,
Thame helpis no conclusionis sle;
    Timor mortis conturbat me.

In medicyne the most practicianis,
Lechis, surrigianis, and phisicianis,
Thame self fra ded may not supple;
    Timor mortis conturbat me.

I se that makaris amang the laif
Playis heir ther pageant, syne gois to graif;
Sparit is nocht ther faculte;
    Timor mortis conturbat me.

He hes done petuously devour,
The noble Chaucer, of makaris flour,
The Monk of Bery, and Gower, all thre
    Timor mortis conturbat me.

The gude Syr Hew of Elgintoun,
And eik Heryot, and Wyntoun,
He hes tane out of this cuntre;
    Timor mortis conturbat me.

That scorpion fell hes done infek
Maister Johne Clerk, and James Afflek,
Fra balat making and tragidie;
    Timor mortis conturbat me.

Holland and Barbour he hes breavit;
Allace! that he nocht with us levit
Schir Mungo Lokert of the Le;
    Timor mortis conturbat me.

Clerk of Tranent eik he hes tane,
That maid the Anteris of Gawane;
Schir Gilbert Hay endit hes he;
    Timor mortis conturbat me.

He hes Blind Hary and Sandy Traill
Slaine with his schour of mortall haill,
Quhilk Patrik Johnestoun mycht nocht fle
    Timor mortis conturbat me.

He hes reft Merseir his endite,
That did in luf so lifly write,
So schort, so quyk, of sentence hie;
    Timor mortis conturbat me.

He hes tane Roull of Aberdene,
And gentill Roull of Corstorphin;
Two bettir fallowis did no man se;
    Timor mortis conturbat me.

In Dumfermeleyne he hes done roune
With Maister Robert Henrisoun;
Schir Johne the Ros enbrast hes he;
    Timor mortis conturbat me.

And he hes now tane, last of aw,
Gud gentill Stobo and Quintyne Schaw,
Of quham all wichtis hes pete;
    Timor mortis conturbat me.

Gud Maister Walter Kennedy
In poynt of dede lyis veraly,
Gret reuth it wer that so suld be;
    Timor mortis conturbat me.

Sen he hes all my brether tane,
He will nocht lat me lif alane,
On forse I man his nyxt pray be;
    Timor mortis conturbat me.

Sen for the deid remeid is none,
Best is that we for dede dispone,
Eftir our deid that lif may we;
    Timor mortis conturbat me.

WILLIAM DUNBAR

Lammermoor

O wild and stormy Lammermoor!
Would I could feel once more
The cold north-wind, the wintry blast,
That sweeps thy mountains o'er.
Would I could see thy drifted snow
Deep, deep in cleuch and glen,
And hear the scream of the wild birds,
And was free on thy hills again!

I hate this dreary southern land,
I weary day by day
For the music of thy many streams
In the birchwoods far away!
From all I love they banish me,
But my thoughts they cannot chain;
And they bear me back, wild Lammermoor!
To thy distant hills again!

LADY JOHN SCOTT (ALICIA ANN SPOTTISWOODE)

The Land o' the Leal

I'm wearin' awa', John,
Like snaw-wreaths in thaw, John,
I'm wearin' awa'

To the land o' the leal.
There's nae sorrow there, John,
There's neither cauld nor care, John,
The day is aye fair
    In the land o' the leal.

Our bonnie bairn's there, John,
She was baith gude and fair, John,
And oh! we grudged her sair
    To the land o' the leal.
But sorrow's sel' wears past, John,
And joy is comin' fast, John,
The joy that's aye to last
    In the land o' the leal.

Sae dear's the joy was bought, John,
Sae free the battle fought, John,
That sinfu' man e'er brought
    To the land o' the leal.
O, dry your glist'nin' e'e, John,
My saul langs to be free, John,
And angels beckon me
    To the land o' the leal.

O, haud ye leal an' true, John,
Your day it's wearin' thro', John,
And I'll welcome you
    To the land o' the leal.
Now fare ye weel, my ain John,
This warld's cares are vain, John,
We'll meet, and we'll be fain,
    In the land o' the leal.

CAROLINA OLIPHANT (LADY NAIRNE)

The Last Rose

'O which is the last rose?'
A blossom of no name.
At midnight the snow came;

264

At daybreak a vast rose,
In darkness unfurl'd,
O'er-petall'd the world.

Its odourless pallor
Blossom'd forlorn,
Till radiant valour
Establish'd the morn —
Till the night
Was undone
In her fight
With the sun.

The brave orb in state rose,
And crimson he shone first;
While from the high vine
Of heaven the dawn burst,
Staining the great rose
From sky-line to sky-line.

The red rose of morn
A white rose at noon turn'd;
But at sunset reborn
All red again soon burn'd.
Then the pale rose of noonday
Rebloom'd in the night,
And spectrally white
        In the light
Of the moon lay.

But the vast rose
        Was scentless,
And this is the reason:
When the blast rose
        Relentless,
And brought in due season
The snow rose, the last rose
Congeal'd in its breath,
Then came with it treason;
The traitor was Death.

In lee-valleys crowded,
The sheep and the birds
Were frozen and shrouded
In flights and in herds.
In highways
And byways
The young and the old
Were tortured and madden'd
And kill'd by the cold.
But many were gladden'd
By the beautiful last rose,
The blossom of no name
That came when the snow came,
In darkness unfurl'd –
The wonderful vast rose
That fill'd all the world.

JOHN DAVIDSON

The Last Sark

Gude guide me, are you hame again, an' ha'e ye got nae wark?
We've naething noo tae put awa' unless yer auld blue sark;
My head is rinnin' roon about far lichter than a flee –
What care some gentry if they're weel though a' the puir wad dee!

Our merchants an' mill masters they wad never want a meal,
Though a' the banks in Scotland wad for a twelve month fail;
For some o' them have far mair goud than ony ane can see –
What care some gentry if they're weel though a' the puir wad dee!

This is a funny warld, John, for it's no divided fair,
And while I think some o' the rich have got the puir folk's share,
Tae see us starving here the nicht wi' no ae bless'd bawbee –
What care some gentry if they're weel though a' the puir wad dee!

Oor hoose ance bean an' cosey, John; oor beds ance snug an warm
Feels unco cauld an' dismal noo, an' empty as a barn;
The weans sit greeting in oor face, and we ha'e noucht to gie –
What care some gentry if they're weel though a' the puir wad dee!

It is the puir man's hard-won toil that fills the rich man's purse;
I'm sure his gouden coffers they are het wi' mony a curse;
Were it no for the working men what wad the rich men be?
What care some gentry if they're weel though a' the puir wad dee!

My head is licht, my heart is weak, my een are growing blin';
The bairn is faen' aff my knee – oh! John, catch haud o' him,
You ken I hinna tasted meat for days far mair than three;
Were it no for my helpless bairns I wadna care to dee.

ELLEN JOHNSTON

From The Lay of the Last Minstrel

Canto VI

I

Breathes there the man, with soul so dead,
Who never to himself hath said,
This is my own, my native land!
Whose heart hath ne'er within him burn'd
As home his footsteps he hath turn'd,
From wandering on a foreign strand!
If such there breathe, go, mark him well;
For him no Minstrel raptures swell;
High though his titles, proud his name,
Boundless his wealth as wish can claim;
Despite those titles, power, and pelf,
The wretch, concentred all in self,
Living, shall forfeit fair renown,
And, doubly dying, shall go down
To the vile dust, from whence he sprung,
Unwept, unhonor'd, and unsung.

II

O Caledonia! Stern and wild,
Meet nurse for a poetic child!
Land of brown heath and shaggy wood,

Land of the mountain and the flood,
Land of my sires! What mortal hand
Can e'er untie the filial band
That knits me to thy rugged strand!

SIR WALTER SCOTT

Let Us All Be Unhappy on Sunday

A Lyric for Saturday Night

We zealots, made up of stiff clay,
The sour-looking children of sorrow,
While not over-jolly today,
Resolve to be wretched tomorrow.
We can't for a certainty tell
What mirth may molest us on Monday;
But, at least, to begin the week well,
Let us all be unhappy on Sunday.

That day, the calm season of rest,
Shall come to us freezing and frigid;
A gloom all our thoughts shall invest,
Such as Calvin would call over-rigid,
With sermons from morning to night,
We'll strive to be decent and dreary:
To preachers a praise and delight,
Who ne'er think that sermons can weary . . .

All tradesmen cry up their own wares;
In this they agree well together:
The Mason by stone and lime swears;
The Tanner is always for leather.
The Smith still for iron would go;
The Schoolmaster stands up for teaching;
And the Parson would have you to know,
There's nothing on earth like his preaching.

The face of kind Nature is fair;
But our system obscures its effulgence:

How sweet is a breath of fresh air!
But our rules don't allow the indulgence.
These gardens, their walks and green bowers,
Might be free to the poor man for one day;
But no, the glad plants and gay flowers
Mustn't bloom or smell sweetly on Sunday.

What though a good precept we strain
Till hateful and hurtful we make it!
What though, in thus pulling the rein,
We may draw it as tight as to break it!
Abroad we forbid folks to roam,
For fear they get social or frisky;
But of course they can sit still at home,
And get dismally drunk upon whisky.

Then, though we can't certainly tell
How mirth may molest us on Monday;
At least, to begin the week well,
Let us all be unhappy on Sunday.

CHARLES, LORD NEAVES

Liberty Preserved: or, Love Destroyed

At length the Bondage I have broke
Which gave me so much Pain;
I've slipt my Heart out of the Yoke,
Never to drudge again;
And, conscious of my long Disgrace,
Have thrown my Chain at Cupid's Face.

If ever he attempt again
My freedom to enslave,
I'll court the Godhead of Champain
Which makes the Coward brave,
And, when the Deity has heal'd my Soul,
I'll drown the little Bastard in my Bowl.

ALEXANDER ROBERTSON, 13TH DONNACHAIDH CHIEF

The Life and Death of Habbie Simson, the Piper of Kilbarchan

Kilbarchan now may say alas!
For she hath lost her game and grace,
Both *Trixie* and *The Maiden Trace*;
    But what remead?
For no man can supply his place:
    Hab Simson's dead.

Now who shall play *The Day it Dawis*,
Or *Hunt's Up*, when the cock he craws?
Or who can for our kirk-town cause
    Stand us in stead?
On bagpipes now nobody blaws
    Sen Habbie's dead.

Or wha will cause our shearers shear?
Wha will bend up the brags of weir,
Bring in the bells, or good play-meir
    In time of need?
Hab Simson cou'd, what needs you speir?
    But now he's dead.

So kindly to his neighbours neast
At Beltan and St. Barchan's feast
He blew, and then held up his breast,
    As he we weid:
But now we need not him arrest,
    For Habbie's dead.

At fairs he play'd before the spear-men
All gaily graithed in their gear men:
Steel bonnets, jacks, and swords so clear then
    Like any bead:
Now wha shall play before such weir-men
    Sen Habbie's dead?

At clark-plays when he wont to come
His Pipe play'd trimly to the drum;
Like bikes of bees he gart it bum,
    And tun'd his reed:

270

Now all our pipers may sing dumb,
    Sen Habbie's dead.

And at horse races many a day,
Before the black, the brown, the gray,
He gart his pipe, when he did play,
    Baith skirl and skreed:
Now all such pastime's quite away
    Sen Habbie's dead.

He counted was a weil'd wight-man,
And fiercely at football he ran:
At every game the gree he wan
    For pith and speed.
The like of Habbie was na than,
    But now he's dead.

And than, besides his valiant acts,
At bridals he won many placks;
He bobbed ay behind fo'k's backs
    And shook his head.
Now we want many merry cracks
    Sen Habbie's dead.

He was convoyer of the bride,
With Kittock hinging at his side;
About the kirk he thought a pride
    The ring to lead:
But now we may gae but a guide,
    For Habbie's dead.

So well's he keeped his decorum
And all the stots of *Whip-meg-morum*;
He slew a man, and wae's me for him,
    And bure the fead!
But yet the man wan hame before him,
    And was not dead.

And whan he play'd, the lasses leugh
To see him teethless, auld, and teugh,
He wan his pipes besides Barcleugh,
    Withouten dread!

Which after wan him gear eneugh;
    But now he's dead.

Ay when he play'd the gaitlings gedder'd,
And when he spake, the carl bledder'd,
On Sabbath days his cap was fedder'd,
    A seemly weid;
In the kirk-yeard his mare stood tedder'd
    Where he lies dead.

Alas! for him my heart is saur,
For of his spring I gat a skair,
At every play, race, feast, and fair,
    But guile or greed;
We need not look for pyping mair,
    Sen Habbie's dead.

ROBERT SEMPILL

Listen. Put on morning

Listen. Put on morning.
Waken into falling light.
A man's imagining
Suddenly may inherit
The handclapping centuries
Of his one minute on earth.
And hear the virgin juries
Talk with his own breath
To the corner boys of his street.
And hear the Black Maria
Searching the town at night.
And hear the playropes caa
The sister Mary in.
And hear Willie and Davie
Among bracken of Narnain
Sing in a mist heavy
With myrtle and listeners.
And hear the higher town
Weep a petition of fears

At the poorhouse close upon
The public heartbeat.
And hear the children tig
And run with my own feet
Into the netting drag
Of a suiciding principle.
Listen. Put on lightbreak.
Waken into miracle.
The audience lies awake
Under the tenements
Under the sugar docks
Under the printed moments.
The centuries turn their locks
And open under the hill
Their inherited books and doors
All gathered to distil
Like happy berry pickers
One voice to talk to us.
Yes listen. It carries away
The second and the years
Till the heart's in a jacket of snow
And the head's in a helmet white
And the song sleeps to be wakened
By the morning ear bright.
Listen. Put on morning.
Waken into falling light.

W. S. GRAHAM

Loch Lomond

By yon bonnie banks and by yon bonnie braes,
Where the sun shines bright on Loch Lomond,
Where me and my true love were ever wont to gae,
On the bonnie, bonnie banks o' Loch Lomond.

O ye'll tak' the high road, and I'll tak' the low road,
And I'll be in Scotland a'fore ye,
But me and my true love will never meet again,
On the bonnie, bonnie banks o' Loch Lomond.

'Twas there that we parted, in yon shady glen,
On the steep, steep side o' Ben Lomond,
Where in soft purple hue, the highland hills we view,
And the moon coming out in the gloaming.

The wee birdies sing and the wildflowers spring,
And in sunshine the waters are sleeping.
But the broken heart it kens nae second spring again,
Though the waeful may cease frae their grieving.

ANON.

Loch Thom

I

Just for the sake of recovering
I walked backward from fifty-six
Quick years of age wanting to see,
And managed not to trip or stumble
To find Loch Thom and turned round
To see the stretch of my childhood
Before me. Here is the loch. The same
Long-beaked cry curls across
The heather-edges of the water held
Between the hills a boyhood's walk
Up from Greenock. It is the morning.

And I am here with my mammy's
Bramble jam scones in my pocket.
The Firth is miles and I have come
Back to find Loch Thom maybe
In this light does not recognise me.

This is a lonely freshwater loch.
No farms on the edge. Only
Heath grouse-moor stretching
Down to Greenock and One Hope
Street or stretching away across
Into the blue moors of Ayrshire.

2

And almost I am back again
Wading in the heather down to the edge
To sit. The minnows go by in shoals
Like iron-filings in the shallows.

My mother is dead. My father is dead
And all the trout I used to know
Leaping from their sad rings are dead.

3

I drop my crumbs into the shallow
Weed for the minnows and pinheads.
You see that I will have to rise
And turn round and get back where
My running age will slow for a moment
To let me on. It is a colder
Stretch of water than I remember.

The curlew's cry travelling still
Kills me fairly. In front of me
The grouse flurry and settle. GOBACK
GOBACK GOBACK FAREWELL LOCH THOM.

W. S. GRAHAM

Lochinvar

O, young Lochinvar is come out of the west,
Through all the wide Border his steed was the best;
And save his good broadsword he weapons had none,
He rode all unarm'd, and he rode all alone.
So faithful in love, and so dauntless in war,
There never was knight like the young Lochinvar.

He staid not for brake, and he stopp'd not for stone,
He swam the Eske river where ford there was none;
But ere he alighted at Netherby gate,

The bride had consented, the gallant came late:
For a laggard in love, and a dastard in war,
Was to wed the fair Ellen of brave Lochinvar.

So boldly he enter'd the Netherby Hall,
Among bride's-men, and kinsmen, and brothers and all:
Then spoke the bride's father, his hand on his sword,
(For the poor craven bridegroom said never a word,)
'O come ye in peace here, or come ye in war,
Or to dance at our bridal, young Lord Lochinvar?'

'I long woo'd your daughter, my suit you denied;—
Love swells like the Solway, but ebbs like its tide—
And now I am come, with this lost love of mine,
To lead but one measure, drink one cup of wine.
There are maidens in Scotland more lovely by far,
That would gladly be bride to the young Lochinvar.'

The bride kiss'd the goblet: the knight took it up,
He quaff'd off the wine, and he threw down the cup.
She look'd down to blush, and she look'd up to sigh,
With a smile on her lips and a tear in her eye.
He took her soft hand, ere her mother could bar,—
'Now tread we a measure!' said young Lochinvar.

So stately his form, and so lovely her face,
That never a hall such a galliard did grace;
While her mother did fret, and her father did fume,
And the bridegroom stood dangling his bonnet and plume;
And the bride-maidens whisper'd, ''twere better by far
To have match'd our fair cousin with young Lochinvar.'

One touch to her hand, and one word in her ear,
When they reach'd the hall-door, and the charger stood near;
So light to the croupe the fair lady he swung,
So light to the saddle before her he sprung!
'She is won! we are gone, over bank, bush, and scaur;
They'll have fleet steeds that follow,' quoth young Lochinvar.

There was mounting 'mong Graemes of the Netherby clan;
Forsters, Fenwicks, and Musgraves, they rode and they ran:

There was racing and chasing on Cannobie Lee,
But the lost bride of Netherby ne'er did they see.
So daring in love, and so dauntless in war,
Have ye e'er heard of gallant like young Lochinvar?

SIR WALTER SCOTT

Lord Randal

'O where ha you been, Lord Randal, my son?
And where ha you been, my handsome young man?'
'I ha been at the greenwood; mother, mak my bed soon
For I'm wearied wi hunting, and fain wad lie down.'

'An what met ye there, Lord Randal, my son?
An wha met you there, my handsome young man?'
'O I met wi my true-love; mother, mak my bed soon,
For I'm wearied wi huntin, an fain wad lie down.'

'And what did she give you, Lord Randal, my son?
And what did she give you, my handsome young man?'
'Eels fried in a pan; mother, mak my bed soon,
For I'm wearied wi huntin, and fain wad lie down.'

'And wha gat your leavins, Lord Randal, my son?
And wha gat your leavins, my handsome young man?'
'My hawks and my hounds; mother, mak my bed soon,
For I'm wearied wi hunting, and fain wad lie down.'

'And what became of them, Lord Randal, my son?
And what became of them, my handsome young man?'
'They stretched their legs out an died; mother, mak my bed soon,
For I'm wearied wi huntin, and fain wad lie down.'

'O I fear you are poisoned, Lord Randal, my son!
I fear you are poisoned, my handsome young man!'
'O yes, I am poisoned; mother, mak my bed soon,
For I'm sick at the heart, and I fain wad lie down.'

'What d'ye leave to your mother, Lord Randal, my son?
What d'ye leave to your mother, my handsome young man?'
'Four and twenty milk kye; mother, mak my bed soon,
For I'm sick at the heart, and I fain wad lie down.'

'What d'ye leave to your sister, Lord Randal, my son?
What d'ye leave to your sister, my handsome young man?'
'My gold and my silver; mother, mak my bed soon,
For I'm sick at the heart, an I fain wad lie down.'

'What d'ye leave to your brother, Lord Randal, my son?
What d'ye leave to your brother, my handsome young man?'
'My houses and my lands; mother, mak my bed soon,
For I'm sick at the heart, and I fain wad lie down.'

'What d'ye leave to your true-love, Lord Randal, my son?
What d'ye leave to your true-love, my handsome young man?'
'I leave her hell and fire; mother, mak my bed soon,
For I'm sick at the heart, and I fain wad lie down.'

ANON.

Love

I hadn't met his kind before.
His misericord face – really,
like a joke on his father – blurred
as if from years of polish;
his hands like curled dry leaves;

the profligate heat he gave
out, gave out, his shallow,
careful breaths: I thought
his filaments would blow,
I thought he was an emperor,

278

dying on silk cushions.
I didn't know how to keep
him wrapped, I didn't know
how to give him suck, I had
no idea about him. At night

I tried to remember the feel
of his head on my neck, the skull
small as a cat's, the soft spot
hot as a smelted coin,
and the hair, the down, fine

as the innermost, vellum layer
of some rare snowcreature's
aureole of fur, if you could meet
such a beast, if you could
get so near. I started there.

KATE CLANCHY

Lucky Spence's Last Advice

Three times the carline grain'd and rifted,
Then frae the cod her pow she lifted,
In bawdy policy well gifted,
When she now fan,
That death nae longer wad be shifted,
She thus began:

My loving lasses, I maun leave ye,
But dinna wi' your greeting grieve me,
Nor wi' your draunts and droning deave me,
But bring 's a gill:
For faith, my bairns, ye may believe me,
'T is 'gainst my will.

O black-ey'd Bess, and mim-mou'd Meg,
O'er good to work, or yet to beg,
Lay sunkets up for a sair leg;
For when ye fail,

279

Ye'r face will not be worth a feg,
Nor yet ye'r tail.

Whane'er ye meet a fool that's fou,
That ye're a maiden gar him trow,
Seem nice, but stick to him like glue;
And when set down,
Drive at the jango till he spew,
Syne he'll sleep sown.

When he's asleep, then dive and catch
His ready cash, his rings, or watch;
And gin he likes to light his match
At your spunk-box,
Ne'er stand to let the fumbling wretch
E'en take the pox.

Cleek a' ye can by hook or crook,
Ryp ilky pouch frae nook to nook;
Be sure to truff his pocket-book;
Saxty pounds Scots
Is nae deaf nits; in little bouk
Lie great bank notes.

To get amends of whindging fools,
That's frighted for repenting-stools,
Wha often whan their metal cools,
Turn sweer to pay,
Gar the kirk-boxie hale the dools,
Anither day.

But dawt red-coats, and let them scoup,
Free for the fou of cutty stoup;
To gee them up, ye need na hope
E'er to do weel:
They'll rive ye'r brats, and kick your doup,
And play the deel.

There's ae sair cross attends the craft,
That curst correction-house, where aft
Wild hangy's taz ye'er riggings saft

Makes black and blae,
Enough to pit a body daft;
But what'll ye say?

Nane gathers gear withoutten care,
Ilk pleasure has of pain a share;
Suppose then they should tirle ye bare,
And gar ye sike;
E'en learn to thole; 'tis very fair
Ye're nibour like.

Forby, my looves, count upo' losses,
Ye'r milk-white teeth, and cheeks like roses,
Whan jet-black hair and brigs of noses
Faw down wi' dads,
To keep your hearts up 'neath sic crosses,
Set up for bawds.

Wi' well-crish'd loofs I hae been canty,
Whan e'er the lads wad fain ha'e faun t' ye,
To try the auld game taunty-raunty,
Like coosers keen,
They took advice of me, your aunty,
If ye were clean.

Then up I took my siller ca',
And whistl'd benn, whiles ane whiles twa;
Roun'd in his lug, that there was a
Poor country Kate,
As halesome as the wall of Spa,
But unka blate.
Sae when e'er company came in,
And were upo' a merry pin,
I slade awa' wi' little din,
And muckle mense,
Left conscience judge, it was a' ane
To Lucky Spence.

My bennison come on good doers,
Who spend their cash on bawds and whores;
May they ne'er want the wale of cures

For a sair snout;
Foul fa' the quacks wha that fire smoors,
And puts nae out.

My malison light ilka day
On them that drink and dinna pay,
But tak' a snack and run away;
May't be their hap
Never to want a gonorrhea,
Or rotten clap.

Lass, gi'e us in anither gill,
A mutchken, jo, let's tak' our fill;
Let Death syne registrate his bill
Whan I want sense,
I'll slip away with better will,
Quo' Lucky Spence.

ALLAN RAMSAY

Bho M' Anam do Sgar Riomsa A-raoir

M' anam do sgar riomsa a-raoir,
calann ghlan dob ionnsa i n-uaigh;
rugadh bruinne maordha mín
is aonbhla lín uime uainn.

Do tógbhadh sgath aobhdha fhionn
a-mach ar an bhfaongha bhfann:
laogh mo chridhise do chrom,
craobh throm an tighise thall.

M' aonar a-nocht damhsa, a Dhé,
olc an saoghal camsa ad-chí;
dob álainn trom an taoibh naoi
do bhaoi sonn a-raoir, a Rí.

[. . .]

Táinig an chlí as ar gcuing,
agus dí ráinig mar roinn:
corp idir dá aisil inn
ar dtocht don fhinn mhaisigh mhoill.

Leath mo throigheadh, leath mo thaobh,
a dreach mar an droighean bán,
níor dhílse neach dhí ná dhún,
leath mo shúl i, leath mo lámh.

Leath mo chuirp an choinneal naoi;
's guirt riom do roinneadh, a Rí;
agá labhra is meirtneach mé –
dob é ceirtleath m' anma i.

MUIREADHACH ALBANACH Ó DÁLAIGH

From My Soul Was Ripped from Me Last Night

My soul was ripped from me last night,
a fine beloved body's in the grave,
a majestic soft chest was taken from us
wrapped in a linen shroud.

A fair lovely cutting was pruned
from off the delicate stem:
the love of my heart is bent,
the heavy branch of that house.

I am alone tonight, O God,
the evil of this crooked world is clear;
the young flank was heavy and lovely
that was here last night, O King.

[. . .]

The life-force left our yoke,
and fled as her share:
I'm a body between two axles,
because of the lovely fair one.

Half my feet, half my side,
her appearance like the whitethorn,
there was no one more loyal to her than me,
she was half my eyes, half my hands.

Half my body, the fresh candle,
I've been treated roughly, O King;
telling it exhausts me –
she was truly half my soul.

Trans. Peter Mackay and Iain S. MacPherson

MUIREADHACH ALBANACH Ó DÁLAIGH

Maggie Lauder

Wha wadna be in love
Wi bonnie Maggie Lauder?
A piper met her gaun to Fife,
And spier'd what was't they ca'd her:
Richt scornfully she answered him,
Begone, you hallan-shaker!
Jog on your gate, you bladder skate,
My name is Maggie Lauder.

Maggie! quoth he; and, by my bags,
I'm fidgin' fain to see thee!
Sit doun by me, my bonnie bird;
In troth I winna steer thee;
For I'm a piper to my trade;
My name is Rob the Ranter:
The lasses loup as they were daft,
When I blaw up my chanter.

Piper, quo' Meg, hae ye your bags,
Or is your drone in order?
If ye be Rob, I've heard o' you;
Live you upo' the Border?
The lasses a', baith far and near,
Have heard o' Rob the Ranter;

284

I'll shake my foot wi' richt gude will,
Gif ye'll blaw up your chanter.

Then to his bags he flew wi' speed;
About the drone he twisted:
Meg up and wallop'd ower the green;
For brawly could she frisk it!
Weel done! quo' he. Play up! quo' she.
Weel bobb'd! quo' Rob the Ranter;
It's worth my while to play, indeed,
When I hae sic a dancer!

Weel hae ye play'd your part! quo' Meg;
Your cheeks are like the crimson;
There's nane in Scotland plays sae weel,
Sin' we lost Habbie Simson.
I've lived in Fife, baith maid and wife,
This ten years and a quarter;
Gin ye should come to Anster Fair,
Spier ye for Maggie Lauder.

FRANCIS SEMPILL

Marbhrann do Chloinn Fhir Thaigh Ruspainn

Nan luighe seo gu h-ìosal
Far na thiodhlaic sinn an triùir
Bha fallain, làidir, inntinneach
Nuair dh'inntrig a' bhliadhn' ùr;
Cha deachaidh seachad fathast
Ach deich latha dhith o thùs;
Ciod fhios nach tig an teachdair oirnn
Nas braise na ar dùil?

Am bliadhna thìm bha dithis diubh
Air tighinn on aon bhroinn,
Bha iad nan dà chomrad
O choinnich iad nan cloinn;
Cha d'bhris an t-aog an comann ud,
Ged bu chomasach dha 'n roinn;

Ach gheàrr e snàth'nn na beath-s' ac'
Gun dàil ach latha 's oidhch'.

Aon duine 's bean on tàinig iad,
Na bràithrean seo a chuaidh,
Bha an aon bheatha thìmeil ac'
'S bha 'n aodach den aon chluaimh;
Mun aon uair a bhàsaich iad,
'S bha 'n nàdar den aon bhuaidh;
Chaidh 'n aon siubhal dhaoine leo
'S chaidh 'n sìneadh san aon uaigh.

Daoine nach d'rinn briseadh iad,
'S e fiosrachail do chàch,
'S cha mhò a rinn iad aon dad
Ris an can an saoghal gràs;
Ach ghineadh iad is rugadh iad,
Is thogadh iad is dh'fhàs;
Chaidh stràc den t-saoghal thairis orr'
'S mu dheireadh fhuair iad bàs.

Nach eil an guth seo labhrach
Ris gach aon neach tha beò?
Gu h-àraidh ris na seann daoinibh
Nach d'ionnsaich an staid phòst';
Nach gabh na tha na dhleastanas,
A dheasachadh an lòn,
Ach caomhnadh nì gu falair dhoibh
'S a' folach an cuid òir.

Cha chaith iad fèin na rinn iad,
Agus oighreachan cha dèan;
Ach ulaidhnean air shliabh ac'
Bhios a' biathadh chon is eun.
Tha iad fon aon dìteadh,
Fo nach robh 's nach bi mi fhèin,
Gur duirche, taisgte 'n t-òr ac'
Na nuair bha e anns a' mhèinn.

Freastal glic an Àrd-Rìgh,
Dh'fhàg e pàirt de bhuidheann gann,

286

Gu feuchainn iochd is oileanachd
D' an dream d' an tug e meall;
Carson nach tugtadh pòrsan
Dhen cuid stòrais aig gach àm
Do bhochdannaibh a dheònaicheadh
An còrr a chur na cheann?

An dèidh na rinn mi rùsgadh dhuibh –
Tha dùil agam gun lochd –
'S a liuthad focal fìrinneach
A dhìrich mi nur n-uchd,
Tha eagal orm nach èist sibh
Gu bhith feumail do na bochd
Nas mò na rinn na fleasgaich ud
A sheachdain gus a-nochd.

ROB DONN MACAOIDH

An Elegy for the Children of the House of Rispond

Lying here below
Are three that we have buried
Who were healthy, strong and sharp,
When we took the New Year in.
Only ten days have passed
Since then – who can know
The harbinger won't come for us
More quickly than we think?

Within a year two of them
Emerged from the one womb;
They were a pair of comrades
From their childhood days;
Death didn't break that fellowship
Though it could have split them up;
Instead it cut their life-threads
Just a day and night apart.

They came from one man and wife,
These brothers who have left,

They had the same life around them,
Their clothes from the same wool;
They died around the same hour,
Their natures were alike;
They were carried in the same procession,
Laid out in the same grave.

They broke none of the commandments,
As far as we can tell,
But they also never did anything
Of what the world calls grace;
They were conceived and were born,
Were nursed and they grew up;
A stroke of world passed over them,
And eventually they died.

Does this tale not resonate
With everyone who is alive?
Especially for those old men
Who were never married;
Men who'll hang on to their money,
And not spend it on food,
Saving up for their funeral feast
And hiding all their gold.

They'll never spend what they've made,
And they will leave no heirs;
But their treasure troves on hillsides,
Will feed the dogs and birds.
They all face the same charges,
Which I don't, will never, face:
Their gold's more darkly hoarded
Than when it was in the mine.

The High King in his wise providence,
Has left some of us without,
To test the mercy and the doctrines
Of those who have a lot;
Why shouldn't they give a portion
Of their riches at all times,

To support His poor,
To increase their meagre share.

Despite what I've revealed for you –
I trust it isn't wrong –
And all the truthful words
I've laid out before you,
I fear that you won't listen
And won't help out the poor,
Any more than these bachelors did
Until a week ago tonight.

Trans. Peter Mackay

ROB DONN MACKAY

Marie Hamilton

I

Word's gane to the kitchen,
And word's gane to the ha,
That Marie Hamilton gangs wi bairn
To the hichest Stewart of a'.

2

He's courted her in the kitchen,
He's courted her in the ha,
He's courted her in the laigh cellar,
And that was warst of a'.

3

She's tyed it in her apron
And she's thrown it in the sea;
Says, Sink ye, swim ye, bonny wee babe!
You'l neer get mair o me.

4

Down them cam the auld queen,
Goud tassels tying her hair:
'O Marie, where's the bonny wee babe
That I heard greet sae sair?'

5

'There never was a babe intill my room,
As little designs to be;
It was but a touch o my sair side,
Come oer my fair bodie.'

6

'O Marie, put on your robes o black,
Or else your robes o brown,
For ye maun gang wi me the night,
To see fair Edinbro town.'

7

'I winna put on my robes o black,
Nor yet my robes o brown;
But I'll put on my robes o white,
To shine through Edinbro town.'

8

When she gaed up the Cannogate,
She laughd loud laughters three;
But whan she cam down the Cannogate
The tear blinded her ee.

9

When she gaed up the Parliament stair,
The heel cam aff her shee;
And lang or she cam down again
She was condemnd to dee.

10

When she cam down the Cannogate,
The Cannogate sae free,
Many a ladie lookd oer her window,
Weeping for this ladie.

11

'Ye need nae weep for me,' she says,
'Ye need nae weep for me;
For had I not slain mine own sweet babe,
This death I wadna dee.'

12

'Bring me a bottle of wine,' she says,
'The best that eer ye hae,
That I may drink to my weil-wishers,
And they may drink to me.

13

'Here's a health to the jolly sailors,
That sail upon the main;
Let them never let on to my father and mother
But what I'm coming hame.

14

'Here's a health to the jolly sailors,
That sail upon the sea;
Let them never let on to my father and mother
That I cam here to dee.

15

'Oh little did my mother think,
The day she cradled me,
What lands I was to travel through,
What death I was to dee.

16

'Oh little did my father think,
The day he held up me,
What lands I was to travel through,
What death I was to dee.

17

'Last night I washd the queen's feet,
And gently laid her down;
And a' the thanks I've gotten the nicht
To be hangd in Edinbro town!

18

'Last nicht there was four Maries,
The nicht there'l be but three;
There was Marie Seton, and Marie Beton,
And Marie Carmichael, and me.'

ANON.

Mary's Song

I wad ha'e gi'en him my lips tae kiss,
Had I been his, had I been his;
Barley breid and elder wine,
Had I been his as he is mine.

The wanderin' bee it seeks the rose;
Tae the lochan's bosom the burnie goes;
The grey bird cries at evenin's fa',
'My luve, my fair one, come awa'.'

My beloved sall ha'e this he'rt tae break,
Reid, reid wine and the barley cake,
A he'rt tae break, and a mou' tae kiss,
Tho' he be nae mine, as I am his.

MARION ANGUS

Memory

I still keep open memory's chamber: still
Drink from the fount of youth's perennial stream.
It may be in old age an idle dream
Of those dear children; but beyond my will
They come again, and dead affections thrill
My pulseless heart, for now once more they seem
To be alive, and wayward fancies teem
In my fond brain, and all my sense fill.
Come, Alice, leave your books; tis I who call.
Bind up your hair, and teasing – did you say
Kissing – that kitten? Evey, come with me.
Mary, grave darling, take my hand: yes, all.
I have three hands today, a holiday.
A holiday, Papa? Woe's me – tis memory.

FRANCIS ERSKINE

The Midges Dance Aboon the Burn

The midges dance aboon the burn;
    The dews begin to fa';
The pairtricks down the rushy holm
    Set up their e'ening ca'.
Now loud and clear the blackbird's sang
    Rings through the briery shaw,
While, flitting gay, the swallows play
    Around the castle wa'.

Beneath the golden gloamin' sky
    The mavis mends her lay;
The redbreast pours his sweetest strains
    To charm the lingering day;
While weary yeldrins seem to wail
    Their little nestlings torn,
The merry wren, frae den to den,
    Gaes jinking through the thorn.

The roses fauld their silken leaves,
    The foxglove shuts its bell;
The honeysuckle and the birk
    Spread fragrance through the dell.
Let others crowd the giddy court
    Of mirth and revelry,
The simple joys that nature yields
    Are dearer far to me.

ROBERT TANNAHILL

Mo nighean Donn à Còrnaig

Mo nighean donn à Còrnaig,
Gun robh thu buidhe bòidheach,
Mo nighean donn à Còrnaig.

Nuair chaidh càch don t-searman
Chaidh na sealgairean don Mhòintich.

Gur olc an sgeul a chuala mi
Diluain an dèidh Didòmhnaich:

Gun robh do chuailein slaodte riut
'S do lèine chaol na stròicean.

Do chìochan mìne, geala
'S iad a' call na fala còmhla.

Mo nighean bhuidhe, bhadanach
Na cadal anns a' Mhòintich.

Gur olc an obair mhaidne dhomh
Bhith cur nam fear an òrdan.

'S gur olc an obair feasgair dhomh
Bhith deasachadh do thòrraidh.

'S truagh nach robh mi 'n taice
Ris na gillean rinn an dò-bheart.

Nan robh claidheamh ruisgt' agam
Gum feuchainn lùths mo dhòrn air.

Am fìon a bha gu d' bhanais
Bha na galain air do thòrradh.

GUN URRA

My Brown-Haired Girl From Còrnaig

My brown-haired girl from Còrnaig,
You were fair and beautiful;
My brown-haired girl from Còrnaig.

When the others went to church
The hunters went to Moss.

Evil was the tale I heard
On Monday following (that) Sunday.

Your curly locks were hanging limp
And your chemise was in tatters.

Your soft white breasts
Were both bleeding profusely.

My fair wavy-haired girl
Was lying asleep in Moss.

What a dreadful morning's work I had
Sorting out the men.

And dreadful was my evening's work
Preparing your funeral.

If only I could get near
The young men who committed this wicked act.

If only I had a sword unsheathed
I would put all the strength of my fist behind it.

The wine supplied for your wedding
Flowed by the gallon at your funeral.

Trans. Iona Brown and Flora NicPhàil

ANON.

Mo Rùn Geal Òg

Och, a Theàrlaich òig Stiùbhairt,
'S e do chùis rinn mo lèireadh,
Thug thu bhuam gach nì bh' agam
Ann an cogadh 'nad adhbhar;
Cha chrodh is cha chàirdean
Rinn mo chràdh ach mo chèile
On là dh'fhàg e mi 'm aonar
Gun sìon san t-saoghal ach lèine,
Mo rùn geal òg.

Cò nis thogas an claidheamh
No nì a' chathair a lìonadh?
'S gann gur e a th' air m' aire
O nach maireann mo chiad ghràdh;
Ach ciamar gheibhinn o m' nàdar
A bhith 'g àicheadh na 's miann leam
Is mo thogradh cho làidir
Bhith cur an àite mo rìgh mhath,
Mo rùn geal òg?

Bu tu 'm fear slinneanach, leathann,
Bu chaoile meadhan 's bu dealbhaich:
Cha bu tàillear gun eòlas
Dhèanadh còta math geàrr dhut
No dhèanadh dhut triubhas
Gun bhith cumhang no gann dhut –
Mar gheala-bhradain do chosan
Le d' gheàrr-osan mu d' chalpa,
Mo rùn geal òg.

Bu tu 'm fear mòr bu mhath cumadh
O d' mhullach gu d' bhrògan,

Bha do shlios mar an eala
'S blas na meal' air do phògan;
T' fhalt dualach donn lurach
Mu do mhuineal an òrdugh
'S e gu cama-lùbach cuimir
'S gach aon toirt urram d'a bhòidhchead,
Mo rùn geal òg.

Bu tu iasgair na h-abhann,
'S tric a thathaich thu fhèin i,
Agus sealgair a' mhunaidh-
Bhiodh do ghunn' air dheagh ghleusadh;
Bu bhinn leam tabhann do chuilean
Bheireadh fuil air mac èilde,
As do làimh bu mhòr m' earbsa –
Gur tric a mharbh thu le chèil' iad,
Mo rùn geal òg.

[· · ·]

'S ioma baintighearna phrìseil
Le 'n sìoda 's le 'n sròltaibh
Da'n robh mise 'm chùis fharmaid
Chionns gun tairgeadh tu pòg dhomh;
Ged a bhithinn cho sealbhmhor
'S gum bu leam airgead Hanòbhair,
Bheirinn cnag anns na h-àithntean
Nan cumadh càch bhuam do phògan,
Mo rùn geal òg.

'S iomadh bean a bha brònach
Eadar Tròndairnis 's Slèibhte,
'S iomadh tè bha na bantraich
Nach d' fhuair samhla do m' chèile;
Bha mise làn sòlais
Fhad 's bu bheò sinn le chèile,
Ach a-nis on a dh'fhalbh thu
Cha chùis fharmaid mi fhèin daibh,
Mo rùn geal òg.

CAIRISTÌONA NICFHEARGHAIS

My Bright Young Love

Och, young Charles Stuart,
Your cause has tormented me,
You took all that I had
For a war for your sake;
It's not cattle or kin
But my husband that pains me
Since the day he left me alone
With nothing but a shirt,
My bright young love.

Who will now lift the sword
Or fill the throne?
That's not really my focus
Since my first love is dead.
But could I find it in my nature
To deny what I want,
When I strongly desire
To have instead of my good king
My bright young love?

You were broad-shouldered, well-built,
Narrow-waisted and shapely,
It took a highly skilled tailor
To make you a trim coat,
Or to cut you some trousers
That weren't narrow or ill-fitting –
Your legs were like white salmon,
Short hose round your calves,
My bright young love.

You were a big well-shaped man
From your head to your shoes,
Your side was like a swan's,
Your kiss tasted of honey.
Your neat wavy brown hair
Was set out round your neck
In tidy loose curls,
Each one honouring your beauty,
My bright young love.

You were the fisher of the river,
You often went there,
And the hunter of the moor,
With your gun well-primed;
I loved the bark of your dogs
Who'd blood a hind's son,
I had great trust in your hands
That often killed them both,
My bright young love.

[. . .]

Many affluent ladies
With their silks and their satins
Were jealous of me
For getting your kisses;
If I was so prosperous
As to have Hanover's money,
I'd still break the commandments
If they stopped you from kissing me,
My bright young love.

Many wives were in mourning,
Between Trotternish and Sleat,
And many women were widows
Who never met my man's like;
I was full of happiness
While we lived together,
But now that you're gone
I'm no cause of envy,
My bright young love.

Trans. Peter Mackay

CHRISTINA FERGUSON

Bho Moladh Beinn Dòbhrain

Ùrlar
An t-urram thar gach beinn
Aig Beinn Dòbhrain;
De na chunnaic mi fon ghrèin,
'S i bu bhòidhche leam:
Munadh fada rèidh,
Cuilidh 'm faighte fèidh,
Soilleireachd an t-slèibh
Bha mi sònrachadh;
Doireachan nan geug,
Coill' anns am bi feur,
'S foinneasach an sprèidh
Bhios a chòmhnaidh ann;
Greadhain bu gheal cèir,
Faghaid air an dèidh,
'S laghach leam an sreud
A bha sròineiseach.
'S aigeannach fear eutrom
Gun mhòrchuis
Thèid fasanta na èideadh
Neo-spòrsail:
Tha mhanntal uime fèin,
Caithtiche nach trèig,
Bratach dhearg mar chèir
Bhios mar chòmhdach air.
'S culaidh ga chur eug –
Duine dhèanadh teuchd,
Gunna bu mhath gleus
An glaic òganaich;
Spor anns am biodh beàrn,
Tarrann air a ceann,
Snap a bhuaileadh teann
Ris na h-òrdaibh i;
Ochd-shlisneach gun fheall,
Stoc den fhiodh gun mheang,
Lotadh an damh seang
Is a leònadh e;
'S fear a bhiodh mar cheàird
Riutha sònraichte,

Dh'fhòghnadh dhaibh gun taing
Le chuid seòlainean;
Gheibhte siud ri àm,
Pàdraig anns a' ghleann,
Gillean is coin sheang,
'S e toirt òrdugh dhaibh;
Peilearan nan deann,
Teine gan cur ann;
Eilid nam beann àrd'
Thèid a leònadh leo.

Siubhal
'S i 'n eilid bheag bhinneach
Bu ghuiniche sraonadh,
Le cuinnean geur biorach
A' sireadh na gaoithe:
Gasganach, speireach,
Feadh chreachainn na beinne,
Le eagal ro theine
Cha teirinn i h-aonach;
Ged thèid i na cabhaig,
Cha ghearain i maothan:
Bha sinnsireachd fallain;
Nuair shìneadh i h-anail,
'S toil-inntinn leam tannasg
Dha langan a chluinntinn,
'S i 'g iarraidh a leannain
'N àm daraidh le coibhneas.
'S e damh a' chinn allaidh
Bu gheal-cheireach feaman,
Gu cabarach ceannard,
A b' fharamach raoiceadh;
'S e chòmhnaidh 'm Beinn Dòbhrain,
'S e eòlach ma fraoinibh.
'S ann am Beinn Dòbhrain,
Bu mhòr dhomh ra innseadh
A liuthad damh ceann-àrd
Tha fantainn san fhrìth ud;
Eilid chaol-eangach,
'S a laoighean ga leantainn,
Len gasgana geala,

Ri bealach a' dìreadh,
Ri fraigh Choire Chruiteir,
A' chuideachda phìceach.
Nuair a shìneas i h-eangan
'S a thèid i na deannaibh,
Cha saltradh air thalamh
Ach barra nan ìnean:
Cò b' urrainn ga leantainn
A dh'fhearaibh na rìoghachd?
'S arraideach, faramach,
Carach air grìne
A' chòisridh nach fhanadh
Gnè smal air an inntinn;
Ach caochlaideach, curaideach,
Caol-chasach, ullamh,
An aois cha chuir truim' orra,
Mulad no mì-ghean.

DONNCHADH BÀN MAC AN T-SAOIR

From In Praise of Ben Dorain

I

Honour past all bens
to Ben Dorain.
Of all beneath the sun,
I adore her.

Mountain ranges clear,
storehouse of the deer,
the radiance of the moor
I've observed there.

Leafy branchy groves,
woods where the grass grows,
inquisitive the does
that are roaming there.

Herds with white rumps race –
hunters in the chase.
O I love the grace
of these noble ones.

Spirited and delicate
and shy,
in fashionable coat
he goes by

in mantle well arrayed,
suit that will not fade,
dress of waxen-red
that he's wearing now.

Weapon that brings death,
bullet that stops breath,
expert studied youth
with his rifle there.

Flint that's notched and true,
on its head a screw,
a cock that would strike to
the hammers, it.

Eight-sided, without flaw,
gun-stock would lay low
the great stag in the flow
of his own blood there.
One whose craft was dear –
Mozart of them –
would kill them with a pure
trick and stratagem.

One would find such men –
Patrick in the glen –
boys and dogs at one,
and he'd order them.

Bullets left and right,
fires creating light,
the hind on mountain height
gets its wound from them.

II

The hind that's sharp-headed
is fierce in its speeding:
how delicate, rapid,
its nostrils, wind-reading!
Light-hooved and quick-limbèd,
she runs on the summit,

from that uppermost limit
no gun will remove her.
You'll not see her winded,
that elegant mover.

Her forebears were healthy.
When she stopped to take breath then,
how I loved the pure wraith-like

sound of her calling,
she seeking her sweetheart
in the lust of the morning.

It's the stag, the proud roarer,
white-rumped and ferocious,
branch-antlered and noble,
would walk in the shaded
retreats of Ben Dorain,
so haughtily-headed.

O they are in Ben Dorain,
so numerous, various,
the stags that go roaring
so tall and imperious.

Hind, nimble and slender,
with her calves strung behind her
lightly ascending
the cool mountain passes
through Harper's Dell winding
on their elegant courses.

Accelerant, speedy,
when she moves her slim body
earth knows nought of this lady
but the tips of her nails.
Even light would be tardy
to the flash of her pulse.

Dynamic, erratic,
by greenery spinning,
this troupe never static,
their minds free from sinning.

Coquettes of the body,
slim-leggèd and ready,
no age makes them tardy,
no grief nor disease.

Trans. Iain Crichton Smith

DUNCAN MacINTYRE

Bho Moladh Mòraig

Ùrlar
'S truagh gun mi sa choill
Nuair bha Mòrag ann,
Thilgeamaid na cruinn
Cò bu bhòidhch' againn;
Inghean a' chùil duinn
Air a bheil a loinn,
Bhiomaid air ar broinn
Feadh nan ròsanan;

Bhreugamaid sinn fhìn,
Mireag air ar blìon,
A' buain shòbhrach mìn-bhuidh'
Nan còsagan;
Theannamaid ri strì
'S thadhlamaid san fhrìth
'S chailleamaid sinn fhìn
Feadh nan strònagan.

Ùrlar
Sùil mar ghorm-dhearc driùchd
Ann an ceò-mhaidinn,
Deirg' is gil' nad ghnùis
Mar bhlàth òirseidean;
Shuas cho mìn ri plùr,
Shìos garbh mo chulaidh-chiùil,
Grian na planaid-cùrs'
Am measg òigheannan;
Reula glan gun smùr
Measg nan rionnag-iùil,
Sgàthan-mais' air flùr
Na bòidhchid thu;
Àilleagan glan ùr
A dhallas ruisg gu 'n cùl;
Mas ann do chrèadhaich thù
'S adhbhar mòr-iongnaidh.

Ùrlar
On thàinig gnè de thùr
O m' aois òige dhomh,
Nìor facas creutair dhiubh
Bu cho-ghlòrmhoire:
Bha Maili 's dearbha caoin,
'S a gruaidh air dhreach nan caor,
Ach caochlaideach mar ghaoith
'S i ro òranach;
Bha Peigi fad' an aois –
Mur b' e sin b' i mo ghaol;
Bha Marsaili fìor aotrom
Làn neònachais;
Bha Lili a' taitne rium

Mur b' e a ruisg bhith fionn;
Ach cha bu shàth bùrn-ionnlaid
Don Mhòraig s' iad.

Siubhal
O, 's coma leam, 's coma leam
Uil' iad ach Mòrag:
Rìbhinn dheas chulach
Gun uireas'aibh foghlaim;
Chan fhaighear a tional
Air mhaise no bhunailt,
No 'm beusaibh neo-chumanta
Am Muile no 'n Leòdhas;
Gu geamnaidh, deas, furanach,
Duineil, gun mhòrchuis,
Air thagha na cumachd
O 'mullach gu 'brògaibh;
A neul tha neo-churraidh
'S a h-aigne ro-lurach,
Gu brìodalach, cuireideach,
Urramach, seòlta.

Siubhal
O guiliugag, guiliugag,
Guiliugag Mòrag!
Aice ata 'chulaidh
Gu curaidh nan òigfhear;
B' e 'n t-aighear 's an sòlas
Bhith sìnte ri d' ulaidh
Seach daonnan bhith fuireach
Ri munaran pòsaidh,
Dam phianadh 's dam ruagadh
Le buaireadh na feòla,
Le aislingean connain
Na colna dam leònadh;
Nuair chithinn mu m' choinneimh
A cìochan le coinnil,
Thèid m' aign' air bhoilich
'S na theine dearg sòlais.

Siubhal
O fairigean, fairigean,
Fairigean Mòrag!
Aice ata 'chroiteag
As toite san Eòrpa;
A cìochan geal criostail,
Nan faiceadh tu stòit' iad
Gun tàirneadh gu beag-nàir'
Ceann-eaglais na Ròimhe;
Air bhuige 's air ghile
Mar lili nan lònan;
Nuair dhèanadh tu 'n dinneadh
Gun cinneadh tu deònach;
An deirgead, an grinnead,
Am mìnead 's an teinnead,
Gum b' àsainn chur spionnaidh
Agus spioraid à feòil iad.

[. . .]

ALASDAIR MAC MHAIGHSTIR ALASDAIR

From In Praise of Morag

Ground
It's a shame I wasn't in the woods
When Morag was,
We would cast lots
For the prettiest of us;
Young girls with brown-hair
Who sparkle, are fair –
We'd join them over there
On our bellies in the roses;
We'd playfully entice
Each other, on our sides,
Gathering the fine
Yellow primrose from the crags;
Playfights would start,
And we'd roam the deerpark
Until we'd lose track
Of ourselves in the hills.

Ground
Your eye's a blue-dewberry
In the morning mist,
Your face white and cherry-
Blossomed like an orange-kiss,
Your top's a fine-flower scent
(Below, a coarse instrument),
A sun that courses the firmament
Among virgins.
A clean, blemish-free star,
You're a vanity-mirror
On beauty's flower
Among guiding lights.
A jewel so dazzling
That you are blinding;
If you are made of clay
It's amazing.

Ground
Since I first came to my senses
In my youngest days
I haven't seen a creature
So glorious:
Maili was very sweet,
With her rowan-coloured cheeks,
But she was fickle as the breeze
And too songful;
Peggy wasn't young
Or she'd have been the one;
Marsaili was gone
In the head, and strange;
Lili would've made me hanker
If her eyes'd been darker;
But none of them are fit to crank
Your bath-water.

Variation
I don't care, I don't care
For anyone but Morag:
Morag, with her culture
And her glad-rags;

You won't find her equal,
One so virtuous and loyal
And uncommonly beautiful
On Lewis or Mull;
Able, welcoming, pure,
Humane, not pompous,
The choicest of figures
From her head to her toes;
Her complexion is tireless
Her mind so gorgeous,
Shrewd and flirtatious,
Noble and sharp.

Variation
O giddy-up, giddy-up
Giddy-up Morag!
She's got the stirrups
To spur on the young wags;
It'd be a pleasure
To lie with your treasure
And not have to measure
The days to our wedding.
I'm pained and harassed
By fleshly temptation,
My dreaming body is bruised
By sensations.
When, by candles, I see
Her breasts before me
My mind goes crazy
In red fires of bliss.

Variation
O, fairigean, fairigean,
Fairigean Morag!
She's got the tightest
Pussy in Europe;
Breasts of such white crystal
That if he saw their domes,
They'd lead unto scandal
The Pontiff of Rome.
Like the lily of the valley

They are soft and white;
She grows pliable, willing,
If you knead them just right.
With their redness, their pertness,
Their smoothness, their firmness:
The means to give flesh
Spirit and life.

[. . .]

Trans. Peter Mackay and Iain S. MacPherson

ALEXANDER MacDONALD

Mr Scales Walks His Dog

The dog is so old dust flies out from its arse as it runs;
the dog is so old its tongue rattles in its mouth, its eyes were changed
in the 17th century, its legs are borrowed from a Louis Fourteen
bedside cabinet.
The dog is barking with an antique excitement.
Scales dog is so old its barks hang in the air like old socks,
like faded paper flowers.
It is so old it played the doorman of the Atlantic Hotel in *The Last Laugh*,
so old it played the washroom attendant too.
Scales dog is so old he never learned to grow old gracefully.
Scales dog bites in stages.
Scales dog smells of naphtha.
Scales dog misjudges steps and trips.
Scales dog begs for scraps, licks plates.
Scales dog is seven times older than you think:
so he runs elliptically; so he cannot see spiders; so he is often distracted;
so he loses peanuts dropped at his feet; so he has suddenly become diabetic
and drinks from puddles; so there is bad wind in his system that came over
with the *Mayflower*; so he rolls on his back only once a week.
Scales dog is Gormenghast, is Nanny Slagg.
Scales dog is Horus, is Solomon Grundy.
His body makes disconnected music.
He is so old his eyes are glazed with blood;
so old wonders have ceased; so old all his diseases are benign; so old

he disappoints instantly; so old his aim is bad.
Scales dog is so old each day Scales urges him to die.
Scales dog puts on a show like a bad magician.
Scales dog squats as if he was signing the Declaration of Independence.
Scales dog is so old worms tired of him.
So old his fleas have won prizes for longevity.
So old his dreams are on microfilm in the Museum of Modern Art.
So old he looks accusingly.
So old he scratches for fun.
Scales dog was buried with the Pharaohs, with the Aztecs; draws social
security from fourteen countries; travels with his blanket; throws up on
the rug; has a galaxy named after him; Scales dog runs scared;
would have each day the same, the same;
twitches in his sleep;
wheezes.

ALEXANDER HUTCHISON

Mrs Midas

Now the garden was long and the visibility poor, the way
the dark of the ground seems to drink the light of the sky,
but that twig in his hand was gold. And then he plucked
a pear from a branch. – we grew Fondante d'Automne –
and it sat in his palm, like a lightbulb. On.
I thought to myself, Is he putting fairy lights in the tree?

He came into the house. The doorknobs gleamed.
He drew the blinds. You know the mind; I thought of
the Field of the Cloth of Gold and of Miss Macready.
He sat in that chair like a king on a burnished throne.
The look on his face was strange, wild, vain. I said,
What in the name of God is going on? He started to laugh.

I served up the meal. For starters, corn on the cob.
Within seconds he was spitting out the teeth of the rich.
He toyed with his spoon, then mine, then with the knives, the forks.
He asked where was the wine. I poured with a shaking hand,
a fragrant, bone-dry white from Italy, then watched
as he picked up the glass, goblet, golden chalice, drank.

It was then that I started to scream. He sank to his knees.
After we'd both calmed down, I finished the wine
on my own, hearing him out. I made him sit
on the other side of the room and keep his hands to himself.
I locked the cat in the cellar. I moved the phone.
The toilet I didn't mind. I couldn't believe my ears:

how he'd had a wish. Look, we all have wishes; granted.
But who has wishes granted? Him. Do you know about gold?
It feeds no one; aurum, soft, untarnishable; slakes
no thirst. He tried to light a cigarette; I gazed, entranced,
as the blue flame played on its luteous stem. At least,
I said, you'll be able to give up smoking for good.

Separate beds. in fact, I put a chair against my door,
near petrified. He was below, turning the spare room
into the tomb of Tutankhamun. You see, we were passionate then,
in those halcyon days; unwrapping each other, rapidly,
like presents, fast food. But now I feared his honeyed embrace,
the kiss that would turn my lips to a work of art.

And who, when it comes to the crunch, can live
with a heart of gold? That night, I dreamt I bore
his child, its perfect ore limbs, its little tongue
like a precious latch, its amber eyes
holding their pupils like flies. My dream milk
burned in my breasts. I woke to the streaming sun.

So he had to move out. We'd a caravan
in the wilds, in a glade of its own. I drove him up
under the cover of dark. He sat in the back.
And then I came home, the woman who married the fool
who wished for gold. At first, I visited, odd times,
parking the car a good way off, then walking.

You knew you were getting close. Golden trout
on the grass. One day, a hare hung from a larch,
a beautiful lemon mistake. And then his footprints,
glistening next to the river's path. He was thin,
delirious; hearing, he said, the music of Pan
from the woods. Listen. That was the last straw.

What gets me now is not the idiocy or greed
but lack of thought for me. Pure selfishness. I sold
the contents of the house and came down here.
I think of him in certain lights, dawn, late afternoon,
and once a bowl of apples stopped me dead. I miss most,
even now, his hands, his warm hands on my skin, his touch.

CAROL ANN DUFFY

My Pain

. . . one begins, ungratefully, to long for the contrasting tone of some
honest, unironic misery, confident that when it arrives Roddy Lumsden
will have the technical resources to handle it.

Neil Powell, TLS

I'm trying to string together three words
which I hate more than I hate myself:
gobsmacked, hubby and . . . when I realise
that words no longer count for much at all.

And that's me back down, head on the floor.
It's like Cathal Coughlan goes in his song:

till I've seen how low I can go.

It's like what my ancestor told me in a dream:
You'll be a sponge for the pain of others.
It's like what I told the lassie from the local paper:
I do not suffer for my art, I just suffer.

And face it, while we're at it, it's like
what curly Shona said that night at Graffiti
when all the gang were gathered for the show:
how she reckoned I would be the first to die,

or the time I slipped back from the bogs in Bo's
to hear my best friend tell a stranger girl
who'd been sweet in my company, *mind how you go
with Roddy, he's damaged goods, you know.*

RODDY LUMSDEN

My Shadow

I have a little shadow that goes in and out with me,
And what can be the use of him is more than I can see.
He is very, very like me from the heels up to the head;
And I see him jump before me, when I jump into my bed.

The funniest thing about him is the way he likes to grow –
Not at all like proper children, which is always very slow;
For he sometimes shoots up taller like an india-rubber ball,
And he sometimes gets so little that there's none of him at all.

He hasn't got a notion of how children ought to play,
And can only make a fool of me in every sort of way.
He stays so close beside me, he's a coward you can see;
I'd think shame to stick to nursie as that shadow sticks to me!

One morning, very early, before the sun was up,
I rose and found the shining dew on every buttercup;
But my lazy little shadow, like an arrant sleepy-head,
Had stayed at home behind me and was fast asleep in bed.

ROBERT LOUIS STEVENSON

Nae Day Sae Dark

Nae day sae dark; nae wüd sae bare;
Nae grund sae stour wi' stane;
But licht comes through; a sang is there;
A glint o' grass is green.

Wha hasna thol'd his thorter'd hours
And kent, whan they were by,
The tenderness o' life that fleurs
Rock-fast in misery?

WILLIAM SOUTAR

The Night Is Near Gone

Hay! now the day dawis,
The jolly cock crawis,
Now shroudis the shawis
    Throw Nature anon.
The throstle-cock cryis
On lovers wha lyis;
Now skaillis the skyis:
    The night is near gone.

The fieldis ourflowis
With gowans that growis
Where lilies like lowe is,
    As red as the ro'an.
The turtle that true is,
With notes that renewis,
Her pairtie pursueis:
    The night is near gone.

Now hartis with hindis,
Conform to their kindis,
Hie tursis their tyndis,
    On grund where they groan.
Now hurchonis, with haris,
Ay passes in pairis;
Whilk duly declaris
    The night is near gone.

The season excellis
Through sweetness that smellis;
Now Cupid compellis
    Our hairtis each one

On Venus wha wakis,
To muse on our makis,
Syne sing, for their sakis:
    'The night is near gone'.

All courageous knichtis
Aganis the day dichtis
The briest-plate that bricht is,
    To fecht with their fone.
The stoned steed stampis
Through courage, and crampis,
Syne on the land lampis:
    The night is near gone.

The freikis on fieldis
That wight wapins wieldis
With shining bright shieldis
    As Titan in trone;
Stiff spearis in restis,
Owre courseris crestis,
Are broke on their breistis:
    The night is near gone.

So hard are their hittis,
Some swayis, some sittis,
And some perforce flittis
    On grund whill they groan.
Syne groomis that gay is,
On bonkis and brayis
With swordis assayis:
    The night is near gone.

ALEXANDER MONTGOMERIE

No Roaring Seas

No roaring seas which roanting strikes on rocks
And hills of spindrifts raises on the shore,
Na rearding thunders that abates and knocks
The highest trees which them withstand the more,
Na damned souls are terrified so sore

Wha sees the gibbet of their fatal day,
Na windy tempests nor yet storms that roar,
And doth their blasts on lands and seas display,
Doth lossed ships with terror more affray,
Nor wandring pilgrims strikes with shaking fear,
Wha walking on are doubtful of the way,
And turning there, and now returning here,
    As I do fear the starnes of her ees,
    More fearful far than thunders, rocks and seas.

WILLIAM FOWLER

Bho Nuair bha mi Òg

Moch 's mi 'g èirigh air bheagan èislein,
Air madainn Chèitein 's mi ann an Òs,
Bha sprèidh a' geumnaich an ceann a chèile,
'S a' ghrian ag èirigh air Leac an Stòrr;
Bha gath a' boillsgeadh air slios nam beanntan,
Cur tuar na h-oidhche na dheann fo sgòd,
Is os mo chionn sheinn an uiseag ghreannmhor,
Toirt na mo chuimhne nuair bha mi òg.

Toirt na mo chuimhne le bròn is aoibhneas,
Nach fhaigh mi cainnt gus a chur air dòigh,
Gach car is tionndadh an corp 's an inntinn
Bhon dh'fhàg mi 'n gleann 'n robh sinn gun ghò;
Bha sruth na h-aibhne dol sìos cho tàimhidh,
Is toirm nan allt freagairt cainnt mo bheòil,
'S an smeòrach bhinn suidhe seinn air meanglan,
Toirt na mo chuimhne nuair bha mi òg.

Nuair bha mi gòrach a' siubhal mòintich,
'S am fraoch a' sròiceadh mo chòta-bàn,
Feadh thoman còinnich gun snàthainn a bhrògan,
'S an eigh na còsan air lochan tàimh;
A' falbh an aonaich ag iarraidh chaorach,
'S mi cheart cho aotrom ri naosg air lòn –
Gach bot is poll agus talamh toll
Toirt na mo chuimhne nuair bha mi òg.

Toirt na mo chuimhn' iomadh nì a rinn mi
Nach faigh mi 'm bann gu ceann thall mo sgeòil –
A' falbh sa gheamhradh gu luaidh is bainnsean
Gun solas lainnteir ach ceann an fhòid;
Bhiodh òigridh ghreannmhor ri ceòl is dannsa,
Ach dh'fhalbh an t-àm sin 's tha 'n gleann fo bhròn;
Bha 'n tobht aig Anndra 's e làn de fheanntaig,
Toirt na mo chuimhne nuair bha mi òg.

[. . .]

MÀIRI MHÒR NAN ÒRAN

From When I Was Young

Rising early, slightly sorrowful,
on a May morning when I was in Ose,
the cattle were lowing in their herd,
and the sun rising on the rock of Storr;
light beams glittering on the slopes of mountains,
hurrying away the hue of the night,
and above my head the lively skylark singing
make me remember when I was young.

Make me remember with joy and sadness,
that I can't find the words to relate,
each twist and turn of the mind and body
since I left this glen of faultless heroes;
the river flowing downstream so gently,
the murmuring burn answering my words,
and the sweet-voiced thrush singing on a branch,
make me remember when I was young.

When I was foolish, walking the moorland,
the heather catching my white petticoat,
through mounds of moss, with my feet bare,
and the ice in patches on still lochs;
crossing the uplands, looking for sheep,
and feeling so light as a snipe in a field –
every bog and pool and muddy hole
make me remember when I was young.

Make me remember many things I did
that I can't close until my story's told –
going in the winter to waulks and weddings
with no lantern light, just a burning peat;
lively young folk would be singing, dancing,
but those times have gone and the glen is sad;
Andrew's ruined house, now full of nettles,
makes me remember when I was young.

[. . .]

Trans. Peter Mackay

MARY MacPHERSON

O Domine Deus!

O Domine Deus! speravi in Te:
O care mi Jesu! nunc libera me,
In durà catenà, in miserà poenà, desidero te;
Languendo, gemendo, et genu flectendo,
Adoro, imploro, ut liberes me!

My Lord and My God

My Lord and My God, I have hoped in Thee:
O Jesu, sweet Saviour, now liberate me!
I have languished for Thee in afflictions and chains,
Through long years of anguish and bodily pains.
Adoring, imploring, on humbly bowed knee,
I crave of thy mercy to liberate me.

Trans. Agnes Strickland

MARY, QUEEN OF SCOTS

O Wert Thou in the Cauld Blast

O wert thou in the cauld blast,
On yonder lea, on yonder lea,
My plaidie to the angry airt,
I'd shelter thee, I'd shelter thee;
Or did Misfortune's bitter storms
Around thee blaw, around thee blaw,
Thy bield should be my bosom,
To share it a', to share it a'.

Or were I in the wildest waste,
Sae black and bare, sae black and bare,
The desert were a Paradise,
If thou wert there, if thou wert there;
Or were I Monarch o' the globe,
Wi' thee to reign, wi' thee to reign,
The brightest jewel in my Crown
Wad be my Queen, wad be my Queen.

ROBERT BURNS

Ode to the Gowdspink

Frae fields whare Spring her sweets has blawn
Wi caller verdure owr the lawn,
The gowdspink comes in new attire,
The brawest 'mang the whistling choir,
That, ere the sun can clear his een,
Wi glib notes sain the simmer's green.

Sure Nature herried mony a tree,
For spraings and bonny spats to thee:
Nae mair the rainbow can impart
Sic glowing ferlies o' her art,
Whase pencil wrought its freaks at will
On thee the sey-piece o' her skill.
Nae mair thro' straths in simmer dight
We seek the rose to bless our sight;
Or bid the bonny wa-flowers sprout

On yonder ruin's lofty snout.
Thy shining garments far outstrip
The cherries upo' Hebe's lip,
And fool the tints that Nature chose
To busk and paint the crimson rose.

'Mang man, wae's heart! We aften find
The brawest drest want peace of mind,
While he that gangs wi ragged coat
Is weel contentit wi his lot.
Whan wand wi glewy birdlime's set,
To steal far aff your dautit mate,
Blyth wad ye change your cleething gay
In lieu of lav'rock's sober grey.
In vain thro' woods you sair may ban
Th'envious treachery of man,
That, wi your gowden glister taen,
Still hunts you on the simmer's plain,
And traps you 'mang the sudden fa's
O' winter's dreary dreepin snaws.
Now steekit frae the gowany field,
Frae ilka fav'rite houff and bield,
But mergh, alas! To disengage
Your bonny bouk frae fettering cage,
Your free-born bosom beats in vain
For darling liberty again.
In window hung, how aft we see
Thee keek around at warblers free,
That carrol saft, and sweetly sing
Wi' a the blythness of the spring?
Like Tantalus they hing you here,
To spy the glories o' the year;
And tho' you're at the burnie's brink,
They downa suffer you to drink.

Ah, Liberty! thou bonny dame,
How wildly wanton is thy stream,
Round whilk the birdies a' rejoice,
An' hail you wi a grateful voice.
The gowdspink chatters joyous here,
And courts wi' gleesome sangs his peer:

The mavis frae the new-bloom'd thorn
Begins his lauds at ear'est morn;
And herd loun louping owr the grass,
Need far less fleetching til his lass,
Than paughty damsels bred at courts,
Wha thraw their mou's and take the dorts:
But, reft of thee, fient flee we care
For a' that life ahint can spare.
The gowdspink, that sae lang has kend
Thy happy sweets (his wonted friend),
Her sad confinement ill can brook
In some dark chamber's dowy nook;
Tho' Mary's hand his neb supplies,
Unkend to hunger's painfu cries,
Ev'n beauty canna cheer the heart
Frae life, frae liberty apart;
For now we tyne its wonted lay,
Sae lightsome sweet, sae blythly gay.

Thus Fortune aft a curse can gie,
To wyle us far frae liberty:
Then tent her siren smiles wha list,
I'll ne'er envy your girnal's grist;
For whan fair freedom smiles nae mair,
Care I for life? Shame fa' the hair;
A field o'ergrown wi' rankest stubble,
The essence of a paltry bubble.

ROBERT FERGUSSON

Of the Day Estivall

O perfite light, quhilk schaid away,
The darkenes from the light,
And set a ruler ou'r the day,
Ane uther ou'r the night.

Thy glorie when the day foorth flies,
Mair vively dois appeare,
Nor at midday unto our eyes,
The shining Sun is cleare.

The schaddow of the earth anon,
Remooves and drawes by,
Sine in the East, when it is gon,
Appeares a clearer sky.

Quhilk Sunne perceaves the little larks,
The lapwing and the snyp,
And tunes their sangs like natures clarks,
Ou'r midow, mure, and stryp.

Bot everie bais'd nocturnall beast,
Na langer may abide,
They hy away baith maist and least,
Them selves in howis to hide.

They dread the day fra thay it see,
And from the sight of men,
To saits, and covers fast they flee,
As Lyons to their den.

Oure Hemisphere is poleist clein,
And lightened more and more,
While everie thing be clearely sein,
Quhilk seemed dim before.

Except the glistering astres bright,
Which all the night were cleere,
Offusked with a greater light,
Na langer dois appeare.

The golden globe incontinent,
Sets up his shining head,
And ou'r the earth and firmament,
Displayes his beims abread.

For joy the birds with boulden throts,
Agains his visage shein,
Takes up their kindelie musicke nots,
In woods and gardens grein.

Up braids the carefull husbandman,
His cornes, and vines to see,
And everie tymous artisan,
In buith worke busilie.

The pastor quits the slouthfull sleepe,
And passis forth with speede,
His little camow-nosed sheepe,
And rowtting kie to feede.

The passenger from perrels sure,
Gangs gladly foorth the way:
Breife, everie living creature,
Takes comfort of the day,

The subtile mottie rayons light,
At rifts thay are in wonne;
The glansing phains, and vitre bright,
Resplends against the sunne.

The dew upon the tender crops,
Lyke pearles white and round,
Or like to melted silver drops,
Refreshes all the ground.

The mystie rocke, the clouds of raine,
From tops of mountaines skails,
Cleare are the highest hils and plaine,
The vapors takes the vails.

Begaried is the saphire pend,
With spraings of skarlet hew,
And preciously from end till end,
Damasked white and blew.

The ample heaven of fabrik sure,
In cleannes dois surpas,
The chrystall and the silver pure,
Or clearest poleist glas.

The time sa tranquill is and still,
That na where sall ye find,
Saife on ane high, and barren hill,
Ane aire of peeping wind.

All trees and simples great and small,
That balmie leife do beir,
Nor thay were painted on a wall,
Na mair they move or steir.

Calme is the deepe, and purpour se,
Yee, smuther nor the sand,
The wals that woltring wont to be,
Are stable like the land.

Sa silent is the cessile air,
That every cry and call,
The hils, and dails, and forrest fair,
Againe repeates tham all.

The rivers fresh, the callor streames,
Ou'r rockes can softlie rin,
The water cleare like chrystall seames,
And makes a pleasant din.

The fields, and earthly superfice,
With verdure greene is spread,
And naturallie but artifice,
In partie coulors cled.

The flurishes and fragrant flowres,
Throw Phoebus fostring heit,
Refresht with dew and silver showres,
Casts up ane odor sweit.

The clogged busie humming beis,
That never thinks to drowne,
On flowers and flourishes of treis,
Collects their liquor browne.

The Sunne maist like a speedie post,
With ardent course ascends,
The beautie of the heavenly host,
Up to our zenith tends.

Nocht guided be na Phaeton,
Nor trained in a chyre,
Bot be the high and haly On,
Quhilk dois all where impire.

The burning beims downe from his face,
Sa fervently can beat:
That man and beast now seekes a place
To save them fra the heat.

The brethles flocks drawes to the shade,
And frechure of their fald,
The startling nolt as they were made,
Runnes to the rivers cald.

The heards beneath some leaffie trie,
Amids the flowers they lie,
The stabill ships upon the sey,
Tends up their sails to drie.

The hart, the hynd, and fallow deare,
Are tapisht at their rest,
The foules and birdes that made the beir,
Prepares their prettie nest.

The rayons dures descending downe,
All kindlis in a gleid,
In cittie nor in borroughstowne,
May nane set foorth their heid.

Back from the blew paymented whun,
And from ilk plaister wall:
The hote reflexing of the sun,
Inflams the aire and all.

The labourers that timellie raise
All wearie faint and weake:
For heate downe to their houses gais,
Noone-meate and sleepe to take.

The callowr wine in cave is sought,
Mens brothing breists to cule:
The water cald and cleare is brought,
And sallets steipt in ule.

Sume plucks the honie plowm and peare,
The cherrie and the pesche,
Sume likes the reamand London beare,
The bodie to refresh.

Forth of their skepps some raging bees,
Lyes out and will not cast,
Some uther swarmes hyves on the trees,
In knots togidder fast.

The corbeis, and the kekling kais,
May scarce the heate abide,
Halks prunyeis on the sunnie brais,
And wedders back, and side.

With gilted eyes and open wings,
The cock his courage shawes,
With claps of joy his breast he dings,
And twentie times he crawes.

The dow with whistling wings sa blew,
The winds can fast collect,
Hir pourpour pennes turnes mony hew,
Against the sunne direct.

Now noone is went, gaine is mid-day,
The heat dois slake at last,
The sunne descends downe west away,
Fra three of clock be past.

A little cule of braithing wind,
Now softly can arise,
The warks throw heate that lay behind
Now men may enterprise.

Furth fairis the flocks to seeke their fude,
On everie hill and plaine,
Ilk labourer as he thinks gude,
Steppes to his turne againe.

The rayons of the Sunne we see,
Diminish in their strength,
The schad of everie towre and tree,
Extended is in length.

Great is the calme for everie quhair,
The wind is sitten downe,
The reik thrawes right up in the air,
From everie towre and towne.

Their firdoning the bony birds,
In banks they do begin,
With pipes of reides the jolie hirds,
Halds up the mirrie din.

The Maveis and the Philomeen,
The Stirling whissilles lowd,
The Cuschetts on the branches green,
Full quietly they crowd.

The gloming comes, the day is spent,
The Sun goes out of sight,
And painted is the occident,
With pourpour sanguine bright.

The Skarlet nor the golden threid,
Who would their beawtie trie,
Are nathing like the colour reid,
And beautie of the sky.

Our West Horizon circuler,
Fra time the Sunne be set,
Is all with rubies (as it wer)
Or Rosis reid ou'rfret.

What pleasour were to walke and see,
Endlang a river cleare,
The perfite forme of everie tree,
Within the deepe appeare?

The Salmon out of cruifs and creils
Up hailed into skowts,
The bels, and circles on the weills,
Throw lowpping of the trouts.

O: then it were a seemely thing,
While all is still and calme,
The praise of God to play and sing,
With cornet and with shalme.

Bot now the hirds with mony schout,
Cals uther be their name,
Ga, Billie, turne our gude about,
Now time is to go hame.

With bellie fow the beastes belive,
Are turned fra the corne,
Quhilk soberly they hameward drive,
With pipe and lilting horne.

Throw all the land great is the gild,
Of rustik folks that crie,
Of bleiting sheepe fra they be fild,
Of calves and rowting ky.

All labourers drawes hame at even,
And can till uther say,
Thankes to the gracious God of Heaven,
Quhilk send this summer day.

ALEXANDER HUME

The Oister

With open shells in seas, on heauenly due
A shining oister lushiouslie doth feed,
And then the Birth of that ætheriall seed
Shows, when conceau'd, if skies lookt darke or blew:
Soe doe my thoughts (celestiall twins) of you,
At whose aspect they first beginne & breed,
When they are borne to light demonstrat true,
If yee then smyld, or lowr'd in murning weed.
Pearles then are framd orient, faire in forme,
In their conception if the heauens looke cleare;
But if it thunder, or menace a storme,
They sadlie darke and wannish doe appeare:
    Right so my thoughts are, so my notes do change,
    Sweet if yee smyle, & hoarse if yee looke strange.

WILLIAM DRUMMOND OF HAWTHORNDEN

Old Woman

And she, being old, fed from a mashed plate
as an old mare might droop across a fence
to the dull pastures of its ignorance.
Her husband held her upright while he prayed

to God who is all-forgiving to send down
some angel somewhere who might land perhaps
in his foreign wings among the gradual crops.
She munched, half dead, blindly searching the spoon.

Outside, the grass was raging. There I sat
imprisoned in my pity and my shame
that men and women having suffered time
should sit in such a place, in such a state

and wished to be away, yes, to be far away
with athletes, heroes, Greeks or Roman men
who pushed their bitter spears into a vein
and would not spend an hour with such decay.

'Pray God,' he said, 'we ask you, God,' he said.
The bowed back was quiet. I saw the teeth
tighten their grip around a delicate death.
And nothing moved within the knotted head

but only a few poor veins as one might see
vague wishless seaweed floating on a tide
of all the salty waters where had died
too many waves to mark two more or three.

IAIN CRICHTON SMITH

On Himself, upon Hearing What Was His Sentence

Let them bestow on every airth a limb;
Open all my veins, that I may swim
To thee my Maker, in that crimson lake;
Then place my par-boiled head upon a stake;

Scatter my ashes, strew them in the air:
Lord since thou know'st where all these atoms are,
I'm hopeful thou'lt recover once my dust,
And confident thou'lt raise me with the just.

JAMES GRAHAM, MARQUESS OF MONTROSE

On His Headache

My head did ache yester nicht,
This day to mak write that I na micht,
So sare the migrime does me menyie
Piercing my brow as ony ganyie,
That scant I look may on the licht.

And now, Shir, lately, efter Mess,
To dight thocht I begouth to dress,
The sentence lay full evil till find,
Unsleepit in my head behind,
Dullit in dullness and distress.

Full oft at morrow I uprise,
When that my courage sleeping lies,
For mirth, for menstrally and play,
For din nor dancing nor deray,
It will nocht walkin me no wise.

WILLIAM DUNBAR

On the pier at Kinlochbervie

The stars go out one by one
as though a bluetit the size of the world
were pecking them like peanuts out of the sky's string bag,

A ludicrous image, I know.

Take away the gray light.
I want the bronze shields of summer
or winter's scalding sleet.

My mind is struggling with itself.

That fishing boat is a secret
approaching me. It's a secret
coming out of another one.
I want to know the first one of all.

Everything's in the distance,
as I am. I wish I could flip that distance
like a cigarette into the water.

I want an extreme of nearness.
I want boundaries on my mind.
I want to feel the world like a straitjacket.

NORMAN MacCAIG

Ora nam Buadh

    Ionnlaime do bhasa
Ann am frasa fiona,
Ann an liu nan lasa,
Ann an seachda sìona,
Ann an subh craobh,
Ann am bainne meala,
Is cuirime na naoi buaidhean glana caon
Ann do ghruaidhean caomha geala,
    Buaidh cruth,
    Buaidh guth,
    Buaidh rath,
    Buaidh math,
    Buaidh chnoc,
    Buaidh bhochd,
    Buaidh na rogha finne,
    Buaidh na fìor eireachdais,
    Buaidh an deagh labhraidh.

Is dubh am bail' ud thall,
Is dubh na daoine th' ann,
Is tu an eala dhonn,
Ta dol a-steach nan ceann.
Ta an cridhe fo do chonn,
Ta an teanga fo do bhonn,
'S a chaoidh cha chan iad bonn
    Facail is oil leat.

Is dubhar thu ri teas,
Is seasgar thu ri fuachd,
Is sùilean thu dhan dall,
Is crann dhan deòraidh thruagh,
Is eilean thu air muir,
Is cuisil thu air tìr,
Is fuaran thu am fàsach,
    Is slaint' dhan ti tha tinn.

Is tu gleus na Mnatha Sìthe,
Is tu beus na Brìde bithe,
Is tu creud na Moire mine,

Is tu gnìomh na mnatha Grèig,
Is tu sgèimh na h-Eimir àlainn,
Is tu mein na Dearshul àgha,
Is tu meanm na Meabha làidir,
      Is tu tàladh Binne-bheul.

Is tu sonas gach nì èibhinn,
Is tu solus gath na grèine,
Is tu dorus flath na fèile,
Is tu corra reul an iùil,
Is tu ceum fèidh nan àrdaibh,
Is tu ceum steud nam blàraibh,
Is tu sèimh eal' an t-snàmhibh,
      Is tu àilleagan gach rùin.

Cruth àlainn an Dòmhnaich
Ann do ghnùis ghlain,
An cruth is àilinde
Bha air talamh.

An tràth is feàrr 's an latha duit,
An là is feàrr 's an t-seachdain duit,
An t-seachdain is feàrr 's à bhliadhna duit,
      A' bhliadhn is feàrr an domhan Mhic De duit.

Thàinig Peadail 's thàinig Pòl,
Thàinig Seumas 's thàinig Eòin,
Thàinig Muiril is Muir Òigh,
Thàinig Uiril uile chòrr,
Thàinig Airil àill nan òg,
Thàinig Gabriel fàdh na h-Òigh,
Thàinig Raphail flath nan seòd,
'S thàinig Mìcheal mil air slòigh,
Thàinig 's Ìosa Crìosda ciùin,
Thàinig 's Spiorad fìor an iùil,
Thàinig 's Rìgh nan rìgh air stiùir,
A bheireadh duit-se gràdh is rùn,
      A bheireadh duit-se gràdh is rùn.

ALASDAIR MacGHILLEMHÌCHEIL

The Invocation of the Graces

I bathe thy palms
In showers of wine,
In the lustral fire,
In the seven elements,
In the juice of the rasps,
In the milk of honey,
And I place the nine pure choice graces
In thy fair fond face,
    The grace of form,
    The grace of voice,
    The grace of fortune,
    The grace of goodness,
    The grace of wisdom,
    The grace of charity,
    The grace of choice maidenliness,
    The grace of whole-souled loveliness,
    The grace of goodly speech.

Dark is yonder town,
Dark are those therein,
Thou art the brown swan
Going in among them.
Their hearts are under thy control,
Their tongues are beneath thy sole,
Nor will they ever utter a word
    To give thee offence.

A shade art thou in the heat,
A shelter art thou in the cold,
Eyes art thou to the blind,
A staff art thou to the pilgrim,
An island art thou at sea,
A fortress art thou on land,
A well art thou in the desert,
    Health art thou to the ailing.

Thine is the skill of the Fairy Woman,
Thine is the virtue of Bride the calm,
Thine is the faith of Mary the mild,

Thine is the tact of the woman of Greece,
Thine is the beauty of Emir the lovely,
Thine is the tenderness of Darthula delightful,
Thine is the courage of Maebh the strong,
    Thine is the charm of Binne-bheul.

Thou art the joy of all joyous things,
Thou art the light of the beam of the sun,
Thou art the door of the chief of hospitality,
Thou art the surpassing star of guidance,
Thou art the step of the deer of the hill,
Thou art the step of the steed of the plain,
Thou art the grace of the swan of swimming,
    Thou art the loveliness of all lovely desires.

The lovely likeness of the Lord
Is in thy pure face,
The loveliest likeness that
Was upon earth.

The best hour of the day be thine,
The best day of the week be thine,
The best week of the year be thine,
    The best year in the Son of God's domain be thine.

Peter has come and Paul has come,
James has come and John has come,
Muriel and Mary Virgin have come,
Uriel the all-beneficent has come,
Ariel the beauteousness of the young has come,
Gabriel the seer of the Virgin has come,
Raphael the prince of the valiant has come,
And Michael the chief of the hosts has come,
And Jesus Christ the mild has come,
And the Spirit of true guidance has come,
And the King of kings has come on the helm,
To bestow on thee their affection and their love,
    To bestow on thee their affection and their love.

Translated by author

ALEXANDER CARMICHAEL

Òran air Latha Blàr Inbhir Lòchaidh eadar Clann Dòmhnaill agus na Caimbeulaich

Hì rim ho ro, hò ro leatha,
Hì rim ho ro, hò ro leatha,
Hì rim ho ro, hò ro leatha,
Chaidh an latha le Clann Dòmhnaill.

[. . .]

Sin nuair chruinnich mòr-dhragh na falachd,
'N àm rùsgadh nan greidlein tana,
Bha iongnan nan Duibhhneach ri talamh,
An dèidh an lùithean a ghearradh.

'S lìonmhor corp nochdte gun aodach
Tha nan sìneadh air Cnoc an Fhraoich
On bhlàr an greasta na saoidhean,
Gu ceann Leitir Blàr a' Chaorainn.

Dh'innsinn sgeul eile le fìrinn,
Cho math 's a nì clèireach a sgrìobhadh:
Chaidh na laoich ud gu 'n dìcheall
'S chuir iad maoim air luchd am mìoruin.

Iain Mhùideartaich nan seòl soilleir,
Sheòladh an cuan ri là doilleir,
Ort cha d' fhuaireadh bristeadh coinne,
'S ait' leam Barra-breac fo d' chomas.

Cha b' e sud an siubhal cearbach
A thug Alasdair do dh'Albainn,
Creachadh, losgadh, agus marbhadh,
'S leagadh leis Coileach Shrath Bhalgaidh.

An t-eun dona chaill a cheuta,
An Sasann, an Albainn, 's an Èirinn,
Ite à cùrr na sgèithe:
Gur misde leam on a ghèill e.

Alasdair nan geurlann sgaiteach,
Gheall thu an-dè a bhith cur às daibh,
Chuir thu 'n ratreuta seach an caisteal –
Seòladh glè mhath air an leantainn.

Alasdair nan geurlann guineach.
Nam biodh agad àrmainn Mhuile;
Thug thu air na dh'fhalbh dhiubh fuireach,
'S ratreut air pràbar an duilisg.

Alasdair Mhic Cholla ghasda,
Làmh dheas a sgoltadh nan caisteal;
Chuir thu 'n ruaig air Ghallaibh glasa,
'S ma dh'òl iad càl gun chuir thu asd' e.

'M b' aithne dhuibhse 'n Goirtean Odhar?
'S math a bha e air a thodhar,
Chan innear chaorach no ghobhar
Ach fuil Dhuibhneach an dèidh reothadh.

Sgrios oirbh mas truagh leam ur càradh,
'G èisteachd anshocair ur pàisdean,
Caoidh a' phannail bha anns an àraich,
Donnalaich bhan Earra-ghàidheal.

IAIN LOM

A Song on the Battle of Inverlochy, between Clan Donald and the Campbells

Hi rim ho ro, ho ro leatha,
Hi rim ho ro, ho ro leatha,
Hi rim ho ro, ho ro leatha,
The day went with Clan Donald.

[. . .]

Then the great blood-letting happened,
the time for baring thin blades:
the Campbells' claws in the ground
after their joints were severed.

Many corpses, stripped naked,
are lying on Cnoc an Fhraoich;
from the battlefield where heroes were hurried
on to Leitir Blàr a' Chaorainn.

Truly I could tell another tale
as well as any cleric could write it:
those warriors were diligent
and routed their enemies.

Iain of Moidart, of the bright sails,
who'd sail the ocean on dull days,
never known to break a meeting,
I'm glad Barbreck is in your power.

It was no ill-planned journey
that brought Alasdair to Scotland,
plundering, burning and killing,
felling the Cock of Strathbogie.

That bad bird lost its elegance
in England, Scotland and Ireland;
he's a feather from inside the wing –
it pains me he surrendered.

Alasdair of the sharp cutting blades,
you promised yesterday to destroy them,
you made them retreat past the castle –
a great direction to chase them.

Alasdair of the sharp biting blades,
if you'd had the heroes from Mull
you would have caught those who escaped
when that dulse-eating rabble retreated.

Alasdair, son of splendid Colla,
a ready hand at splitting castles,
you routed the sallow-skinned Lowlanders:
you made them skitter the kale they'd drunk.

Did you know the Goirtean Odhar?
It was well-manured:
not by sheep dung or goat dung
but by the congealed blood of Campbells.

Damn you if I pity your state,
as I listen to the distress of your children,
the mourning of those on the battlefield,
the wailing of the women of Argyll.

Trans. Peter Mackay

JOHN MacDONALD

Bho Òran an t-Samhraidh

An dèis dhomh dùsgadh san mhaidean
'S an dealt air a' choill,
Ann am maidean ro shoilleir,
Ann a lagan beag doilleir,
Gun cualas a feadan
Gu leadarra seinn,
'S mac-talla nan creagan
Da fhreagra bròn-bhinn.

Bidh am beithe deagh-bholtrach,
Ùrail, dosrach nan càrn,
Ri maoth-bhlàs driùchd Cèitein,
Mar ri caoin-dheàrrsadh grèine,
Brùchdadh barraich roi gheugaibh
San mhìos cheutach-sa Mhàigh:
Am mìos breac-laoghach buailteach,
Bainneach, buadhach gu dàir.

Bidh gach doire dlùth uaignidh
'S trusgan uaine umpa a' fàs;
Bidh an snodhach a' dìreadh
As gach feumhaich as ìsle
Roi na cuislinnean snìomhain
Gu mìodachadh blàth;

Cuach is smeòrach san fheasgar
Seinn a leadain 'nam bàrr.

Am mìos breac-uigheach braonach,
Creamhach maoth-ròsach àigh,
Chuireas sgeadas neo-thruaillidh
Air gach àite, da dhuaichneachd,
A dh'fhògras sneachd le chuid fuachda
O gheur-ghruaim nam beann àrd
'S aig meud eagail roi Phèbus
Thèid sna speuraibh 'na smàl.

Am mìos lusanach mealach,
Feurach failleanach blàth,
'S e gu gucagach duilleach,
Luachrach dìtheanach lurach,
Beachach seilleanach dearcach,
Ciùthrach dealtach trom tlàth,
'S i mar chùirneanan daoimein:
'Bhratach bhoillsgeill air làr.

ALASDAIR MAC MHAIGHSTIR ALASDAIR

From Song of Summer

On waking this morning,
with the dew on the woods,
on this very bright morning,
in a shady wee hollow,
I heard then the chanter
with elegance played,
and the rocks' Echo sounded
their sweet-sad reply.

The fine-scented birch tree,
new-branched over the cairn,
wet with tender warm May-dew,
warm with sun's kindly shining,
exudes foliage from twiglets
in this lovely month, May:

month of dappled calves folded,
month for mating and milk.

Each grove, close and secret,
has its mantle of green,
the wood-sap is rising
from the woods at the bottom,
through arteries twisting
to swell out the growth;
thrush and cuckoo at evening
sing their litany above.

Month of specked eggs, dewy,
fine month for garlic and rose,
that with elegance decks out
places formerly gloomy,
expels snow with its coldness
from high mountains' harsh gloom;
so great its fear is of Phoebus,
it dissolves in the sky.

Month of plants and of honey,
warm, with grasses and shoots,
month of buds and of leafage,
rushes, flowers that are lovely,
wasps, bees and berries,
mellow mists, heavy dews,
like spangles of diamonds,
a sparkling cover for earth.

[. . .]

Trans. Derick Thomson

ALEXANDER MacDONALD

Bho Òran do Dh'Alasdair Mac Colla

Alasdair, a laoigh mo chèille,
Cò chunnaic no dh'fhàg thu 'n Eirinn,
Dh'fhàg thu na mìltean 's na ceudan

343

'S cha d' fhàg thu t' aon leithid fèin ann,
Calpa cruinn an t-siubhail eutruim,
Cas chruinneachaidh 'n t-sluaigh ri chèile,
Cha dèanar cogadh as t-eugais,
'S cha dèanar sìth gun do rèite,
'S ged nach bi na Duimhnich rèidh riut,
Gun robh an rìgh mar tha mi fèin duit.

E-hò, hi u hò, rò hò eile,
E-hò, hi u hò, 's i ri ri ù,
Hò hi ù ro, o hò ò eile,
Mo dhìobhail dìth nan ceann-fheadhna.

Mo chruit, mo chlàrsach, a's m' fhiodhall,
Mo theud chiùil 's gach àit am bithinn,
Nuair a bha mi òg 's mi 'm nighinn,
'S e thogadh m' inntinn thu thighinn,
Gheibheadh tu mo phòg gun bhruithinn,
'S mar tha mi 'n diugh 's math do dhligh oirr'.

Mhoire, 's e mo rùn am firionn,
Cha bhuachaille bhò san innis,
Ceann-feadhna greadhnach gun ghiorraig,
Marcaich nan steud 's leòir a mhire,
Bhuidhneadh na crùintean d'a ghillean,
'S nach seachnadh an toir iomairt,
Ghaolaich, nan dèanadh tu pilleadh,
Gheibheadh tu na bhiodh tu sireadh,
Ged a chaillinn ris mo chinneach –
Pòg o ghruagach dhuinn an fhirich.

'S truagh nach eil mi mar a b' ait leam,
Ceann Mhic-Cailein ann am achlais,
Cailean liath 'n dèidh a chasgairt,
'S an Crùnair an dèidh a ghlacadh,
Bu shunndach a gheibhinn cadal,
Ged a b' i chreag chruaidh mo leabaidh.

DIORBHAIL NIC A' BHRUTHAIN

From A Song to Alasdair Mac Colla

Alasdair, my beloved darling,
Who did you see or leave in Ireland?
You left thousands and hundreds,
But no one who is your equal.
Your light-stepping strong calves,
The leg that rallied the people:
War cannot be made without you,
Nor peace without your mediation.
Though you're not on terms with the Campbells
I hope the King treats you as I would.

E-hò, hi u hò, rò hò eile,
E-hò, hi u hò, 's i ri ri ù,
Hò hi ù ro, o hò ò eile,
My ruin is the lack of chieftains.

My harp, my clàrsach, my fiddle,
my stringed instruments wherever I go:
when I was young, a little girl,
your coming would cheer my spirits,
you'd get a kiss without having to ask,
and I feel now you have a right to one.

Mary, he is the man I love,
not a cowherd in the valley
but a splendid, nerveless chieftain,
a rider of warhorses, who is playful,
who'd win crowns for his lads,
and not avoid campaigning.
Love, if you would return,
you'd get what you've been seeking
even if I'd be shunned by my clansfolk –
a kiss from the brown-haired girl of the mountains.

It's a shame I'm not as I'd wish,
with MacCailein's head in my armpit
grey Colin having been butchered,
and the Crowner having been captured,

how cheerfully I'd sleep then,
though my bed was a hard rock-face.

Trans. Peter Mackay

DOROTHY BROWN

Bho Òran do Dh'Ameireaga

An uair thèid na dròbhairean sin gur n-iarraidh
Is ann leis na breugan a nì iad feum,
Gun fhacal fìrinne bhith ga innse,
Is an cridhe a' dìteadh na their am beul.
Ri cur am fiachaibh gu bheil san tìr seo
Gach nì as prìseile tha fon ghrèin;
An uair thig sibh innte gur beag a chì sibh
Ach coille dhìreach toirt dhibh an speur.

An uair thig an geamhradh is àm na dùbhlachd
Bidh sneachd a' dlùthadh ri cùl nan geug,
Is gu domhain dùmhail dol thar na glùine,
Is ge math an triùbhsair cha dèan i feum
Gun stocainn dhùbailt sa mhocais chlùdaich
Bhios air a dùnadh gu dlùth le èill:
B' e am fasan ùr dhuinn a cosg le fionntach
Mar chaidh a rùsgadh den bhrùid an-dè.

Mur bi mi eòlach airson mo chòmhdaich
Gum faigh mi reòite mo shròn 's mo bheul,
Le gaoith a tuath a bhios neimheil fuaraidh
Gum bi mo chluasan an cunnart geur.
Tha an reothadh fuathasach, cha seas an tuagh ris,
Gum mill e a' chruaidh ged a bha i geur;
Mur toir mi blàths di, gum brist an stàilinn,
Is gun dol don cheàrdaich cha gheàrr i beum.

An uair thig an samhradh 's am mìosa Cèitein
Bidh teas na grèine gam fhàgail fann;
Gun cuir i spèirid sa h-uile creutair
A bhios fo èislean air feadh nan toll.

Na mathain bhèisteil gun dèan iad èirigh
Dhol feadh an treud, is gur mòr an call:
Is a' chuileag ìneach gu socach puinnseant'
Gam lot gu lìonmhor le rinn a lainn.

Gun dèan i m' aodann gu h-olc a chaobadh,
Chan fhaic mi an saoghal, 's ann bhios mi dall;
Gun at mo shùilean le neart a cungaidh,
Ro ghuineach drùidheach tha sùgh a teang'.
Chan fhaigh mi àireamh dhuibh ann an dànachd
Gach beathach gràineil a thogas ceann;
Is cho liutha plàigh ann 's a bha air Rìgh Phàro
Airson nan tràillean, nuair bhàth e an camp.

Gur h-iomadh caochladh tighinn air an t-saoghal
'S ro-bheag a shaoil mi nuair bha mi thall;
Bu bheachd dhomh 'n uair sin mun d' rinn mi gluasad
Gum fàsainn uasal nuair thiginn nall.
An car a fhuair mi cha b' ann gum bhuannachd
Tighinn thar a' chuain air a' chuairt bha meallt'
Gu tìr nan craobh anns nach eil an t-saorsainn,
Gun mhart, gun chaora, 's mi dh'aodach gann.

IAIN MacILLEATHAIN

From A Song to America

When those drovers come to get you
They make good use of lies,
They won't tell a word of the truth,
Their hearts condemn what's in their mouths.
They'd have you believe that this land
Has everything precious under the sun;
But when you arrive, there's little to see
But colossal forests that block out the sky.

When winter comes and the time of darkness
Snow's packed tight on the back of each branch,
It is thick and deep to above the knee,
However good your trousers, they're not enough
Without doubled stockings and patched moccasins
Tied tightly with leather thongs:
It was our new fashion to wear them furred
As stripped from a beast the day before.

If I'm not careful with my clothing
I'll get frostbite on my nose and mouth:
From the bitterly cold northerly wind
My ears are in severe danger.
The frost is dreadful, the axe can't stand it,
It would ruin metal even if it was sharp;
Unless it's warmed, the steel will fracture,
Without going to the smithy, it won't make a cut.

When the summer comes, the month of May,
The heat of the sun leaves me weak;
It gives energy to every creature
That has been lying in a hole asleep.
The beastly bears will all wake up,
Go through our herds, cause lots of damage:
And the stinging fly with its poison beak
Gives me many wounds with the tip of its lance.

Its bites make my face come out in hives,
I can't see the world, I am blinded;
My eyes swell up with the force of its poison,
The venom of its tongue stings, penetrates.
I can't put their number down in verse –
All those hateful creatures that emerge;
There are as many plagues as befell the Pharaoh
Because of slaves, when he drowned his followers.

Many a change has come on the world
Which I barely imagined over there;
Back then I thought, before I emigrated,
That I would be noble when I got here.
What I've gone through has brought me no profit,

Crossing the sea on a trip based on lies,
To the land of trees where there is no freedom,
No cattle, no sheep, with my clothes growing scarce.

[. . .]

Trans. Peter Mackay

JOHN MacLEAN

Bho Oran do na Cìobairibh Gallda

Thàinig oirnn do dh'Albainn crois,
Tha daoine bochd' nochdte ris,
Gun bhiadh, gun aodach, gun chluain;
Tha 'n àird a tuath an dèidh a sgrios:
Chan fhaicear ach caoirich is uain,
Goill mun cuairt dhaibh air gach slios;
Tha gach fearann air dol fàs,
Na Gàidheil 's an cinn fo fhliodh.

Chan fhaicear crodh-laoigh air gleann,
No eich, ach gann, a' dol an èill;
'S ann don fhàisinneachd a bh' ann:
Gun rachadh an crann bho fheum;
Chaidh na sealgairean fo gheall,
'S tha gach cuilbheir cam, gun ghleus:
Cha mharbhar maoiseach no meann,
'S dh'fhuadaich sgriachail Ghall na feidh.

Chan eil àbhachd feadh nam beann,
Chaidh gìomanaich teann fo smachd:
Tha fear na cròice air chall,
Chaidh gach eilid is mang as:
Chan fhaighear ruadh-bhoc nan allt
Le cù seang ga chur gu srath;
An èirig gach cùis a bh' ann,
Feadaireachd nan Gall 's gach glaic.

Cha chluinnear geum ann am buailidh,
Chaidh an crodh guailfhionn à suim;
Chan èisdear luinneag no duanag,
Bleodhain mairt aig gruagaich dhuinn;
Bhon chaidh ar cuallach an tainead,
'S tric a tha pathadh gar claoidh,
'N àite gach càirdean a bh' againn,
Luinnseach ghlas am bun gach tuim.

Mar gun tuiteadh iad fon chraoibh,
Cnothan caoch dol aog sa bharrach;
'S ann mar siud a tha seann daoine,
'S clann bheag a h-aogais bainne;
Thilgeadh iad gu iomall cùirte,
Bhon dùthchas a bh' aig an seanair;
B' fheàrr leinn gun tigeadh na Frangaich
A thoirt nan ceann dheth na Gallaibh.

[. . .]

AILEAN DALL DÙGHALLACH

From Song to the Lowland Shepherds

Mishap has come to us in Scotland,
And poor people are exposed to it,
Without food, shelter or peace;
The North has been devastated;
There's nothing but lambs and sheep,
Lowlanders round them on each slope,
All the farmland is laid waste:
Chickweed has grown on the Gaels' heads.

No milk-cows are seen in the glens,
And only few horses in harness;
It was in a prophecy:
The plough would fall out of use;
The hunters have been proscribed,
And every gun is bent, unprimed;
No doe or roe can be killed,
The Lowland skreichs have cleared the deer.

There's no mirth among the hills,
Hunting is tightly controlled:
The antlered one is lost,
Every hind and fawn has fled;
You can't get the roebuck of the streams,
No slim hound will chase it to the valley,
The compensation for all this
Is a Lowland whistling in every nook.

There's no lowing heard in the folds,
White-shouldered cows are not esteemed;
You won't hear a tune or ditty,
From dark-haired maids at the milking;
Since cattle-tending is now rare
Thirst often fatigues us,
Instead of the close friends we once had,
A grey idler at the base of each hillock.

As if they had fallen from the tree,
Empty nuts that died on the top-branches;
That is how our old people are,
And young children without milk;
Cast to the edge of privilege,
From the inheritance of their grandfathers;
We'd rather the French to come
And decapitate the Lowlanders.

[. . .]

Trans. Peter Mackay

ALLAN MacDOUGALL

Bho Òran do MhacLeòid Dhùn Bheagain

Meud a' mhulaid tha am thadhal
Dh'fhàg treaghaid am chliabh cho goirt,
On a rinneas air m' adhart
Ad dheaghaidh an triall gun toirt;
Tha mis' ort an tòir,

Is mi meas gu robh còir agam ort,
A mhic athar mo ghràidh,
Is tu m' aighear, 's tu m' àdh, 's tu m' olc.

Chaidh a' chuibhle mun cuairt,
Ghrad thionndaidh gu fuachd am blàths:
Gum faca mi uair
Dùn ratha nan cuach 'n seo thràigh,
Far 'm biodh tathaich nan duan,
Iomadh mathas gun chruas, gun chàs:
Dh'fhalbh an latha sin uainn,
'S tha na taighean gu fuarraidh fàs.

[. . .]

Thoir teachdaireachd uam
le deatam gu Ruaidhri òg,
agus innis da fèin
cuid d'a chunnart giodh e Mac Leòid;
biodh e 'g amharc 'na dhèidh
air an Iain a dh'eug 's nach beò:
gum bu shaidhbhir a chliù,
is chan fhàgadh e 'n Dùn gun cheòl.

AN CLÀRSAIR DALL

From A Song to Macleod of Dunvegan

I am haunted by such sorrow:
it's left a darting pain in my chest,
since I set out after you
on a fruitless journey;
I'm on your trail,
I reckon I had a right to you,
son of a father I loved,
you're my cheer, my fortune, my mischief.

The wheel has gone round,
and warmth turned quickly to cold:
here I once saw a castle

filled with cups that are now dry,
where songs were common,
good things shared without worry or stint:
that day has gone from us,
and the buildings are empty and damp.

[. . .]

Take this message from me
as quick as you can to young Ruaidhri,
and tell him the danger
he is in, though he is MacLeod;
let him look back
at the Iain who died, who's no more:
his reputation was rich,
he'd never leave the castle without music.

Trans. Peter Mackay

RODERICK MORISON (THE BLIND HARPER)

Òran do na Fògarraich

Togaibh misneach is sòlas,
Bithibh inntinneach ceòlmhor
Agus cuiribh ur dòchas
    Ann an còmhnadh an Àrd-Rìgh,
On as fheudar dhuibh seòladh,
('S nach ann do ur deòin e)
Do rioghachd nach eòl duibh
    Mar a thòisich ur càirdean,
O nach fuiling iad beò sibh
Ann an crìochaibh ur n-eòlais,
'S fheàrr dhuibh falbh do ur dèoin
    Na bhith fodha mar thràillean;
'S iad na h-uachdarain ghòrach
A chuir fuaradh fo'r srònaibh —
A bhris muineal Rìgh Deòrsa
    Nuair a dh'fhògradh na Gàidhil!

Ma thig cogadh is creachan
(Mar as minig a thachair)
'S ann a bhios sibh 'nur starsaich
    Fo chasaibh ur nàmhaid;
Tha sibh soirbh ri bhur casgairt
'S gun neach ann gu'm bacadh,
Tha bhur guaillean gun tacsa
    'S na gaisgich gur fàgail.
Rìgh, gur sgiolta ri'm faicinn
'Nan seasamh air faithche
Le'n aodaichean gasta
    De bhreacanan càrnaid
Na tha falbh uaibh an ceartuair
De dh'òganaich dhreachmhor –
Gun truailleadh, gun ghaiseadh,
    Gun taise gun tàire.

Thug siod sgriob air MacDhòmhnaill,
Thug e spùilleadh air Mòrar,
Thug e lomadh air Cnòideart,
    Thug e leòn air Clann Raghnaill:
Falbh nam fear òga,
Falbh nam fear mòra,
Falbh nam fear cròdha
    'N àm na tòrachd a phàigheadh.
Bidh cinn-chinnidh 'nan ònar,
'S an slinnean gun chòmhdach,
Gun treise gun chòmhnadh
    Nuair thig fòirneart an làthair,
Ur nàimhdean gu spòrsail
Gur stampadh fo'm bhrògan –
Luchd fòirneart gu treòrach
    Gun neach beò gus an àicheadh.

'S truagh an gnothach ri smaoineach',
Tha 'm fearann ga dhaoradh –
Ghrad dh'fhalbh ar cuid dhaoine
    'S thàinig caoirich 'nan àite;
'S lag an sluagh iad, 's is faoin iad
Dol an carraid no 'n caonnaig,

Làn bracsaidh is caoile
    'S iad fo dhraoidh ghille-màrtainn.
Cha dean smiùradh ur saoradh
'N làthair batail air raonaidh,
No fead ciobair an aonaich
    Gnè chaochladh dhe'r n-ànradh,
'S ged a chruinnicheadh sibh caogad
Mholt is reitheachan maola,
'S beag a thogadh a h-aon diubh
    Claidheamh faobharach stàilinn.

[. . .]

Triallaibh nis, fhearaibh,
Gu dùthaich gun ghainne,
Cuiribh cùl ris an fhearann
    Chaidh thairis am màl oirbh
Gu dùthaich a' bhainne,
Gu dùthaich na meala,
Gu dùthaich an ceannaich sibh
    Fearann gu'r n-àilgheas,
Gu dùthaich gun aineis,
Gun chrìonadh gun stanard,
Far an cnuasaich sibh barrachd
    'S a mhaireas ri'r làithean –
'S e 'n saighdear glic fearail
Nuair chitheadh e barrachd
A theicheadh le 'anam
    'S nach fanadh air làraich.

Seallaibh mun cuairt duibh
Is faicibh na h-uaislean
Gun iochd annt' ri truaghain,
    Gun suairceas ri dàimhich;
'S ann a tha iad am barail
Nach buin sibh don talamh,
'S ged dh'fhàg iad sibh falamh
    Chan fhaic iad mar chall e:
Chaill iad an sealladh
Air gach reachd agus gealladh

Bha eadar na fearaibh
    Thug am fearann s' on nàmhaid –
Ach innseadh iad dhòmhsa
Nuair thèid sibh air fògradh
Mur caill iad an còir air
    Gun dòigh air a theàrnadh.

IAIN MAC FHEARCHAIR

A Song to the Exiles

Pluck up courage and joy,
Be hopeful and cheerful
And put your reliance
    In the help of the High King,
Because you must sail
(Though it's not what you want)
To a kingdom unknown to you
    In the wake of your kinsfolk.
Since they won't let you live
In the country you know,
You had better leave willingly
    And not be trampled like slaves;
How stupid are landlords
Who put your bows to the wind –
Who broke the neck of King George
    When the Gael were expelled!

If war and plundering come
(As has frequently happened)
You'll be a threshold
    Under enemy feet;
You are easy to slaughter
When there's no one to stop them,
No support at your shoulders
    As the heroes are leaving you.
O King, how trim to be seen
Standing on greensward
With their splendid attire
    Of red tartan plaids

Are those handsome young men
Who are leaving you soon –
Uncorrupted, unblemished,
      Without fear or reproach.

What has ravaged MacDonald,
Brought destruction to Morar,
Laid Knoydart waste
      And wounded Clanranald
Is the going of the young men,
The going of the big men,
The going of the brave men
      Who'd pay their rent in the battlefield.
Chiefs will be isolated,
Their shoulderblades naked,
Without strength or support
      When violence appears,
Your enemies gleefully
Tramping you underfoot –
Oppressors will thrive
      With none alive to oppose them.

It's sad to reflect
How the land's being enslaved –
Our people suddenly went
      And sheep came in their place;
They're weak troops, ineffective
In attack or in battle,
Full of braxy and famine
      And under foxes' enchantments.
No smearing will save you
In time of battle on battlefield,
No shepherd's whistle on mountain
      Will relieve your distress,
And if you mustered fifty
Hornless rams and wedders
Not one of them would lift
      A bladed sword of steel.

[. . .]

Go now, my lads,
To a realm without want,
Abandon the land
    Whose rent's gone too high for you
For the realm of the milk,
For the realm of the honey,
For a realm where you'll buy
    All the land you'll desire,
For a realm without poverty,
Without blight or rationing,
Where you will glean more
    Than can last all your days –
It's the wise manly soldier
When he saw more arriving
Who'd escape with his life
    And not stay on the field.

Look all around you
And behold the nobility
With no pity for unfortunates
    And no decency to kinsfolk;
They are convinced
That you don't belong to the land,
And though they've left you with nothing
    They don't see it as loss:
They have lost sight
Of each law and commitment
Binding the men
    Who took this land from the foe –
But let them just tell me
When you go into exile
If they won't lose their right to it
    With no way of saving it.

Trans. Ronald Black

JOHN MacCODRUM

Bho Òran don Ollamh MacIain

Gur tu an losgann sleamhainn tàrrbhuidh,
    'S tu màigein tàirrngeach nan dìgean,
Gur tu dearc-luachrach a' chàthair
    Ri snàg 's màgaran mìltich;
'S tu bratag sgreataidh an fhàsaich,
    'S tu 'n t-seilcheag ghrànda, bhog, lìtheach,
'S tu 'n cartan nach fhurasta thàrsainn
    Uait na thàrras tu 'nad ìngnean.

Gur tu 'n sgonnachù gollach, sgallach,
    'S tu tramasgal salach gach fàs-phòir,
'S tu soplach is moll na fasgnaig
    An àm sìol reachdmhor a chàthadh;
'S tu tom odhar an tombaca,
    Gur tu stad feachda o bhlàraibh,
Gur tu croman-luch' na h-ealtainn –
    'S tu nis mìr-cagnaidh nam bàrdan.

Gur tu fuidheagan an aodaich,
    Gur tu cnò-chaoch na fìor fhàsaig,
'S tu am madadh-allaidh air chonfhadh,
    Gur tu meas toirmisgt' a' ghàrraidh,
'S mòr tha de bheusan, a bhalaich,
    A' bhrùid air carradh ad' nàdar –
Chan iongnadh ged tha thu sgreamhail
    'S an fhail anns an deachaidh d' àrach.

Cha bu tu 'n droigheann no 'n cuileann
    No 'n t-iubhar fulannach làidir,
Chan eil mìr annad den darach
    No de sheileach dearg nam blàran;
Tha chuid as mò dhiot de chritheann,
    Ìngnean sgithich 's làmhan feàrna –
Tha do cheann gu lèir de leamhan,
    Gu h-àraidh do theanga 's do chàirein.

Ceann puinnsein a chinnich 'na fhàsach
    Den fhailbhe 's den àileadh lomlàn,
Gann uiread maighdeige-tràghad

De dh'eanchainn nàdarr' ad' throm-cheann,
Chan iongnadh ged thigeadh toth gràineil
    O dheudach beàrnach do ronnachraois
'S do chom gun chridhe gu d' àinean
    Ach uiread màileid de dhomblas.

Am measg nan iasg 's tu 'n dallag mhùrlaich,
    A' bhiast mhùgach sin 'm mac-làmhaich,
'S tu 'n t-isean à meadhan na brèine,
    Am broc 's a shorn 'na chèir trì ràithean,
A' mhial chaorach dhan ainm an t-seulain,
    Salach an sprèidh tha dhuit càirdeach –
'S mur bitheadh nach toil leam ainm èisge,
    Gun dùraiginn fhèin do sgràilleadh.

Ach nì mi nis a bhrìgh do sgòrnail
    Glomhar ad' bheul mòr a sparradh,
Nach dealaich riut fhads as beò thu,
    Gach aon deireadh lò ga theannadh;
Bharrachd air na gheibh thu de riasladh
    Air ballan-stiallach gad spannadh –
B' fheàrr dhuit nach beirte bho thòs thu
    Ach ad' mharbh-laogh bò gun anam.

SEUMAS MAC AN T-SAOIR

From A Song to Dr Johnson

You're the slimy yellow-bellied toad,
    You're the sluggish crawler of ditches,
You're the lizard of the swamp
    Which creeps and slithers through sweet-grass;
You're the ugly wasteland caterpillar,
    You're the foul, soft, slimy snail,
You're the botfly hard to relieve
    Of what you've seized in your claws.

You're the mean, vile, greedy cur,
    You're the foul trash of each growing-crop,
You're the dirt and refuse of the corn-fan

When good strong seed's being winnowed;
You're the pale stools of tobacco,
    You're what stops armies going to battles,
You're the kestrel of the birdflock –
    You're now the chewing-gum of the poets.

You're the thrum-end of the cloth,
    You're the shell with no nut in it,
You're the hydrophobic wolf,
    You're the banned fruit of the garden,
Many brutish habits, you churl,
    Have formed a scab in your nature –
It's no surprise you'd be disgusting
    In the pigsty you were reared in.

You'd not be the thorn or the holly
    Or the tough enduring yew,
There's not a bit in you of the oak
    Or the red willow of the plains;
Most of you is of aspen,
    With whitethorn nails and alder hands –
Your whole head is made of elm,
    Especially your tongue and your gums.

A head of poison that became a vacuum
    Full of emptiness and air
With scarce as much as a little shore-whelk
    Of natural brain in your bloated head,
It's no surprise if a foul smell wafts
    From your huge spittlemouth's gapped teeth
Since your trunk has no heart for your liver
    But just a satchelful of gall instead.

Amongst sea creatures you're the purblind dogfish,
    That snuffling monstrosity the catfish,
You are the chicken from amidst the stench,
    The brock with his nose three seasons in his arse,
You are the sheep-louse that they call the tick,
    Vile are the creatures that are kin to you –
And if it weren't that I hate the name of satirist,
    I myself would wish to make fun of you.

But now on account of your throaty gargling
    I'll stick a gag in your massive mouth
That won't part from you as long as you live,
    Being tightened at the end of each day;
On top of all you suffer I'll have you
    Being flayed alive at a lashing-post –
You would wish you were still-born from the start
    As the soulless foetus of a calving cow.

Trans. Ronald Black

JAMES MacINTYRE

Oran Eile air an Adhbhar Cheudna

Tha mise fo mhulad san àm,
Chan òlar leam dram le sunnd;
Tha durrag air ghur ann mo chàil
A dh'fhiosraich do chàch mo rùn;
Chan fhaic mi dol seachad air sràid
An cailin bu tlàithe sùil –
'S e sin a leag m' aigne gu làr
Mar dhuilleach o bhàrr nan craobh.

A ghruagach as bachlaiche cùl,
Tha mise gad ionndrainn mòr;
Ma thagh thu deagh àite dhut fèin,
Mo bheannachd gach rè g' ad chòir;
Tha mise ri osnaich nad dhèidh
Mar ghaisgeach an dèis a leòn,
Na laighe san àraich gun fheum,
'S nach tèid anns an t-sreup nas mò.

'S e dh'fhàg mi mar iudmhail air treud,
Mar fhear nach toir spèis do mhnaoi,
Do thuras thar chuan fo bhrèid,
Thug bras shileadh dheur om shùil;
B' fheàrr nach mothaichinn fèin
Do mhaise, do chèill 's do chliù,
No suairceas milis do bhèil
As binne na sèis gach ciùil.

Gach an-duin' a chluinneas mo chàs
A' cur air mo nàdar fiamh,
A' cantainn nach eil mi ach bàrd
'S nach cinnich leam dàn as fiach –
Mo sheanair ri pàigheadh a mhàil
Is m' athair ri màileid riamh –
Chuireadh iad gearrain an crann
Is ghearrainn-sa rann ro cheud.

'S fad' a tha m' aigne fo ghruaim,
Cha mhosgail mo chluain ri ceòl,
'M breislich mar ànrach a' chuain
Air bharraibh nan stuagh ri ceò;
'S e iùnndaran d' àbhachd uam
A chaochail air snuadh mo neòil,
Gun sùgradh, gun mhire, gun uaill,
Gun chaithream, gun bhuadh, gun treòir.

Cha dùisgear leam ealaidh air àill',
Cha chuirear leam dàn air dòigh,
Cha togar leam fonn air clàr,
Cha chluinnear leam gàir nan òg;
Cha dìrich mi bealach nan àrd
Le suigeart mar bha mi 'n tòs,
Ach triallam a chadal gu bràth
Do thalla nam bàrd nach beò.

UILLEAM ROS

Another Song on the Same Topic

Now I'm depressed.
I won't happily take a dram –
a maggot festers in my brain
which lets everyone know my desire.
I can't see, going past in the street,
the young woman with the gentlest eye:
this is what's felled my spirit
like leaves from the top of the trees.

O girl of the curliest hair,
I'm badly missing you;
if you chose a good place for yourself,
my blessing on you for all time.
I am sighing for you,
like a warrior who has been wounded,
lying useless in a battlefield,
who won't enter the fray any more.

What's left me astray from the flock,
like one who can love no woman –
your sea journey as a head-dressed bride
that brought torrents of tears from my eyes;
I wish I couldn't notice
your beauty, your sense and your fame,
or your mouth's sweet affability
more tuneful than any music.

Every hater who hears of my plight
claims my nature is flawed,
says that I'm just a poet
who can't make a worthwhile song;
but my grandfather paid his rent
and my father carried his pack –
they could hitch geldings to ploughs,
and I could cut verse with the best.

My spirits have long been clouded,
music doesn't waken my senses;
delirious like a wanderer at sea
on top of the mist-covered waves;
it is missing your humour
that has changed the hue of my sky:
no love-making, mirth or pride,
no excitement, virtue or direction.

I can't wake an ode on beauty.
I can't get a poem to sit true,
I can't raise a tune from the stave,
I can't hear the laugh of the young;

I can't climb high mountain passes
cheerfully, as I once did,
but let me go forever to sleep
in the hall of the unliving poets.

Trans. Peter Mackay and Iain S. MacPherson

WILLIAM ROSS

Bho Òran Eile air Latha Chùil Lodair

[. . .]

Ach thig a' chuibhle mun cuairt
Car o dheas no o thuath,
'S gheibh ar n-eascairdean duais an eucoir.

Gum bi Uilleam Mac Dheòrs'
Mar chraoibh sheargte fo leòn,
Gun fhreumh, gun duilleach, gun mheòirean gèige.

Guma lom bhios do leac,
Gun bhean, gun bhràthair, gun mhac,
Gun fhuaim clàrsaich, gun lasair chèire.

Gun sòlas, sonas no seanns,
Ach dòlas dona mud cheann,
Mar bh' air ginealach Chlann na h-Èipheit.

'S chì sinn fhathast do cheann
Dol gun athadh ri crann,
'S eòin an adhair gu teann ga reubadh.

Is bidh sinn uile fa-dheòidh
Araon sean agus òg,
Fon Rìgh dhligheach dhan còir duinn gèilleadh.

IAIN RUADH STIÙBHART

From Another Song About the Day of Culloden

[. . .]

But the wheel will yet turn
From the south or the north,
Our foes will be paid for their crimes.

May Prince William be
A withered, scarred tree
Without roots or leaves or twigs.

May your gravestone be bare
With no wife, son or brother,
No harp song or flicker of candle.

No comfort, happiness, luck
But destruction on your head
As befell the children of Egypt.

And we'll yet see your head
With no flinching strung up
And the birds of the air tearing at it.

We'll all finally be ruled –
Whether we're young or old –
By the rightful King, due our obedience.

Trans. Peter Mackay

JOHN ROY STUART

Bho Oran Murtadh Ghlinn Comhainn

B' iad mo ghràdh na cuirp gheala
    Bha gu fiùghantach fearail neo-chrìon:
'S mairg a chunnairc ar n-uaislean
    Dol fo bhinn an luchd fuatha gun dìon;
Ach nam biomaid nar n-armaibh
    Mun do chruinnich an t-sealg air an tìr,

Gun robh còtaichean dearga
	Gun dol tuilleadh a dh'armailt an Rìgh.

Cha b'e cruadal an cridhe
	Thug dhoibh buainteachd air buidhinn mo ruin:
Tilgeadh luaidhe na cithibh,
	Sud a' chùis a bha mishealbhach dhùinn;
Eadar uaislean is mhithibh
	Gun robh bhuaidh ud a' rith oirinn bho thus:
Bu linn toiseach na slighe,
	Bhiodh na sluaisdean a' frithealadh dhùinn.

Cha b' i sud an fhuil shalach
	Bha ga taomadh mun talamh sa' ghleann,
'S a liuthad ùrnaidh mar ghearan
	Bha cur fùdair na dheannaibh mu'r ceann.
A Rìgh dhùilich nan aingeal,
	Gabh-sa cùram d' ur n-anam 's sibh thall:
Chaidh ur cunntas an tanad
	Le garbh dhùsgadh na malairt a bha ann.

MURCHADH MacMHATHAIN

From A Song on the Massacre of Glencoe

I loved the white corpses
	that had been generous, manly and brave:
woe to the one who saw our nobles
	condemned by their enemies without a chance;
but if we had been ready for combat
	before the hunt gathered force in the land,
impossible for the red-coats
	to return to the ranks of the King.

It was not bravery of heart
	that let them reap down the people I loved:
but firing lead-shot in showers,
	an unfortunate aspect for us;
both commoners and nobles,

we were bound to be overcome from the start:
we were setting out on the journey,
    shovels preparing our grave.

That blood was not tainted
    that was spilled on the ground in the glen,
with so many complaining cowards
    sending gun-powder rushing past our heads.
O Creator King of the angels,
    take care of your souls on the other side:
your number has been diminished
    by the rough awakening of what took place.

Trans. Meg Bateman

MURDOCH MATHESON

The Parawd o Dustie-Fute

DUSTIE-FUTE
    eftir Eugenio de Andrade

He cam fae a fremmit land,
had kent thrist an the watter o Mairch bere,
his feet i the wey o the slaw stour o eternitie.

The dour snaw cam eftir.

GREATER HORSESHOE BAT

Rhinolophus feurrumequinum!
Soon you'll be extinct as Latin.
Your horseshoe noseleaf
Sculpts the ultrasound of Gaia's grief.

AYE-AYE

To us the Aye-Aye is a no-no,
A lemur like a tiny academic:
Big starey eyes, bat ears, baldly hirsute, it knows
The jury's out; scary, peaky, rainforest geek.

368

LEAR'S MACAW

Lear sketched your blues:
Wished you a Boss-Woss, a Pobble or Jumbly;
You parrot his limericks humbly:
There was a there was a there was a
Caged mostly in pea-green zoos.

MAN

Shaped like a pumpkin
Lardy and farty and screwy
and a pure mingin killer
Makes the ocean floor a bin
Hypocrite lecteur, mon semblable, mon frère.

DUSTIE-FUTE

Tae apen hauns.
As if the wun war the mairvel.
Tae straik the outloup o his mane,
lently the lent fever craig.

Tae let him lae,
still green.
Wi the outpour,
cream o the well.

THE DHOLE

The Dhole's a wild dug
That clucks lik a hen:
He's loast his fuckin habitat
An the habit o rhyme.

THE BLUE WHALE

Big on omega 3, I gulp
9,000 pounds of plankton per day;
Pavarotti of the sea, I belt
it out: bray spray, spray prey,
outweigh everyone!

DUSTIE-FUTE

Whan she glowered
back intae thi pit

than ma shouders gowped,
ilka stab lik thi clash o an aik

ilka faa lik the glisk
o lichtnin fused

i the mirk.

Noo the nicht-hawk
flauchters thru brainches,

deeback an leesions
hap ma hide,

the parawd
intae the untholeable licht.

SNOW LEOPARD

What can the leopard tell us of snow?
That it is melting away.
What does the snow say of the leopard?
It has melted away.

DUSTIE-FUTE

Now Dustie-Fute is Nemo
Trees and beasts ex-beau
Hot bod hard-got
But a liar the light forgot.

DAVID KINLOCH

Phrase-Book

Words are a monstrous excrescence.
Everything green is extended. It
is apricot, orange, lemon, olive, and cherry,
and other snakes in the linguistic grass;
also a white touch of marble which evokes
no ghosts, the taste of squid, the . . .
Go away. I shall call a policeman.
Acrocorinth which evokes no
goats under the lemon blossom.

World is a monstrous excrescence;
he is following me everywhere, one
Nescafé and twenty Athenes, everything
green; I am not responsible for it.
I don't want to speak to you.
Leave me alone. I shall stay here.
I refuse a green extension. Beware.
I have paid you. I have paid you
enough, sea, sun, and octopodi.
It is raining cats and allomorphs.

'Where' is the British Embassy.

VERONICA FORREST-THOMSON

Pietà

Her face was thrawed.
She wisna aa come.

In the trams o her airms
the wummin held oot her first bairn.
It micht hae been a mercat day
and him for sale.
Naebody stoppit tae niffer.

His life bluid cled his breast
wi a new reid semmit.
He'd hippens for deid claes.

Aifter the boombers cleck
and the sodgers traik thro the skau
there's an auld air sterts up –
bubblin and greetin.

It's a ballant mithers sing
on their hunkers i the stour
for a bairn deid.

They ken it by hert.

It's the cauldest grue i the universe
yon skelloch.
It niver waukens the deid.

ALASTAIR MACKIE

The Praise of Age

Wythin a garth, under a rede rosere,
Ane ald man, and decrepit, herd I syng;
Gay was the note, suete was the voce et clere:
It was grete joy to here of sik a thing.
'And to my dome,' he said, in his dytyng,
'For to be yong I wald not, for my wis
Off all this warld to mak me lord et king:
The more of age the nerar hevynnis blis.

'False is this warld, and full of variance,
Besoucht with syn and other sytis mo;
Treuth is all tynt, gyle has the gouvernance,
Wrechitnes has wroht all welthis wele to wo;
Fredome is tynt, and flemyt the lordis fro,
And covatise is all the cause of this;
I am content that youthede is ago:
The more of age the nerar hevynnis blisse.

372

'The state of youth I repute for na gude,
For in that state sik perilis now I see;
Bot full smal grace, the regeing of his blude
Can none gaynstand quhill that he agit be;
Syne of the thing that tofore joyit he
Nothing remaynis for to be callit his;
For quhy it were bot veray vanitee:
The more of age the nerar hevynnis blisse.

'Suld no man traist this wrechit warld, for quhy
Of erdly joy ay sorow is the end;
The state of it can noman certify,
This day a king, to morne na gude to spend.
Quhat have we here bot grace us to defend?
The quhilk god grant us for to mend oure mys,
That to his glore he may oure saulis send;
The more of age the nerar hevynnis blisse.'

ROBERT HENRYSON

The Princess of Scotland

'Who are you that so strangely woke,
And raised a fine hand?'
Poverty wears a scarlet cloke
In my land.

'Duchies of dreamland, emerald, rose
Lie at your command?'
Poverty like a princess goes
In my land.

'Wherefore the mask of silken lace
Tied with a golden band?'
Poverty walks with wanton grace
In my land.

'Why do you softly, richly speak
Rhythm so sweetly-scanned?'
Poverty hath the Gaelic and Greek
In my land.

'There's a far-off scent about you seems
Born in Samarkand.'
Poverty hath luxurious dreams
In my land.

'You have wounds that like passion-flowers you hide:
I cannot understand.'
Poverty hath one name with Pride
In my land.

'Oh! Will you draw your last sad breath
'Mid bitter bent and sand?'
Poverty begs from none but Death
In my land.

RACHEL ANNAND TAYLOR

The Proloug of the Sevynt Buik *from* Eneados

As brycht Phebus, schene souerane, hevynnis e,
The opposit held of his chymmis hie,
Cleir schynand bemys, and goldin symmeris hew,
In lattoun colour altering haill of new;
Kithing no syng of heyt be his visage,
So neir approachit he his wynter staige;
Redy he was to entir the thrid morne
In cloudy skyis vndir Capricorne.
All thocht he be the hart and lamp of hevin,
Forfeblit wolx his lemand giltly lewyne,
Throw the declyning of his large round speir.
The frosty regioun ringis of the yeir,
The tyme and sessoune bitter cald and paill,
Thai schort days that clerkis clepe brumaill;
Quhen brym blastis of the northyne art
Ourquhelmit had Neptunus in his cart,
And all to schaik the levis of the treis,
The rageand storm ourwalterand wally seis;
Reveris ran reid on spait with watteir broune,
And burins hurlis all thair bankis downe,
And landbrist rumland rudely wyth sic beir,

374

So loud ne rummist wyld lioun or beir.
Fludis monstreis, sic as meirswyne or quhailis,
For the tempest law in the deip devallyis.
Mars occident, retrograide in his speir,
Provocand stryff, regnit as lord that yer;
Rany Orioune wyth his stormy face
Bewalit of the schipman by his rays;
Frawart Saturne, chill of complexioune,
Throw quhais aspect derth and infectioune
Bene causit oft, and mortale pestilens,
Went progressiue the greis of his ascens;
And lust Hebe, Junois douchtir gay,
Stud spulyeit of hir office and array.
The soill ysowpit into wattir wak,
The firmament ourkest with rokis blak,
The ground fadyt, and fauch wolx all the feildis,
Montayne toppis sleikit wyth snaw ourheildis,
On raggit rolkis of hard harsk quhyne stane,
With frosyne frontis cauld clynty clewis schane;
Bewtie wes lost, and barrand schew the landis,
With frostis haire ourfret the feildis standis.
Soure bittir bubbis, and the schowris snell,
Semyt on the sward ane similitude of hell,
Reducyng to our mynd, in every steid,
Goustly schaddois of eild and grisly deid,
Thik drumly scuggis dirknit so the hevyne.
Dym skyis oft furth warpit feirfull levyne,
Flaggis of fyir, and mony felloun flawe,
Scharp soppis of sleit, and of the snypand snawe.
The dowy dichis war all donk and wait,
The law vaille flodderit all wyth spait,
The plane stretis and every hie way
Full of fluschis, doubbis, myre and clay.
Laggerit leys wallowit farnys schewe
Broune muris kithit thair wysnit mossy hewe,
Bank, bra, and boddum blanschit wolx and bair;
For gurll weddir growyt bestis haire;
The wynd maid wayfe the reid weyd on the dyk,
Bedovin in donkis deyp was every syk;
Our craggis, and the front of rochis seyre,
Hang gret isch schoklis lang as ony spere:

375

The grund stude barrand, widderit, dosk and gray,
Herbis, flouris, and gersis wallowit away;
Woddis, forestis, wyth nakyt bewis blout,
Stud strypyt of thair weyd in every hout.
So bustuysly Boreas his bugill blew,
The deyr full dern dovne in the dalis drew;
Smal byrdis, flokand throw thik ronnis thrang,
In chyrmyng and with cheping changit thair sang.
Sekand hidlis and hirnys thaim to hyde
Fra feirfull thudis of the tempestuus tyde.
The wattir lynnis routtis, and every lynde
Quhyslyt and brayt of the swouchand wynde.
Puire laboraris and byssy husband men
Went wayt and wery draglyt in the fen;
The silly scheip and thair lytill hyrd gromis
Lurkis vndir le of bankis, wodys, and bromys;
And uthir dantit gretar bestial,
Within thair stabillis sesyt into stall,
Sic as mulis, horsis, oxin and ky,
Fed tuskit baris, and fat swyne in sty,
Sustenit war by mannis gouernance
On hervist and on symmeris purviance.
Widequhair with fors so Eolus schouttis schyll
In this congelyt sessioune scharp and chyll,
The callour air, penetrative and puire,
Dasyng the bluide in every creature,
Maid seik warm stoivis, and beyne fyris hoyt,
In double garmont cled and wyly coyt,
Wyth mychty drink, and meytis confortive,
Agayne the storme wyntre for to strive.
    Repaterit weill, and by the chymnay beykyt,
At evin be tyme dovne a bed I me streikit,
Warpit my heid, kest on claythis thrinfauld,
For till expell the perrellus peirsand cauld.
I crocit me, syne bownit for to sleip,
Quhair, lemand throw the glas, I did tak keip
Latonia, the lang irksum nycht;
Hir subtell blenkis sched and wattry lycht,
Full hie wp quhyrlyt in hir regioune,
Till Phebus rycht in oppositioune,
Into the Crab hir propir mansioune draw,

Haldand the hycht allthoucht the son went law.
Hornit Hebawde, quhilk clepe we the nycht owle,
Within hir caverne hard I schout and yowle;
Laithlie of forme, wyth crukit camschow beik,
Vgsum to heir was hir wyld elriche screik:
The wyld geis claking eik by nychtis tyde
Attoure the citie fleand hard I glyde.

On slummyr I slaid full sad, and slepit sownd
Quhill the oryent wpwart gan rebound.
Phebus crownit byrd, the nychtis orloger,
Clappand his wyngis thryse had crawin cleir.
Approching neir the greiking of the day.
Wythin my bed I waikynnit quhair I lay,
So fast declinis Synthea the mone,
And kais keklis on the ruiff abone.
Palamedes byrdis crouping in the sky,
Fleand on randoune schapin lik ane Y,
And as ane trumpat rang thair vocis soun,
Quhais cryis bene pronosticatioun
Off wyndy blastis and ventositeis.
Fast by my chalmir, in heych wysnit treis,
The soir gled quhislis loud wyth mony ane pew,
Quhairby the day was dawin weil I knew;
Bad beit the fyrie, and the candill alycht,
Syne blissit me, and, in my wedis dycht
Ane schot wyndo vnschet a lytill on char,
Persawit the mornyng bla, wan, and har.
Wyth cloudy gum and rak ourquehelmyt the air,
The sulye stythlie, hasart, rowch and hair,
Branchis brattlyng, and blayknit schew the brays,
With hyrstis harsk of waggand wyndilstrays;
The dew droppis congelyt on stibyll and rynd,
And scharp hailstanis, mortfundit of kynd,
Hoppand on the thak and on the causay by.
The schot I clossit and drew inwart in hy,
Chiverand for cauld, the sessoun was so snell;
Schup wyth hait flambe to fleme the fresyng fell.

And, as I bownit me to the fyre me by,
Bayth wp and downe the hous I did aspy;
And seand Virgill on ane letterune stand,
To writ anone I hynt ane pen in hand,

For tyll performe the poet grave and sad,
Quham sa fer furth, or than, begun I had;
And wolx ennoyit sum deyll in my hart,
Thair restit vncompleittit so gret ane part.
And til myself I said: 'In guid effect,
Thow man draw furth, the yok lyis on thi nek.'
Wythin my mynd compasing thocht I so,
Na thing is done quhill ocht remanis to do.
For byssines, quhilk occurrit on cace,
Ourvoluit I this volume, lay ane space;
And, thocht I wery was, me lyst nocht tyre,
Full laith to leve our werk, swa in the myre,
Or yit to stynt for byttir storme or rane:
Heyr I assayit to yok our pleuch agane:
And, as I culd, with afauld diligence,
This nixt buike following of profund sentence
Has thus begoune in the chyll wyntir cauld,
Quhen frostis days ourfret bayth fyrth and fauld.

Explicit tristis prologus

GAVIN DOUGLAS

Proud Maisie

Proud Maisie is in the wood,
Walking so early;
Sweet Robin sits on the bush,
Singing so rarely.

'Tell me, thou bonny bird,
When shall I marry me?'
'When six braw gentlemen
Kirkward shall carry ye.'

'Who makes the bridal bed,
Birdie, say truly?'
'The grey-headed sexton,
That delves the grave duly.

378

'The glowworm o'er grave and stone
Shall light thee steady;
The owl from the steeple sing,
"Welcome, proud lady." '

SIR WALTER SCOTT

The Prows o' Reekie

O wad this braw hie-heapit toun
Sail aff like an enchanted ship,
Drift owre the warld's seas up and doun,
And kiss wi' Venice lip to lip,
Or anchor into Naples' Bay
A misty island far astray
Or set her rock to Athens' wa',
Pillar to pillar, stane to stane,
The cruikit spell o' her backbane,
Yon shadow-mile o' spire and vane,
Wad ding them a', wad ding them a'!
Cadiz wad tine the admiralty
O' yonder emerod fair sea,
Gibraltar frown for frown exchange
Wi' Nigel's crags at elbuck-range,
The rose-red banks o' Lisbon make
Mair room in Tagus for her sake.

A hoose is but a puppet-box
To keep life's images frae knocks,
But mannikins scrieve oot their sauls
Upon its craw-steps and its walls;
Whaur hae they writ them mair sublime
Than on yon gable-ends o' time?

LEWIS SPENCE

Psalm 23

The Lord God is my Pastor gude,
Aboundantlie me for to feid:
Than how can I be destitute
Of ony gude thing in my neid?
He feidis me in feildis fair,
To Reveris sweit, pure, and preclair,
He dryvis me but ony dreid.

My Saull and lyfe he dois refresche,
And me convoyis in the way
Of his Justice and rychteousnes.
And me defendis from decay,
Nocht for my warkis verteousnes,
Bot for his name sa glorious,
Preservis me baith nycht and day.

And thocht I waver, or ga wyll,
Or am in danger for to die,
Na dreid of deide sall cum me till,
Nor feir of cruell Tyrannie.
Because that thow art me besyde,
To governe me and be my gyde,
From all mischeif and miserie.

Thy staffe, quhair of I stand greit awe,
And thy scheip huke me for to fang,
Thay nurtour me, my faultis to knaw,
Quhen fra the hie way I ga wrang.
Thairfoir my spreit is blyith and glaid,
Quhen on my flesche thy scurge is laid,
In the rycht way to gar me gang.

And thow ane Tabill dois provyde
Befoir me, full of all delyte,
Contrair to my persewaris pryde,
To thair displesour and dispyte.
Thow hes annoyntit weill my heide,
And full my coupe thow hes maid,
With mony dischis of delyte.

They gudnes and beningnitie
Lat ever be with me thairfoir;
And quhill I leve untill I die,
Thow lay thame up with me in stoir,
That I may haif my dwelling place,
Into thy hous befoir thy face,
To ring with the for ever moir.

GUDE & GODLIE BALLADS

Psyche Left Herlane

Out whaur yon drystane dyke pairts aff
    The carry frae the muir,
The gray muin straws the sterns like caff
    Throu the caller air.

It wes at this hour he wad come
    As a seuch that steirs the hair,
Reeshlan like the leaves that thrum
    Outbye on the gairden stair.

TOM SCOTT

Quatrains

i
our land's gey bonnie i the settin sun
gress and flouers perfumin the waretime wund
swallas flee abune the slaistery slatch
doverin deuks beik on the warm saun

ii
the watter's emerant, the birds whiter yit
the hills is green, their flourish skyrie-gettin
here's anither waretime winnin awa –
an whan'll come ma ain hame-gaun?

BRIAN HOLTON

Translated from the Mandarin below by the author

絕句

一

———   ———   ———

二

江碧鳥逾白
山青花欲燃
今春看又過
何日是歸年

DU FU

Qwhen Alexander our kynge was dede

Qwhen Alexander our kynge was dede,
That Scotlande lede in lauche and le,
Away was sons of alle and brede,
    Off wyne and wax, of gamyn and gle.
Our golde was changit in to lede.
    Christ, borne in virgynyte,
Succoure Scotlande, and ramede,
    That stade is in perplexite.

ANON.

The Railway Bridge of the Silvery Tay

Beautiful Railway Bridge of the Silvery Tay!
With your numerous arches and pillars in so grand array
And your central girders, which seem to the eye
To be almost towering to the sky.
The greatest wonder of the day,

And a great beautification to the River Tay,
Most beautiful to be seen,
Near by Dundee and the Magdalen Green.

Beautiful Railway Bridge of the Silvery Tay!
That has caused the Emperor of Brazil to leave
His home far away, incognito in his dress,
And view thee ere he passed along en route to Inverness.

Beautiful Railway Bridge of the Silvery Tay!
The longest of the present day
That has ever crossed o'er a tidal river stream,
Most gigantic to be seen,
Near by Dundee and the Magdalen Green.

Beautiful Railway Bridge of the Silvery Tay!
Which will cause great rejoicing on the opening day
And hundreds of people will come from far away,
Also the Queen, most gorgeous to be seen,
Near by Dundee and the Magdalen Green.

Beautiful Railway Bridge of the Silvery Tay!
And prosperity to Provost Cox, who has given
Thirty thousand pounds and upwards away
In helping to erect the Bridge of the Tay,
Most handsome to be seen,
Near by Dundee and the Magdalen Green.

Beautiful Railway Bridge of the Silvery Tay!
I hope that God will protect all passengers
By night and by day,
And that no accident will befall them while crossing
The Bridge of the Silvery Tay,
For that would be most awful to be seen
Near by Dundee and the Magdalen Green.

Beautiful Railway Bridge of the Silvery Tay!
And prosperity to Messrs Bouche and Grothe,
The famous engineers of the present day,
Who have succeeded in erecting

The Railway Bridge of the Silvery Tay,
Which stands unequalled to be seen
Near by Dundee and the Magdalen Green.

WILLIAM MCGONAGALL

Reading Pascal in the Lowlands

His aunt has gone astray in her concern
And the boy's mum leans across his wheelchair
To talk to him. She points to the river.
An aged angler and a boy they know
Cast lazily into the rippled sun.
They go there, into the dappled grass, shadows
Bickering and falling from the shaken leaves.

His father keeps apart from them, walking
On the beautiful grass that is bright green
In the sunlight of July at 7 p.m.
He sits on the bench beside me, saying
It is a lovely evening, and I rise
From my sorrows, agreeing with him.
His large hand picks tobacco from a tin;

His smile falls at my feet, on the baked earth
Shoes have shuffled over and ungrassed.
It is discourteous to ask about
Accidents, or of the sick, the unfortunate.
I do not need to, for he says 'Leukaemia'.
We look at the river, his son holding a rod,
The line going downstream in a cloud of flies.

I close my book, the *Pensées* of Pascal.
I am light with meditation, religiose
And mystic with a day of solitude.
I do not tell him of my own sorrows.
He is bored with misery and premonition.
He has seen the limits of time, asking 'Why?'
Nature is silent on that question.

A swing squeaks in the distance. Runners jog
Round the perimeter. He is indiscreet.
His son is eight years old, with months to live.
His right hand trembles on his cigarette.
He sees my book, and then he looks at me,
Knowing me for a stranger. I have said
I am sorry. What more is there to say?

He is called over to the riverbank.
I go away, leaving the Park, walking through
The Golf Course, and then a wood, climbing,
And then bracken and gorse, sheep pasturage.
From a panoptic hill I look down on
A little town, its estuary, its bridge,
Its houses, churches, its undramatic streets.

DOUGLAS DUNN

Re-reading Katherine Mansfield's 'Bliss and Other Stories'

A pressed fly, like a skeleton of gauze,
Has waited here between page 98
And 99, in the story called 'Bliss',
Since the summer of '62, its date,

Its last day in a trap of pages. Prose
Fly, what can '*Je ne parle pas français*' mean
To you who died in Scotland, when I closed
These two sweet pages you were crushed between?

Here is a green bus-ticket for one week
In May, my place-mark in 'The Dill Pickle'.
I did not come home that Friday. I flick
Through all our years, my love; and I love you still.

These stories must have been inside my head
That day, falling in love, preparing this
Good life; and this, this fly, verbosely buried
In 'Bliss', one dry tear punctuating 'Bliss'.

DOUGLAS DUNN

Right inuff

right inuff
ma language is disgraceful

ma maw tellt mi
ma teacher tellt mi
thi doactir tellt mi
thi priest tellt mi

ma boss tellt mi
ma landlady in carrington street tellt mi
thi lassie ah tried tay get aff way in 1969 tellt mi
sum wee smout thit thoat ah hudny read chomsky tellt mi
a calvinistic communist thit thoat ah wuz revisionist tellt mi

po-faced literati grimly kerryin thi burden a thi past tellt mi
po-faced literati grimly kerryin thi burden a thi future tellt mi
ma wife tellt mi jist-tay-get-inty-this-poem tellt mi
ma wainz came hame fray school an tellt mi
jist aboot ivry book ah oapnd tellt mi
even thi introduction tay thi Scottish National Dictionary tellt mi

ach well
all livin language is sacred
fuck thi lohta thim

TOM LEONARD

The Road Home

As I came home from Kirkwall
The ships were on the tide:
I saw the kirk of Magnus
Down by the water side:
The blesséd brave Saint Magnus
Who bowed his head and died.
His shining life was shorn away,
His kirk endureth to this day.
As I came home from Kirkwall
The ships were on the tide.

As I came home from Birsay
A sower, all in tatters,
Strode, scattering the seed, immense
Against the sunset bars,
And through his fingers, with the night,
Streamed all the silver stars.
I watched him (leaning on a gate)
Scatter the glowing seeds of fate:
As I came home from Birsay
Against the sunset bars.

As I came home from Sandwick
A star was in the sky.
The northern lights above the hill
Were streaming broad and high.
The tinkers lit their glimmering fires,
Their tents were pitched close by.
But the city of the vanished race
Lay dark and silent in that place.
As I came home from Sandwick
A star was in the sky.

GEORGE MACKAY BROWN

'S mòr mo mhulad

'S mòr mo mhulad 's cha lugha m' eu-slaint
Ge b'e dh'èisdeadh rium.

'S tric mi 'g amharc thar a' bhealaich
'S m' air' air dol a-nunn

Far am bheil a' ghruagach chùl-donn
Is i gu sùil-ghorm cruinn.

Do shlios mar aoilean, do ghruaidh mar chaorann,
Do mhala chaol fo thuinn.

Do shlios àlainn, do ghruaidh mar sgàrlaid,
Do bheul o 'm màlda cainnt.

Do bheulan lurach a' cur orm furain,
A ghaoil, cha duilich leam.

'S iom' oidhche anmoch a thug mo mheanmna
Mi do 'n ghleann ud thall.

Shnàmhainn thairis gun ràmh gun darach,
Nam biodh mo leannan thall.

Sruth ga chaisid cha chùm air ais mi
Nam biodh mo leachd fo thuinn.

Shiùbhlainn giùthsaich re oidhche dhùbh-dhoirch
Ge do bhiodh an drìuchda trom.

Cha b'ann air mhèirle a bheirinn ionnsaigh,
Ghlacainn mo ghràdh air làimh.

Anna mhaiseach a' chiùil chleachdaich,
Tionndaidh d' aigne rium.

Anna bhòidheach, gruaidh mar ròs ort,
'S truagh nach pòisd thu rium.

'S ged thèid mi 'm leabaidh, chan fhaigh mi cadal,
Chan eil m' aigne leam.

'S tric mi d' fhaicinn ann am bruadar,
A bhean a' chuailein duinn.

Gaol na rìbhinn a rinn mo lìonadh,
Bean nam mìn-rosg mall.

'S mis' tha brònach thu dol a phòsadh
Is mi bhith chòir nan gleann.

Gun bheàrn nam dheudach, gun chais' am eudainn,
Tha uchd mo chlèibh gun srann.

'S cha b'e lughaid m' eudail thug ort mo thrèigsinn,
Ach comann geur nan Gall.

Gar am bheil mi eòlach air cur an eòrna
Ghleidhinn duit feòil nam mang.

Fiadh à fireach is breac à linne
'S damh biorach donn nan càrn.

Damh chinn-riamhaich sa bheinn liath-ghlais,
Bhiodh san t-sliabh uam marbh.

Ge bu leamsa gu Loch Abar
Is ni b'fhaide thall,

Ealgainn Moireibh 's Dun Eideann mar-ris
'S na bheil de dh'fhearann ann,

Chuirinn suarach na rinn mi luaidh riut
Mun tugainn uam an geall.

GUN URRA

Great is my sorrow

Great is my sorrow, not small my ill health,
No matter who would listen to me.

I often look across the hill-pass:
My attention is pulled there

To the dark-haired maiden
With round blue eyes.

Your side like a seagull, your cheek like the ash,
Your slim brow under waves.

Your side lovely, your cheek like scarlet,
Your mouth of the gentlest speech.

Your lovely little mouth invites me,
My love, I'm not sorry.

Many late nights my imagination
Took me over to that glen.

I'd swim across without oar or ship,
If my love was over there.

No strong current would keep me back
If my stone was under waves.

I'd travel a pinewood on a pitch-black night
Even if the dew was heavy.

My invasion would not be theft;
I'd grab my love by the hand.

Gorgeous Anna of the fashionable tresses,
Turn your thoughts to me.

Lovely Anna, with a rose-like cheek,
It's a shame you didn't marry me.

Though I go to bed I cannot sleep,
My spirit isn't with me.

I often see you in a dream,
The girl with the brown curls.

Love for the maiden has filled me,
Woman of the soft fine eyelashes.

I'm sad you're going to marry
And I'm bound to the glens.

No holes in my teeth, no wrinkles on my face,
No wheezing in my ribcage.

Not my lack of passion made you forsake me
But the sharp company of lowlanders.

Though I'm not acquainted with sowing barley
I'd preserve for you meat from fawns.

Deer from the moorland, trout from pools,
And the sharp brown stags of the cairns.

Brindle-headed stags in the light-grey hills –
I would kill them on the slopes.

Though I would go to Lochaber
And even further away,

Elgin in Moray, and Edinburgh,
What there is of land there,

I'd demean the praise I gave you
Before I'd take from myself the vow.

Trans. Peter Mackay

ANON.

Scotch Astrology

Omen
In the gloamin.

ALEXANDER SCOTT

Scotch Poets

Wha's the
T'ither?

ALEXANDER SCOTT

'Scotland small?'

Scotland small? Our multiform, our infinite Scotland *small*?
Only as a patch of hillside may be a cliché corner
To a fool who cries 'Nothing but heather!' where in September another

Sitting there and resting and gazing around
Sees not only the heather but blaeberries
With bright green leaves and leaves already turned scarlet,
Hiding ripe blue berries; and amongst the sage-green leaves
Of the bog-myrtle the golden flowers of the tormentil shining;
And on the small bare places, where the little Blackface sheep
Found grazing, milkworts blue as summer skies;
And down in neglected peat-hags, not worked
Within living memory, sphagnum moss in pastel shades
Of yellow, green, and pink; sundew and butterwort
Waiting with wide-open sticky leaves for their tiny winged prey;
And nodding harebells vying in their colour
With the blue butterflies that poise themselves delicately upon them;
And stunted rowans with harsh dry leaves of glorious colour.
'Nothing but heather!' – How marvellously descriptive! And incomplete!

HUGH MacDIARMID

Sea Buckthorn

Saut an' cruel winds tae shear it,
Nichts o' haar an' rain –
Ye micht think the sallow buckthorn
Ne'er a hairst could hain;
But amang the sea-bleached branches
Ashen-grey as pain,
Thornset orange berries cluster
Flamin', beauty-fain.

Daith an' dule will stab ye surely,
Be ye man or wife,
Mony trauchles an' mischances
In ilk weird are rife;
Bide the storm ye canna hinder,
Mindin' through the strife,
Hoo the luntin' lowe o' beauty
Lichts the grey o' life.

HELEN CRUICKSHANK

Sea-loch

High tide this week is early morning, so you wake
to a full still loch glassily holding the greens of the hillside.

Northwards, its placid surface is pale mirrored cloud
and white reflections of houses scattered on the other shore

then ripples come, a quivering of waves, slight as a shrug,
as the sea starts pulling all five miles of water back

towards itself, dragging the loch away from the land
till it shrinks and a shoreline appears: bladderwrack,

crabshells, mackerel creels, beached rowing boats,
grass for the sheep. Now you can walk easily across

dark rock and yellow seaweed, over the gravelly floor,
all the workings of inlets exposed, an underside revealed

then covered over—a slow seeping, now bigger folds of water,
the push of tide heaving waves into this narrow space,

shoving seawater in so quickly it looks like a river in spate,
rushing towards the head of the loch, where it stops,

becomes shallower, eases into fields of bog myrtle
and meadowsweet. Quiet now, with little lapping waves

like breaths of the far-off tide, this great lung
of sea-loch rising and falling all day long.

ELIZABETH BURNS

Bho Seathan Mac Righ Èireann

B'annsa Seathan a' falbh slèibhe,
   Hù rù o nà hi ò ro,
Mise lag is esan treubhach,
   Nà hi ò ro hó hug ò ro,

Mise lag is esan treubhach;
        Hù rù etc.
Cha ghiùlaininn ach beag èididh,
        Nà hi ò ro etc.

Cha ghiùlaininn ach beag èididh,
        Hù rù etc.
Còta ruadh mu leath mo shlèisne,
'S criosan caol-dubh air mo lèine,
'S mi falbh le Seathan mar eudail.
        Nà hi ò ro hó hug ò ro

'S iomadh beinn is gleann a shuibhail sinn,
Bha mi an Ìle, bha mi am Muile leat,
Bha mi an Èirinn an Còig' Mumha leat,
'S dh'èisd mi 'n Aifhreann 'sa Choill' Bhuidhe leat.
        Hù rù o nà hi ò ro.

'S minig a chuala, 's nach do dh'innis e.
Gu robh mo leannan am Minginis;
Nam biodh e 'n sin, 's fhad' o thigeadh e;
Chuireadh e bàta dha m' shireadh-sa,
'S chuirinn-sa long mhòr 'ga shireadh-san,
Sgiobadh cliùiteach, ùrail, iriseal.
        Nà hi ò ro hó hug ò ro,
        Nà hi ò ro hó hug ò ro,
        Nà hi ò ro hó hug ò ro.

Nam faighte Seathan ri fhuasgladh,
Dh'fhàsadh an t-òr fo na bruachaibh,
Cha bhiodh gobhair an creig ghruamaich,
'S cha bhiodh lìon gun iasg an cuantan.
        Nà hi ò ro hó hug ò ro,
        Nà hi ò ro hó hug ò ro,
        Nà hi ò ro hó hug ò ro.

B'annsa Seathan air cùl tobhtadh
Na bhith le mac rìgh air lobhtaidh,
Ged bhiodh aige leaba shocair,
'S stròl dhan t-sìoda bhith fo chasan,
'S cluasag dhan òr dhearg a' lasradh.
        Nà hi ò ro hó hug ò ro.

394

Tha Seathan an nochd 'na mharbhan,
Sgeul as ait le luchd a shealga,
'S le mac caillich nan trì dealga,
Sgeul as olc le fearaibh Alba.
A Sheathain! a Sheathain m'anma!
Dhealbh-mhic mo rìgh o thìr Chonbhaigh!
    Hù rù o nà hi ò ro.

GUN URRA

From Seathan, Son of the King of Ireland

Beloved Seathan travelling moorland,
I was weak and he was mighty,
I was weak and he was mighty,
I wouldn't bother with much clothing.

I wouldn't bother with much clothing,
a russet coat down to mid-thigh,
round my shift a thin black girdle,
me travelling with Seathan as his lover.

Many a hill and glen we wandered in,
I was in Islay, I was in Mull with you,
I was with you in Ireland in the province of Munster,
in the Yellow Wood I heard mass with you.

Woe to him who heard it but never reported it,
that my darling was over in Minginish;
had he been there, he'd have come long ago,
he'd send a boat to come and look for me,
I'd send a ship to go and look for him,
with a youthful crew, renowned and dutiful.

If Seathan would be released from bondage
gold would grow below the banks of the river,
there'd be no goats on gloomy clifftop,
nor net without fish in the oceans.

395

Better lying with Seathan behind a ruined building
than be with a prince in an upper storey,
even though his were a soft mattress,
with a red gold gleaming pillow,
and under his feet a strip of satin.

Tonight Seathan is a lifeless body,
tidings of joy for his pursuers
and the son of the crone of the three needles,
an evil tale to the men of Scotland,
O Seathan, O my soul's Seathan!
the image of my king from Conway country.

[. . .]

Trans. Meg Bateman

ANON.

She Walks in Beauty

I.

She walks in Beauty, like the night
Of cloudless climes and starry skies;
And all that's best of dark and bright
Meet in her aspect and her eyes:
Thus mellowed to that tender light
Which Heaven to gaudy day denies.

II.

One shade the more, one ray the less,
Had half impaired the nameless grace
Which waves in every raven tress,
Or softly lightens o'er her face;
Where thoughts serenely sweet express,
How pure, how dear their dwelling-place.

III.

And on that cheek, and o'er that brow,
So soft, so calm, yet eloquent,
The smiles that win, the tints that glow,
But tell of days in goodness spent,
A mind at peace with all below,
A heart whose love is innocent!

LORD BYRON

The Shortest and Sweetest of Songs

Come
Home.

GEORGE MacDONALD

Sir Patrick Spens

The King sits in Dunferline toun,
Drinkin the blude-reid wine
'O whaur will A get a skeely skipper
Tae sail this new ship o mine?'

O up and spak an eldern knight,
Sat at the king's richt knee;
'Sir Patrick Spens is the best sailor
That ever sailt the sea.'

Our king has written a braid letter
And sealed it wi his hand,
And sent it to Sir Patrick Spens,
Wis walkin on the strand.

'Tae Noroway, to Noroway,
Tae Noroway ower the faem;
The King's dauchter o Noroway,
Tis thou maun bring her hame.'

The first word that Sir Patrick read
Sae loud, loud laucht he;
The neist word that Sir Patrick read
The tear blindit his ee.

'O wha is this has duin this deed
An tauld the king o me,
Tae send us out, at this time o year,
Tae sail abuin the sea?

'Be it wind, be it weet, be it hail, be it sleet,
Our ship maun sail the faem;
The King's dauchter o Noroway,
Tis we maun fetch her hame.'

They hoystit their sails on Monenday morn,
Wi aw the speed they may;
They hae landit in Noroway
Upon a Wodensday.

'Mak ready, mak ready, my merry men aw!
Our gude ship sails the morn.'
'Nou eer alack, ma maister dear,
I fear a deadly storm.'

'A saw the new muin late yestreen
Wi the auld muin in her airm
And gif we gang tae sea, maister,
A fear we'll cam tae hairm.'

They hadnae sailt a league, a league,
A league but barely three,
When the lift grew dark, an the wind blew loud
An gurly grew the sea.

The ankers brak, an the topmaist lap,
It was sic a deadly storm.
An the waves cam ower the broken ship
Til aw her sides were torn.

'Go fetch a web o silken claith,
Anither o the twine,
An wap them into our ship's side,
An let nae the sea cam in.'

They fetcht a web o the silken claith,
Anither o the twine,
An they wapp'd them roun that gude ship's side,
But still the sea cam in.

O laith, laith were our gude Scots lords
Tae weet their cork-heelt shuin;
But lang or aw the play wis playd
They wat their hats abuin.

And mony wis the feather bed
That flattert on the faem;
And mony wis the gude lord's son
That never mair cam hame.

O lang, lang may the ladies sit,
Wi their fans intae their hand,
Afore they see Sir Patrick Spens
Come sailin tae the strand!

And lang, lang may the maidens sit
Wi their gowd kames in their hair,
A-waitin for their ane dear loes!
For them they'll see nae mair.

Half-ower, half-ower to Aberdour,
Tis fifty fathoms deep;
An there lies gude Sir Patrick Spens,
Wi the Scots lords at his feet!

ANON.

Sir Thomas Maitland's Satyr upon Sir Niel Laing

Canker'd, cursed creature, crabbed, corbit kittle,
Buntin-ars'd, beugle-back'd, bodied like a beetle;
Sarie shitten, shell-padock, ill shapen shit,
Kid-bearded gennet, all alike great:
Fiddle-douped, flindrikin, fart of a man,
Wa worth the, wanwordie, wanshapen wran!

THOMAS MAITLAND

The six o'clock news

this is thi
six a clock
news thi
man said n
thi reason
a talk wia
BBC accent
iz coz yi
widny wahnt
mi ti talk
aboot thi
trooth wia
voice lik
wanna yoo
scruff. if
a toktaboot
thi trooth
lik wanna yoo
scruff yi
widny thingk
it wuz troo.
jist wanna yoo
scruff tokn.
thirza right
way ti spell
ana right way
to tok it. this

is me tokn yir
right way a
spellin. this
is ma trooth.
yooz doant no
thi trooth
yirsellz cawz
yi canny talk
right. this is
the six a clock
nyooz. belt up.

TOM LEONARD

Slattern

I leave myself about, slatternly,
bits of me, and times I liked:
I let them go on lying where they fall,
crumple, if they will. I know fine
how to make them walk
and breathe again. Sometimes at night,
or on the train, I dream I'm dancing,
or lying in someone's arms who says
he loves my eyes in French, and again
and again I am walking up your road,
that first time, bidden and wanted,
the blossom on the trees, light,
light and buoyant. *Pull yourself
together*, they say, quite rightly,
but she is stubborn, that girl,
that hopeful one, still walking.

KATE CLANCHY

Smeòrach Chloinn Dòmhnaill

Hoilibheag, hilibheag, hò-ail-il ò
Hoilibheag, hilibheag, hò ro ì,
Hoilibheag, hilibheag, hò-ail-il ò
Smeòrach le Clann Dòmhnàill mi.

Smeòrach mis' air ùrlar Phabil:
Crùbadh ann an dùsal cadail,
Gun deòrachd a thèid nas fhaide;
Truimid mo bhròn, thòirleum m' aigne.

Smeòrach mis' air mullach beinne,
'G amharc grèin' is speuran soilleir;
Thig mi stòlda chòir na coille –
Bidh mi beò air treòdas eile.

Smeòrach mis' air bhàrr gach bidein,
Dèanamh mùirn ri driùchd na madainn,
Bualadh mo chliath-lùth air m' fheadan,
Seinn mo chiùil gun smùr gun smodan.

Ma mholas gach eun a thìr fèin,
Cuim' thar èis nach moladh mise?
Tìr nan curaidh, tìr nan cliar,
An tìr bhiadhchar, fhialaidh, mhiosail.

'N tìr nach caol ri cois na mara,
An tìr ghaolach, chaomhach, channach,
An tìr laoghach, uanach, mheannach,
Tìr an arain, bhainneach, mhealach.

An tìr riabhach, ghrianach, thaitneach;
An tìr dhìonach, fhiarach, fhasgach;
An tìr lèanach, ghèadhach, lachach,
'N tìr 'm bi biadh gun mhiadh air tacar.

An tìr chròiceach, eòrnach, phailte;
An tìr bhuadhach, chluaineach, ghartach;
An tìr chruachach, sguabach, dhaiseach,
Dlùth ri cuan gun fhuachd ri sneachda.

'S i 'n tìr sgiamhach tìr a' mhachair,
Tìr nan dìthean mìogach dathte;
An tìr làireach, àigeach, mhartach,
Tìr an àigh gu bràth nach gaisear.

'N tìr as bòidhche ta ri faicinn;
'M bi fir òg' an còmhdach dreachail;
Pailt na 's leòr le pòr a' mhachair;
Sprèidh air mòintich, òr air chlachan.

An Cladh Chòmhghain mise rugadh,
'N Àird an Runnair fhuair mi togail;
Fradharc a' chuain uaibhrich, chuislich,
Nan stuagh guanach, cluaineach, cluiceach.

Measg Chlann Dòmhnaill fhuair mi m' altram,
Buidheann nan seòl 's nan sròl dathte,
Nan long luath air chuantaibh farsaing,
Aiteam nach ciùin rùsgadh ghlaslann.

Na fir eòlach, stòlda, staideil,
Bha 's a' chòimhstrith stròiceach, sgaiteach,
Fir gun bhròn, gun leòn, gun airtneal,
Leanadh tòir is tòir a chaisgeadh.

Buidheann mo ghaoil nach caoin caitean,
Buidheann nach gann greann 's an aisith;
Bhuidheann shanntach 'n àm bhith aca,
Rùsgadh lann fo shranntraich bhratach.

Bhuidheann uallach 'n uair na caismeachd,
Leanadh ruaig gun luaidh air gealtachd;
Cinn is guaillean cruaidh gan spealtadh,
Aodach ruadh le fuaim ga shracadh.

Buidheann rìoghail 's fìorghlan alladh,
Buidheann gun fhiamh 's ìotadh fal' orr';
Buidheann gun sgàth 'm blàr no 'n deannal,
Foinnidh, nàrach, làidir, fearail.

Buidheann mhòr 's am pòr nach troicheil,
Dh'fhàs gu meanmnach, dealbhach, toirteil,
Fearail fo 'n airm – 's mairg d' a nochdadh,
Ri uchd stairm nach leanabail coltas.

Suidhmid mu 'n bhòrd stòlda, beachdail;
'N t-sùil san dòrn nach òl a-mach i –
Slàint' Shir Seumas, dheagh thighinn dachaigh;
Aon Mhac Dè mar sgèith do d' phearsain.

IAIN MaCCODRUM

The Song Thrush of Clan Donald

Holivag hilivag hò-ail-il ò
Holivag hilivag hò ro ì
Holivag hilivag hò-ail-il ò
I'm a song thrush of Clan Donald.

I'm a song thrush on the plain of Paible,
Crouched down in a napping sleep,
Banished if I go any further;
My sadness heavy, my spirit weak.

I'm a song thrush up a mountain,
Watching the sun and the clear skies;
Composed, I go towards the forest –
I will live by other means.

I'm a song thrush on each summit peak,
Cheerful in the morning dew,
Hitting tuning notes on my chanter,
Singing my music clean and true.

If every bird praises its own land,
Why then should I not praise my own?
This land of heroes, land of poets,
Fruitful, hospitable, far-renowned.

The fertile land beside the sea,
Land that is lovely, kind and mild,
Land of calves and lambs and kids,
Land of bread and milk and honey.

The dappled, sunny, delightful land,
The safe, grassy, sheltered land,
The land of meadows, geese and wild ducks,
The land of food, provision for all.

The land of seaweed, barley, plenty,
Land of virtues, meadows and corn,
Land of stacks and sheaves and ricks,
Beside the sea, without cold or snow.

The machair land is a graceful land,
This land of sparkling coloured flowers,
Land of mares, stallions and cattle,
A land where fortune will never fade.

The loveliest land that could be seen,
Where young men dress in handsome clothes,
With plentiful crops on the machair,
Stock on the moors, gold on stones.

I was born in Comgan's churchyard,
And raised in Àird an Runnair;
In sight of the proud, pulsating ocean,
The giddy, fickle, playful waves.

I was nursed among Clan Donald,
The folk of the sails and coloured flags,
The swift ships on the wide oceans,
People who're ready to bare grey blades.

Men who are skilful, steady, stately,
Who were sharp and shredding in war;
Men without sadness, wounds or tiredness,
Who'd follow a rout or push it back.

The folk I love are not smoothly ruffled,
Folk who'd bristle in times of strife;
Who would be eager to go at them,
To bare their blades under whipping flags.

Folk who are proud in times of marching,
Who'd follow the rout with no hint of fear;
Who'd cleave hard through heads and shoulders,
Ripping loudly through red cloth.

This royal folk, of purest fame,
Who have no fear when thirsting blood –
Folk without dread in battle or conflict,
Lively, modest, strong and brave.

Great folk, not from a stunted line,
Who grew up shapely, bold and strong:
Poor you if you face their weapons!
They look manly, not childlike, in war.

Let's sit round the table, steady, thoughtful –
Your eye in your fist if you don't toast this out:
'The health of Sir James, may you safely come home,
God's only son be a shield to your person.'

Trans. Peter Mackay

JOHN MacCODRUM

The Smoky Smirr o Rain

A misty mornin' doon the shore wi a hushed an' caller air,
an' ne'er a breath frae East or Wast tie sway the rashes there,
a sweet, sweet scent frae Laggan's birks gaed breathin' on its ane,
their branches hingin beaded in the smoky smirr o rain.

As I gaed doon by Laggan shore on a misty mornin' aa,
the warld was turned a mystery in the mist o rain sae smaa,
for time an' airt in aa that place tie ken o there war name,
as reek o haze ilk wye did steek in the smoky smirr o rain.

The day was hushed an' doverin' as the fog o rain cam doon,
Owre shore an' watter hoverin' it drifted frae abune,
Nae waft o air tie steer it was there; the lift was lown,
an' rallyoch winds gied owre their virr in the smoky smirr o rain.

The hills aroond war silent wi the mist alang the braes,
The woods war derk an' quiet wi dewy, glintin' spreays,
The mavies didna raise for me, as I gaed bye alane,
but a wee, wae cheep at passin' in the smoky smirr o rain.

Rock an' stane lay glisterin' on aa the heichs abune,
Cool an' kind an' whisperin' it drifted gently doon,
till hill an' howe war rowed in it, an' land an' sea war gane,
Aa was still an' saft an' silent in the smoky smirr o rain.

A blessin', a caressin' was the rain upon my face,
Deep dwaamed the silence. Calm lay deep an' kind owre aa that place.
Nae cry o whaup cam frae the lift an' lift an' yirrd war ane,
as I gaed doon by Laggan in the smoky smirr o rain.

As I turned frae Laggan Roaig, I brocht back wi me
a history o mystery an' mist on land an' sea,
o muted mavies, waveless shores an' gairs in harr their lane
as I cam back frae Laggan shore in the smoky smirr o rain.

Aa licht was faint, horizons tint, asclent the rain cam doon.
The day was derk, the braes war mirk an' misty heich abune
an' strand an' land war dernin an' the mavies made their maen
as beuchs an' branches bieldit thaim in the smoky smirr o rain.

GEORGE CAMPBELL HAY

Snow

I

'Who affirms that crystals are alive?'
    I affirm it, let who will deny: —
Crystals are engendered, wax and thrive,
    Wane and wither; I have seen them die.

Trust me, masters, crystals have their day.
    Eager to attain the perfect norm,
Lit with purpose, potent to display
    Facet, angle, colour, beauty, form.

II

Water-crystals need for flower and root
    Sixty clear degrees, no less, no more;
Snow, so fickle, still in this acute
    Angle thinks, and learns no other lore:

Such its life, and such its pleasure is,
    Such its art and traffic, such its gain,
Evermore in new conjunctions this
    Admirable angle to maintain.

Crystalcraft in every flower and flake
    Snow exhibits, of the welkin free:
Crystalline are crystals for the sake,
    All and singular, of crystalry.

Yet does every crystal of the snow
    Individualize, a seedling sown
Broadcast, but instinct with power to grow
    Beautiful in beauty of its own.

Every flake with all its prongs and dints
    Burns ecstatic as a new-lit star:
Men are not more diverse, finger-prints
    More dissimilar than snow-flakes are.

Worlds of men and snow endure, increase,
    Woven of power and passion to defy
Time and travail: only races cease,
    Individual men and crystals die.

III

Jewelled shapes of snow whose feathery showers,
    Fallen or falling wither at a breath,
All afraid are they, and loth as flowers
    Beasts and men to tread the way to death.

Once I saw upon an object-glass,
    Martyred underneath a microscope,
One elaborate snow-flake slowly pass,
    Dying hard, beyond the reach of hope.

Still from shape to shape the crystal changed,
    Writhing in its agony: and still,
Less and less elaborate, arranged
    Potently the angle of its will.

Tortured to a simple final form,
    Angles six and six divergent beams,
Lo, in death it touched the perfect norm
    Verifying all its crystal dreams!

IV

Such the noble tragedy of one
    Martyred snow-flake. Who can tell the fate
Heinous and uncouth of showers undone,
    Fallen in cities! – showers that expiate

Errant lives from polar worlds adrift
    Where the great millennial snows abide;
Castaways from mountain-chains that lift
    Snowy summits in perennial pride;

Nomad snows, or snows in evil day
    Born to urban ruin, to be tossed,
Trampled, shovelled, ploughed and swept away
    Down the seething sewers: all the frost

Flowers of heaven melted up with lees,
    Offal, recrement, but every flake

Showing to the last in fixed degrees
    Perfect crystals for the crystal's sake.

V

Usefulness of snow is but a chance
    Here in temperate climes with winter sent,
Sheltering earth's prolonged hibernal trance:
    All utility is accident.

Sixty clear degrees the joyful snow,
    Practising economy of means,
Fashions endless beauty in, and so
    Glorifies the universe with scenes

Arctic and antarctic: stainless shrouds,
    Ermine woven in silvery frost, attire
Peaks in every land among the clouds
    Crowned with snows to catch the morning's fire.

JOHN DAVIDSON

So We'll Go No More a Roving

So, we'll go no more a roving
    So late into the night,
Though the heart be still as loving,
    And the moon be still as bright.

For the sword outwears its sheath,
    And the soul wears out the breast,
And the heart must pause to breathe,
    And love itself have rest.

Though the night was made for loving,
    And the day returns too soon,
Yet we'll go no more a roving
    By the light of the moon.

LORD BYRON

Solace in Age

Thocht that this warld be verie ftrange,
And theiffis hes done my rowmis range,
    And teynd my fauld;
Yet wald I leif, and byde ane change,
Thocht I be auld.

Now me to fpoulyie fum men nocht fpairis;
To tak my geir na captaine cairis,
    Thay ar fa bald;
Yet tym may com, may mend my fairis,
    Thocht I be auld.

Sum now, be force of men of weir,
My hous, my landis, and my geir,
    Fra me thay hald;
Yit, as I may, fall mak gude cheir,
    Thocht I be auld.

Sa weill is kend my innocence,
That I will nocht for myne offence,
    Flyte lyk ane fkald;
Bot thank God, and tak patience;
    For I am auld.

For eild, and my infirmitie,
Warme claythis ar bettir far, for me
    To keip fra cauld;
Nor in dame Venus chamber be,
    For I am auld.

Of Venus play paft is the heit;
For I may not the mifteris beit
    Of Meg, nor Mald;
For ane young lafs I am not meit,
    I am fa auld.

The faireft wenche hi all this toun,
Thocht I hir had in hir beft goun,
    Rycht braivlie brald;

With hir I micht not play the loun,
    I am fa auld.

My wyf fumtyme wald taillis trow,
And mony leifingis weill allow,
    War of me tald:
Scho will not eyndill on me now,
    And I fa auld.

My hors, my harneis, and my fpeir,
And all uther, my hoifting geir,
    Now may be fald;
I am not abill for the weir,
    I am fa auld.

Quhan young men cumis fra the grene,
Playand at the fute-ball had bene,
    With broken fpald;
I thank my God, I want my ene,
    And am fa auld.

Thocht I be fweir to ryd or gang,
Thair is fumthing, I've wantit lang,
    Fane have I wald;
Thame punyfit that did me wrang,
    Thocht I be auld.

SIR RICHARD MAITLAND

The Soldiers' Cairn

Gie me a hill wi' the heather on't,
An' a reid sun drappin' doon,
Or the mists o' the mornin' risin' saft
Wi' the reek owre a wee grey toon.
Gie me a howe by the lang Glen road,
For it's there 'mang the whin and fern
(D'ye mind on't, Will? Are ye hearin', Dod?)
That we're biggin' the Soldiers' Cairn.

Far awa' is the Flanders land
Wi' fremmit France atween,
But mony a howe o' them baith the day
Has a hap o' the Gordon green.
It's them we kent that's lyin' there,
An' it's nae wi' stane or airn
But wi' brakin' herts, an' mem'ries sair,
That we're biggin' the Soldiers' Cairn.

Doon, laich doon the Dullan sings —
An' I ken o' an aul' sauch tree,
Where a wee loon's wahnie's hingin' yet
That's dead in Picardy;
An' ilka win' fae the Conval's broo
Bends aye the buss o' ern,
Where aince he futtled a name that noo
I'll read on the Soldiers' Cairn.

Oh! build it fine and build it fair,
Till it leaps to the moorland sky —
More, more than death is symbolled there,
Than tears or triumphs by.
There's the Dream Divine of a starward way
Our laggard feet would learn —
It's a new earth's corner-stone we'd lay
As we fashion the Soldiers' Cairn.

....

Lads in your plaidies lyin' still
In lands we'll never see,
This lanely cairn on a hameland hill
Is a' that oor love can dee;
An' fine an' braw we'll mak' it a',
But oh, my Bairn, my Bairn,
It's a cradle's croon that'll aye blaw doon
To me fae the Soldiers' Cairn.

MARY SYMON

Some Practises of Medicine

Dia Custrum

The ferd feilik is fyne, and of ane felloun pryce,
Gud for hailing, and hofling, or heit at the hairt
Recipe, thre fponfull of the blak fpyce,
With ane grit gowpene of the gowk fart,
The lug of ane ly vin, the gufe of ane gryce;
Ane mice of ane ofler poik at the nether parte
Annoyntit with nurice doung, for it is rycht nyce,
Myngit with myfe dirt and with muflart
Ye may clamp to this cure, and ye will mak coft,
Bayth the bellox of ane brok,
With three crawis of the cok,
The fchadow of ane Yule ftok,
Is gud for the hoft.

ROBERT HENRYSON

Sonet of Venus and Cupid

Fra banc to banc, fra wod to wod, I rin
Ourhailit with my feble fantasie,
Lyk til a leif that fallis from a trie
Or til a reid ourblawin with the wind.
Twa gods gyds me: the ane of tham is blind,
Ye, and a bairn brocht up in vanitie;
The nixt a wyf ingenrit of the se,
And lichter nor a dauphin with hir fin.

Unhappie is the man for evirmair
That teils the sand and sawis in the aire;
Bot twyse unhappier is he, I lairn,
That feidis in his hairt a mad desyre,
And follows on a woman throw the fyre,
Led be a blind and teichit be a bairn.

MARK ALEXANDER BOYD

Song XIV

Oh little apple and whither
    are you rolling? Ever further
from the riverside, where she waits,
    as still as a heron, for you.

Oh little apple, will this be
    your last word? There are no last words.
The river flows on, as it must,
    past you and the lonely heron.

TOM POW

Song Composed in August

Now westlin winds and slaught'ring guns
Bring Autumn's pleasant weather;
The moorcock springs on whirring wings
Amang the blooming heather:
Now waving grain, wide o'er the plain,
Delights the weary farmer;
And the moon shines bright, when I rove at night,
To muse upon my charmer.

The partridge loves the fruitful fells,
The plover loves the mountains;
The woodcock haunts the lonely dells,
The soaring hern the fountains:
Thro' lofty groves the cushat roves,
The path of man to shun it;
The hazel bush o'erhangs the thrush,
The spreading thorn the linnet.

Thus ev'ry kind their pleasure find,
The savage and the tender;
Some social join, and leagues combine,
Some solitary wander:
Avaunt, away! the cruel sway,
Tyrannic man's dominion;

The sportsman's joy, the murd'ring cry,
The flutt'ring, gory pinion!

But, Peggy dear, the ev'ning's clear,
Thick flies the skimming swallow,
The sky is blue, the fields in view,
All fading-green and yellow:
Come let us stray our gladsome way,
And view the charms of Nature;
The rustling corn, the fruited thorn,
And ev'ry happy creature.

We'll gently walk, and sweetly talk,
Till the silent moon shine clearly;
I'll grasp thy waist, and, fondly prest,
Swear how I love thee dearly:
Not vernal show'rs to budding flow'rs,
Not Autumn to the farmer,
So dear can be as thou to me,
My fair, my lovely charmer!

ROBERT BURNS

Sonnet viii

My Lute, bee as thou wast when thou didst grow
With thy greene Mother in some shadie Grove,
When immelodious Windes but made thee move,
And Birds on thee their Ramage did bestow.
Sith that deare Voyce which did thy Sounds approve,
Which us'd in such harmonious Straines to flow,
Is reft from Earth to tune those Spheares above,
What art thou but a Harbenger of Woe?
Thy pleasing Notes be pleasing Notes no more,
But orphane Wailings to the fainting Eare,
Each Stoppe a Sigh, each Sound draws forth a Teare,
Be therefore silent as in Woods before,
Or if that any Hand to touch thee deigne,
Like widow'd Turtle, still her losse complaine.

WILLIAM DRUMMOND OF HAWTHORNDEN

Sonnet

Striving to sing glad songs, I but attain
Wild discords sadder than Grief's saddest tune;
As if an owl with his harsh screech should strain
To over-gratulate a thrush of June.
The nightingale upon its thorny spray
Finds inspiration in the sullen dark;
The kindling dawn, the world-wide joyous day
Are inspiration to the soaring lark;
The seas are silent in the sunny calm,
Their anthem surges in the tempest boom;
The skies outroll no solemn thunder psalm
Till they have clothed themselves with clouds of gloom.
My mirth can laugh and talk, but cannot sing;
My grief finds harmonies in everything.

JAMES THOMSON

Sonnet

My love grows, and yet mair on mair shall grow
As lang as I hae life: O happy pairt,
Alane tae haud a place in that dear hairt
Tae which in time my love itsel shall show
Sae clear that he can nane misdoot me then!
For him I will staun stieve agin sair fate,
For him I will strive for the heichest state,
And dae sae muckle for him he shall ken
I naethin hae – nae gowd, nae gear, nae pleisure –
But tae obey and serve him in haill meisure.
For him I hope for aw guid chance and graith;
For him I will me keep baith quick and weel;
True smeddum I desire for him and feel,
And never will I change while I hae braith.

Translated from the French by James Robertson

MARY, QUEEN OF SCOTS

Sonnet: On the River Tweed

Faire famous flood, which sometyme did devyde,
But now conjoynes, two Diadems in one,
Suspend thy pace and some more softly slyde,
Since wee have made the Trinchman of our mone,
And since non's left but thy report alone
To show the world our Captaines last farewell
That courtesye I know when wee are gon
Perhapps your Lord the Sea will it reveale,
And you againe the same will not conceale,
But straight proclaim't through all his bremish bounds,
Till his high tydes these flowing tydeings tell
And soe will send them with his murmering sounds
    To that Religious place whose stately walls
    Does keepe the heart which all our hearts inthralls.

ROBERT AYTOUN

The Spell Is Broke, the Charm Is Flown

The spell is broke, the charm is flown!
Thus is it with Life's fitful fever:
We madly smile when we should groan;
Delirium is our best deceiver.
Each lucid interval of thought
Recalls the woes of Nature's charter;
And *He* that acts as *wise men ought*,
But *lives* – as Saints have died – a martyr.

LORD BYRON

St Andrews

Sacred St Andrews, the whole wide world
Saw you as the burgh of God.
Jove, eyeing your great Cathedral,
Blushed for his own wee Tarpeian kirk.
The architect of the Ephesian temple,

418

Seeing yours, felt like a fake.
Culdee priests in holy cassocks
Gazed through your East Neuk of light.
St Andrews' Archbishop, clad in gold,
Bellowed at Scotland's Parliament.
Now that's gone, walls ankle-high,
Priestly *fiat lux* tarnished.
Still you pull poets, though. You wow
Lecturers and lab technicians.
Aurora of the Peep o' Day in Fife.
Frisks ashore with salt-reddened fingers,
Herring-sparkle of dawn.
Thetis coughs through 10 a.m. haar,
Waking hirpling, hungover students
Who sober up with golfclubs.
Phocis was Phoebus's long-time lover,
Attica of Pallas. In St Andrews
Each dances. Forever. Now.

Translated from the Latin of Robert Crawford

ARTHUR JOHNSTON

St Kilda's Parliament: 1879–1979

The photographer revisits his picture

On either side of a rock-paved lane,
Two files of men are standing barefooted,
Bearded, waistcoated, each with a tam-o'-shanter
On his head, and most with a set half-smile
That comes from their companionship with rock,
With soft mists, with rain, with roaring gales,
And from a diet of solan goose and eggs,
A diet of dulse and sloke and sea-tangle,
And ignorance of what a pig, a bee, a rat,
Or rabbit look like, although they remember
Three apples brought here by a traveller
Five years ago, and have discussed them since.
And there are several dogs doing nothing
Who seem contemptuous of my camera,

And a woman who might not believe it
If she were told of the populous mainland.
A man sits on a bank by the door of his house,
Staring out to sea and at a small craft
Bobbing there, the little boat that brought me here,
Whose carpentry was slowly shaped by waves,
By a history of these northern waters.
Wise men or simpletons – it is hard to tell –
But in that way they almost look alike.
You also see how each is individual.
Proud of his shyness and of his small life
On this outcast of the Hebrides
With his eyes full of weather and seabirds,
Fish, and whatever morsel he grows here.
Clear, too, is manhood, and how each man looks
Secure in the love of a woman who
Also knows the wisdom of the sun rising,
Of weather in the eyes like landmarks,
Fifty years before depopulation –
Before the boats that came at their own request
To ease them from their dying babies –
It was easy, even then, to imagine
St Kilda return to its naked self,
Its archaeology of hazelraw
And footprints stratified beneath the lichen.
See, how simple it all is, these toes
Playfully clutching the edge of a boulder.
It is a remote democracy, where men,
In manacles of place, outstare a sea
That rattles back its manacles of salt,
The moody jailer of the wild Atlantic.
        Traveller, tourist with your mind set on
Romantic Staffas and materials for
Winter conversations, if you should go there,
Landing at sunrise on its difficult shores,
On St Kilda you will surely hear Gaelic
Spoken softly like a poetry of ghosts
By those who never were contorted by
Hierarchies of cuisine and literacy.
You need only look at the faces of these men
Standing there like everybody's ancestors,

This flick of time I shuttered on a face.
Look at their sly, assuring mockery.
They are aware of what we are up to
With our internal explorations, our
Designs of affluence and education.
They know us so well, and are not jealous,
Whose be-all and end-all was an eternal
Casual husbandry upon a toehold
Of Europe, which, when failing, was not their fault.
You can see they have already prophesied
A day when survivors look across the stern
Of a departing vessel for the last time
At their gannet-shrouded cliffs, and the farewells
Of the St Kilda mouse and St Kilda wren
As they fall into the texts of specialists,
Ornithological visitors at the prow
Of a sullenly managed boat from the future.
They pose for ever outside their parliament,
Looking at me, as if they have grown from
Affection scattered across my own eyes.
And it is because of this that I, who took
This photograph in a year of many events –
The Zulu massacres, Tchaikovsky's opera –
Return to tell you this, and that after
My many photographs of distressed cities,
My portraits of successive elegants,
Of the emaciated dead, the lost empires,
Exploded fleets, and of the writhing flesh
Of dead civilians and commercial copulations,
That after so much of that larger franchise
It is to this island that I return.
Here I whittle time, like a dry stick,
From sunrise to sunset, among the groans
And sighings of a tongue I cannot speak,
Outside a parliament, looking at them,
As they, too, must always look at me
Looking through my apparatus at them
Looking. Benevolent, or malign? But who,
At this late stage, could tell, or think it worth it?
For I was there, and am, and I forget.

DOUGLAS DUNN

Still and All

I give my word on it. There is no way
Other than this. There is no other way
Of speaking. I am my name. I find my place
Empty without a word, and my word is
Given again. It is nothing less than all
Given away again, and all still truly
Returned on a belief. Believe me now.
There is no other. There is no other way.

These words run vertical in their slim green tunnels
Without any turning away. They turn into
The first flower and speak from a silent bell.
But underneath it is as always still
Truly awakening, slowly and slowly turning
About a shadow scribbled down by sunlight
And turning about my name. I am in my
Survival's hands. I am my shadow's theme.

My shadow's ground feeds me with roots, and rhymes
My statement over. Its radius feeds my flames
Into a cool tunnel. And I who find your ways
About me (In every part I find your ways
Of speech.) pierce ground and shadow still. The light
Is struck. Its definition makes me my quiet
Survival's answer. All still and all so truly
Wakening underneath me and turning slowly.

It's all so truly still. I'll take you into
The first statement. I'll take you along cool tunnels
That channelled light and petalled an iridescent
Symmetry over my bruised shadow. And yes
I'll take you, and your word will follow me,
Till definitions gather distilled honey
And make their mark the fingerprints of light.
I am, believe me then, the name I write.

I lie here still. Yes, truly still. And all
My deliberate identities have fallen
Away with the word given. I find my place

In every place, in every part of speech,
And lie there still. I let my statements go.
A cool green tunnel has stepped in the light of my shadow
There is no way round it. It leads to the flower
Bell – that swings slowly and slowly over.

BURNS SINGER

Tam Lin

O I forbid you, maidens a',
That wear gowd on your hair,
To come or gae by Carterhaugh,
For young Tam Lin is there.

There's nane that goes by Carterhaugh
But they leave him a wad,
Either their rings, or green mantles,
Or else their maidenhead.

Janet has kilted her green kirtle
A little aboon her knee,
And she has broded her yellow hair
A little aboon her bree,

And she's awa to Carterhaugh,
As fast as she can hie.
When she came to Carterhaugh
Tam Lin was at the well,
And there she fand his steed standing,
But away was himsel.

She had na pu'd a double rose,
A rose but only twa,
Till up then started young Tam Lin,
Says, 'Lady, thou's pu nae mae.

'Why pu's thou the rose, Janet,
And why breaks thou the wand?
Or why comes thou to Carterhaugh
Withoutten my command?'

'Carterhaugh, it is my ain,
My daddie gave it me.
I'll come and gang by Carterhaugh,
And ask nae leave at thee.'

Janet has kilted her green kirtle
A little aboon her knee,
And has snooded her yellow hair
A little aboon her bree,
And she is to her father's ha,
As fast as she can hie.

Four and twenty ladies fair
Were playing at the ba,
And out then came the fair Janet,
Ance the flower amang them a'.

Four and twenty ladies fair
Were playing at the chess,
And out then came the fair Janet,
As green as onie glass.

Out then spake an auld gray knight,
Lay oer the castle wa,
And says, 'Alas, fair Janet, for thee
But we'll be blamed a'.'

'Haud your tongue, ye auld fac'd knight,
Some ill death may ye die.
Father my bairn on whom I will,
I'll father nane on thee.'

Out then spake her father dear,
And he spake meek and mild.
'And ever alas, sweet Janet,' he says,
'I think thou gaes wi child.'

'If that I gae wi child, father,
Mysel maun bear the blame.
There's naer a laird about your ha
Shall get the bairn's name.

'If my love were an earthly knight,
As he's an elfin gray,
I wad na gie my ain true-love
For nae lord that ye hae.

'The steed that my true-love rides on
Is lighter than the wind.
Wi siller he is shod before,
Wi burning gowd behind.'

Janet has kilted her green kirtle
A little aboon her knee,
And she has snooded her yellow hair
A little aboon her bree,
And she's awa to Carterhaugh,
As fast as she can hie.

When she came to Carterhaugh,
Tam Lin was at the well,
And there she fand his steed standing,
But away was himsel.

She had na pu'd a double rose,
A rose but only twa,
Till up then started young Tam Lin,
Says, 'Lady, thou pu's nae mae.

'Why pu's thou the rose, Janet,
Amang the groves sae green,
And a' to kill the bonnie babe
That we gat us between?'

'O tell me, tell me, Tam Lin,' she says,
'For's sake that died on tree,
If ere ye was in holy chapel,
Or Christendom did see?'

'Roxbrugh he was my grandfather,
Took me with him to bide,
And ance it fell upon a day
That wae did me betide.

'And ance it fell upon a day,
A cauld day and a snell
When we were frae the hunting come,
That frae my horse I fell.
The Queen o Fairies she caught me,
In yon green hill to dwell.

'And pleasant is the fairy land,
But, an eerie tale to tell,
Ay at the end of seven years
We pay a tiend to hell.
I am sae fair and fu of flesh,
I'm feared it be mysel.

'But the night is Halloween, lady,
The morn is Hallowday.
Then win me, win me, an ye will,
For weel I wat ye may.

'Just at the mirk and midnight hour
The fairy folk will ride,
And they that wad their true-love win,
At Miles Cross they maun bide.'

'But how shall I thee ken, Tam Lin,
Or how my true-love know,
Amang sae mony unco knights
The like I never saw?'

'O first let pass the black, lady,
And syne let pass the brown,
But quickly run to the milk-white steed,
Pu ye his rider down.

'For I'll ride on the milk-white steed,
And ay nearest the town.
Because I was an earthly knight
They gie me that renown.

'My right hand will be gloved, lady,
My left hand will be bare,
Cockt up shall my bonnet be,
And caimed down shall my hair,
And thae's the takens I gie thee,
Nae doubt I will be there.

'They'll turn me in your arms, lady,
Into an esk and adder;
But hold me fast, and fear me not,
I am your bairn's father.

'They'll turn me to a bear sae grim,
And then a lion bold.
But hold me fast, and fear me not,
As ye shall love your child.

'Again they'll turn me in your arms
To a red het gaud of airn.
But hold me fast, and fear me not,
I'll do to you nae harm.

'And last they'll turn me in your arms
Into the burning gleed.
Then throw me into well water,
O throw me in wi speed.

'And then I'll be your ain true-love,
I'll turn a naked knight.
Then cover me wi your green mantle,
And cover me out o sight.'

Gloomy, gloomy was the night,
And eerie was the way,
As fair Jenny in her green mantle
To Miles Cross she did gae.

About the middle o the night
She heard the bridles ring.
This lady was as glad at that
As any earthly thing.

First she let the black pass by,
And syne she let the brown.
But quickly she ran to the milk-white steed,
And pu'd the rider down.

Sae weel she minded what he did say,
And young Tam Lin did win.
Syne covered him wi her green mantle,
As blithe's a bird in spring.

Out then spake the Queen o Fairies.
Out of a bush o broom:
'Them that has gotten young Tam Lin
Has gotten a stately groom.'

Out then spake the Queen o Fairies,
And an angry woman was she:
'Shame betide her ill-fared face,
And an ill death may she die,
For she's taen awa the boniest knight
In a' my company.

'But had I kend, Tam Lin,' she says,
'What now this night I see,
I wad hae taen out thy twa gray een,
And put in twa een a tree.'

ANON.

Tam o' the Lin

Tam o' the Lin was fu' o' pride,
And his weapon he girt to his valorous side,
A scabbard o' leather wi' de'il-haiit within.
'Attack me wha dour!' quo' Tam o' the Lin.

Tam o' the Lin he bought a mear;
She cost him five shillings, she wasna dear.
Her back stuck up, and her sides fell in.
'A fiery yaud,' quo' Tam o' the Lin.

Tam o' the Lin he courted a May;
She stared at him sourly, and said him nay;
But he stroked down his jerkin and cocked up his chin.
'She aims at a laird, then,' quo' Tam o' the Lin.

Tam o' the Lin he gaed to the fair,
Yet he looked wi' disdain on the chapman's ware;
Then chucked out a sixpence; the sixpence was tin.
'There's coin for the fiddlers,' quo' Tam o' the Lin.

Tam o' the Lin wad show his lear,
And he scann'd o'er the book wi' wise-like stare.
He muttered confusedly, but didna begin.
'This is dominie's business,' quo' Tam o' the Lin.

Tam o' the Lin had a cow wi' ae horn,
That likit to feed on his neighbour's corn.
The stanes he threw at her fell short o' the skin:
'She's a lucky auld reiver,' quo' Tam o' the Lin.

Tam o' the Lin he married a wife,
And she was the torment, the plague o' his life;
She lays sae about her, and maks sic a din,
'She frightens the baby,' quo' Tam o' the Lin.

Tam o' the Lin grew dowie and douce,
And he sat on a stane at the end o' his house.
'What ails, auld chield?' He looked haggard and thin.
'I'm no very cheery,' quo' Tam o' the Lin.

Tam o' the Lin lay down to die,
And his friends whispered softly and woefully –
'We'll buy you some masses to scour away sin.'
'And drink at my lyke-wake,' quo' Tam o' the Lin.

JOANNA BAILLIE

Tam o' Shanter

When chapman billies leave the street,
And drouthy neibors neibors meet;
As market days are wearing late,
And folk begin to tak the gate,
While we sit bousing at the nappy,
An' getting fou and unco happy,
We think na on the lang Scots miles,
The mosses, waters, slaps and stiles,
That lie between us and our hame,
Where sits our sulky, sullen dame,
Gathering her brows like gathering storm,
Nursing her wrath to keep it warm.

This truth fand honest Tam o' Shanter,
As he frae Ayr ae night did canter:
(Auld Ayr, wham ne'er a town surpasses,
For honest men and bonie lasses).

O Tam! had'st thou but been sae wise,
As taen thy ain wife Kate's advice!
She tauld thee weel thou was a skellum,
A blethering, blustering, drunken blellum;
That frae November till October,
Ae market-day thou was na sober;
That ilka melder wi' the Miller,
Thou sat as lang as thou had siller;
That ev'ry naig was ca'd a shoe on
The Smith and thee gat roarin' fou on;
That at the Lord's house, ev'n on Sunday,
Thou drank wi' Kirkton Jean till Monday,
She prophesied that late or soon,
Thou wad be found, deep drown'd in Doon,
Or catch'd wi' warlocks in the mirk,
By Alloway's auld, haunted kirk.

Ah, gentle dames! it gars me greet,
To think how mony counsels sweet,
How mony lengthen'd, sage advices,
The husband frae the wife despises!

But to our tale: Ae market night,
Tam had got planted unco right,
Fast by an ingle, bleezing finely,
Wi' reaming swats, that drank divinely;
And at his elbow, Souter Johnie,
His ancient, trusty, drougthy crony:
Tam lo'ed him like a very brither;
They had been fou for weeks thegither.
The night drave on wi' sangs an' clatter;
And aye the ale was growing better:
The Landlady and Tam grew gracious,
Wi' favours secret, sweet, and precious:
The Souter tauld his queerest stories;
The Landlord's laugh was ready chorus:
The storm without might rair and rustle,
Tam did na mind the storm a whistle.

Care, mad to see a man sae happy,
E'en drown'd himsel amang the nappy.
As bees flee hame wi' lades o' treasure,
The minutes wing'd their way wi' pleasure:
Kings may be blest, but Tam was glorious,
O'er a' the ills o' life victorious!

But pleasures are like poppies spread,
You seize the flow'r, its bloom is shed;
Or like the snow falls in the river,
A moment white – then melts for ever;
Or like the Borealis race,
That flit ere you can point their place;
Or like the Rainbow's lovely form
Evanishing amid the storm. –
Nae man can tether Time nor Tide,
The hour approaches Tam maun ride;
That hour, o' night's black arch the key-stane,
That dreary hour he mounts his beast in;
And sic a night he taks the road in,
As ne'er poor sinner was abroad in.

The wind blew as 'twad blawn its last;
The rattling showers rose on the blast;
The speedy gleams the darkness swallow'd;
Loud, deep, and lang, the thunder bellow'd:
That night, a child might understand,
The Deil had business on his hand.

Weel-mounted on his grey mare, Meg,
A better never lifted leg,
Tam skelpit on thro' dub and mire,
Despising wind, and rain, and fire;
Whiles holding fast his gude blue bonnet,
Whiles crooning o'er some auld Scots sonnet,
Whiles glow'rin round wi' prudent cares,
Lest bogles catch him unawares;
Kirk-Alloway was drawing nigh,
Where ghaists and houlets nightly cry.

By this time he was cross the ford,
Where in the snaw the chapman smoor'd;
And past the birks and meikle stane,
Where drunken Charlie brak's neck-bane;
And thro' the whins, and by the cairn,
Where hunters fand the murder'd bairn;
And near the thorn, aboon the well,
Where Mungo's mither hang'd hersel'.
Before him Doon pours all his floods,
The doubling storm roars thro' the woods,
The lightnings flash from pole to pole,
Near and more near the thunders roll;
When, glimmering thro' the groaning trees,
Kirk-Alloway seem'd in a bleeze,
Thro' ilka bore the beams were glancing,
And loud resounded mirth and dancing.

Inspiring bold John Barleycorn!
What dangers thou canst make us scorn!
Wi' tippenny, we fear nae evil;
Wi' usquabae, we'll face the devil!
The swats sae ream'd in Tammie's noddle,
Fair play, he car'd na deils a boddle,

But Maggie stood, right sair astonish'd,
Till, by the heel and hand admonish'd,
She ventur'd forward on the light;
And, wow! Tam saw an unco sight!

Warlocks and witches in a dance;
Nae cotillon, brent new frae France,
But hornpipes, jigs, strathspeys, and reels,
Put life and mettle in their heels.
A winnock-bunker in the east,
There sat Auld Nick, in shape o' beast;
A towzie tyke, black, grim, and large,
To gie them music was his charge;
He screw'd the pipes and gart them skirl,
Till roof and rafters a' did dirl.—
Coffins stood round, like open presses,
That shaw'd the Dead in their last dresses;
And (by some devilish cantraip sleight)
Each in its cauld hand held a light.
By which heroic Tam was able
To note upon the haly table,
A murderer's banes, in gibbet-airns;
Twa span-lang, wee, unchristened bairns;
A thief, new-cutted frae a rape,
Wi' his last gasp his gab did gape;
Five tomahawks, wi' blude red-rusted:
Five scimitars, wi' murder crusted;
A garter which a babe had strangled:
A knife, a father's throat had mangled.
Whom his ain son of life bereft,
The grey-hairs yet stack to the heft;
Wi' mair of horrible and awfu',
Which even to name wad be unlawfu'.
Three lawyers tongues, turned inside oot,
Wi' lies, seamed like a beggars clout,
Three priests hearts, rotten, black as muck,
Lay stinkin, vile in every neuk.

As Tammie glowr'd, amaz'd, and curious,
The mirth and fun grew fast and furious;
The Piper loud and louder blew,

The dancers quick and quicker flew,
They reel'd, they set, they cross'd, they cleekit,
Till ilka carlin swat and reekit,
And coost her duddies to the wark,
And linkit at it in her sark!

Now Tam, O Tam! had they been queans,
A' plump and strapping in their teens!
Their sarks, instead o' creeshie flainen,
Been snaw-white seventeen hunder linen!—
Thir breeks o' mine, my only pair,
That ance were plush o' guid blue hair,
I wad hae gien them off my hurdies,
For ae blink o' the bonie burdies!
But wither'd beldams, auld and droll,
Rigwoodie hags wad spean a foal,
Louping an' flinging on a crummock,
I wonder did na turn thy stomach.

But Tam kent what was what fu' brawlie:
There was ae winsome wench and waulie
That night enlisted in the core,
Lang after ken'd on Carrick shore;
(For mony a beast to dead she shot,
And perish'd mony a bonie boat,
And shook baith meikle corn and bear,
And kept the country-side in fear);
Her cutty sark, o' Paisley harn,
That while a lassie she had worn,
In longitude tho' sorely scanty,
It was her best, and she was vauntie.
Ah! little ken'd thy reverend grannie,
That sark she coft for her wee Nannie,
Wi twa pund Scots ('twas a' her riches),
Wad ever grac'd a dance of witches!

But here my Muse her wing maun cour,
Sic flights are far beyond her power;
To sing how Nannie lap and flang,
(A souple jade she was and strang),
And how Tam stood, like ane bewitch'd,

And thought his very een enrich'd:
Even Satan glowr'd, and fidg'd fu' fain,
And hotch'd and blew wi' might and main:
Till first ae caper, syne anither,
Tam tint his reason a thegither,
And roars out, 'Weel done, Cutty-sark!'
And in an instant all was dark:
And scarcely had he Maggie rallied.
When out the hellish legion sallied.

As bees bizz out wi' angry fyke,
When plundering herds assail their byke;
As open pussie's mortal foes,
When, pop! she starts before their nose;
As eager runs the market-crowd,
When 'Catch the thief!' resounds aloud;
So Maggie runs, the witches follow,
Wi' mony an eldritch skreich and hollow.

Ah, Tam! Ah, Tam! thou'll get thy fairin!
In hell, they'll roast thee like a herrin!
In vain thy Kate awaits thy comin!
Kate soon will be a woefu' woman!
Now, do thy speedy-utmost, Meg,
And win the key-stone o' the brig;
There, at them thou thy tail may toss,
A running stream they dare na cross.
But ere the keystane she could make,
The fient a tail she had to shake!
For Nannie, far before the rest,
Hard upon noble Maggie prest,
And flew at Tam wi' furious ettle;
But little wist she Maggie's mettle!
Ae spring brought off her master hale,
But left behind her ain grey tail:
The carlin claught her by the rump,
And left poor Maggie scarce a stump.

Now, wha this tale o' truth shall read,
Ilk man and mother's son, take heed:
Whene'er to Drink you are inclin'd,

Or Cutty-sarks rin in your mind,
Think ye may buy the joys o'er dear;
Remember Tam o' Shanter's mare.

ROBERT BURNS

The Tap-room

This warl's a Tap-room owre an owre,
    Whar ilk ane tak's his caper,
Some taste the sweet, some drink the sour,
    As waiter Fate sees proper;
Let mankind live, ae social core,
    An drap a selfish quar'ling,
An whan the Landlord ca's his score,
    May ilk ane's clink be sterling.

ROBERT TANNAHILL

The Tay Bridge Disaster

Beautiful Railway Bridge of the Silv'ry Tay!
Alas! I am very sorry to say
That ninety lives have been taken away
On the last Sabbath day of 1879,
Which will be remember'd for a very long time.

'Twas about seven o'clock at night,
And the wind it blew with all its might,
And the rain came pouring down,
And the dark clouds seem'd to frown,
And the Demon of the air seem'd to say –
'I'll blow down the Bridge of Tay.'

When the train left Edinburgh
The passengers' hearts were light and felt no sorrow,
But Boreas blew a terrific gale,
Which made their hearts for to quail,
And many of the passengers with fear did say –
'I hope God will send us safe across the Bridge of Tay.'

But when the train came near to Wormit Bay,
Boreas he did loud and angry bray,
And shook the central girders of the Bridge of Tay
On the last Sabbath day of 1879,
Which will be remember'd for a very long time.

So the train sped on with all its might,
And Bonnie Dundee soon hove in sight,
And the passengers' hearts felt light,
Thinking they would enjoy themselves on the New Year,
With their friends at home they lov'd most dear,
And wish them all a happy New Year.

So the train mov'd slowly along the Bridge of Tay,
Until it was about midway,
Then the central girders with a crash gave way,
And down went the train and passengers into the Tay!
The Storm Fiend did loudly bray,
Because ninety lives had been taken away,
On the last Sabbath day of 1879,
Which will be remember'd for a very long time.

As soon as the catastrophe came to be known
The alarm from mouth to mouth was blown,
And the cry rang out all o'er the town,
Good Heavens! the Tay Bridge is blown down,
And a passenger train from Edinburgh,
Which fill'd all the people's hearts with sorrow,
And made them for to turn pale,
Because none of the passengers were sav'd to tell the tale
How the disaster happen'd on the last Sabbath day of 1879,
Which will be remember'd for a very long time.

It must have been an awful sight,
To witness in the dusky moonlight,
While the Storm Fiend did laugh, and angry did bray,
Along the Railway Bridge of the Silv'ry Tay,
Oh! ill-fated Bridge of the Silv'ry Tay,
I must now conclude my lay
By telling the world fearlessly without the least dismay,

That your central girders would not have given way,
At least many sensible men do say,
Had they been supported on each side with buttresses,
At least many sensible men confesses,
For the stronger we our houses do build,
The less chance we have of being killed.

WILLIAM McGONAGALL

Tenth Elegy: The Frontier

One must die because one knows them, die
of their smile's ineffable blossom, die
of their light hands

But dust blowing round them
has stopped up their ears
           o for ever
not sleeping but dead

The airliner's passengers,
crossing without effort the confines
of wired-off Libya, remember
little, regret less. If they idly
inspect from their windows the ennui
of limestone desert
           —and beneath them
their skimming shadow –
           they'll be certain
they've seen it, they've seen all

(Seen all, maybe, including
the lunar qattaras, the wadis like family trees,
the frontier passes with their toyshop spirals –
seen nothing, and seen all

And the scene yields them? Nothing)

Yet that coast-line
could yield much: there were recces and sorties
drumfire and sieges. The outposts
lay here: there ran the supply route.
Forgotten.
                    By that bend of Halfaya
the convoys used to stick, raw meat for the Jabos.

And here, the bay's horseshoe:
how nobly it clanged through laconic communiqués!
Still, how should this interest the airborne travellers,
being less real to them than the Trojan defence-works
and touching them as little as the Achaean strategies?
Useless to deny. The memorial's obsequious
falsehoods are irrelevant. It has little to arrest them,
survivors by accident
                    that dried blood in the sangars.

So I turn aside in the benighted deadland
to perform a duty, noting an outlying
grave, or restoring a fallen cross-piece.
Remembrancer.
                    And shall sing them who amnestied
escaped from the tumult to stumble across sand-dunes
and darken their waves in the sea, the deliverer.

Run, stumble and fall in their instant of agony
past burnt-out brennpunkt, along hangdog dannert.
Here gutted, or stuck through the throat like Buonconte,
or charred to grey ash, they are caught in one corral.
We fly from their scorn, but they close all the passes:
their sleep's our unrest, we lie bound in their inferno –
this alliance must be vaunted and affirmed, lest they condemn
                                                            us!

Lean seedlings of lament spring like swordsmen around us;
the coronach scales white arêtes. Bitter keening
of women goes up by the solitary column.
Denounce and condemn! Either build for the living
love, patience and power to absolve these tormented,
or else choke in the folds of their black-edged vendetta!
Run, stumble and fall in our desert of failure,

impaled, unappeased. And inhabit that desert
of canyon and dream – till we carry to the living
blood, fire and red flambeaux of death's proletariat.
Take iron in your arms! At last, spanning this history's
apollyon chasm, proclaim them the reconciled.

HAMISH HENDERSON

Tha mi sgìth 'n fhògar seo

Tha mi sgìth 'n fhògar seo,
Tha mi sgìth dhen t-strì,
Seo an tìm dhòrainneach;
Tha mi sgìth 'n fhògar seo.

Ged a tha mi sa choille
Chan eil coire ri chnòdach orm,

Ach mi seasamh gu dìleas
Leis an rìgh bhon bha chòir aige.

Mi air fògar bhon fhoghar,
Dèanamh thaighean gun cheò annta.

Ann am buthaig bhig bharraich,
Cha tig caraid gam fheòraich ann.

Ach nam bithinn aig a' bhaile
Gheibhinn càirdean 's luchd-eòlais ann.

Ach nan tigeadh Cornwallis,
Sinn a ghluaiseadh gu sòlasach.

Gu sgrios a thoirt air bèistean,
Thug an t-èideadh 's an stòras uainn.

Thoir mo shoraidh thar linne
Dh'ionnsaigh ghlinne 'm bu chòir dhomh bhith.

Thoir mo shoraidh Chinn t-Sàile,
Far 'm bi mànran is òranan;

Far am minig a bha mi
Ag èisteachd gàirich laoigh òg' aca.

Thoir mo shoraidh le dùrachd
Gu Sgùrr Ùrain,'s math m' eòlas ann.

'S tric a bha mi mun cuairt dith
'G èisteachd ùdlaiche crònanaich.

'S a' bheinn ghorm a tha ma coinneamh,
Leam bu shoilleir a neòineanan.

Thoir mo shoraidh le coibhneas
Gu Tòrr Laoighsich nan smèoraichean,

Far an tric bha mi ma bhuideal
Mar ri cuideachda shòlasaich.

Cha b' e 'n dram a bha mi 'g iargain,
Ach na b' fhiach an cuid stòireannan.

Sìos is suas tro Ghleann Seile
'S tric a leag mi damh cròiceach ann.

Gheibhte bric air an linne,
Fir gan sireadh is leòis aca.

Tha mi nis air mo dhìteadh
Ann am prìosan droch-bheòshlàinteach.

IAIN MAC MHURCHAIDH

I am tired of this banishment

I am tired of this banishment,
I am tired of the strife;
This is the time of torments;
I am tired of this banishment.

Though I am outlawed,
I can be accused of no faults

Except for standing faithfully
With the rightful king.

I've been in hiding since the autumn,
Making houses with no smoke.

In a little hut of wattles,
Where no friend will come to find me.

But if I was at home,
I'd have friends and acquaintances.

But if Cornwallis came,
We would happily march.

To devastate the beasts
Who took our clothes and things.

Take my farewell across the sea
To the glen where I should be.

Take my farewell to Kintail,
Where there is music and song.

Where I'd often listen
To the lowing of young calves.

Take my sincere farewell,
To Sgùrr Ùrainn, I well knew it.

I often listened around there
To the bellows of stags.

And the blue hill before it,
So bright were its daisies.

Take my farewell, with kindness,
To Tòrr Laoighseach of the thrushes,

Where I often sat round a bottle
In sociable company.

It wasn't the dram that I missed
But the quality of their stories.

Up and down Glen Shiel,
I often felled antlered stags.

Trout would be got in the pool,
Men hunting them with lights.

Now I'm condemned
In a health-wrecking prison.

Trans. Peter Mackay

JOHN MacRAE

Thair is nocht ane Winche

Thair is nocht ane winche that I se
Sall win ane vantage of me.
Be scho fals, I sal be sle,
And say to dispyt hir;
Be scho trew, I will confyd;
Will scho remane, I sall abyd;
Will scho slip, I will bot slyd,
And so sall I quyt hir.

Be scho constant and trew,
I sall evir hir persew;
Be scho fals, than adew,
No langer I tary;
Be scho faithfull in mynd,
I sal be to hir inclynd;
Be scho strange and unkynd,
I gif hir to fary.

Be scho haltand and he,
Rycht so sall scho fynd me;
Be scho lawly and fre.
The suth I sall say hir;
Be scho secreit and wyis,
I sall await on hir servyis;
Will scho glaik and go nyis,
I leif hir to play hir.

And I magyn my mailis,
I sall feid hir with caillis;
Thocht my sawis haif no sellis,
I sall leir hir to fan;
Be scho wylie as ane tod,
Quhen scho winkis, I sall nod.
Scho sall nocht begyle me, be God,
For ocht that scho can.

ANON.

There's Nae Luck About the House

And are ye sure the news is true?
 And are ye sure he's weel?
Is this a time to think o' wark?
 Ye jauds, fling by your wheel.
Is this a time to think o' wark,
 When Colin's at the door?
Rax me my cloak, I'll to the quay,
 And see him come ashore.
  For there's nae luck about the house.
   There's nae luck at a'
  There's little pleasure in the house.
   When our gudeman's awa'.

And gie to me my bigonet,
 My bishop-satin gown;
For I maun tell the baillie's wife
 That Colin's come to town.

My turkey slippers maun gae on,
    My hose o' pearl blue;
It's a' to please my ain gudeman,
    For he's baith leal and true.

Rise up and mak a clean fireside,
    Put on the muckle pot;
Gie little Kate her Sunday gown
    And Jock his button coat;
And mak their shoon as black as slaes,
    Their hose as white as snaw;
It's a' to please my ain gudeman,
    For he's been lang awa'.

Since Colin's weel, I'm weel content,
    I hae nae mair to crave;
Could I but live to mak him blest,
    I'm blest aboon the lave:
And will I see his face again?
    And will I hear him speak?
I'm downricht dizzy wi' the thocht,
    In troth I'm like to greet.

There's twa fat hens upo' the bauk,
    They've fed this month and mair,
Mak haste and thraw their necks about,
    That Colin weel may fare;
And spread the table neat and clean,
    Gar ilka thing look braw;
For wha can tell how Colin fared
    When he was far awa'?

Sae true his heart, sae smooth his speech
    His breath like caller air;
His very foot has music in't
    As he comes up the stair.
And will I see his face again?
    And will I hear him speak?
I'm downricht dizzy wi' the thocht,
    In troth I'm like to greet.

For there's nae luck about the house.
    There's nae luck at a'
There's little pleasure in the house,
    When our gudeman's awa'.

JEAN ADAM

They (may forget (their names (if let out)))

petcitement incitement of a pet to excitement
petcitement incitement into the excitement
of being a pet petcitement incitement to be
a pet a fed pet a fleece pet incitement to be
a floorpet a fleapit a carpet a polkadot
blanket pet blanket pet answer brass doorbell what name
tin waterbowl what name thrilled vomitfall polkadot
padded on patted on turded on welcome mat name
turns to no-one's reminder walks wilder walks further
downriver from calling calling owner predator
who that who tagalong meaner whose canines further
from food fleece floor flea cloth car poll card dot blank bit door
no no owner owns in nomine domini pet
outruns petfetch petcome will wild default reset.

VAHNI CAPILDEO

Thir Lenterne Dayis ar Luvely Lang

Thir Lenterne dayis ar luvely lang,
And I will murne ne mair,
Nor for no mirthles may me mang,
That will not for me cair.
I wil be glaid and latt hir gang,
With falsat in hir fair;
I fynd ane freschar feir to fang,
Baith of hyd, hew and hair.

The wintter nycht is lang but weir,
I may murne gif I will,
Scho will not murne for me, that cleir,
Thairfoir I wil be still.
O, King of Luve, that is so cleir,
I me acquyt you till,
Sa scho fra me and I fra hir,
And not bot it be skill.

O, Lord of Luve, how lykis the,
My lemmen's laitis unleill?
Scho luvis ane uthir bettir than me,
I haif caus to appeill.
I pray to him that deit on tre,
That for us all thold baill,
Mot send my lemmane twa or thre,
Sen scho can not be leill.

Uthir hes hir hairt. Sowld scho haif myne,
Trewly that war grit wrang.
Quhen thay haif play, gif I haif pyne,
On gallowis mot I hang.

WILLIAM STEWART

This Evening

You placed yellow roses by the window, then,
leaning forwards, began combing your red hair;
perhaps you were crying.
To make the distance less I turned away
and faced you across the earth's circumference.

The windowpane turns black:
across its flawed glass suddenly your image
runs on mine.
I stare at the vase until yellow
is no longer a colour, nor roses flowers.

RON BUTLIN

Thomas the Rhymer

True Thomas lay on Huntlie bank,
    A ferlie he spied wi' his ee
And there he saw a lady bright,
    Come riding down by the Eildon Tree.

Her shirt was o the grass-green silk,
    Her mantle o the velvet fyne
At ilka tett of her horse's mane
    Hang fifty siller bells and nine.

True Thomas, he pulld aff his cap,
    And louted low down to his knee:
'All hail, thou mighty Queen of Heaven!
    For thy peer on earth I never did see.'

'O no, O no, Thomas,' she said,
'That name does not belang to me;
    I am but the queen of fair Elfland,
That am hither come to visit thee.

'Harp and carp, Thomas,' she said,
'Harp and carp along wi' me,
    And if ye dare to kiss my lips,
Sure of your bodie I will be.'

'Betide me weal, betide me woe,
That weird shall never daunton me;'
    Syne he has kissed her rosy lips,
All underneath the Eildon Tree.

'Now, ye maun go wi me,' she said,
'True Thomas, ye maun go wi me,
    And ye maun serve me seven years,
Thro weal or woe, as may chance to be.'

She mounted on her milk-white steed,
She's taen True Thomas up behind,
    And aye wheneer her bridle rung,
The steed flew swifter than the wind.

O they rade on, and farther on –
    The steed gaed swifter than the wind –
Untill they reached a desart wide,
    And living land was left behind.

'Light down, light down, now, True Thomas,
    And lean your head upon my knee;
Abide and rest a little space,
    And I will shew you ferlies three.

'O see ye not yon narrow road,
    So thick beset with thorns and briers?
That is the path of righteousness,
    Tho after it but few enquires.

'And see not ye that braid braid road,
    That lies across that lily leven?
That is the path to wickedness,
    Tho some call it the road to heaven.

'And see not ye that bonny road,
    That winds about the fernie brae?
That is the road to fair Elfland,
    Where thou and I this night maun gae.

'But, Thomas, ye maun hold your tongue,
    Whatever ye may hear or see,
For, if you speak word in Elflyn land,
    Ye'll neer get back to your ain countrie.'

O they rade on, and farther on,
    And they waded thro rivers aboon the knee,
And they saw neither sun nor moon,
    But they heard the roaring of the sea.

It was mirk mirk night, and there was nae stern light,
    And they waded thro red blude to the knee;
For a' the blude that's shed on earth
    Rins thro the springs o that countrie.

Syne they came on to a garden green,
      And she pu'd an apple frae a tree:
'Take this for thy wages, True Thomas,
      It will give the tongue that can never lie.'

'My tongue is mine ain,' True Thomas said;
      'A gudely gift ye was gie to me!
I neither dought to buy nor sell,
      At fair or tryst where I may be.

'I dought neither speak to prince or peer,
      Nor ask of grace from fair ladye:'
'Now hold thy peace,' the lady said,
      'For as I say, so must it be.'

He has gotten a coat of the even cloth,
      And a pair of shoes of velvet green,
And till seven years were gane and past
      True Thomas on earth was never seen.

ANON.

To a Lady

      Sweet rois of vertew and of gentilness,
Delytsum lily of everie lustynes,
      Richest in bontie and in bewtie clear,
      And everie vertew that is wenit dear,
Except onlie that ye are mercyless.

Into your garth this day I did persew;
There saw I flowris that fresche were of hew;
      Baith quhyte and reid most lusty were to seyne,
      And halesome herbis upon stalkis greene;
Yet leaf nor flowr find could I nane of rew.

I doubt that Merche, with his cauld blastis keyne,
Has slain this gentil herb, that I of mene;
  Quhois piteous death dois to my heart sic paine
  That I would make to plant his root againe,–
So confortand his levis unto me bene.

WILLIAM DUNBAR

To a Louse

Ha! whaur ye gaun, ye crowlin ferlie?
Your impudence protects you sairly;
I canna say but ye strunt rarely,
Owre gauze and lace;
Tho', faith! I fear ye dine but sparely
On sic a place.

Ye ugly, creepin, blastit wonner,
Detested, shunn'd by saunt an' sinner,
How daur ye set your fit upon her –
Sae fine a lady?
Gae somewhere else and seek your dinner
On some poor body.

Swith! in some beggar's haffet squattle;
There ye may creep, and sprawl, and sprattle,
Wi' ither kindred, jumping cattle,
In shoals and nations;
Whaur horn nor bane ne'er daur unsettle
Your thick plantations.

Now haud you there, ye're out o' sight,
Below the fatt'rels, snug and tight;
Na, faith ye yet! Ye'll no be right,
Till ye've got on it –
The verra tapmost, tow'rin height
O' Miss' bonnet.

My sooth! right bauld ye set your nose out,
As plump an' grey as ony groset:
O for some rank, mercurial rozet,
Or fell, red smeddum,
I'd gie you sic a hearty dose o't,
Wad dress your droddum.

I wad na been surpris'd to spy
You on an auld wife's flainen toy;
Or aiblins some bit dubbie boy,
On's wyliecoat;
But Miss' fine Lunardi! fye!
How daur ye do't?

O Jenny, dinna toss your head,
An' set your beauties a' abroad!
Ye little ken what cursed speed
The blastie's makin:
Thae winks an' finger-ends, I dread,
Are notice takin.

O wad some Power the giftie gie us
To see oursels as ithers see us!
It wad frae mony a blunder free us,
An' foolish notion:
What airs in dress an' gait wad lea'e us,
An' ev'n devotion!

ROBERT BURNS

To a Mountain Daisy

On Turning One Down with the Plough, in April, 1786

Wee, modest, crimson-tippèd flow'r,
Thou's met me in an evil hour;
For I maun crush amang the stoure
        Thy slender stem:
To spare thee now is past my pow'r,
        Thou bonie gem.

Alas! it's no thy neibor sweet,
The bonie lark, companion meet,
Bending thee 'mang the dewy weet
      Wi' spreck'd breast,
When upward-springing, blythe, to greet
      The purpling east.

Cauld blew the bitter-biting north
Upon thy early, humble birth;
Yet cheerfully thou glinted forth
      Amid the storm,
Scarce rear'd above the parent-earth
      Thy tender form.

The flaunting flowers our gardens yield
High shelt'ring woods an' wa's maun shield:
But thou, beneath the random bield
      O' clod or stane,
Adorns the histie stibble-field
      Unseen, alane.

There, in thy scanty mantle clad,
Thy snawie-bosom sun-ward spread,
Thou lifts thy unassuming head
      In humble guise;
But now the share uptears thy bed,
      And low thou lies!

Such is the fate of artless maid,
Sweet flow'ret of the rural shade!
By love's simplicity betray'd
      And guileless trust;
Till she, like thee, all soil'd, is laid
      Low i' the dust.

Such is the fate of simple bard,
On life's rough ocean luckless starr'd!
Unskilful he to note the card
      Of prudent lore,
Till billows rage and gales blow hard,
      And whelm him o'er!

Such fate to suffering Worth is giv'n,
Who long with wants and woes has striv'n,
By human pride or cunning driv'n
         To mis'ry's brink;
Till, wrench'd of ev'ry stay but Heav'n,
         He ruin'd sink!

Ev'n thou who mourn'st the Daisy's fate,
That fate is thine – no distant date;
Stern Ruin's ploughshare drives elate,
         Full on thy bloom,
Till crush'd beneath the furrow's weight
         Shall be thy doom.

ROBERT BURNS

To a Mouse

On Turning Her Up in Her Nest with the Plough, November, 1785

Wee, sleekit, cowrin, tim'rous beastie,
O, what a panic's in thy breastie!
Thou need na start awa sae hasty,
Wi' bickering brattle!
I wad be laith to rin an' chase thee,
Wi' murdering pattle!

I'm truly sorry Man's dominion
Has broken Nature's social union,
An' justifies that ill opinion
Which makes thee startle
At me, thy poor, earth-born companion
An' fellow-mortal!

I doubt na, whyles, but thou may thieve;
What then? poor beastie, thou maun live!
A daimen-icker in a thrave
'S a sma' requet;
I'll get a blessin wi' the lave,
An' never miss't!

Thy wee-bit housie, too, in ruin!
Its silly wa's the win's are strewin!
An' naething, now, to big a new ane,
O' foggage green!
An' bleak December's win's ensuing,
Baith snell an' keen!

Thou saw the fields laid bare an' waste,
An' weary Winter comin fast,
An' cozie here, beneath the blast,
Thou thought to dwell,
Till crash! the cruel coulter past
Out thro' thy cell.

That wee bit heap o' leaves and stibble,
Has cost thee monie a weary nibble!
Now thou's turned out, for a' thy trouble,
But house or hald,
To thole the Winter's sleety dribble,
An' cranreuch cauld!

But Mousie, thou art no thy lane,
In proving foresight may be vain:
The best-laid schemes o' Mice an' Men
Gang aft agley,
An' lea'e us nought but grief an' pain,
For promis'd joy!

Still thou are blest, compared wi' me!
The present only toucheth thee:
But Och! I backward cast my e'e,
On prospects drear!
An' forward, tho' I cannot see,
I guess an' fear!

ROBERT BURNS

To Alexander Graham

Lying asleep walking
Last night I met my father
Who seemed pleased to see me.
He wanted to speak. I saw
His mouth saying something
But the dream had no sound.

We were surrounded by
Laid-up paddle steamers
In The Old Quay in Greenock.
I smelt the tar and the ropes.

It seemed that I was standing
Beside the big iron cannon
The tugs used to tie up to
When I was a boy. I turned
To see Dad standing just
Across the causeway under
That one lamp they keep on.

He recognised me immediately.
I could see that. He was
The handsome, same age
With his good brows as when
He would take me on Sundays
Saying we'll go for a walk.

Dad, what am I doing here?
What is it I am doing now?
Are you proud of me?
Going away, I knew
You wanted to tell me something.

You stopped and almost turned back
To say something. My father,
I try to be the best
In you you give me always.

Lying asleep turning
Round in the quay-lit dark
It was my father standing
As real as life. I smelt
The quay's tar and the ropes.

I think he wanted to speak.
But the dream had no sound.
I think I must have loved him.

W. S. GRAHAM

To Any Reader

As from the house your mother sees
You playing round the garden trees,
So you may see, if you will look
Through the windows of this book,
Another child, far, far away,
And in another garden, play.
But do not think you can at all,
By knocking on the window, call
That child to hear you. He intent
Is all on his play-business bent.
He does not hear; he will not look,
Nor yet be lured out of this book.
For, long ago, the truth to say,
He has grown up and gone away,
And it is but a child of air
That lingers in the garden there.

ROBERT LOUIS STEVENSON

To luve unluvit

To luve unluvit is ane pain:
For sho that is my sovereign,
Some wanton man so he has set her,
That I can get no luve again,
Bot breaks my heart, and nocht the better.

When that I went with that sweet may,
To dance, to sing, to sport and play,
And oft times in my armis plet her;
I do now mourn both nicht and day,
And breaks my heart, and nocht the better.

Where I was wont to see her go
Richt trimly passand to and fro,
With comely smilis when that I met her:
And now I live in pain and woe,
And breaks my heart, and nocht the better.

Whattan ane glaikit fool am I
To slay myself with melancholy,
Sen well I ken I may nocht get her.
Or what suld be the cause, and why,
To break my heart, and nocht the better?

My heart, sen thou may nocht her please,
Adieu, as good luve comes as gais,
Go choose ane odder and forget her:
God give him dolor and disease,
That breaks their heart and nocht the better.

ALEXANDER SCOTT

Toad

Stop looking like a purse. How could a purse
squeeze under the rickety door and sit,
full of satisfaction, in a man's house?

You clamber towards me on your four corners —
right hand, left foot, left hand, right foot.

I love you for being a toad,
for crawling like a Japanese wrestler,
and for not being frightened.

I put you in my purse hand, not shutting it,
and set you down outside directly under
every star.

A jewel in your head? Toad,
you've put one in mine,
a tiny radiance in a dark place.

NORMAN MacCAIG

Todd

My father's white uncle became
Arthritic and testamental in
Lyrical stages. He held cardinal sin
Was misuse of horses, then any game

Won on the sabbath. A Clydesdale
To him was not bells and sugar or declension
From paddock, but primal extension
Of rock and soil. Thundered nail

Turned to sacred bolt. And each night
In the stable he would slaver and slave
At cracked hooves, or else save
Bowls of porridge for just the right

Beast. I remember I lied
To him once, about oats: then I felt
The brand of his loving tongue, the belt
Of his own horsey breath. But he died,

When the mechanised tractor came to pass.
Now I think of him neighing to some saint
In a simple heaven or, beyond complaint,
Leaning across a fence and munching grass.

STEWART CONN

Trio

Coming up Buchanan Street, quickly, on a sharp winter evening
a young man and two girls, under the Christmas lights –
The young man carries a new guitar in his arms,
the girl on the inside carries a very young baby,
and the girl on the outside carries a chihuahua.
And the three of them are laughing, their breath rises
in a cloud of happiness, and as they pass
the boy says, 'Wait till he sees this but!'
The chihuahua has a tiny Royal Stewart tartan coat like a
teapot-
holder,
the baby in its white shawl is all bright eyes and mouth like
favours
in a fresh sweet cake,
the guitar swells out under its milky plastic cover, tied at the
neck
with silver tinsel tape and a brisk sprig of mistletoe.
Orphean sprig! Melting baby! Warm chihuahua!
The vale of tears is powerless before you.
Whether Christ is born, or is not born, you
put paid to fate, it abdicates
under the Christmas lights.
Monsters of the year
go blank, are scattered back,
can't bear this march of three.

– And the three have passed, vanished in the crowd
(yet not vanished, for in their arms they wind
the life of men and beasts, and music,
laughter ringing them round like a guard)
at the end of this winter's day.

EDWIN MORGAN

The Tryst

O luely, luely, cam she in
And luely she lay doun:
I kent her be her caller lips
And her breists sae sma' and roun'.

A' thru the nicht we spak nae word
Nor sinder'd bane frae bane:
A' thru the nicht I heard her hert
Gang soundin' wi' my ain.

It was about the waukrife hour
When cocks begin to craw
That she smool'd saftly thru the mirk
Afore the day wud daw.

Sae luely, luely, cam she in
Sae luely was she gaen;
And wi' her a' my simmer days
Like they had never been.

WILLIAM SOUTAR

Tullochgorum

Come gie's a sang, Montgomery cry'd,
And lay your disputes all aside,
What signifies't for folks to chide
    For what was done before them:
Let Whig and Tory all agree,
Whig and Tory, Whig and Tory,
Whig and Tory all agree,
    To drop their Whig-mig-morum;
Let Whig and Tory all agree
To spend the night wi' mirth and glee,
And cheerfu' sing alang wi' me
    The Reel o' Tullochgorum.

O' Tullochgorum's my delight,
It gars us a' in ane unite,
And ony sumph that keeps a spite,
        In conscience I abhor him:
For blyth and cheerie we'll be a',
Blyth and cheerie, blyth and cheerie,
Blyth and cheerie we'll be a',
        And mak' a happy quorum;
For blyth and cheerie we'll be a'
As lang as we hae breath to draw,
And dance till we be like to fa'
        The Reel o' Tullochgorum.

What needs there be sae great a fraise
Wi' dringing dull Italian lays,
I wadna gie our ain Strathspeys
        For half a hunder score o' them;
They're dowf and dowie at the best,
Dowf and dowie, dowf and dowie,
Dowf and dowie at the best,
        Wi' a' their variorum;
They're dowf and dowie at the best,
Their allegros and a' the rest,
They canna' please a Scottish taste
        Compar'd wi' Tullochgorum.

Let warldly worms their minds oppress
Wi fears o' want and double cess,
And sullen sots themsells distress
        Wi' keeping up decorum:
Shall we sae sour and sulky sit,
Sour and sulky, sour and sulky,
Sour and sulky shall we sit
        Like old philosophorum!
Shall we sae sour and sulky sit,
Wi' neither sense, nor mirth, nor wit,
Nor ever try to shake a fit
        To th' Reel o' Tullochgorum?

May choicest blessings aye attend
Each honest, open-hearted friend,
And calm and quiet be his end,
    And a' that's good watch o'er him;
May peace and plenty be his lot,
Peace and plenty, peace and plenty,
Peace and plenty be his lot,
    And dainties a great store o' them;
May peace and plenty be his lot,
Unstain'd by any vicious spot,
And may he never want a groat,
    That's fond o Tullochgorum!

But for the sullen frumpish fool,
That loves to be oppression's tool,
May envy gnaw his rotten soul,
    And discontent devour him;
May dool and sorrow be his chance,
Dool and sorrow, dool and sorrow,
Dool and sorrow be his chance,
    And nane say, wae's me for him
May dool and sorrow be his chance,
Wi' a' the ills that come frae France,
Wha e'er he be that winna dance
    The Reel o' Tullochgorum.

JOHN SKINNER

The Twa Corbies

As I was walking all alane,
I heard twa corbies making a mane;
The tane unto the t'other say,
'Where sall we gang and dine to-day?'

'In behint yon auld fail dyke,
I wot there lies a new-slain knight;
And naebody kens that he lies there,
But his hawk, his hound, and his lady fair.

'His hound is to the hunting gane,
His hawk, to fetch the wild-fowl hame,
His lady's ta'en another mate,
So we may mak our dinner sweet.

'Ye'll sit on his white hause-bane,
And I'll pike out his bonny blue een.
Wi' ae lock o' his gowden hair,
We'll theek our nest when it grows bare.

'Mony a ane for him makes mane,
But nane sall ken whare he is gane:
O'er his white banes, when they are bare,
The wind sall blaw for evermair.'

ANON.

The Two Mice

Esope, myne authour, makis mentioun
Of twa myis, and thay wer sisteris deir,
Of quham the eldest duelt in ane borous toun;
The uther wynnit uponland weill neir,
Richt soliter, quhyle under busk and breir,
Quhilis in the corne, in uther mennis skaith,
As owtlawis dois and levis on thair waith.

This rurall mous in to the wynter tyde
Had hunger, cauld, and tholit grit distres;
The uther mous, that in the burgh can byde,
Was gild brother and made ane fre burges,
Toll-fre als, but custum mair or les,
And fredome had to ga quhair ever scho list
Amang the cheis and meill, in ark and kist.

Ane tyme quhein scho wes full and unfute-sair,
Scho tuke in mynd hir sister upon land,
And langit for to heir of hir weilfair,
To se quhat lyfe scho led under the wand.
Bairfute allone, with pykestaf in hir hand,

As pure pylgryme, scho passit owt off town
To seik hir sister, baith ovre daill and down.

Throw mony wilsum wayis can scho walk,
Throw mosse and mure, throw bankis, busk, and breir,
Fra fur to fur, cryand fra balk to balk,
'Cum furth to me, my awin sister deir!
Cry peip anis!' With that the mous culd heir
And knew hir voce, as kinnisman will do
Be varray kynd, and furth scho come hir to.

The hartlie cheir, Lord God! geve ye had sene
Beis kith quhen that thir sisteris met,
And grit kyndnes wes schawin thame betuene,
For quhylis thay leuch, and quhylis for joy thay gret,
Quhyle kissit sweit, quhylis in armis plet,
And thus thay fure quhill soberit wes their mude;
Syne fute for fute unto the chalmer yude.
As I hard say, it was ane semple wane,
Off fog and farne full misterlyk wes maid
Ane sillie scheill under ane erdfast stane,
Off quhilk the entres wes not hie nor braid;
And in the samin thay went, but mair abaid,
Withoutin fyre or candill birnand bricht,
For comonly sic pykeris luffis not lycht.

Quhen thay wer lugit thus, thir sely myse,
The youngest sister into hir butterie hyid,
And brocht furth nuttis and peis, in steid off spyce;
Giff this wes gude fair, I do it on thame besyde,
This burges mous prunyit forth in pryde,
And said, 'Sister, this is your dayly fude?'
'Quhy not,' quod scho, 'is not this meit rycht gude?'

'Na, be my saull, I think it bot ane scorne.'
'Madame,' quod scho, 'ye be the mair to blame.
My mother sayd, efter that we wer borne,
That I and ye lay baith within ane wame;
I keip the ryte and custome off my dame,
And off my syre, levand in povertie,
For landis have we nane in propertie.'

'My fair sister,' quod scho, 'have me excusit;
This rude dyat and I can not accord.
To tender meit my stomok is ay uist,
For quhy I fair als weill as ony lord.
Thir wydderit peis and nuttis, or thay be bord,
Wil brek my teith and mak my wame ful sklender,
Quhilk usit wes before to metis tender.'

'Weil, weil, sister,' quod the rurall mous,
'Geve it yow pleis, sic thing as ye se heir,
Baith meit and dreink, harberie and hous,
Sal be your awin, will ye remane al yeir.
Ye sall it have wyth blyith and mery cheir,
And that suld mak the maissis that ar rude,
Amang freindis, richt tender, sueit, and gude.

'Quhat plesans is in feistis delicate,
The quhilkis ar gevin with ane glowmand brow?
Ane gentill hart is better recreate
With blyith visage, than seith to him ane kow.
Ane modicum is mair for till allow,
Swa that gude will be kerver at the dais,
Than thrawin vult and mony spycit mais.'

For all hir mery exhortatioun
This burges mous had littill will to sing,
Bot hevilie scho kest hir browis doun,
For all the daynteis that scho culd hir bring;
Yit at the last scho said, halff in hething,
'Sister, this victuall and your royall feist
May weill suffice unto ane rurall beist.

'Lat be this hole and cum unto my place:
I sall to yow schaw, be experience,
My Gude Friday is better nor your Pace,
My dische likingis is worth your haill expence.
I have housis anew off grit defence;
Off cat, na fall, na trap, I have na dreid.'
'I grant,' quod scho, and on togidder thay yeid.

In skugry ay, throw rankest gers and corne,
Under cowert full prevelie couth thay creip;
The eldest wes the gyde and went beforne,
The younger to hir wayis tuke gude keip.
On nicht thay ran and on the day can sleip,
Quhill in the morning, or the laverok sang,
Thay fand the town, and in blythlie couth gang.

Not fer fra thyne, unto ane worthie vane,
This burges brocht thame sone quhare thay suld be.
Withowt God speid thair herberie wes tane
In to ane spence with vittell grit plentie:
Baith cheis and butter upon skelfis hie,
And flesche and fische aneuch baith fresche and salt,
And sekkis full off grotis, meill, and malt.

Efter, quhen thay disposit wer to dyne,
Withowtin grace, thay wesche and went to meit,
With all coursis that cukis culd devyne,
Muttoun and beif, strikin in tailyes greit.
Ane lordis fair thus couth thay counterfeit
Except ane thing: thay drank the watter cleir
In steid off wyne; bot yit thay maid gude cheir.

With blyith upcast, and merie countenance,
The eldest sister sperit at her gest
Giff that scho by ressone fand difference
Betuix that chalmer and hir sarie nest.
'Ye, dame,' quod scho, 'bot how lang will this lest?'
'For evermair, I wait, and langer to.'
'Giff it be swa, ye ar at eis,' quod scho.

Till eik thair cheir ane subcharge furth scho brocht,
Ane plait off grottis and ane disch full off meill;
Thraf caikkis als I trow scho spairit nocht
Aboundantlie about hir for to deill,
And mane full fyne scho brocht in steid off geill,
And ane quhyte candill owt off ane coffer stall
In steid off spyce, to gust thair mouth withall.

This maid thay merie, quhill thay micht na mair,
And 'Haill, Yule, haill!' cryit upon hie.
Yit efter joy oftymes cummis cair,
And troubill efter grit prosperitie.
Thus as they sat in all thair jolitie,
The spenser come with keyis in his hand,
Oppinnit the dure, and thame at denner fand.

They taryit not to wesche, as I suppose,
Bot on to ga, that micht formest win.
The burges had ane hole, and in scho gois;
Hir sister had na hole to hyde hir in.
To se that selie mous, it wes grit sin;
So desolate and will off ane gude reid;
For verray dreid scho fell in swoun neir dead.

Bot, as God wald, it fell ane happie cace:
The spenser had na laser for to byde,
Nowther to seik nor serche, to char nor chace,
Bot on he went, and left the dure up wyde.
The bald burges his passing weill hes spyde;
Out off hir hole scho come and cryit on hie,
'How fair ye, sister? Cry peip, quhair ever ye be!'

This rurall mous lay flatling on the ground,
And for the deith scho wes full sair dredand
For till hir hard straik mony wofull stound;
As in ane fever trimbillit fute and hand;
And quhan hir sister in sic ply hir fand,
For verray pietie scho began to greit,
Syne confort hir with wordis hunny sweit.

'Quhy ly ye thus? Ryse up, my sister deir!
Cum to your meit; this perrell is overpast.'
The uther answerit hir with hevie cheir,
'I may not eit, sa sair I am agast.
I had lever thir fourty dayis fast
With watter caill, and to gnaw benis or peis
Than all your feist in this dreid and diseis.'

468

With fair tretie yit scho gart hir upryse,
And to the burde thay went and togidder sat.
And scantlie had thay drunkin anis or twyse,
Quhen in come Gib Hunter, our jolie cat,
And bad 'God speid'. The burges up with that,
And till hir hole scho fled as fyre of flint;
Bawdronis the uther be the bak hes hint.

Fra fute to fute he kest hir to and fra,
Quhylis up, quhylis doun, als tait as ony kid.
Quhylis wald he lat hir rin under the stra;
Quhylis wald he wink, and play with hir buk heid;
Thus to the selie mous grit pane he did;
Quhill at the last throw fortune and gude hap,
Betwix the dosor and the wall scho crap.

And up in haist behind the parraling
Scho clam so hie that Gilbert micht not get hir,
Syne be the cluke thair craftelie can hing
Till he wes gane; hir cheir wes all the better.
Syne doun scho lap quhen thair wes nane to let hir,
Apon the burges mous loud can scho cry,
'Fairweill, sister, thy feist heir I defy!

'Thy mangerie is mingit all with cair,
Thy guse is gude, thy gansell sour as gall;
The subcharge off thy service is bot sair;
Sa sall thow find heir-efterwart may fall.
I thank yone courtyne and yone perpall wall
Off my defence now fra yone crewell beist.
Almichtie God keip me fra sic ane feist.

'Wer I into the kith that I come fra,
For weill nor wo suld I never cum agane.'
With that scho tuke hir leif and furth can ga,
Quhylis throw the corne and quhylis throw the plane.
Quhen scho wes furth and fre scho wes full fane,
And merillie markit unto the mure;
I can not tell how eftirwart scho fure,

Bot I hard say scho passit to hir den,
Als warme as woll, suppose it wes not greit,
Full beinly stuffit, baith but and ben,
Off beinis and nuttis, peis, ry, and quheit;
Quhen ever scho list scho had aneuch to eit,
In quyet and eis withoutin ony dreid,
Bot to hir sisteris feist na mair scho yeid.

Moralitas

Freindis, heir may he find, and ye will tak heid
In this fabill ane gude moralitie:
As fitchis myngit ar with nobill seid,
Swa interminglit is adversitie
With eirdlie joy, swa that na state is frie
Without trubill and sum vexatioun,
And namelie thay quhilk clymmis up maist hie,
That ar not content with small possessioun.

Blissed be sempill lyfe withoutin dreid;
Blissed be sober feist in quietie.
Quha hes aneuch, of na mair hes ne neid,
Thocht it be littill into quantatie.
Grit aboundance and blind prosperitie
Oftymes makis ane evill conclusioun.
The sweitest lyfe, thairfoir, in this cuntrie,
Is sickernes, with small possessioun.

O wantoun man, that usis for to feid
Thy wambe and makis it a god to be,
Luke to thy self, I warne the weill on deid.
The cat cummis and to the mous hes ee;
Quhat vaillis than thy feist and royaltie,
With dreidfull hart and tribulatioun?
Thairfoir, best thing in eird, I say for me,
Is merry hart with small possessioun.

Thy awin fyre, my freind, sa it be bot ane gleid,
It warmis weill, and is worth gold to the;
And Solomon sayis, gif that throw will reid,
'Under the hevin thair can not better be

Than ay be blyith and leif in honestie.'
Quhairfoir I may conclude be this ressoun:
Of eirthly joy it beiris maist degré,
Blyithnes in hart, with small possessioun.

ROBERT HENRYSON

Uamh an Òir

Is truagh, a Rìgh, gun trì làmhan
Dà làimh sa phìob, dà làimh sa phìob,
Is truagh, a Rìgh, gun trì làmhan
Dà làimh sa phìob, 's làmh sa chlaidheamh.

Eadarainn a' chruit, a' chruit, a' chruit,
Eadarainn a' chruit, mo chuideachd air m' fhàgail;
Eadarainn, a luaidh, a luaidh, a luaidh,
Eadarainn, a luaidh, 's i ghall' uain' a shàraich mi.

Mo thaobh fodham, 's m' fheòil air breothadh,
Daol am shùil, daol am shùil:
Dà bhior iarainn ga sìor siaradh
Ann am ghlùin, ann am ghlùin.

Bidh na minn bheaga nan gobhair chreagach
Man tig mise, man till mis' à
Uamh an Òir, Uamh an Òir,
'S na lothan cliathta nan eich dhiallta
Man tig mise, man till mis' à
Uamh an Òir, Uamh an Òir.

Bidh na laoigh bheaga nan crodh eadraidh
Man tig mise, man till mis' à
Uamh an Òir, Uamh an Òir,
'S na mic uchda nam fir fheachda
Man tig mise, man till mis' à
Uamh an Òir, Uamh an Òir

'S iomadh maighdeann òg fo ceud-bhàrr
Thèid a-null, thèid a-null
Man tig mise, man till mis' à
Uamh an Òir, Uamh an Òir.

GUN URRA

The Cave of Gold

It's a shame, O Lord, I didn't have three hands,
Two hands on the pipes, two hands on the pipes,
It's a shame, O Lord, I didn't have three hands,
Two hands on the pipes, one hand on my sword.

Between us is the harp, the harp, the harp,
Between us is the harp, my friends have left me,
Between us is the harp, the harp, the harp,
Between us, my love, is the green bitch who wronged me.

Lying on my side, my flesh is rotting,
A beetle in my eye, a beetle in my eye,
Two iron barbs repeatedly thrusting
Into my knee, into my knee.

The wee kids will be rock-climbing goats
Before I come, before I return from
The Cave of Gold, the Cave of Gold,
And harrowed colts be saddled horses
Before I come, before I return from
The Cave of Gold, the Cave of Gold

Little calves will be milking cows
Before I come, before I return from
The Cave of Gold, the Cave of Gold,
And suckling sons be men of war
Before I come, before I return from
The Cave of Gold, the Cave of Gold

Many young girls in their first bridal veil
Will have passed over, will have passed over
Before I come, before I return from
The Cave of Gold, the Cave of Gold.

Trans. Peter Mackay

ANON.

Unexpected Join

The
earth
meets the
sky over
the
hill.

I was
told
by
a sparrow with
a lump on
its head.

IVOR CUTLER

The Unwanted Child

I was the wrong music
The wrong guest for you
When I came through the tundras
And thro' the dew.

Summon'd, tho' unwanted,
Hated, tho' true
I came by golden mountains
To dwell with you.

I took strange Algol with me
And Betelgeuse, but you
Wanted a purse of gold
And interest to accrue.

You could have had them all,
The dust, the glories too,
But I was the wrong music
And why I never knew.

OLIVE FRASER

Upon Tobacco

Forsaken of all comforts but these two,
My faggot and my pipe, I sit and muse
On all my crosses, and almost accuse
The heavens for dealing with me as they do.
Then hope steps in and with a smiling brow
Such cheatful expectations doth infuse
As makes me think ere long I cannot choose
But be some Grandee, whatsoever I'm now.
But having spent my pipe I then perceive
That hopes and dreams are cousins: both deceive.
Then make I this conclusion in my mind:
It's all one thing; both tends unto one scope:
To live upon tobacco and on hope,
The one's but smoke; the other is but wind.

ROBERT AYTOUN

The Video Box: No. 25

If you ask what my favourite programme is
it has to be that strange world jigsaw final.
After the winner had defeated all his rivals
with harder and harder jigsaws, he had to prove his mettle
by completing one last absolute mind crusher
on his own, under the cameras, in less than a week.

We saw, but he did not, what the picture would be:
the mid-Atlantic, photographed from a plane,
as featureless a stretch as could be found,
no weeds, no flotsam, no birds, no oil, no ships,
the surface neither stormy nor calm, but ordinary,
a light wind on a slowly rolling swell.
Hand-cut by a fiendish jigger to simulate,
but not to have, identical beaks and bays,
it seemed impossible; but the candidate –
he said he was a stateless person, called himself Smith –
was impressive: small, dark, nimble, self-contained.
The thousands of little grey tortoises were scattered
on the floor of the studio; we saw the clock; he started.
His food was brought to him, but he hardly ate.
He had a bed, with the light only dimmed to a weird blue,
never out. By the first day he had established
the edges, saw the picture was three metres long
and appeared to represent (dear God!) the sea.
Well, it was a man's life, and the silence
(broken only by sighs, click of wood, plop of coffee
in paper cups) that kept me fascinated.
Even when one hand was picking the edge-pieces
I noticed his other hand was massing sets
of distinguishing ripples or darker cross-hatching or
incipient wave-crests; his mind,
if not his face, worked like a sea.
It was when he suddenly rose from his bed
at two, on the third night, went straight over
to one piece and slotted it into a growing central patch,
then back to bed, that I knew he would make it.
On the sixth day he looked haggard and slow,
with perhaps a hundred pieces left,
of the most dreary unmarked lifeless grey.
The camera showed the clock more frequently.
He roused himself, and in a quickening burst
of activity, with many false starts, began
to press that inhuman insolent remnant together.
He did it, on the evening of the sixth day.
People streamed onto the set. Bands played.
That was fine. But what I liked best
was the last shot of the completed sea,

filling the screen; then the saw-lines disappeared,
till almost imperceptibly the surface moved
and it was again the real Atlantic, glad
to distraction to be released, raised
above itself in growing gusts, allowed
to roar as rain drove down and darkened,
allowed to blot, for a moment, the orderer's hand.

EDWIN MORGAN

Waly, Waly

O waly, waly, up the bank,
And waly, waly, doun the brae,
And waly, waly, yon burn-side,
Where I and my Love wont to gae!
I lean'd my back unto an aik,
I thocht it was a trustie tree;
But first it bow'd and syne it brak –
Sae my true love did lichtlie me.

O waly, waly, gin love be bonnie
A little time while it is new!
But when 'tis auld it waxeth cauld,
And fades awa' like morning dew.
O wherefore should I busk my heid,
Or wherefore should I kame my hair?
For my true Love has me forsook,
And says he'll never lo'e me mair.

Now Arthur's Seat sall be my bed,
The sheets sall ne'er be 'filed by me;
Saint Anton's well sall be my drink;
Since my true Love has forsaken me.
Marti'mas wind, when wilt thou blaw,
And shake the green leaves aff the tree?
O gentle Death, when wilt thou come?
For of my life I am wearie.

'Tis not the frost, that freezes fell,
Nor blawing snaw's inclemencie,

'Tis not sic cauld that makes me cry;
But my Love's heart grown cauld to me.
When we cam in by Glasgow toun,
We were a comely sicht to see;
My Love was clad in the black velvet,
And I mysel in cramasie.

But had I wist, before I kist,
That love had been sae ill to win,
I had lock'd my heart in a case o' gowd,
And pinn'd it wi' a siller pin.
And O! if my young babe were born,
And set upon the nurse's knee;
And I mysel were dead and gane,
And the green grass growing over me!

ANON.

Wanted a Husband

Baking and cooking, scrubbing and dressing –
Accomplishments grand, well worth the possessing;
Economy too, with wisdom discreet,
My wife must practise to make all ends meet.

ELEVE

Wanted a husband who doesn't suppose,
That all earthly employments one feminine knows, –
That she'll scrub, do the cleaning, and cooking, and baking,
And plain needlework, hats and caps, and dressmaking.
Do the family washing, yet always look neat,
Mind the bairns, with a temper unchangeably sweet,
Be a cheerful companion, whenever desired,
And contentedly toil day and night, if required.
Men expecting as much, one may easily see,
But they're not what is wanted, at least, not by me.

Wanted a husband who's tender and true,
Who will stick to his duty, and never get 'fou',
But when all his day's work he has blithely gone through,

Help his wife, 'set to rights', till her work is done too;
Who will not absurdly, and helplessly go,
And trouble the wife about 'buttons to sew',
On his shirt, or his gloves, or his coat, or his vest,
But will sew them himself, and not think he's oppressed.
Now, if such a lad you should happen to see,
He's wanted by many, but yet – not by me!

MARION BERNSTEIN

From The War of Inis-Thona

O lay me, ye that see the light, near some rock of my hills! let the thick
hazels be around, let the rustling oak be near. Green be the place of my
rest; let the sound of the distant torrent be heard. Daughter of Toscar, take
the harp, and raise the lovely song of Selma; that sleep may overtake my
soul in the midst of joy; that the dreams of my youth may return, and the
days of the mighty Fingal.

Selma! I behold thy towers, thy trees, thy shaded wall! I see the heroes of
Morven; I hear the song of bards: Oscar lifts the sword of Cormalo; a
thousand youths admire its studded thongs. They look with wonder on my
son: they admire the strength of his arm. They mark the joy of his father's
eyes; they long for an equal fame,

And ye shall have your fame. O sons of streamy Morven! My soul is often
brightened with song; I remember the friends of my youth. But sleep
descends in the sound of the harp! pleasant dreams begin to rise! Ye Sons
of the chase, stand far distant nor disturb my rest The bard of other times
holds discourse with his fathers! the chiefs of the days of old! Sons of the
chase, stand far distant! disturb not the dreams of Ossian!

JAMES MCPHERSON

Warming Her Pearls

for Judith Radstone

Next to my own skin, her pearls. My mistress
bids me wear them, warm them, until evening
when I'll brush her hair. At six, I place them
round her cool, white throat. All day I think of her,

resting in the Yellow Room, contemplating silk
or taffeta, which gown tonight? She fans herself
whilst I work willingly, my slow heat entering
each pearl. Slack on my neck, her rope.

She's beautiful. I dream about her
in my attic bed; picture her dancing
with tall men, puzzled by my faint, persistent scent
beneath her French perfume, her milky stones.

I dust her shoulders with a rabbit's foot,
watch the soft blush seep through her skin
like an indolent sigh. In her looking-glass
my red lips part as though I want to speak.

Full moon. Her carriage brings her home. I see
her every movement in my head . . . Undressing,
taking off her jewels, her slim hand reaching
for the case, slipping naked into bed, the way

she always does . . . And I lie here awake,
knowing the pearls are cooling even now
in the room where my mistress sleeps. All night
I feel their absence and I burn.

CAROL ANN DUFFY

The Watergaw

Ae weet forenicht i' the yow-trummle
I saw yon antrin thing,
A watergaw wi' its chitterin' licht
Ayont the on-ding;
An' I thocht o' the last wild look ye gied
Afore ye deed!

There was nae reek i' the laverock's hoose
That nicht – an' nane i' mine;
But I hae thocht o' that foolish licht
Ever sin' syne;
An' I think that mebbe at last I ken
What your look meant then.

HUGH MacDIARMID

Wee Willie Winkie

Wee Willie Winkie rins through the toon,
Upstairs and doonstairs in his nichtgoon.
Chappin' at the windaes,
Peerin' through the locks –
'Are a' the bairnies in their beds?
It's past eight o'clock!'

'Hey, Willie Winkie, are ye comin' ben?
The cat's singin' grey thrums to the sleepin' hen.
The dug's spelder'd on the flair, and disna' gi'e a cheep,
But here's a waukrife laddie that winna fa' asleep!'

Onything but sleep, you rogue? Glow'ring like the mune.
Rattlin' in an airn jug wi' an airn spune,
Rumblin', tumblin', roond aboot, crawin' like a cock,
Skirlin' like a kenna-what, wauk'nin' sleepin' fowk.

'Hey Willie Winkie – the wean's in a creel!
Wambling aff a bodie's knee like a verra eel.
Ruggin' at the cat's lug, and rav'lin a' her thrums.
Hey, Willie Winkie!' – see, now, there he comes!

480

Wearit is the mither that has a stoorie wean,
A wee stumpie stoussie, that canna rin his lane,
That has a battle aye wi' sleep before he'll close an e'e,
But ae kiss frae aff his rosy lips gi'es strength anew tae me.

WILLIAM MILLER

A Wet Day: Hughie's Pity for the Tinklers

The mist lies like a plaid on plain,
The dyke-taps a' are black wi' rain,
A soakit head the clover hings,
On ilka puddle rise the rings.

Sair dings the rain upon the road, –
It dings, an' nae devallin' o'd;
Adoun the gutter rins a rill
Micht halflins ca' a country mill.

The very roadman's left the road:
The only kind o' beas' abroad
Are dyucks, rejoicin' i' the flood,
An' pyots, clatterin' i' the wud.

On sic a day wha tak's the gate?
The cadger? maybe; but he's late.
The carrier? na! he doesna flit
Unless, D.V., the pooers permit.

On sic a day wha tak's the gate?
The tinkler, an' his tousie mate;
He foremost, wi' a nose o' flint,
She sour an' sulky, yards ahint.

A blanket, fra her shouthers doun,
Wraps her an' a' her bundles roun';
A second rain rins aff the skirt;
She skelps alang through dub an' dirt.

Her cheeks are red, her een are sma',
Her head wi' rain-draps beadit a';
The yellow hair, like wires o' bress,
Springs, thrivin' in the rain, like gress.

Her man an' maister stalks in front,
Silent mair than a tinkler's wont;
His wife an' warkshop there ahint him, —
This day he caresna if he tint them.

His hands are in his pouches deep,
He snooves alang like ane in sleep,
His only movement's o' his legs,
He carries a' aboon like eggs.

Sma' wecht! his skeleton an' skin,
And a dour heavy thocht within.
His claes, sae weel wi' weet they suit him,
They're like a second skin aboot him.

They're doun the road, they're oot o' sicht;
They'll reach the howff by fa' o' nicht,
In Poussie Nancy's cowp the horn,
An' tak' the wanderin' gate the morn.

They'll gie their weasands there a weet,
Wi' kindred bodies there they'll meet,
Wi' drookit gangerels o' the clan,
The surgeons o' the pat an' pan.

Already on the rain-washed wa'
A darker gloom begins to fa':
Sooms fra the sicht the soakin' plain, —
It's closin' for a nicht o' rain.

J. LOGIE ROBERTSON

Wha Is Perfyte

Wha is perfyte to put in writ
·The inwart murning and mischance,
Or to endite the great delight
Of lusty luvis observance,
Bot he that may, certain, patiently suffer pain
To win his soverane in recompanse.

Albeit I know of luvis law
The pleasure and the painis smart,
Yet I stand awe for to furthshaw
The quiet secretis of my heart.
For it may Fortune raith to do her body skaith
Whilk wat that of them baith I am expert.

She wat my woe that is ago,
She wat my welfare and remead,
She wat also, I love no mo
Bot her, the well of womanheid.
She wat whithouten fail, I am her luvar laill,
She has my hairt all haill till I be deid.

That bird of bliss in beauty is
In erd the only a per se,
Whase mouth to kiss is worth, I wis,
The warld full of gold to me.
Is nocht in erd I cure, both please my lady pure,
Syne be her servitour unto I dee.

She has my luve at her behufe,
My hairt is subject bound and thrall,
For she dois move my hairt abuve
To see her proper persoun small.
Sen she is wrocht at will, that Nature may fulfil
Gladly I give her till, body and all.

There is nocht wie can estimie
My sorrow and my sighingis sair,
For I am so done faithfully
In favouris with my lady fair

That baith our hairtis are ane, locknyt in luvis chain,
And everilk grief is gane for evermair.

ALEXANDER SCOTT

What the Auld Fowk Are Thinkin

The bairns i' their beds, worn oot wi' nae wark,
Are sleepin, nor ever an eelid winkin;
The auld fowk lie still wi' their een starin stark,
An' the mirk pang-fou o' the things they are thinkin.

Whan oot o' ilk corner the bairnies they keek,
Lauchin an' daffin, airms loosin an' linkin,
The auld fowk they watch frae the warm ingle-cheek,
But the bairns little think what the auld fowk are thinkin.

Whan the auld fowk sit quaiet at the reet o' a stook,
I' the sunlicht their washt een blinterin an' blinkin,
Fowk scythin, or bin'in, or shearin wi' heuk
Carena a strae what the auld fowk are thinkin.

At the kirk, whan the minister's dreich an' dry,
His fardens as gien they war gowd guineas chinkin,
An' the young fowk are noddin, or fidgetin sly,
Naebody kens what the auld fowk are thinkin.

Whan the young fowk are greitin aboot the bed
Whaur like water throu san' the auld life is sinkin,
An' some wud say the last word was said,
The auld fowk smile, an' ken what they're thinkin.

GEORGE MacDONALD

What they think she said

Teach me to believe
that nothing lasts,
to wear my life

like a skin of glass
or water that will borrow
my shape and pass

IMTIAZ DHARKER

When Will the War Be By?

'This year, neist year, sometime, never,'
A lanely lass, bringing hame the kye,
Pu's at a floo'er wi' a weary sigh,
An' laich, laich, she is coontin' ever
'This year, neist year, sometime, never,
When will the war be by?'

'Weel, wounded, missin', deid,'
Is there nae news o' oor lads ava?
Are they hale an' fere that are hine awa'?
A lass raxed oot for the list, to read –
'Weel, wounded, missin', *deid*';
An' the war was by for twa.

CHARLES MURRAY

White

a memory
a white stone
under six inches of pellucid water

because it is white
because it burns a white hole in your mind
because it is so near the surface
          it offends you

you reach to pluck it and throw it into the depths

you reach through
and through and through

for your whole life
you will be obsessed by six fathomless inches

ROBIN FULTON MACPHERSON

Why Do the Houses Stand

Why do the houses stand
When they that built them are gone;
When remaineth even of one
That lived there and loved and planned
Not a face, not an eye, not a hand,
Only here and there a bone?
Why do the houses stand
When they who built them are gone?
Oft in the moonlighted land
When the day is overblown,
With happy memorial moan
Sweet ghosts in a loving band
Roam through the houses that stand—
For the builders are not gone.

GEORGE MacDONALD

Why the Elgin Marbles Must Be Returned to Elgin

Because they are large, round and bluey,
    and would look good on the top of Lady Hill.
Because their glassy depths would give local kids
    the impression that they are looking at
    the Earth from outer space.
Several Earths in fact, which encourages humility
    and a sense of relativity.
Because local building contractors would use
    JCBs to play giant games in Cooper Park
    and attract more tourists to Morayshire:
    'Monster Marble Showdown Time!'

486

Because the prophecy omitted from the Scottish Play
        must be fulfilled:
        'When the marbles come back to Elgin
        the *mormaer* will rise again.'
(A *mormaer* being a Pictish sub-king.
Which Macbeth was, not a thane.
Nor a tyrant, for that matter.
More sort of an Arthur figure, you know,
        got drunk and married Liza Minnelli, with
        Gielgud as Merlin the butler.)
Because they're just gathering dust
        sitting in the British Museum, never mind
        the danger that if someone leans against them
        they might roll and squash a tourist like a bug.
Because the Greeks, like the rest of Europe,
        don't know where Scotland is, and so
        won't be able to find them.
Because if they come looking we can just
        push the marbles into the Firth off Burghead
        and show them the dolphins instead.
Greeks like dolphins. Always have.
Because it will entertain the dolphins
        watching the Elgin marbles roll with the tides
        and perhaps attract whales.
Because whales can balance the marbles
        on the tops of their spouts,
        then ex-Soviet tourist navies can come
        and fire big guns at them
        like in a funfair.
Because the people of Morayshire were
        originally Greek anyway, as proven by
        Sir Thomas Urquhart in his *Pantochronocanon*.
And by the fact they like dolphins.
Because we are not just asking for them,
        we demand their return, and this
        may be the marble that sets the heather
        alight, so to speak.
Because if the Stone of Destiny is
        the MacGraeae's tooth, then
        the Elgin marbles are
        the weird sisters' glass eyes.

Because Scotland must see visions again,
     even if only through
     a marble of convenience.

W. N. HERBERT

The Wild Geese

'Oh tell me what was on yer road, ye roarin' norlan' Wind,
As ye cam' blawin' frae the land that's niver frae my mind?
My feet they traivel England, but I'm deein' for the north.'
'My man, I heard the siller tides rin up the Firth o Forth.'

'Aye, Wind, I ken them weel eneuch, and fine they fa' and rise,
And fain I'd feel the creepin' mist on yonder shore that lies,
But tell me, ere ye passed them by, what saw ye on the way?'
'My man, I rocked the rovin' gulls that sail abune the Tay.'

'But saw ye naething, leein' Wind, afore ye cam' to Fife?
There's muckle lyin' 'yont the Tay that's mair to me nor life.'
'My man, I swept the Angus braes ye hae'na trod for years.'
'O Wind, forgi'e a hameless loon that canna see for tears!'

'And far abune the Angus straths I saw the wild geese flee,
A lang, lang skein o' beatin' wings, wi' their heids towards the sea,
And aye their cryin' voices trailed ahint them on the air —'
'O Wind, hae maircy, haud yer whisht, for I daurna listen mair!'

VIOLET JACOB

The Wife of Auchtermuchty

In Auchtermuchty there dwelt ane man,
Ane husband, as I heard it tauld,
Wha weel could tipple out a can,
And neither loved hunger nor cauld.
While ance it fell upon a day,
He yokit his pleugh upon the plain,

Gif it be true as I heard say;
The day was foul for wind and rain,

He lows't the pleugh at the land's end,
And drave his oxen hame at e'en;
When he cam' in he lookit ben,
And saw his wife baith trig and clean,
Sitting at the fire, full biek and bauld,
With ane fat soup, as I heard say;
The man being very weet and cauld,
Between thae twa it was nae play.

Quoth he 'Where is my horses' corn?
My ox has neither hay nor strae;
Dame, ye maun to the pleugh the morn,
I sall be housewife, gif I may.
The seed time it proves cauld and bad,
And ye sit warm, nae troubles see;
The morn ye sall gae wi' the lad,
And syne ye'll ken what husbands dree.'

'Husband,' quoth she, 'content am I
To tak' the pleugh my day about,
Sae ye will rule baith calves and kye,
And all the house baith in and out,
And now sin' ye hae made the law,
Then guide a' richt, and dinna break;
They siccar ride that never fa',
We'll see gif naething ye neglect.

'But sin' that ye will hoose-life ken,
First ye sall sift, and syne sall kneed;
And aye as ye gang but and ben,
Look that the bairns fyle not the bed.
Ye'se lay ane saft wisp to the kiln,
(We have ane dear farm on our head),
And aye as ye gang furth and till,
Keep weel the goslings frae the gled.'

The wife was up right late at e'en,
(I pray God give her ill to fare!)

She kirn'd the kirn, and skimm'd it clean,
Left the gudeman but bleddoch bare.
Then in the morning up she gat,
And on her heart laid her disjune;
Syne put as muckle in her lap,
As micht hae served them baith at noon.

Says, 'Jock, be thou the maister of wark,
And thou sall haud and I sall ca',
I'se promise thee ane gude new sark
Either of round claith or of sma'.'
She lows't the oxen aucht or nine,
And took ane gad-staff in her hand;
Up the gudeman raise after-syne,
And saw the wife had done command;

He ca'd the goslings forth to feed,
There was but sevensome o' them a',
And by there comes the greedy gled,
And lickt up five, left him but twa,
Then oot he ran in all his mane,
How soon he heard the goslings cry;
But than, or he cam' in again,
The calves brak lowse and sookit the kye.

The calves and kye met in the loan,
The man ran with ane rung to redd,
When by there comes an ill-willy cow,
And brodit his buttock so that it bled.
Then hame he ran to ane rock of tow,
And he sat down to try the spinning;
I trow he loutit ower near the lowe,
Quoth he 'This wark has ane ill beginning.'
Hynd to the kirn then did he stour,
And jummilt at it while he swat;
When he had jummilt a full lang hour,
The sorrow a scrap of butter he gat.
Albeit nae butter he could get,
Yet he was cumment with the kirn,
And syne he het the milk ower het,
And sorrow a spark of it would yirn.

Then ben there cam' ane greedy sow,
I trow he cunn'd her little thank,
For in she shot her greedy mou',
And aye she winkit and aye she drank.
He cleikit up ane crookit club,
And thought to hit the sow ane rout,
The twa goslings the gled had left,
That straik dang baith their harns out.

He gat his foot upon the spyre,
To get the bawcon for the pat;
He backwards fell into the fire,
And brak' his head on the kaiming stock;
On the fire he set the meikle pat,
And gat twa cans and ran to the spout,
Ere he cam' in, what think ye o' that?
The fire had burnt the bottom oot.

The leam up through the lum did flow,
The soot took fire, and fyled him than;
Ane lump fell down and burnt his pow,
I wat he was a sorra man.
Swith he gat water in a pan,
Wi' whilk he slocken'd out the fire;
To sweep the house he syne began,
To haud a' richt was his desire.

Then he bore kindling to the kiln,
But it stert up all in ane lowe;
Whatever he heard, whatever he saw,
That day he had nae will to mou'.
Then he gaed to tak' up the bairns,
Thought to have found them fair and clean,
The first that he gat in his arms,
Was all bedirten to the een.

The first that he gat in his arms,
It was all dirt up to the een;
'The deil cut off her hands,' quoth he,
'That filled ye a' sae fou' yestreen!'
He trail'd the foul sheets down the gate,

Thought to have washed them on ane stane;
The burn was risen great of spate,
Away frae him the sheets were ta'en.

Then up he gat on ane knowe-head,
On her to cry, on her to shout;
She heard him, as she heard him not,
But stoutly steer'd the stots about.
She drave the day unto the night,
She lows'd the pleugh, and syne cam' hame;
She fand all wrang that should been right;
I trow the man thought right great shame.

Quoth he, 'This office I forsake,
For all the dayis of my life,
For I wald put ane house to wrack,
Had I been twenty days guidwife.'
Quoth she, 'Weel mot ye brook your place,
For truly I will ne'er accep' it.'
Quoth he, 'Fiend fall the limmer's face,
But yet ye may be blythe to get it.'

Then up she gat ane muckle rung,
And the guidman made to the door;
Quoth he, 'Dame, I sall hald my tongue,
For an we fecht, I'll get the waur.'
Quoth he, 'When I forsook my pleugh,
I trow, I but forsook mysel',
And I will to my pleugh again,
For I and this house will ne'er do well.'

ANON.

The Wife of Usher's Well

There lived a wife at Usher's Well,
    And a wealthy wife was she;
She had three stout and stalwart sons,
    And sent them oer the sea.

They hadna been a week from her,
    A week but barely ane,
Whan word came to the carline wife
    That her three sons were gane.

They hadna been a week from her,
    A week but barely three,
Whan word came to the carlin wife
    That her sons she'd never see.

'I wish the wind may never cease,
    Nor fashes in the flood,
Till my three sons come hame to me,
    In earthly flesh and blood.'

It fell about the Martinmass,
    When nights are lang and mirk.
The carlin wife's three sons came hame,
    And their hats were o the birk.

It neither grew in syke nor ditch,
    Nor yet in ony sheugh;
But at the gates o Paradise,
    That birk grew fair eneugh.

'Blow up the fire, my maidens,
    Bring water from the well;
For a' my house shall feast this night,
    Since my three sons are well.'

And she has made to them a bed,
    She's made it large and wide,
And she's taen her mantle her about,
    Sat down at the bed-side.

Up then crew the red, red cock,
    And up and crew the gray;
The eldest to the youngest said,
    'Tis time we were away.'

The cock he hadna crawd but once,
    And clappd his wings at a',
When the youngest to the eldest said,
    'Brother, we must awa.

'The cock doth craw, the day doth daw,
    The channerin worm doth chide;
Gin we be mist out o our place,
    A sair pain we maun bide.

'Faer ye weel, my mother dear!
    Fareweel to barn and byre!
And fare ye weel, the bonny lass
    That kindles my mother's fire!'

ANON.

From Winter

[...]

Now, when the western sun withdraws the day,
And humid evening, gliding o'er the sky,
In her chill progress, checks the straggling beams,
And robs them of their gathered vapory prey,
Where marshes stagnate, and where rivers wind,
Cluster the rolling fogs, and swim along
The dusky-mantled lawn: then slow descend,
Once more to mingle with their watry friends.
The vivid stars shine out, in radiant files;
And boundless ether glows, till the fair moon
Shows her broad visage, in the crimsoned east;
Now, stooping, seems to kiss the passing cloud:
Now, o'er the pure cerulean, rides sublime.
Wide the pale deluge floats, with silver waves,
O'er the skyed mountain, to the low-laid vale;
From the white rocks with dim reflexion gleams,
And faintly glitters through the waving shades.
All night abundant dews unnoted fall,
And at return of morning silver o'er
The face of mother-earth; from every branch

Depending, tremble the translucent gems,
And, quivering, seem to fall away, yet cling,
And sparkle in the sun, whose rising eye,
With fogs bedimmed, portends a beauteous day.

Now, giddy youth, whom headlong passions fire,
Rouse the wild game, and stain the guiltless grove
With violence, and death; yet call it sport,
To scatter ruin through the realms of love,
And peace, that thinks no ill: but these, the muse,
Whose charity, unlimited, extends
As wide as nature works, disdains to sing,
Returning to her nobler theme in view —
For, see, where winter comes, himself, confest,
Striding the gloomy blast, first rains obscure
Drive through the mingling skies, with tempest foul;
Beat on the mountain's brow, and shake the woods,
That, sounding, wave below. The dreary plain
Lies overwhelmed and lost. The bellying clouds
Combine, and deepening into night, shut up
The day's fair face. The wanderers of heaven,
Each to his home, retire; save those that love
To take their pastime in the troubled air,
And, skimming, flutter round the dimply flood.
The cattle, from the untasted fields, return,
And ask, with meaning low, their wonted stalls;
Or ruminate in the contiguous shade:
Thither the household feathery people crowd,
The crested cock, with all his female train,
Pensive and wet. Meanwhile, the cottage-swain
Hangs o'er the enlivening blaze, and taleful there
Recounts his simple frolic: much he talks,
And much he laughs, nor recks the storm that blows
Without, and rattles on his humble roof.
At last, the muddy deluge pours along,
Resistless, roaring, dreadful, down it comes
From the chapt mountain, and the mossy wild,
Tumbling through rocks abrupt, and sounding far:
Then o'er the sanded valley, floating, spreads,
Calm, sluggish, silent; till again constrained,

Betwixt two meeting hills, it bursts a way,
Where rocks and woods o'er hang the turbid stream.
There gathering triple force, rapid, and deep,
It boils, and wheels, and foams, and thunders through.

[. . .]

ANON.

The Winter Climbing

(*for Marj*)

It is late January and at last the snow.
I lie back dreaming about Glencoe
as fluent, hungry, dressed in red,
you climb up and over me. That passion
claimed the darkest, useless months
for risk and play. You rise
up on me, I rise through you . . .

The shadowed face of Aonach Dubh
where Mal first took me climbing
and as we clanked exhausted, happy,
downwards through the dark, I asked
'What route was that?' 'Call it
what you want – it's new.'

You reach the top and exit out;
from way above, your cry comes down.
The rope pulls tight. What shall we call
this new thing we're about?
These days we live in taking
care and chances. Why name it?
My heart is in my mouth as I shout *Climbing* . . .

ANDREW GREIG

The Witch of Fife

'Where have ye been, ye ill woman,
These three lang nights frae hame?
What gars the sweat drap frae yer brow,
Like drops o' the saut sea-faem?

'It fears me muckle ye have seen
What gude man never knew;
It fears me muckle ye have been,
Where the gray cock never crew.

'But the spell may crack, and the bridle break,
Then sharp yer word will be;
Ye had better sleep in yer bed at hame,
Wi' yer dear little bairns and me.'

'Sit dune, sit dune, my leal auld man,
Sit dune, and listen to me;
I'll gar the hair stand on yer crown,
And the cauld sweat blind yer e'e.

'But tell nae words, my gude auld man,
Tell never a word again;
Or dear shall be your courtesy,
And driche and sair yer pain.

'The first leet night, when the new moon set,
When all was douffe and mirk,
We saddled our nags wi' the moon-fern leaf,
And rode frae Kilmerrin kirk.

'Some horses were of the brume-cow framed,
And some of the green bay tree;
But mine was made of ane hemlock shaw,
And a stout stallion was he.

'We raide the tod doune on the hill,
The martin on the law;
And we hunted the owlet out o' breath,
And forced him doune to fa'.'

'What guid was that, ye ill woman?
What guid was that to thee?
Ye would better have been in yer bed at hame,
Wi' yer dear little bairns and me.' —

'And aye we rode, as sae merrily rode,
Through the merkest gloffs of the night;
And we swam the flood, and we darnit the wood,
Till we came to the Lommond height.

'And when we came to the Lommond height,
Sae lightly we lighted doune;
And we drank frae the horns that never grew,
The beer that was never browin.

'Then up there rose a wee wee man,
From neath the moss-gray stane;
His face was wan like the colliflower,
For he neither had blude nor bane.

'He set a reed-pipe till his mouth;
And he played sae bonnily,
Till the gray curlew, and the black-cock flew
To listen his melodye.

'It rang sae sweet through the green Lommond,
That the night-wind lowner blew;
And it soupit alang the Loch Leven,
And wakened the white sea-mew.

'It rang sae sweet through the green Lommond,
Sae sweetly and sae shrill,
That the weasels leaped out of their mouldy holes,
And danced on the midnight hill.

'The corby crow came gledging near,
The erne gaed veering bye;
And the trouts leaped out of the Leven Loch,
Charmed with the melodye.

'And aye we danced on the green Lommond,
Till the dawn on the ocean grew:
Nae wonder I was a weary wight
When I cam hame to you.' –

[. . .]

JAMES HOGG

Witch rhymes

I shall go into a hare,
With sorrow and sych and meickle care;
And I shall go in the Devil's name,
Ay while I come home again.

Hare, hare, God send thee care.
I am in a hare's likeness now,
But I shall be in a woman's likeness even now.

ISOBEL GOWDIE

With Huntis Up

With huntis up, with huntis up,
It is now perfite day,
Jesus, our King, is gaine in hunting,
Quha lykis to speid thay may.

Ane curist Fox lay hid in rox,
This lang and mony ane day,
Devoring scheip, quhill he mycht creip,
Nane mycht him schaip away.

It did him gude to laip the blude
Of yung and tender lambis,
Nane culd he mis, for all was his,
The yung anis with thair dammis.

The hunter is Christ, that huntis in haist,
The hundis ar Peter and Paull,
The Paip is the Fox, Rome is the Rox,
That rubbis us on the gall.

That creull beist, he never ceist,
Be his usurpit power,
Under dispens, to get our penneis,
Our saulis to devoir.

Quha culd devise sic merchandis,
As he had thair to sell,
Onles it war proude Lucifer,
The greit maister of Hell.

He had to sell the Tantonie bell,
And Pardonis thairin was,
Remissioun of sinnis, in auld scheip skinnis,
Our saulis to bring from grace.

With bullis of leid, quhyte wax and reid,
And uther quhylis with grene,
Closit in ane box, this usit the Fox,
Sic peltrie was never sene.

With dispensationis and obligationis,
According to his Law,
He wald dispence, for money from hence,
With thame he never saw.

To curs and ban the sempill pure man,
That had nocht to fle the paine,
Bot quhen he had payit all to ane myit,
He mon be absolvit than.

To sum, God wot, he gaif tot quot,
And uther sum pluralitie,
Bot first with penneis, he mon dispens,
Or ellis it will nocht be.

Kingis to marie and sum to tarie,
Sic is his power and mycht,
Quha that hes gold, with him will he hold,
Thoch it be contrair all rycht.

O blissit Peter, the Fox is ane lier,
Thow kawis weill it is nocht sa,
Quhill at the last, he salbe downe cast,
His peltrie, Pardonis and all.

GUDE & GODLIE BALLADS

Woo'd and married and a'

The bride she is winsome and bonnie,
Her hair it is snooded sae sleek,
And faithful and kind is her Johnnie,
Yet fast fa' the tears on her cheek.
New pearlings are cause o' her sorrow,
New pearlings and plenishing too;
The bride that has a' to borrow,
Has e'en right meikle ado.
Woo'd and married and a',
Woo'd and married and a',
And is na she very weel aff
To be woo'd and married and a'?

Her mother then hastily spak':
'The lassie is glaiket wi' pride;
In my poaches I hadna a plack
The day that I was a bride.
E'en tak' to your wheel and be clever,
And draw out your thread in the sun,
The gear that is gifted, it never
Will last like the gear that is won.
Woo'd and married and a',
Tocher and havings sae sma'
I think ye are very weel aff,
To be woo'd and married and a','

'Toot, toot!' quo' the grey-headed father,
'She's less of a bride than a bairn,
She's ta'en like a cowt frae the heather,
Wi' sense and discretion to learn.
Half husband, I trow, and half daddy,
As humour inconstantly leans;
A chiel may be constant and steady
That yokes wi' a mate in her teens.
'Kerchief to cover so neat,
Locks the winds used to blaw,
I'm baith like to laugh and to creet,
When I think o' her married at a'.'

Then out spak' the wily bridegroom,
Weel waled were his wordies I ween;
'I'm rich, though my coffer be toom,
Wi' the blinks o' your bonnie blue een;
I'm prouder o' thee by my side,
Though thy ruffles or ribbons be few,
Than if Kate o' the craft were my bride,
Wi' purples and pearlings enew.
Dear and dearest of ony,
Ye're woo'd and bookit and a',
And do ye think scorn o' your Johnnie,
And grieve to be married at a'?'

She turn'd, and she blush'd, and she smil'd,
And she lookit sae bashfully down;
The pride o' her heart was beguil'd,
And she play'd wi' the sleeve o' her gown;
She twirl'd the tag o' her lace,
And she nippet her boddice sae blue,
Syne blinket sae sweet in his face,
And aff like a mawkin she flew.
Woo'd and married and a',
Married and carried awa';
She thinks hersel' very weel aff,
To be woo'd and married and a'.

JOANNA BAILLIE

Written after Swimming from Sestos to Abydos

1.

If, in the month of dark December,
Leander, who was nightly wont
(What maid will not the tale remember?)
To cross thy stream, broad Hellespont!

2.

If, when the wintry tempest roared,
He sped to Hero, nothing loth,
And thus of old thy current poured,
Fair Venus! how I pity both!

3.

For *me*, degenerate modern wretch,
Though in the genial month of May,
My dripping limbs I faintly stretch,
And think I've done a feat to-day.

4.

But since he crossed the rapid tide,
According to the doubtful story,
To woo, – and – Lord knows what beside,
And swam for Love, as I for Glory;

5.

'Twere hard to say who fared the best:
Sad mortals! thus the Gods still plague you!
He lost his labour, I my jest:
For he was drowned, and I've the ague.

LORD BYRON

The Year of the Whale

The old go, one by one, like guttered flames.
This past winter
Tammag the bee-man has taken his cold blank mask
To the honeycomb under the hill,
Corston who ploughed out the moor
Unyoked and gone; and I ask,
Is Heddle lame, that in youth could dance and saunter
A way to the chastest bed?
The kirkyard is full of their names
Chiselled in stone. Only myself and Yule
In the ale-house now, speak of the great whale year.

This one and that provoked the taurine waves
With an arrogant pass,
Or probing deep through the snow-burdened hill
Resurrected his flock,
Or passed from fiddles to ditch
By way of the quart and the gill,
All night lay tranced with corn, but stirred to face
The brutal stations of bread;
While those who tended their lives
Like sacred lamps, chary of oil and wick,
Died in the fury of one careless match.

Off Scabra Head the lookout sighted a school
At the first light.
A meagre year it was, limpets and crows
And brief mottled grain.
Everything that could float
Circled the school. Ploughs
Wounded those wallowing lumps of thunder and night.
The women crouched and prayed.
Then whale by whale
Blundering on the rock with its red stain
Crammed our winter cupboards with oil and meat.

GEORGE MACKAY BROWN

The Young Laird and Edinburgh Katy

Now wat ye wha I met yestreen
Coming down the street, my Jo,
My mistress in her tartan screen,
Fow bonny, braw and sweet, my Jo.
'My dear,' quoth I, 'thanks to the night,
That never wish'd a lover ill,
Since ye're out of your mither's sight,
Let's take a wauk up to the hill.

　　'O Katy wiltu gang wi' me,
And leave the dinsome town a while,
The blossom's sprouting frae the tree,
And a' the summer's gawn to smile;
The mavis, nightingale and lark,
The bleeting lambs and whistling hynd,
In ilka dale, green, shaw and park,
Will nourish health, and glad ye'r mind.

　　'Soon as the clear goodman of day
Bends his morning draught of dew,
We'll gae to some burnside and play,
And gather flowers to busk ye'r brow.
We'll pou the dazies on the green,
The lucken gowans frae the bog;
Between hands now and then we'll lean,
And sport upo' the velvet fog.

　　'There's up into a pleasant glen,
A wee piece frae my father's tower,
A canny, saft and flow'ry den,
Which circling birks has form'd a bower:
When e'er the sun grows high and warm,
We'll to the cauller shade remove,
There will I lock thee in mine arm,
And love and kiss, and kiss and love.'

ALLAN RAMSAY

Acknowledgements

Bho 'Oran an t-Samhraidh' / from 'Song of Summer' by **Alasdair mac Mhaighstir Alasdair / Alexander MacDonald**, translated by Professor Derick S. Thomson, from *Gaelic Poetry in the Eighteenth Century: A Bilingual Anthology*, ed. Derick S. Thomson (Association for Literary Studies, 1993), copyright © the Estate of Derick Thomson, reproduced by permission; 'Birlinn Clann Raghnaill' / 'The Galley of Clan Ranald' by Alasdair mac Mhaighstir Alasdair / Alexander MacDonald, translated by Peter Mackay and Iain S. MacPherson, from *100 Dàn as Fheàrr Leinn*, eds Peter Mackay and Jo MacDonald (Edinburgh: Luath, 2020); 'Moladh Mòraig' / 'In Praise of Morag' by Alasdair mac Mhaighstir Alasdair / Alexander MacDonald, text and translation from Peter Mackay and Iain S. MacPherson (eds), *An Leabhar Liath: 500 Years of Gaelic Love and Transgressive Verse* (Edinburgh: Luath, 2016); **Gun Urra / Anonymous**: bho **'Ar sliocht Gaodhal ó Ghort Gréag'** / from **'The Race of Gaels from the Land of Greece'**, translated by Meg Bateman, from *Duanaire na Sracaire: Songbook of the Pillagers: Anthology of Scotland's Gaelic Verse to 1600*, ed. Wilson McLeod and Meg Bateman (Origin, 2007), copyright © Meg Bateman, reproduced with permission of Birlinn Ltd through PLSclear; **'Bothan Àirigh am Bràigh Raineach'** / **'A Sheiling Bothy on Brae Rannoch'**, translated by Peter Mackay and Iain S. MacPherson, from *100 Dàn as Fheàrr Leinn*, eds Peter Mackay and Jo MacDonald (Edinburgh: Luath, 2020); **'Chunnaic mi a'n t-Òg Uasal'** / **'I Saw the Well-Born Youth'**, translated by Ronald Black, from *An Lasair / The Flame*, ed. Ronald Black (Origin, 2001), copyright © Ronald Black, reproduced with permission of Birlinn Ltd through PLSclear; **'Fil Súil nGlais'** / **'A Blue Eye Turns'**, translated by Meg Bateman, from *Duanaire na Sracaire: Songbook of the Pillagers: Anthology of Scotland's Gaelic Verse to 1600*, ed. Wilson McLeod and Meg Bateman (Origin, 2007), copyright © Meg Bateman, reproduced with

The Good Neighbour (Jonathan Cape, 2005), used by permission of Jonathan Cape, an imprint of Vintage, a division of Penguin Random House UK and United Agents LLP; 'History' by John Burnside, from *The Light Trap* (Jonathan Cape, 2005), used by permission of Jonathan Cape, an imprint of Vintage, a division of Penguin Random House UK and and United Agents LLP; 'This Evening' by **Ron Butlin**, from *Ragtime in Unfamiliar Bars* (Secker & Warbug, 1985), reproduced by permission of Ron Butlin; 'Fàire' / 'Horizon' by **Aonghas Pàdraig Caimbeul / Angus Peter Campbell**, from *Aibisidh/ABC* (Polygon, 2011), copyright © Angus Peter Campbell 2011. Reproduced with permission of Birlinn Ltd through PLSclear; 'Bod Brioghmhor Atá ag Donncha' / 'Duncan Has a Powerful Prick' by **Sir Donnchadh Caimbeul Ghlinn Urchaidh / Sir Duncan Campbell of Glen Orchy**, text and translation from Peter Mackay and Iain S. MacPherson (eds), *An Leabhar Liath: 500 Years of Gaelic Love and Transgressive Verse* (Edinburgh: Luath, 2016). For the Gaelic, Wilson McLeod and Meg Bateman (eds), *Duanaire na Sracaire* (Edinburgh: Birlinn, 2007); 'Christmas Oranges' by **Gerry Cambridge**, from *Notes for Lighting a Fire* (HappenStance, 2012), reproduced by permission of Gerry Cambridge; 'They (may forget (their names (if let out)))' by **Vahni Capildeo**, from *Venus as a Bear* (Carcanet, 2018), reprinted by kind permission of Carcanet Press, Manchester, UK; 'The Big Mistake' by **Jim Carruth** from *Black Cart* (Polygon, 2019), copyright © Jim Carruth, reproduced with permission of Birlinn Ltd through PLSclear; bho 'Alasdair à Gleanna Garadh' / from 'Alasdair of Glengarry' by **Sìleas na Ceapaich / Julia MacDonald**, translated by Peter Mackay, from *100 Dàn as Fheàrr Leinn*, eds Peter Mackay and Jo MacDonald (Edinburgh: Luath, 2020); 'Comhairle air na Nigheanan Òga' / 'Advice to Young Girls' by Sìleas na Ceapaich / Julia MacDonald, text and translation from Peter Mackay and Iain S. MacPherson (eds), *An Leabhar Liath: 500 Years of Gaelic Love and Transgressive Verse* (Edinburgh: Luath, 2016); 'Is Mairg dá nGalar an Grádh' / 'Pity One for whom Love Is a Sickness') by **Iseabail ní Mheic Cailéin**, translated by Peter Mackay, from *100 Dàn as Fheàrr Leinn*, eds Peter Mackay and Jo MacDonald (Edinburgh: Luath, 2020). For the Gaelic, Wilson McLeod and Meg Bateman (eds), *Duanaire na Sracaire* (Edinburgh: Birlinn, 2007); 'Atá Fleasgach ar mo Thí' / 'There's a Young Man on My Trail' by Iseabail ní Mheic Cailéin, text and translation from Peter Mackay and Iain S. MacPherson (eds), *An Leabhar Liath: 500 Years of Gaelic Love and Transgressive Verse* (Edinburgh: Luath, 2016). For the Gaelic, Wilson McLeod and Meg Bateman (eds), *Duanaire na Sracaire* (Edinburgh: Birlinn, 2007); 'Ailein Duinn' / 'Brown-haired Alan' by **Anna Chaimbeul / Anne Campbell**, translated by Peter Mackay and Iain S. Macpherson, from *100 Dàn as Fheàrr Leinn*, eds Peter Mackay and Jo MacDonald (Edinburgh: Luath, 2020); 'Cumha Ghriogair MhicGriogair Ghlinn Sreith' / 'Lament for MacGriogair of Glenstrae' by **Mòr Chaimbeul / Marion Campbell**, translated by Meg Bateman, from *Duanaire na Sracaire: Songbook of the Pillagers: Anthology of Scotland's Gaelic Verse to 1600*,

Valkyries: poems in English and Shetland dialect (The Shetland Library, 1997), reproduced by permission of Christine De Luca; 'My Pain' by **Roddy Lumsden**, from *Mischief Night: New and Selected Poems* (Bloodaxe Books, 2004), reproduced with permission of Bloodaxe Books. www.bloodaxebooks.com; 'Ceumannan' / 'Steps' by **Domhnall MacAmhlaigh / Donald MacAulay**, from *Deilbh is Faileasan / Images and Reflections* (Acair, 2008), reproduced by permission of the Estate of Donald MacAulay; 'Is Trom Leam an Àirigh' / 'I'm Depressed by the Sheiling' by **Rob Donn MacAoidh / Rob Donn Mackay**, text and translation from Peter Mackay and Iain S. MacPherson (eds), *An Leabhar Liath: 500 Years of Gaelic Love and Transgressive Verse* (Edinburgh: Luath, 2016); 'Marbhrann do Chloinn Fhir Thaigh Ruspainn' / 'An Elegy for the Children of the House of Rispond' by Rob Donn MacAoidh / Rob Donn Mackay, translated by Peter Mackay, from *100 Dàn as Fheàrr Leinn*, eds Peter Mackay and Jo MacDonald (Edinburgh: Luath, 2020); 'Basking Shark', 'On the pier at Kinlochbervie' and 'Toad' by **Norman MacCaig**, from *The Poems of Norman MacCaig* (Polygon (An Imprint of Birlinn Limited), 2009), copyright © the Estate of Norman MacCaig. Reproduced with permission of Birlinn Ltd through PLSclear; 'The Eemis Stane', 'Empty Vessel' and 'The Watergaw' by **Hugh MacDiarmid**, from *Complete Poems Volume I* (Carcanet, 2017), reprinted by kind permission of Carcanet Press, Manchester, UK; 'Scotland small?' by Hugh MacDiarmid, from *Complete Poems Volume II* (Carcanet, 1994), reprinted by kind permission of Carcanet Press, Manchester, UK; 'White (original version)' by **Robin Fulton Macpherson**, from *Selected Poems 1963–1978* (Macdonald Press, 1980), reproduced by permission of the author; 'Gangan Fruit' by **Ellie McDonald**, from *The Gangan Fuit* (Chapman Publishing, 1991), reproduced by permission of Ellie McDonald; 'Ora nam Buadh' / 'The Invocation of the Graces' by **Alasdair MacGhille Mhìcheil / Alexander Carmichael**, text and translation from Alexander Carmichael, *Carmina Gadelica* (1928); bho 'Òran do Dh'Ameireaga' / from 'A Song to America' by **Iain MacIlleathain / John MacLean**, translated by Peter Mackay, from *100 Dàn as Fheàrr Leinn*, eds Peter Mackay and Jo MacDonald (Edinburgh: Luath, 2020). Full text from *Caran an-t-Saoghail / The Wiles of the World* (Origin, 2003), copyright © Donald Meek, reproduced with permission of Birlinn Ltd through PLSclear; 'An Tiona' / 'The Tin' by **Peter Mackay / Pàdraig MacAoidh**, from *Gu Leòr / Galore* (Acair, 2015), reproduced by permission of the author and Acair; 'Back-Green Odyssey' by **Alastair Mackie**, from *Collected Poems 1954–1994* (Two Ravens Press, 2012), reproduced by permission of the Estate of Alastair Mackie; bho 'Fàilte don Eilean Sgitheanach' / from 'Hail to the Isle of Skye' by **Niall MacLeòid / Neil MacLeod**, from *Caran an-t-Saoghail / The Wiles of the World* (Origin, 2003), copyright © Donald Meek, reproduced with permission of Birlinn Ltd through PLSclear; bho 'Oran Murtadh Ghlinn Comhainn' / from 'A Song on the Massacre of Glencoe' by **Murchadh MacMhathain / Murdoch Matheson**, translated by Meg Bateman

Index of Authors